The Dash Reeves Site: A Middle Woodland Village and Lithic Production Center in the American Bottom

American Bottom Archaeology
FAI-270 Site Reports
Volume 28

Series Editors:
Thomas E. Emerson (Principal Investigator and Program Director) and
John A. Walthall (Chief Archaeologist, Illinois Department of Transportation)

Technical Editor:
Linda Forman

This volume produced by the Illinois Transportation
Archaeological Research Program
Production Staff:
Mike Lewis
Linda Alexander
Corinne Carlson
Amy Maroso

Investigations conducted under the auspices of the
Illinois Archaeological Survey in cooperation with:

The United States Department of Transportation
Federal Highway Administration

The United States Department of the Interior
National Park Service

The State of Illinois
Department of Transportation
Larry Piche (Chief of Environment)
John A. Walthall, Ph.D. (Chief Archaeologist)

The Dash Reeves Site:
A Middle Woodland Village and Lithic Production Center in the American Bottom

Andrew C. Fortier

with contributions by
Thomas O. Maher
Mary Simon
Douglas J. Brewer
John T. Penman

Published for the Illinois Department of Transportation
by the University of Illinois Press
Urbana and Chicago
2001

Library of Congress Cataloging-in-Publication Data

Fortier, Andrew C., 1947-
  The Dash Reeves site : a Middle Woodland village and lithic production
center in the American Bottom / Andrew C. Fortier ; with contributions
by Thomas O. Maher ... [et al.].
      p. cm. -- (American bottom archaeology ; v. 28)
Includes bibliographical references.
  ISBN 0-252-07019-4 (pbk. : alk. paper)
  1. Dash Reeves Site (Ill.) 2. Woodland culture--Illinois--American
Bottom. 3. Excavations (Archaeology)--Illinois--American Bottom. 4.
Indians of North America--Illinois--American Bottom--Antiquities. 5.
American Bottom (Ill.)--Antiquities. I. Illinois. Dept. of
Transportation. II. Title. III. Series.
  E78.I3 F67 2001
  977.3'8--dc21
                                    2001001944

Dedicated to the memory of our mentor, colleague, and friend

Charles J. Bareis
(1929–1999)

FAI-270 Program Coordinator 1978–1994

CONTENTS

LIST OF TABLES

LIST OF FIGURES

LIST OF PLATES

PREFACE

The Illinois Transportation Archaeological Research Program (ITARP) is the product of a more than three-decade-long cooperative effort between Charles J. Bareis, the University of Illinois, and the Illinois Department of Transportation (IDOT) in the preservation of the state's important archaeological resources. It began under the direction of Charles J. Bareis in 1959 with the newly created Illinois Archaeological Survey, continued in 1980 when the IDOT statewide survey program was transferred to the Resource Investigation Program, up until the present time with the formation of ITARP in 1994.

The Program's *Statewide Survey, American Bottom Survey, Western and Northern Illinois Survey,* and *Special Projects Divisions* coordinate archaeological surveys and large multi-year research projects across the state. The *Support Division* provides administrative, curatorial, and laboratory assistance and produces ITARP's five publication series and public outreach programs. The establishment of ITARP was the result of IDOT's interest in developing a centralized program to facilitate its cultural resources protection efforts.

ITARP conducts long-term, large-scale projects that concentrate exclusively on the archaeology of Illinois. This research has brought two national awards and produced a 28-volume University of Illinois Press FAI-270 series hailed as a major landmark in North American archaeology. An integral part of the program includes the curation of massive research collections. These include artifacts from over one hundred major Illinois sites whose analysis has transformed our understanding of Eastern North American prehistory.

One of ITARP's primary goals is the dissemination of information to both professional and public audiences. The program staff is active in public outreach, presents numerous talks at local schools and public service organizations, and produces educational materials such as slide shows, posters, and displays utilizing our vast collection base.

The production of these volumes is accomplished through the efforts of the ITARP Production Office under the direction of Mike Lewis, Publications Manager, Media Coordinators Corinne Carlson and Amy Maroso, and Graphic Designer Linda Alexander.

For information on obtaining Volumes 1–25 of the FAI-270 Project, contact the Illinois Transportation Archaeological Research Program, 209 Nuclear Physics Lab, 23 E. Stadium Drive, Champaign, IL 61820, by phone (217) 244-4244, or on the world wide web at *www.anthro.uiuc.edu/itarp*. Volume 26 and subsequent volumes may be obtained from the University of Illinois Press, P.O. Box 4856, Hampden Post Office, Baltimore, MD 21211, by phone (USA only) (800) 545-4703 (Maryland and Canadian residents call (410) 516-6927), fax (410) 516-6969, or on the world wide web at *www.press.uillinois.edu/*.

ACKNOWLEDGMENTS

This report has come to fruition through the efforts of many individuals and through the generous support of the Illinois Department of Transportation, under the guidance of Dr. John A. Walthall, Chief Archaeologist. The senior author has thanked John many times in the past for his support of specific IDOT-sponsored archaeological projects, and here we also acknowledge his pivotal role in promoting what has become the most widely acclaimed CRM site report series in the United States. The authors also wish to acknowledge the current Director of the Illinois Transportation Archaeological Research Program, Dr. Thomas Emerson, for his leadership and for supporting the completion of this report, a project he inherited from the series' founding editor, Charles J. Bareis. It is with sadness that we note Chuck's passing. It was his vision, passion, and bulldogged determinism that gave birth to the FAI-270 Site Reports Series nearly 20 years ago. Despite his illness, Chuck provided constant support and encouragement during the excavation of the Dash Reeves site as well as during the initial stages of analysis and write-up. We dedicate this volume and all future volumes of the Site Reports Series to Chuck's memory.

We would like to acknowledge the assistance of John Puricelli, environmental coordinator at IDOT District 8 headquarters, as well as that of Larry Kremmel, chief resident engineer, and of Bud Frey, chief IDOT surveyor (now retired). Each played a significant role in providing on-site assistance with land clearance, information about construction schedules, and the establishment of real-life mapping coordinates. Excavation equipment (scrapers, backhoes, water trucks) was provided by Baxmeyer Excavation, Inc., of Waterloo, Illinois. The senior author wishes to thank Wally Burman of the Department of Grants and Contracts at the University of Illinois for expediting heavy machine contracts in a timely and efficient manner. Susanne Pechnick, program secretary at the time of the fieldwork, provided valuable assistance in preparing travel vouchers, handling bills, paying the crew, and serving as general quartermaster for both field and lab activities.

Special thanks go to the 1987 field crew, particularly Jim Burns and Ned Hanenberger, for hanging in there with me to finish those last two test units, despite a blowing 8-inch snowstorm. The 1990 field crew included Liz Kane, Trista Kane, Lucretia Kelly, Pat Nelson, John Schwegman, Larry Vogt, and John Watson. Thanks to all for enduring yet another typical miserable American Bottom summer. I am very much indebted to Thomas O. Maher for serving as my chief field supervisor and for running the show when duties called me elsewhere. As kindred Middle Woodland enthusiasts, we bounced many an idea off of one another and together plotted day-to-day excavation strategies and kept the avalanche of paperwork in order. Tom also analyzed the ceramics from the site (see Chapter 7), the results of which he incorporated into his dissertation (Maher 1996). The senior author would like to thank Kristin Hedman for her assistance in inventorying the chert debitage, entering the data into Excel worksheets, and running preliminary statistics. Over the years, the senior author has greatly benefited from interactions concerning the Dash Reeves materials and Middle Woodland questions in general with the following individuals: Thomas Emerson, Dale McElrath, John Walthall, Thomas Maher, N'omi Greber, Richard E. Hughes, Fred A. Finney, and James W. Porter, who first introduced me to the Dash Reeves site in 1972.

Washing and labeling of artifacts was accomplished by field crew members on rain days. Water flotation of several thousand liters of soil was accomplished by Mike Lewis and Angela Steiner-Neller. Project archaeobotanist Mary Simon wishes to thank Supaporn Nakbunglung (Pan) for assisting in the inventory and sorting of flotation samples. Curation and organization of materials has been the responsibility of ITARP Curator Angela Steiner-Neller and Lab Director Eve Hargrave. Artifact illustrations were drafted by the able hand of Linda Alexander. Artifact photographs were taken by David Minor and Linda Alexander. Site maps, feature profiles, and area maps were prepared by Steve Holland. Graphs and other figures, including those enhanced by computer, were created by Mike Lewis, our well-seasoned and

much-abused production manager. Mike was assisted
by Corinne Carlson and Amy Maroso. Mike also
undertook final preparation of the report manuscript.
The authors also wish to thank editor Linda Forman for
correcting literary, stylistic, and intellectual missteps.

The contents of this volume reflect the views of the
authors, who are solely responsible for the interpretations
and accuracy of the data presented herein. The contents
do not necessarily reflect the official views or policies of
the Illinois Department of Transportation or the federal
government.

THE DASH REEVES SITE

*A Middle Woodland Village and
Lithic Production Center in the American Bottom*

American Bottom Chronology

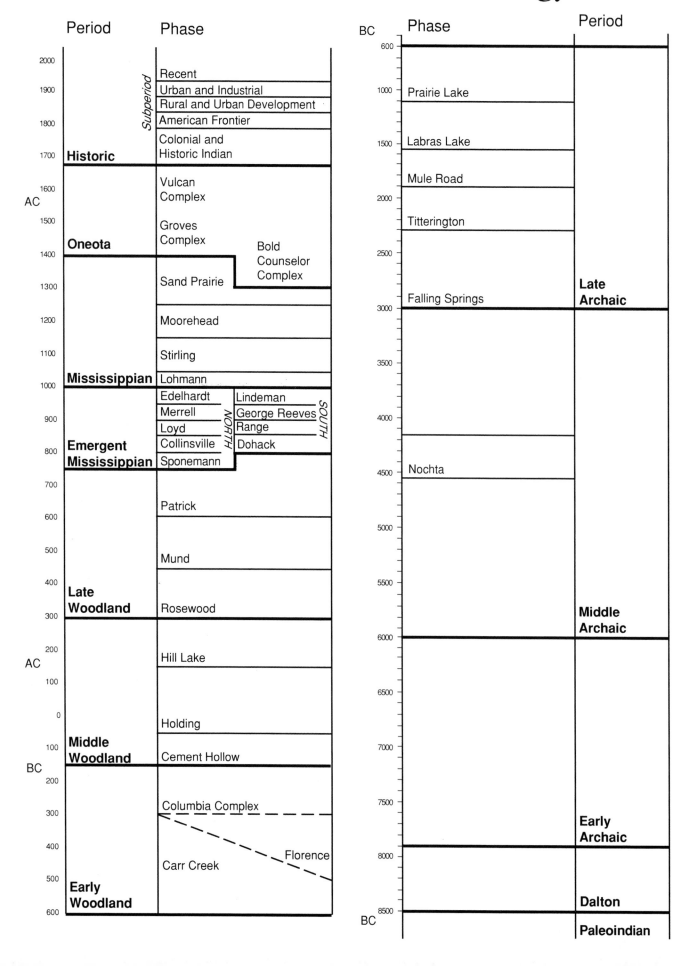

Period	Phase		
Historic	*Subperiod* Recent		
	Urban and Industrial		
	Rural and Urban Development		
	American Frontier		
	Colonial and Historic Indian		
Oneota	Vulcan Complex		
	Groves Complex	Bold Counselor Complex	
	Sand Prairie		
Mississippian	Moorehead		
	Stirling		
	Lohmann		
Emergent Mississippian	Edelhardt	Lindeman	*SOUTH*
	Merrell	George Reeves	
	Loyd	Range	
	Collinsville	Dohack	
	Sponemann		
Late Woodland	Patrick		
	Mund		
	Rosewood		
Middle Woodland	Hill Lake		
	Holding		
	Cement Hollow		
Early Woodland	Columbia Complex		
	Carr Creek	Florence	

BC	Phase	Period
	Prairie Lake	
	Labras Lake	
	Mule Road	
	Titterington	
	Falling Springs	**Late Archaic**
	Nochta	
		Middle Archaic
		Early Archaic
		Dalton
		Paleoindian

1

INTRODUCTION

Archaeological investigations at the Dash Reeves site (11-Mo-80) came about as a result of the Illinois Department of Transportation (IDOT) Columbia Bypass and Interchange Project (FAP 14, Illinois Route 3). This project involved the construction of a major interchange connecting traffic flow between existing FAI-255 (270), the city of Columbia, and County Highway 6 (Palmer Creek Road), which provides access to the Mississippi River floodplain and associated rural farmland. This project was a direct offshoot of the older FAI-270 Project, for which the University of Illinois at Urbana-Champaign (UIUC) had served as the prime archaeological contractor (Bareis and Porter 1984) (Figure 1.1). Because of its involvement in the earlier project, UIUC was asked to conduct archaeological investigations for the Columbia Project.

The Columbia Project involved archaeological investigations at two sites. One was the Dash Reeves site, which was to be partially impacted by construction of a curved access road extending from the interchange area to County Highway 6 (Figure 1.2). The other was the Marge site (11-Mo-99), located 300 m to the east of Dash Reeves, which fell entirely within the proposed access road and bridge cone areas. Investigations at the Marge site have been reported elsewhere (Fortier 1996).

The Dash Reeves site had been known since 1971 and was widely regarded as one of the largest Middle Woodland habitation sites in the American Bottom. Initial surface collections produced nearly 10 orange crate-size boxes of material, almost all of it associated with the middle to late Middle Woodland period. The site was also well known to local collectors, and many

diagnostic artifacts had been removed from the site prior to professional reconnaissance. One collector who visited the site during the 1990 UIUC excavation boasted that he had sold "many celts and points" to dealers in New York. Therefore, despite the fact that the proposed highway right-of-way was to impact less than 20 percent of the site, there was a sense of urgency to recover as much data as possible during our investigations. In addition, in 1987 the landowner had already begun selling off the remainder of the site area to local developers. At the time of this writing (1998), a sizable portion of the site has been destroyed or altered by development. The central portion of the site has been obliterated by subterranean gasoline holding tanks and a service station. Much of the site has been graded and landscaped, and some portions have been buried by fill to indeterminate depths. The site presently has no surface integrity, and it is fully anticipated that in 10 years no vestige of it will remain.

There are not many large Middle Woodland sites extant in the American Bottom, so efforts to recover even portions of such sites are extremely important. Despite previous investigations at Middle Woodland sites such as Holding (Fortier et al. 1989), Truck #7 (Fortier 1985a), Mund (Finney 1983), Willoughby (Jackson 1990), Nochta (Higgins 1990), Meridian Hills (Williams 1993), and a handful of other unpublished sites, very little is known about this important period. The collapse of Middle Woodland cultures in this area represents an enigmatic cultural discontinuity in American Bottom prehistory, perhaps not on the same scale as Cahokia's collapse during the Mississippian period, but nonetheless, a phenomenon for which important re-

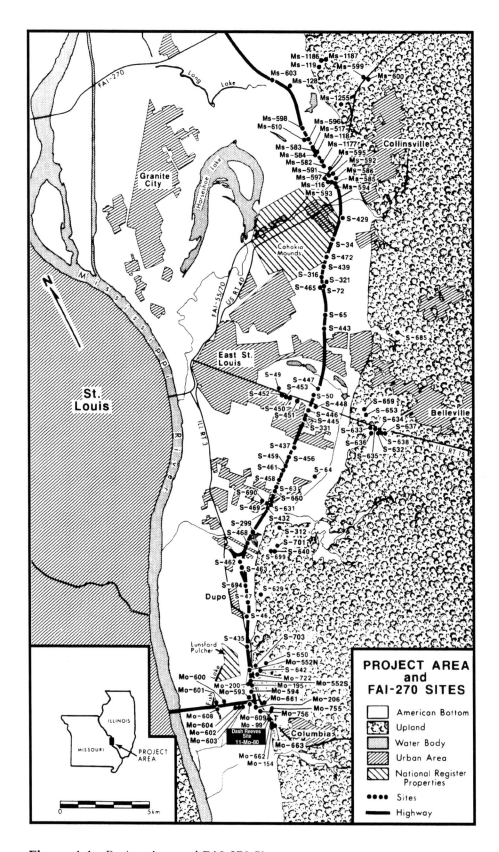

Figure 1.1. Project Area and FAI-270 Sites

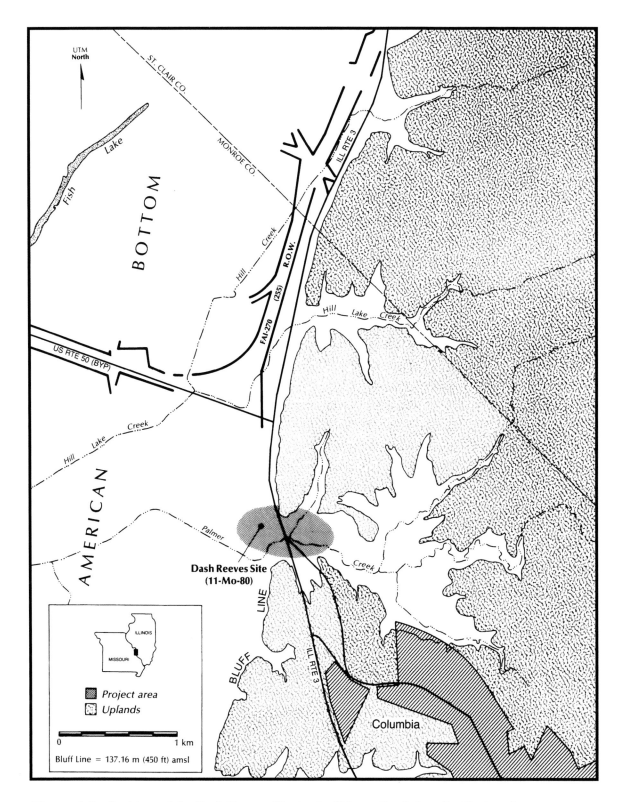

Figure 1.2. Position of the Dash Reeves Site in the Palmer Creek Locality Project Area

search questions remain unresolved (Fortier 2001; McElrath and Fortier 2000). Dash Reeves may not provide definitive answers to these questions, but it does enhance our knowledge of site variability, lithic technology, subsistence, ceramic decorative style, and site formational processes, on the eve of the Middle Woodland/Late Woodland transition.

The following chapters present information on site environment, the history of site investigations, research design, analytical techniques, site formational processes, features, ceramics, lithics, floral and faunal remains, and radiocarbon dating. The report concludes with a summary of the data presentations, followed by a general interpretation of the site and an assessment of its significance. Although this is intended primarily as a descriptive site report, in keeping with the philosophy of the original FAI-270 Site Reports series, questions of regional archaeological significance also are addressed.

2

SITE LOCATION
AND ENVIRONMENT

The Dash Reeves site (11-Mo-80) is located in the Mississippi River floodplain in the central American Bottom in Section 8, Township 15, Range 10W, in northern Monroe County, Illinois. The center of the site (UTM E742050, N4260650) lies approximately 2 km north of the town of Columbia and about 500 m southwest of Illinois State Highway 3. The site falls within the Palmer Creek locality near the outlet of Palmer Creek from the uplands into the Mississippi River floodplain. This creek valley follows a low gradient into the uplands, and settlement at this particular locus would have permitted easy access to both the uplands to the east and the floodplain to the west. The site is situated on a slightly dissected, but mostly flat surface (410–420 ft contours), and as defined by multiple surface collections (see Chapter 3), occupies an oval area encompassing roughly 30,000 m². Aerial photographs show the most intense area of occupation (as defined by surface debris) occurring 50–75 m northwest of a large, prominent cottonwood tree (see Figure 3.3).

The Dash Reeves site is situated on the medial portion of an alluvial fan formed by the action of Palmer Creek. Geomorphologic coring of the fan locality by Dr. Edward Hajic (1988) and subsequent analysis of topographic maps and high-altitude photographs reveal that the Palmer Creek fan was deposited over an old Mississippi River channel and associated buried ridge and swale landforms (Figures 2.1 and 2.2). The distal portion of the fan, which is composed of upland loessal silts, extends out to the west and north where it is eventually truncated by the Hill Lake Meander, a later channel of the Mississippi River. The Palmer Creek fan actually buries the clayey overbank deposits of the Hill Lake Meander. At the time of the Middle Woodland occupation, the Hill Lake Meander had ceased to be a free-flowing channel and had become a large marsh or lake (Hajic 1988). The history of the Hill Lake Meander has been detailed in a prior report, and the reader is directed to that source for more information (Fortier 1985a:1–11).

The Palmer Creek fan was created by a series of paleochannels of Palmer Creek. These paleochannels criss-cross the fan and site area. Sinuosity of the channels occurred as a result of the gradual in-filling of the Hill Lake Meander paludal environment, which reduced the gradient of flow to the west and north. Contour maps of the project area reveal the courses of several of these paleochannels. These also can be seen in an aerial photograph where the dark channel scars form a ring within the site area (Plate 2.1). During excavation we found that one of the paleochannels had been filled with cultural debris, suggesting that its cut-off date as an active channel occurred prior to the Middle Woodland occupation. Yet another, more sizable, channel scar was exposed during geomorphologic trenching along the south half of the right-of-way. Middle Woodland material occurred at the base of heavily laminated silt and gravel-lain sediments of the creek and may have been deposited within an active channel outlining the southern and western limits of the site (Figure 2.3).

There is a sizable difference in depth and width between the two aforementioned paleochannels. Both channel depressions must have been clearly visible to the site's Middle Woodland inhabitants. The smaller, north-south-oriented channel, which was inactive, must

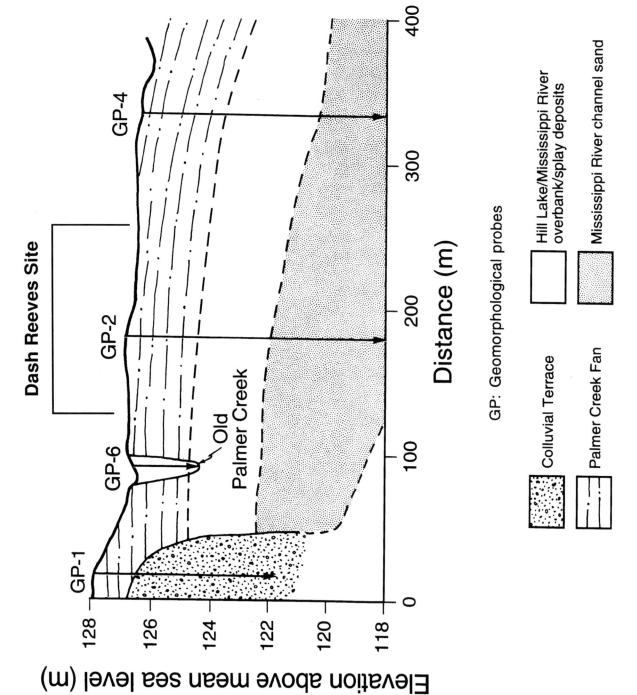

Figure 2.1. Geomorphological Profile of Palmer Creek Locality: view to the south

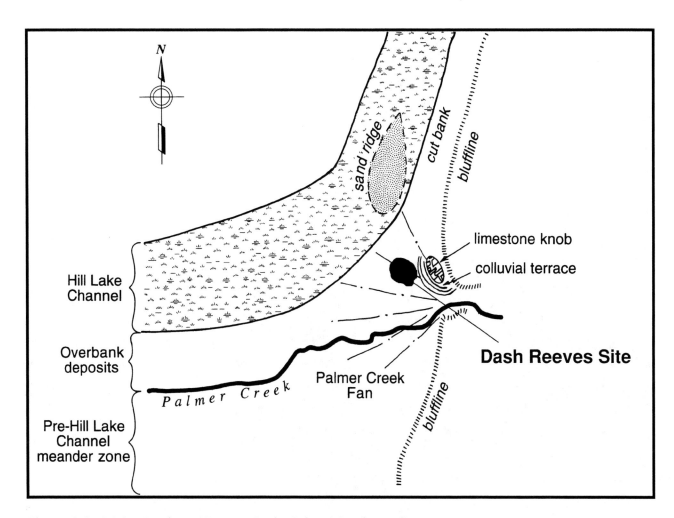

Figure 2.2. Major Landscape Features in the Palmer Creek Locality

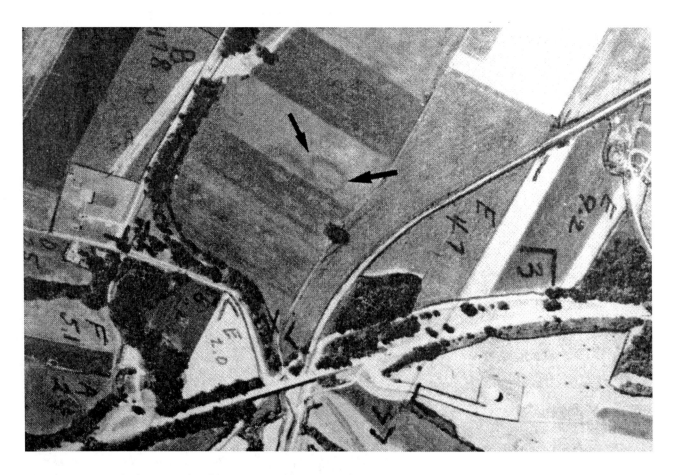

Plate 2.1. Aerial Photograph of Site Area with Ring Midden (Paleochannel) Delineated

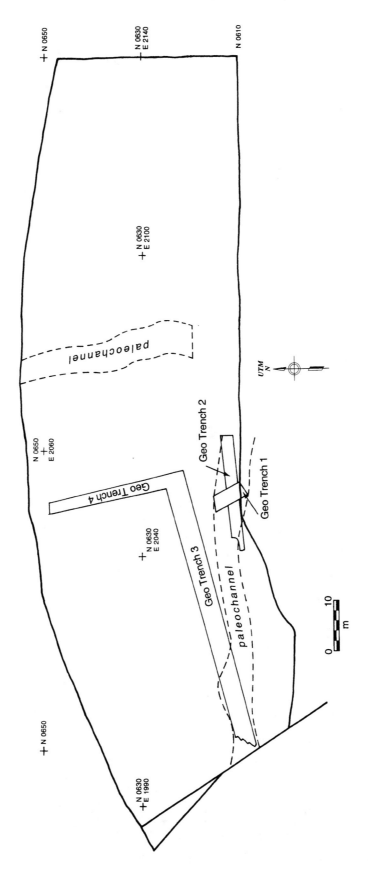

Figure 2.3. Location of Paleochannels and Geomorphological Trenches Within the Excavated Portion of the Right-of-Way

have represented a secondary braid of the main Palmer Creek channel. Braided channels are typical of and have been observed at other alluvial fan localities in this area (Fortier et al. 1983). The smaller channel at Dash Reeves appears on the contour map as a shallow depression and extends at least 100 m north of the proposed right-of-way. Presumably, this channel had been partially filled by the time of the Middle Woodland occupation. As previously mentioned, the site's occupants utilized this older channel or swale as a refuse dump. Auger probing outside the excavation limits tracked this midden-laden swale in a northwesterly direction, where it coincides with the dark ring observed on the aerial photograph. Curiously, the midden ring does not coincide with the north-south depression observed on the contour map. It is possible that this smaller channel contains several tertiary braids as it extends to the north and west. Augering indicated that only the curved braid was utilized as a midden dump.

The second, larger channel, demarcating the southern and western limits of the occupation, clearly represents the main Palmer Creek channel. It is bedded with silt laminae, gravels and pebbles, and clay bands, and is significantly deeper than the smaller channel described above. During excavation of trenches in this area, a relatively restricted deposit of Middle Woodland debris, including pottery, chert debitage, a large portion of a deer carcass with skull and antler parts, and carbonized wood and nut remains, was recovered in the basal sediments of the channel. This material covered an area of no more than 3 x 2 m. It appears to represent a single-episode dump. There is evidence for subsequent rapid filling of the channel with loessal silts, as evidenced by the occurrence of a Middle Woodland pit excavated into those silts. The materials from this feature (Feature 56) date to the Hill Lake phase and are similar to the materials recovered from deep in the channel deposits. In short, it is apparent that Palmer Creek was active along the southern limits of the site for a time during the period of occupation but that it was filled by silts prior to site abandonment. Presumably, the creek moved further to the south or west, leaving behind a shallow swale that occupants utilized to some degree as a cooking or food-processing locus. It is interesting that this now-abandoned channel was not utilized as a dumping area for refuse. The rapid filling of a channel, which may have been several meters deep at one time, demonstrates the energetic and dynamic nature of fan development in this area, a factor that apparently did not restrict continued occupation of this specific locality.

Given the dynamic nature of changing creek channels and the probable wet conditions caused by periodic overflows, it is somewhat intriguing that Middle Woodland peoples actually selected this particular locality for occupation. There are certainly higher, more stable locations within a 1-km radius of this site. Access to nearby aquatic resources such as the Hill Lake marsh was no doubt important, but not appreciably more advantageous than access from other habitable locations within a kilometer of Dash Reeves (Figure 2.4). This location also would not have placed the site's occupants any closer to chert resources, of possible importance considering the huge quantities of chert recovered. It is possible that the loessal soils (Dupo silt loam), perhaps periodically replenished by alluvial erosion and kept wet by overflows, were of critical importance to incipient horticulturalists.

An important resource in this locality's general catchment area is a major outcrop of Ste. Genevieve red chert, located approximately 2 km south of the site on the north side of Carr Creek where it outlets into the Mississippi River floodplain. The Ste. Genevieve limestone formation occurs in the upper portion of the Valmeyeran Series (Mississippian System) and beds upward within the Columbia syncline. Its exposure on the present surface is very restricted and rare in this area (see Figure 2.5). In fact, except for a few isolated occurrences within Carr Creek itself, red Ste. Genevieve cherts have been found only in the Carr Creek outlet exposure. During Middle Woodland times, red cherts were commonly used for tool manufacture. It is probably no accident that a number of Middle Woodland sites cluster within a 10-km radius of this particular outcrop. In fact, approximately 70 percent of the chert recovered from the Dash Reeves site is Ste. Genevieve red.

The Middle Woodland occupation occurs directly beneath the present plowzone. Approximately 150 cm below this occupation is a buried paleosol, or A horizon, measuring 40–60 cm in thickness (Plate 2.2). This soil horizon was formed in loessal soils and probably extends over most of the fan area. It was detected at the nearby Marge site, where it was found at the base of a modern railroad bed. Near the base of the A horizon at Dash Reeves, a Late Archaic Falling Springs phase projectile point (see Figure 12.1a) and several chert flakes were

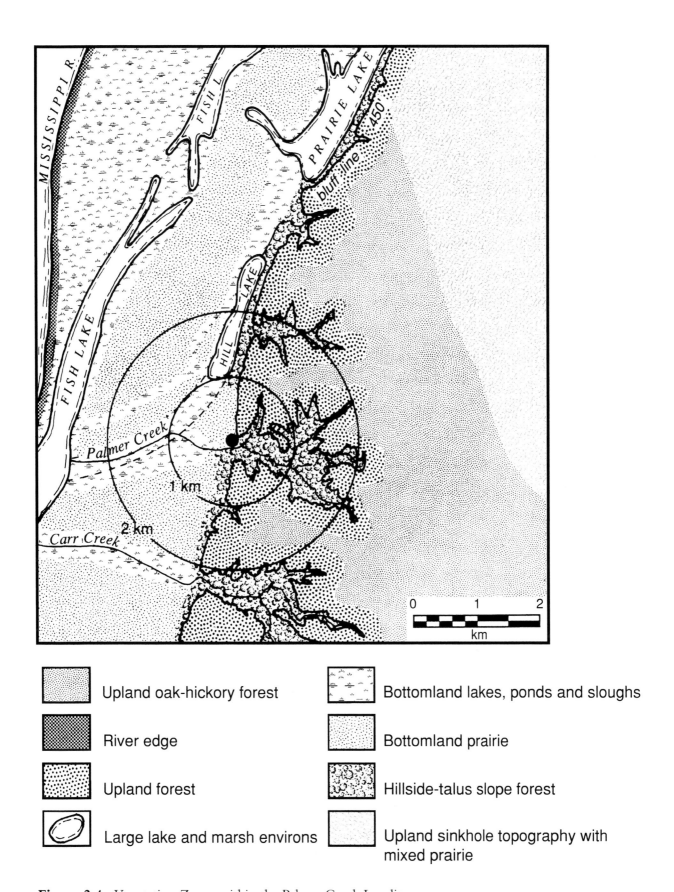

Figure 2.4. Vegetation Zones within the Palmer Creek Locality

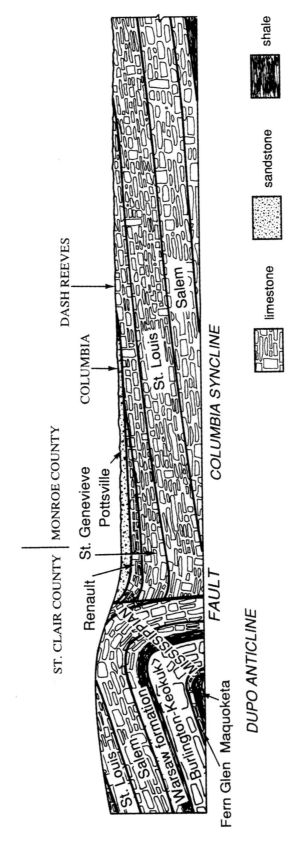

Figure 2.5. Geological Cross–Section of the Project Area (Adapted from Weller 1939:Figure 2)

Plate 2.2. Buried Paleosol in Geo-Trench 3 (upper) and Paleosol Truncated by Old Creek Scar (lower)

recovered. This suggests strongly that a relatively stable surface existed on the fan at least during the early Late Archaic period. Sometime between that period (ca. 1500 B.C.) and the Middle Woodland period, more than a meter of loessal sediment was deposited over the area. The period of stability, possibly coinciding with prairie-like conditions, may have terminated at the time of the Hill Lake Meander cut-off (ca. 1500 B.C.–1100 B.C.) (White et al. 1984:23). At the time of the cut-off from the main Mississippi River channel, silts were allowed to accumulate in the channel scar or oxbow lake. This, in effect, eventually would have raised the gradient and slowed the westward flow of water from Palmer Creek. This, in turn, would have resulted in the accumulation of silts on the fan surface, accelerating the development of the fan. This process would account for the silts deposited between the Late Archaic and Middle Woodland occupations. Curiously, there is little or no evidence for significant silt build-up following the Middle Woodland period. It is possible that at that point silts were being redirected to other areas of the fan, perhaps to the south. Another possibility is that Palmer Creek itself became deeply entrenched and alluviation was more focused around the channel. In any case, no significant occupation, in the sense of habitation, occurred in this location following the late Middle Woodland period. Of course, it is possible that parts of this area were farmed by later prehistoric groups, but there is little direct evidence of this. It is possible that *some* of the polished Mill Creek hoe flakes from the site are associated with Mississippian or Emergent Mississipian farming practices. However, Mill Creek hoe flakes are also found in Middle Woodland pit and submidden contexts at Dash Reeves.

The Middle Woodland occupation exposed within the limits of the right-of-way slopes down gradually to the west. The elevation differential between features located in the far western and eastern ends of the site varies from 40 to 60 cm. There is actually a relatively sharp incline at the far western end that is associated with the deep paleochannel that coursed near that area. Features in the far western area were covered by a dense clay overburden representing splay deposits from the creek. This indicates that the creek was still active in this location at the time of occupation. The gradual downward gradient to the west follows the slope of the fan. Areas along this slope were subsequently dissected in a north-south direction by Palmer Creek paleochannels.

The Middle Woodland occupation appears to have been located primarily on higher ground between a series of active and inactive channels, with some of the inactive channel swales utilized as refuse dumping areas.

The densest occupation area occurs within and adjacent to the dark circular ring clearly visible on aerial photographs (Plate 2.1). As noted, the dark ring coincides with a paleochannel scar, specifically with one utilized as a refuse dump. Essentially, this ring constitutes a midden that appears to enclose the main occupation area. Probes outside the right-of-way indicated that this ring was filled with cultural remains and that materials in the enclosed area were less dense, although evidence of a shallow midden was also detected there. As described in Chapter 6, features uncovered within the right-of-way appear to form an arc along the inside of the ring. Although no structures were found within the right-of-way area, it is quite possible that the main hub of the occupation lies further north within the center of the ring midden. Unfortunately, this is the area impacted most drastically by recent gas tank excavations.

3

HISTORY OF SITE
INVESTIGATIONS

This chapter provides a detailed overview of the sequence of events leading from the site's initial discovery through the production of this report. While the history of investigations at this site may be of only passing interest to many, it is becoming more and more necessary to document the duration of tasks so that cultural resource managers at all levels have reasonable planning information for future projects of equivalent size. Having an appropriate research design at the outset is important, but the decision-making process in the field as well as in the laboratory is equally vital. Unfortunately, there is no easy recipe for excavation and analysis, since every site presents its own difficulties and has its own history. A field director controls much, but not all of that history. The process is dependent upon a number of variables, including the director's field experience, the season of excavation, the amount of available money and time, and the peculiarities of the site itself. For example, on a site type not previously encountered the decision-making process is always slower and less predictable. Middle Woodland sites are particularly exasperating in that regard since middens often cover or envelop features such as pits or houses. To ignore midden materials and focus strictly on submidden features is to ignore up to 70 percent of the cultural record of the inhabitants of the site. On the other hand, complete excavation of such middens is usually not practical both in terms of cost or time. Sampling becomes a critical aspect of the decision-making process in the field but is rarely straightforward, particularly when several different kinds of middens are encountered on the same site and when feature distribution is uneven, such as was the case at Dash Reeves.

It is hoped that the following sections provide insights into the process that culminated in the production of this report.

BACKGROUND AND
INITIAL SURVEY

The Dash Reeves site has figured in a number of projects dating back almost 25 years. The site was first encountered on August 17, 1971, by James W. Porter's Historic Sites Survey (HSS) crew. The site was named after George Reeves, the property owner at that time, and his dog Dash, and not after Col. *Dache* Reeves of local aerial photography fame (see Reeves 1936). Porter and crew collected a large assemblage of mostly Middle Woodland artifacts, and the site was assigned a high priority for further investigation because of its size (6.6 ha), its artifact density, its cultural affiliation, and predicted urban encroachment (Porter 1971:32). Based on this assessment Porter returned to the site the following year (June 27–July 1, 1972), and under his direction, I supervised several crew members in the excavation of four nearly contiguous 1-x-10-m test units. These were placed nearly 90 m northwest of a large cottonwood tree and several meters south of the field road (Figure 3.1). An arbitrary grid oriented northeast-southwest was established and tied to an arbitrary elevation. Some cultural material was retrieved, but more importantly, units revealed a 10 to 25-cm-thick midden situated at the base of the plowzone (Figure 3.2). No features were

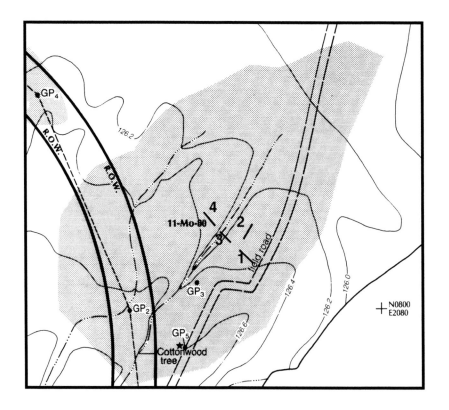

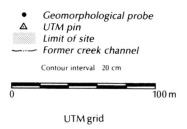

Figure 3.1. Location of 1972 Test Trenches

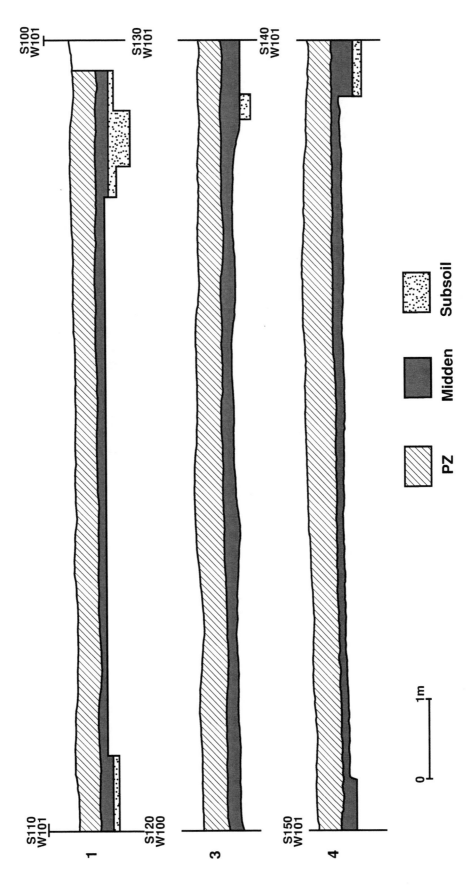

Figure 3.2. 1972 Test Trench Profiles

encountered, although field notes indicated the presence of possible post molds at the base of one unit (Porter 1972:26–27). At that time the midden zone was recognized only as a transitional soil zone. However, it is clear from Porter's soil descriptions and profiles that this zone was identical to the midden described later in the main excavation area. It is also significant that the 1972 midden zone gradually increased in depth as units were extended out into the main site area. The profile of Trench 4 revealed the depth of the midden to be 25 cm. Porter apparently revisited Dash Reeves periodically over the next two or three years, making general surface pick-ups. Eventually, Pam Butler, an undergraduate at the University of Wisconsin at Madison, prepared a short (unpublished) senior thesis based on the material recovered from the site.

In 1976 an FAP-410 field crew from Southern Illinois University at Edwardsville resurveyed the site and collected over 450 items, including 11 projectile points, 23 Middle Woodland sherds, and a polished stone celt (Williams and Woods 1977:34, 119). These materials were not available at the time the current analysis was undertaken and, therefore, have not been incorporated into this report. The proposed FAP-410 highway project was subsequently shelved, and the site was not revisited until 1980, when it fell within the parameters of the Fish Lake Survey, directed by Warren Wittry (Wittry 1981). Although Wittry collected materials from the site, he did not report them, instead listing the FAP-410 materials (Wittry 1981:9). I inspected the curated materials from the Wittry survey and identified several sherds and chert tools diagnostic of the Middle Woodland period. Wittry did not attempt to redefine the limits of the site, as surface visibility apparently was not good at the time of his visit. No subsurface testing was carried out as part of Wittry's project.

During 1987 (June 30 and August 4, 5, and 12) the Resource Investigation Program (RIP) of the University of Illinois at Urbana-Champaign carried out a survey of the site and the surrounding locality in connection with IDOT's proposed Columbia Bypass Project. A portion of the Dash Reeves site was to be impacted by that project. Several walk-overs were made of the site area, which at that time was in high corn affording less than 40 percent surface visibility. No collection of artifacts was made, given that collections existed from previous surveys of the site. It was recommended, in the event the IDOT project proceeded, that additional archaeological investigations be undertaken at the site. Specific recommendations included the preparation of a topographic map, controlled surface collection, and hand excavations, combined with limited use of heavy machinery.

TESTING PHASE

Phase Two work was initiated on December 8, 1987, by a crew of three (Fortier 1988). Although this work was conducted under the umbrella of RIP, the project was funded separately. From December 8 to 14, a contour map was produced of the site area, a controlled surface collection, consisting of 110 10- x-10-m squares, was made inside the right-of-way, and a general surface collection to define the limits of the site was accomplished outside the right-of-way (Figures 3.3–3.5). The site covered a 30,000 m² area, of which only 6,000 m² fell within the proposed right-of-way. Three 1-x-2-m test units were excavated in the central portion of the right-of-way. These were excavated to varying depths from 50 to 100 cm below the present surface. Despite excavation during a heavy snowstorm, evidence of a 10 to 15-cm-thick dark midden deposit, situated directly beneath the plowzone, was identified in each unit. During the testing phase several Giddings rig cores were taken within the right-of-way by Dr. Ed Hajic, the consulting geomorphologist. A testing report was submitted during the spring of 1988 including the results of the geomorphic work (Hajic 1988). Much of the environmental description presented in the previous chapter is based on Hajic's data appended to that testing report. As a result of the Phase Two investigation, further work was recommended should the IDOT proceed with proposed highway and bridge construction. Although no features had been uncovered, it was believed that they would be exposed once the midden was excavated. This speculation was based on work at the Holding site, which had presented similar pre-excavation conditions (Fortier et al. 1989).

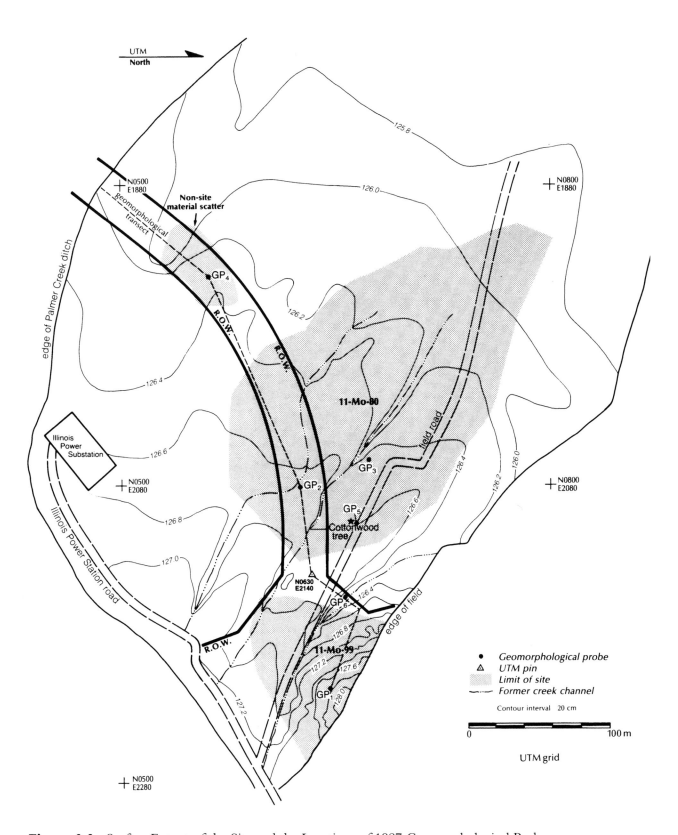

Figure 3.3. Surface Extent of the Site and the Locations of 1987 Geomorphological Probes

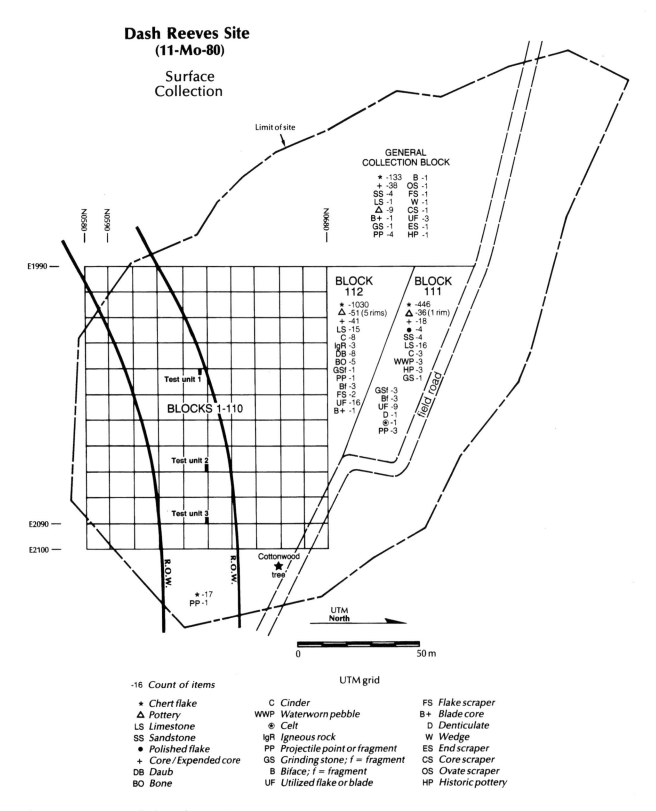

Figure 3.4. Controlled Surface Collection Blocks and 1987 Test Units

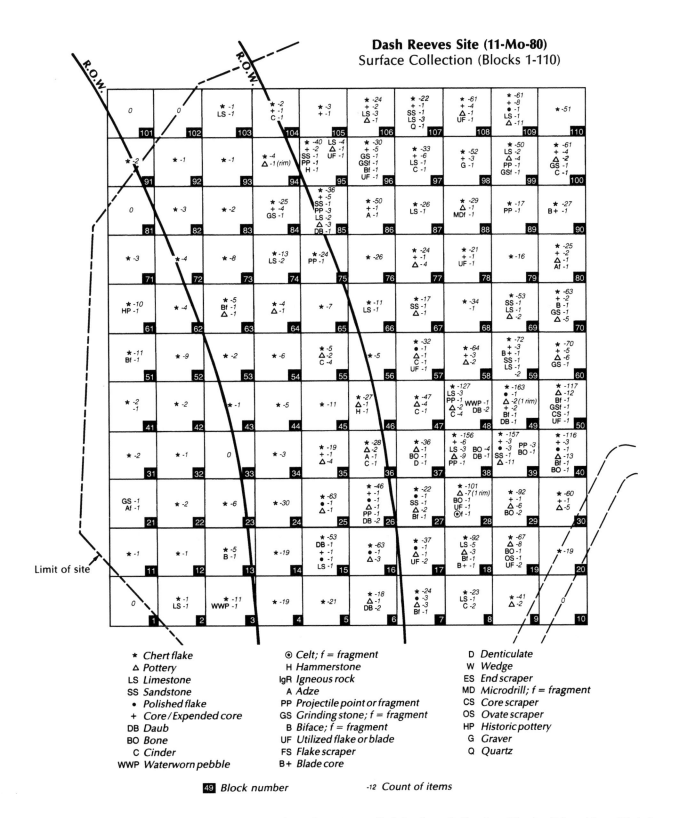

Figure 3.5. Distribution of Cultural Materials within Controlled Surface Collection Blocks (10-x-10-m Units)

EXCAVATION:
STRATEGY AND METHODS

Due to delays in IDOT construction schedules and land purchase, archaeological investigations in the project area did not resume until June 27, 1990. At that time members of the crew that had just completed excavations at the nearby Marge site were shifted to work at the Dash Reeves site. At the outset it was known that an extensive midden lay over the entire site but that it could not be excavated entirely, as had been accomplished at the Holding site. Therefore, a strategy was developed to evaluate the extent and depth of the midden so that excavations could focus on particularly productive areas. A UTM grid was established with the aid of IDOT surveyors, and an extensive soil augering strategy was employed to track the limits and depth of the midden within the right-of-way. Probes were taken along north-south transects varying in length from 30 to 50 m and spaced 5 m apart. Probes were taken at 1-m intervals to a depth of approximately 50–60 cm. Approximately 1,200 probes were taken within the right-of-way. The soil auger had a 1/4-inch bore, which proved to be sufficient for identifying the natural soil profile as well as the cultural midden. A soil profile was recorded for each probe. The probes were evaluated at two levels. Any probe producing a suspicious soil profile or unusual discoloration was defined as being weakly positive. Approximately 28 percent of the probes (n=335) fell into this category. Most of these tests simply reflected subtle natural soil changes. Thirty-five probes (2.9 percent) encountered a combination of cultural material, charcoal flecking, and soil discoloration, and were regarded as culturally significant. Following excavation of the site we learned that 17 of these probes had been associated with the creek midden portion of the site. Only two or three probes (less than 2 percent of all probes) actually penetrated subsoil feature fill at the site. The remaining positive probes essentially had cut through the shallow cultural midden that draped the site north of the UTM N0630 line. A generalized field map of all the positive probes was constructed to guide the placement of subsequent test and excavation units, especially within the dense creek midden area. Augering procedures were completed on July 5, 1990.

The second phase of excavation involved the placement and excavation of 13 2-x-2-m test units (designated Units A–N, with the letter I not being utilized). These units were located within the right-of-way, based on the soil auger tests (Plate 3.1). Not all units were placed in areas yielding positive probes, as we wished to establish several "natural" profiles for comparative purposes. All of the units were excavated in 10-cm levels, and all soil was screened through 1/4-inch mesh hardware cloth. The purpose of these units was to establish more detailed profiles of the midden and to document the density of cultural materials in various portions of the site. Test Units A–F were started and completed between July 6-17. Units G–H were completed July 24. The remaining Units (J–N) were completed during the first week in August (Figure 3.6).

The most important result of the augering and test unit strategy was the recognition that the midden became decidedly more shallow and less dense in a southerly direction. In fact, the centerline of the right-of-way essentially represented the limits of the midden deposition, or at least the limits of what could be mapped in profile. As a result of this observation, a decision was made to use heavy equipment to remove the plowzone south of the centerline, or south of the approximate UTM N0630 line (Plate 3.1). This was accomplished on July 18–19 and involved the removal of approximately 3,000 m^2 of soil. A western extension beyond the limits of the originally defined site area also was scraped on July 19 but failed to reveal midden, features, or cultural materials. In short, during this period the western and southern limits of the site were defined (Figure 3.7).

Because cultural materials were identified in pockets of the southern area, four 4-x-4-m excavation units, designated Excavation Units 1–4, were placed in this area. These units were hand excavated but not screened, although all diagnostic rims, body sherds, and lithic tools were piece-plotted. It became apparent that a thin veneer of shallow midden existed in some portions of the southern area and that, quite possibly, this was masking submidden features. In fact, Unit 1 had produced three pit features (Plate 3.2 continued, lower).

The 4-x-4-m unit was selected as the standard excavation unit at the site because this size had proven useful at the Holding site and its use hopefully would provide a standard of comparison between Dash Reeves and Holding, at least in terms of calculating midden

Plate 3.1. General Excavation Views: upper, Dash Reeves prior to excavation; lower, 2-x-2-m test unit excavation

Plate 3.1. General Excavation Views, continued: upper, backhoe excavation and feature definition at the base of the midden; lower, roto-tilling the midden north of N 0630

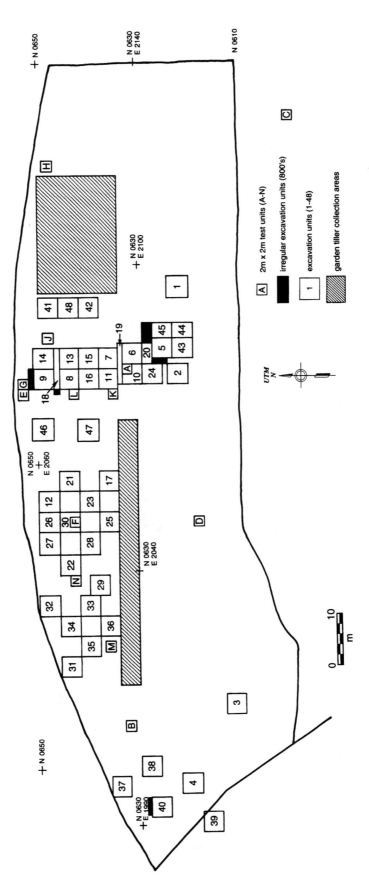

Figure 3.6. Distribution of 1990 Test Units (A–N) and Excavation Units (1–48)

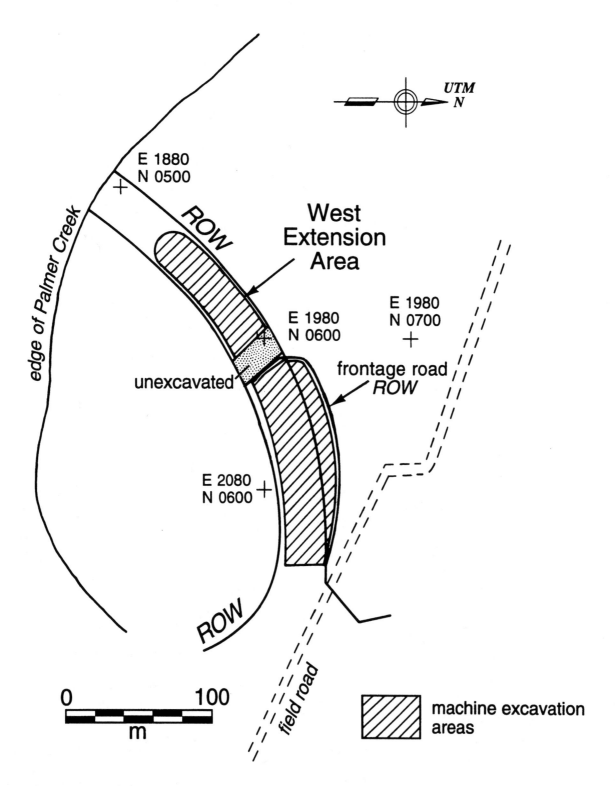

UTM
N

E 1880
N 0500
+

ROW

West
Extension
Area

E 1980
N 0600

E 1980
N 0700
+

frontage road
ROW

unexcavated

edge of Palmer Creek

E 2080
N 0600 +

ROW

field road

0   100
m

machine excavation
areas

Figure 3.7. Extent of Machine Excavations

Plate 3.2. Excavation Views: upper, excavation within the creek midden; lower, hand excavation in Excavation Unit 27 (foreground)

Plate 3.2. Excavation Views, continued: upper, completed excavation units in the eastern portion of the right-of-way; lower, profiles of Features 1–3 in Excavation Unit 1

density. At Dash Reeves it took three people two days to complete a 4-x-4-m unit. A new mapping technique was utilized in these units to more accurately pinpoint and more swiftly remove piece-plotted artifacts. This involved running tapes to the artifact from the unit's northeast and northwest corner stakes. The two taped distances to the artifact constituted two sides of a triangle, with the third side being the north wall of the unit. With the lengths of the three sides of the triangle known, it was possible to calculate the grid coordinates of each piece plot later in the laboratory using a simple computer formula. This technique is more accurate than right-angle field mapping and requires less time (it took approximately five minutes per artifact in the field). It was also quicker than piece-plotting with a standard transit (of course, use of an electronic laser transit, not available to our crews at that time, is far superior to each of the aforementioned techniques). Elevation was taken from a datum near each unit. Using this technique, approximately 500 piece-plotted artifacts had coordinates calculated by computer.

Following the excavation of the first four 4-x-4-m units, a backhoe was utilized on July 30 to excavate the remaining portion of the southern area of the right-of-way. The entire southern area was stripped to sterile subsoil in order to locate features. Backhoe work lasted until August 2 and resulted in the location of 20 features. Between August 9–16 all features in this area were mapped and excavated. Unfortunately, heavy rainfall from August 2–8 precluded any work at the site and delayed machine excavation in other areas of the site.

After August 9 attention shifted to the area north of UTM N0630. From August 9–16 a backhoe was utilized to remove the plowzone in this area in order to reveal the top portion of the midden and to expose its entire extent. A shallow, barely detectable, sheet midden was revealed over a broad area of the western portion of this exposure, while a deeper, darker, and more artifact-rich midden was revealed in the eastern area. The eastern midden later proved to be a more restricted deposit coinciding with an older paleochannel. This area was approximately 10 m wide and extended 35 m in length in a north-south direction. This area was clearly visible following backhoe excavation and became the focus of major excavation in the following month.

At this point in the excavation the entire southern area had been investigated but the northern area lay exposed and needed to be examined in more detail. This area covered approximately 3,500 m². Included was a short stretch to be developed as a frontage road paralleling the northernmost edge of the right-of-way, which was to provide the landowner with access to his fields from the main road. This proposed road area was machine excavated and incorporated into the northern right-of-way area. Since it was not possible to hand excavate the entire northern right-of-way area, a strategy was devised to sample the western and central portions of the midden, which appeared to be less dense in terms of cultural remains, and to excavate in its entirety the dark midden area within the paleochannel. This area appeared to offer the best chance to recover a broad spectrum of artifacts, as well as information about the nature of what appeared to be a more extensive ring midden encircling the entire occupation.

From August 21 to September 27 excavation was completed of the western and eastern paleochannel areas as well as selected units within the central portion of the sheet midden (Plate 3.2). Twenty-nine units were excavated during this period. Not all of the units in the channel area were the standard 4-x-4-m size. Because of the irregularity of the channel itself and our desire to excavate mostly within the channel, some gaps occurred between units. These gaps were filled by smaller units of various sizes.

On September 27 a small garden tiller was utilized in areas not selected for unit excavation, specifically in a 5-x-50-m strip paralleling the N0630 line and in a 17-x-25-m block east of the channel dump (Plate 3.1). The purpose was to disc the midden in these areas in hopes of churning up artifacts that could be collected in much the same manner as materials are recovered during surface collection surveys in plowed fields. In this case we waited until October 16 for a sufficient rain before proceeding with the pick-up. This technique, attempted as a possible substitute for hand excavation in these areas, proved ineffective, largely because the tiller rarely reached the base of the midden where most of the artifacts occurred and because it was destructive to both lithic and ceramic artifacts. The garden tiller, in effect, disturbed the soil matrix more severely than an ordinary plow would have since it was equipped with more blades operating in a more restricted space.

Excavation of 4-x-4-m units, placed more or less checkerboard fashion in the central and western areas of the site continued until October 21, ending with completion of Excavation Unit 48 (Figure 3.6). All in all, 768 m² were excavated, amounting to less than 1 percent of the exposed midden area in the northern portion of the right-of-way. Because of the small size of the crew, which never exceeded six individuals, and the impending construction schedule, additional units were not attempted.

During October 22–25 the remaining portion of the northern right-of-way area was excavated by backhoe to sterile soil in order to uncover any features that might lie at the base of the midden. All diagnostic artifacts were piece-plotted by transit and newly exposed features were flagged. Mapping and excavation of approximately 35 additional features followed and was completed on October 28. In addition, on October 26 several long geomorphological trenches were excavated to check for any buried horizons or paleochannels. These trenches were mapped and profiled over several days. In fact, a deeply buried soil horizon was encountered that had not been recognized in previous geomorphic cores or test augers. This horizon produced a Late Archaic projectile point, some burned clay fragments, and several chert flakes. No features were encountered. No further work was carried out to investigate the extent of this buried occupation, largely because the removal of such a massive amount of soil overburden above this horizon simply was not feasible and cultural material in this horizon was essentially restricted to an area not more than 5–10 m in extent.

On October 28, 1990, the excavation within the right-of-way portion of the Dash Reeves site was terminated. Between June 27 and that date, a crew of four to six, myself included, expended 86 days or 3,408 work-hours investigating the site. Approximately 22,150 m² was exposed by backhoe (102 hours) and paddlewheel scraping (16 hours). Note that this figure exceeds the size of the site within the right-of-way because many areas were scraped twice, once with a paddlewheel and once with a backhoe. Fifty-three features were exposed and excavated.

PROCESSING AND ANALYSIS

Approximately 80 percent of the materials recovered from the Dash Reeves site were washed and labeled on rain days during the field season. These materials, as well as any remaining unwashed materials, were transported to the Urbana laboratory at the University of Illinois for processing and analysis on October 29, 1990. Water flotation samples had previously been sent to Urbana but remained in storage until the following spring (1991), when processing was initiated. The flotation and water screening of all soil samples was completed during the summer and early fall of 1991.

From November to December 1990 I organized incoming materials, completed the washing and labeling of artifacts, and backchecked all feature and field notes and maps. The majority of the ceramics had been pulled during the field season and were organized by Tom Maher, who eventually transported these materials to the University of North Carolina for analysis. From January 1991 to August 1991 I turned my attention to the analysis of the Marge site.

Analysis of the Dash Reeves material assemblage (excluding ceramics) was initiated during September 1991. Lithic materials alone occupied approximately 40 orange crate-size boxes. The initial lithic inventory involved the sorting of debitage from tools. From September to December all of the chert debitage and nonchert materials were inventoried (typed and weighed). Kristin Hedman and I identified chert types and stages of reduction. From January 1992 through May 1992 all of the tools (chert and nonchert), were inventoried, coded, and computerized, and measurements were taken on nearly 200 projectile points. Since the Dash Reeves site produced a sizable and unique assemblage of blades, blade cores, and blade tools, a separate analysis of these materials was undertaken. This analysis lasted from June to December 1992 and included the computer entry of a sizable data base. From January through April 1993 statistics and tables were generated in advance of report writing. In April 1993 I once again focused on the Marge site, then in the report preparation stage. The Marge site report was written between April and August 1993. Production and editing of that report continued into the spring of 1994, at which time the writing of the Dash Reeves site report was initiated. Writing of this report continued through the summer of 1994.

ENDNOTE

Excavation of the Dash Reeves site lasted four months. Processing and analysis of materials, excluding ceramics, took approximately 19 months. Writing and report preparation was accomplished over a five to six-month period. Not included in these figures is the time spent on cartography, illustration, photography, picking and sorting of flotation materials, identification of floral and faunal materials, storage and curation of materials for final disposition, and editing of the report. All of these activities translate into additional time and money. But they are necessary if one takes the position that the conjunctive approach is the proper approach to take in analyzing an archaeological site and reporting on the results of analysis. Sampling is always an issue, and it should be noted that the Dash Reeves site has been sampled, both in terms of the fieldwork and the subsequent analysis.

As a somewhat disconcerting endnote to this historical overview, at this writing the Dash Reeves site is being heavily damaged by the construction of buildings, water lines, and other urban necessities. It is highly likely that 10 years from now the Dash Reeves site, one of the largest Middle Woodland sites in the American Bottom, will be completely obliterated. Even during the course of excavation we knew that this would occur, and for that reason we made an effort to retrieve and report on as much information as possible.

4

RESEARCH DESIGN AND EXCAVATION STRATEGY

It was known at the outset of this project that proposed road construction would impact only a small percentage of the Dash Reeves site and, moreover, would encompass an area that had yielded only a very light scatter of surface materials. This area, in fact, appeared to coincide with the western and southern limits of the site. Nevertheless, a midden was known to exist in this area, and subsurface features were anticipated. Another overriding concern was for the portion of the site beyond the limits of the proposed highway construction, which was endangered by encroaching urban development. To a great extent the initial survey and excavation strategies were dictated by this concern. Ultimately, these strategies were geared toward total site exposure within the proposed highway right-of-way and complete recovery of all data within that area. A decision also was made to incorporate all of the surface materials collected from outside of the right-of-way into the data presentation in this report, since very little of this material had been published previously and it seemed unlikely to be the subject of future in-depth analysis.

The Dash Reeves site is one of only a handful of Middle Woodland sites investigated in the American Bottom. Because of its size and enormous artifact assemblage, it is unique. Its only excavated rival is the Holding site (Fortier et al. 1989), which slightly predates Dash Reeves and which produced significantly less lithic material. By comparison, nearly three times the number of chert tools, three times the number of cores, seven times the number of hafted bifaces, and four times the number of blades were recovered from the

Dash Reeves site. Conversely, the Dash Reeves site assemblage is not nearly as diverse as the Holding site assemblage, particularly in terms of chert types, exotic or nonlocal artifacts, nonchert lithic artifacts, or ceramic types. While the Holding site can be characterized as a horticultural hamlet, Dash Reeves appears to have functioned as a specialized lithic tool production center.

The Dash Reeves site is also significant because it dates to the interval between the Hopewell (or Havana/Hopewell) and early Late Woodland periods in this area. Very little is known about settlement, subsistence, or technology patterns during this interval, referred to as the Hill Lake phase. Prior to the excavations at Dash Reeves, the only data concerning this period came from the Truck #7 site (Fortier 1985a) and from scattered remains and features at the Holding site (Fortier et al. 1989). The Hill Lake phase is generally characterized as having Pike/Baehr series ceramics, poorly executed Hopewell ceramics, virtually no Hopewell Interaction Sphere artifacts, and a greatly reduced blade and core industry compared with Hopewell (Fortier et al. 1989:558–560). In general this characterization is supported by the Dash Reeves assemblage. Dash Reeves differs from this template only in regard to its extensive blade and core industry. It is clear from the Dash Reeves investigations that blade technology, previously assumed to be primarily associated with the Hopewell, or Holding, phase in this area, persisted into the Hill Lake phase, at least at some sites heavily involved in lithic tool production. Blades, blade tools, and blade cores form a significant part of the lithic assemblage from this site. Since this technology was so short-lived in the Midwest and is so poorly understood, the description and documentation of the Dash Reeves industry formed an important focus of the research design.

Equally important is the discovery at the site of a microtool industry, including such tools as microdrills, perforators, and gravers, some made on blades and others made on other reduction-stage materials. There has been a tendency in the regional literature to focus on the larger bifacial tools, including hafted bifaces and scrapers, at the expense of these smaller tools. The reason for this is that these smaller tool types have never been particularly abundant on Middle Woodland sites. The diversity of these kinds of tools at the Dash Reeves site far exceeds the range of small tool types recovered from the Holding site and resulted in a more complex analytical process than originally anticipated.

The delineation of a community plan was one of the explicit research goals of the original excavation project. Unfortunately, only a relatively small number of features (N=53) were identified within the right-of-way area, and these were dispersed mostly along an arc outlining the eastern, western, and southern limits of the site. The bulk of the occupation lies outside of the right-of-way limits and could not be investigated; as a result, the complete community configuration could not be obtained. The features themselves were also relatively unproductive in terms of artifact content, so it became clear that feature analysis would not be a central research issue. Consequently, the major focus of this report is on technological, distributional, and typological aspects of the lithic and ceramic assemblage recovered from the midden, itself a special type of feature on Middle Woodland sites in this area. It is probable that over 90 percent of the materials recovered at the site come from midden contexts. Moreover, since the vast majority of artifacts appear to date exclusively to the Hill Lake phase, this assemblage can be treated as a single data set. Given the significant quantity of surface debris from this site and the documented presence of a midden, it was clear from the outset of the project that the primary research focus would be the delineation of the midden and a description of its artifacts.

More general questions of chronological affiliation, subsistence, and the transition from Hopewell to Late Woodland culture in this area also were incorporated into the overall research design. Although no single site can resolve such general issues, it is important to document the nature and extent of assemblages representing the periods just prior to major cultural discontinuities. Dash Reeves is the largest and most complex site excavated to date from the Hopewell/Late Woodland transition period, and its material assemblage stands in stark contrast to later assemblages in the area. Conversely, with its focus on local lithic resources and apparent minimal contact with the world beyond the American Bottom, Dash Reeves anticipates the Late Woodland template in the area. This suggests that the so-called collapse of Hopewellian culture may have occurred quickly but well within the parameters of what we recognize to be a longer-lived Middle Woodland culture. The existence of a complex blade industry at Dash Reeves is ample proof of this, as is its distinctive Hill Lake phase ceramic assemblage.

Because of the size of the area within the right-of-way it was obvious that the overlying midden could only be sampled and not excavated in its entirety as had been accomplished at the Holding site. Essentially, the excavation strategy focused on establishing the vertical and horizontal parameters of the midden and the locations of features beneath the midden and determining the relative densities and distribution of artifacts within the midden. The initial 2-x-2-m test units were placed in various areas of the site, and units were excavated to various depths to determine the vertical extent of the midden in those localities as well as their material inventories. The midden was clearly visible at the base of the plowzone. Following removal of plowzone over the site area, a series of excavation units, mostly 4 x 4 m in size, was hand excavated, with artifacts collected in a systematic manner, particularly in terms of horizontal and vertical controls. Profiles of the midden were made in each unit in hopes of establishing surface trends for the base of the midden as well as density patterns for artifacts in different parts of the site. Once these excavation units were completed, the remaining portion of unexcavated midden was removed by heavy machinery in order to expose submidden features. These features were excavated and provided a major source of subsistence information.

It should be pointed out that very little effort has been expended in the Midwest on Middle Woodland middens, so much of our energy at the site was devoted as much to understanding formational processes as to learning about the nature of the artifact assemblage. We learned, for example, that middens were formed in a variety of ways at this site. For example, in addition to building up through accretional processes, middens formed as Middle Woodland peoples dumped refuse discriminately away from living areas. This means that on many Middle Woodland sites we need to be aware of the possible existence of specialized dumping areas and not assume that all refuse was simply randomly strewn about living areas. At the Holding site this possibility was not considered. There is also evidence at Dash Reeves that dumping was episodic and variable in terms of artifact content. For example, contiguous excavation units within the creek swale often produced very different artifact spectrums, both in terms of quantity of debris and artifact type and diversity. An isolated dump also was identified at the base of what had been an active creek and is interesting because of the variety of items recovered, including a large segment of a ceramic vessel, lithic debris, remains of a deer, and carbonized plant materials. The association is curious and may or may not represent a single event. Isolated dumps such as this have not previously been recorded in this area but may be more prevalent than anticipated. Their existence provides a possible solution to the whereabouts of missing data on sites, for example, missing portions of vessels represented by only one rim sherd. In any case, such contextual variety on Middle Woodland sites should be anticipated and incorporated into the overall excavation plan and research design for any site dating to this period.

5

THE FEATURE ASSEMBLAGE

Fifty-three features were identified and excavated at the Dash Reeves site. Most were shallow pits and hearths and were concentrated in the eastern and westernmost portions of the exposed site area, with a more dispersed pattern in the central portion of the site. An overall community pattern is unclear from the distribution, but features appear to form an arc coinciding with the ring midden detected in an aerial photograph of the site area (Figure 5.1). It is quite possible that the center of the community lies at the center of this ring, located 50–75 m north of the project right-of-way limits. The excavated portion of the Middle Woodland occupation, therefore, represents the southernmost part of the community, which is bordered on the south and west by a creek channel that was apparently active during some portion of the occupation.

A variety of pit and hearth-like features constitute the feature assemblage. Feature types include open-basin cooking pits, specialized, sunken cooking pits, cooking/refuse pits, extended hearths, special-purpose pits, a cache pit, fire stains, an activity area stain, and postmolds (Plate 5.1). Although the midden is regarded here as a special feature type, it is discussed separately in the following chapter. The attributes of pit features and hearths are presented in Table 5.1. Figure 5.2 presents the formulae utilized to calculate pit volumes. The material inventories for each feature are presented in Appendix A.

Open-Basin Cooking Pits

Twenty-two pits were defined as open-basin cooking pits (Figure 5.3). They include Features 1–7, 19, 21–24, 27, 31, 33, 37, 38, 41, 42, 44, 45, and 56. These were relatively shallow (mean depth=21.8 cm), basin-shaped facilities with low artifact densities (only 41.6 g per feature, excluding limestone). Small pieces of calcined bone occurred, and burned limestone, which is generally not common at this site, occurred in almost 25 percent of these pits. Burned soil and charcoal flecks were also common and sometimes appeared in distinct bands (e.g., in Features 22, 27, and 38) or in concentrations (e.g., Feature 37). Open-basin cooking pits were found over the entire occupation but were most frequent in the western portion. They appeared to be associated spatially with another feature class, fire stains, which may represent the remnant bases of open-basin cooking pits.

Feature 42 was an exceptionally large pit in this class, measuring 175 x 234 cm in plan. This pit was found in Excavation Unit 40, and it is probable that some of the artifacts piece-plotted in that unit near Feature 40 were actually associated with this feature. Otherwise, the pit contained very few artifacts. It is not clear how pits of this size related to the smaller pits in the same class in terms of function. Perhaps the larger pits were used for communal cooking or processing activities. Features 1–3 were small, contiguous pits, presumably utilized at the same time and, therefore, may have functioned in a similar manner to the open-basin pits.

Fire Stains

Five features (Features 13, 14, 16, 39, and 40) were designated fire stains. These features were observed in the field as small, circular to oval areas of burning, but

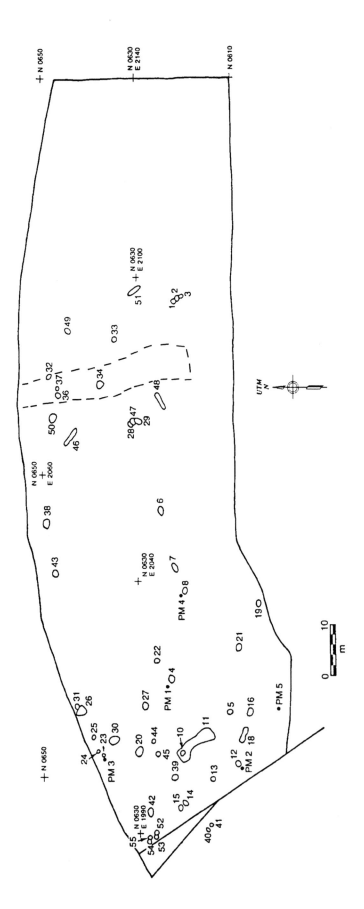

Figure 5.1. Distribution of Features

Plate 5.1. Pit Profiles: upper, Feature 26 (left) and Feature 31 (far right); lower, Feature 29 cache pit

Plate 5.1. Pit Profiles, continued: upper, Feature 37; lower, Feature 51, extended hearth

Table 5.1. Pit Attributes

Feature	Wall Orientation	Base Shape	Max. Plan Length (cm)	Max. Plan Width (cm)	Depth (cm)	Volume (dm³)	Material Wt (g)	No. of Zones	Burned Clay and Daub (g)	Density* (g/dm³)	Calcined Bone (NISP)
1	insl/outsl	flat	88	88	24.0	76.99	28.4	2	–	0.37	–
2	cur/outsl	basin	–	–	44.0	–	8.7	2	–	–	19
3	cur	basin	102	59	41.5	130.08	104.0	1	–	0.80	–
4	cur	basin	94	84	14.0	43.07	53.9	1	–	1.25	21
5	cur	irreg/basin	80	75	21.0	46.96	11.4	1	–	0.24	28
6	cur	basin	149	142	44.5	399.28	43.8	1	–	0.11	5
7	cur	basin	160	118	26.0	193.91	924.2	1	3.3	4.75	3
8	cur	basin	133	130	16.0	106.32	195.8	1	14.9	1.13	371
10	cur	irreg/basin	132	107	31.0	180.01	674.5	1	20.8	3.63	137
12	cur/irreg	basin	113	85	53.5	113.71	44.0	2	–	0.39	26
15	irreg	flat	124	104	58.0	143.93	5.4	1	–	0.04	7
19	irreg	basin	72	62	25.0	49.94	792.0	1	–	15.86	1
20	cur/outsl	basin	76	72	17.0	33.62	765.3	1	12.8	22.38	64
21	cur	basin	101	92	10.0	35.56	41.6	1	–	1.17	–
22	cur	basin	72	61	21.0	39.44	2.1	1	–	0.05	10
23	cur	basin	43	39	19.0	15.46	12.0	2	–	0.78	17
24	cur	basin	41	41	11.0	7.64	13.3	1	–	1.74	8
25	cur	basin	96	91	19.5	67.94	226.9	1	9.4	3.20	15
26	cur	irreg/basin	257	220	35.0	767.45	3,611.4	1	12.3	4.69	107
27	vert/cur	flat	120	112	24.0	441.51	15.4	2	–	0.03	18
28	cur	basin	88	87	35.0	122.55	1,970.7	2	36.5	15.78	31
29	cur	basin	168	127	41.0	364.45	6,433.2	1	27.8	17.65	27
30	cur/belled	flat	215	150	47.5	631.48	13,656.4	4	13,457.8	0.31	4
31	cur	basin	90	50	17.0	31.29	64.1	1	1.0	2.02	4
32	cur	basin	84	81	14.0	37.30	247.6	1	3.0	6.56	37
33	cur	irreg/basin	57	42	16.0	16.49	53.7	1	–	3.26	1
34	cur	basin	252	146	30.0	429.69	653.7	1	2.8	1.51	4
36	cur	basin	112	111	19.0	77.87	523.9	1	7.1	6.64	36
37	cur	basin	46	37	17.0	13.37	57.5	1	–	4.30	6
38	cur	basin	92	64	22.0	54.19	6.0	2	–	0.11	11
41	cur	basin	72	58	16.0	27.24	3.2	1	–	0.12	12
42	cur	basin	234	175	24.0	337.34	9.2	1	–	0.02	12
43	cur	basin	59	56	23.0	34.76	347.4	1	–	10.28	103
44	cur/outsl	irreg/basin	60	58	11.0	15.10	15.6	1	–	1.03	50
45	cur	basin	63	48	11.0	13.21	656.3	1	–	49.68	42
47	cur	basin	110	88	18.0	68.63	530.0	1	4.1	7.66	2
49	cur	basin	102	82	25.0	86.71	186.2	1	0.7	2.14	6
50	cur	basin	212	141	19.5	223.43	321.4	1	21.1	1.34	58
52	cur	basin	196	160	32.0	394.67	652.1	1	–	1.65	42
53	vert/outsl	flat	130	106	24.0	262.46	37.8	1	–	0.14	164
54	cur	basin	145	131	22.0	162.92	112.6	1	–	0.69	82
55	cur	basin	109	108	32.0	158.44	369.9	1	–	2.33	46
56	cur	basin	–	–	42.0	–	14.9	1	–	–	6

* Does not include burned clay and daub.

Key to wall orientation:
insl=inslanted
outsl=outslanted
cur=curvilinear/curved
vert=vertical

Portion of a cone

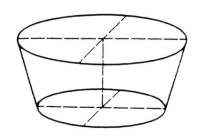

$$V = \frac{h}{2}(a_1 + a_2)$$

a_1 = area of base (πr^2)
a_2 = area of surface (πr^2)
h = height (depth)

Circular or eliptical basin

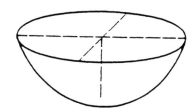

$$V = .16\pi h(3ab + h^2)$$

a = maximum length of surface radius
b = maximum width of surface radius
h = height (depth)

Cylinder

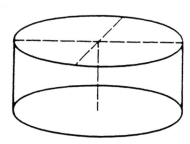

$$V = \pi r^2 h$$

r = surface radius
h = height (depth)

Compound pit

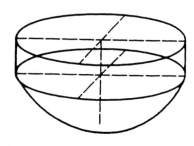

V = Volume of cylinder plus volume of basin

Figure 5.2. Pit Volume Formulae

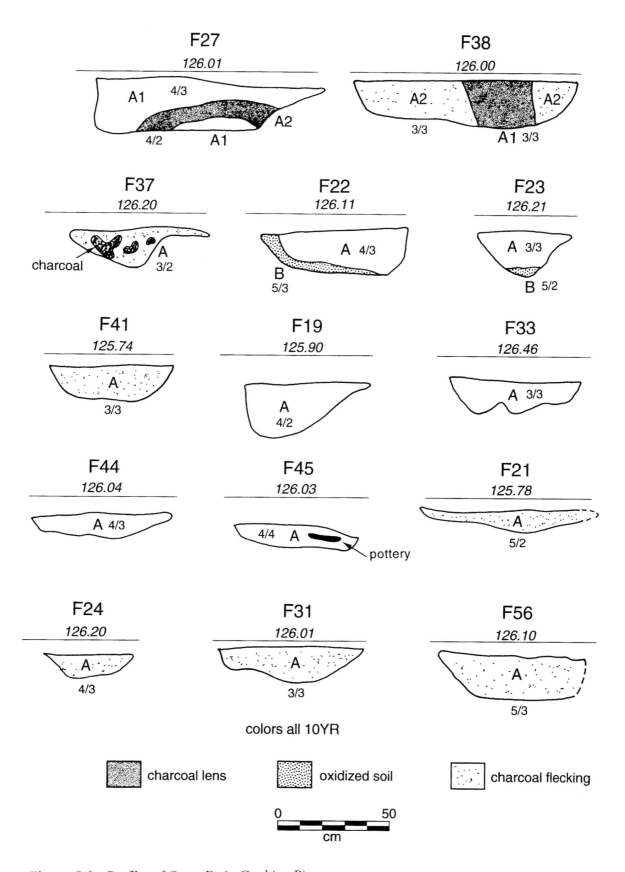

Figure 5.3. Profiles of Open-Basin Cooking Pits

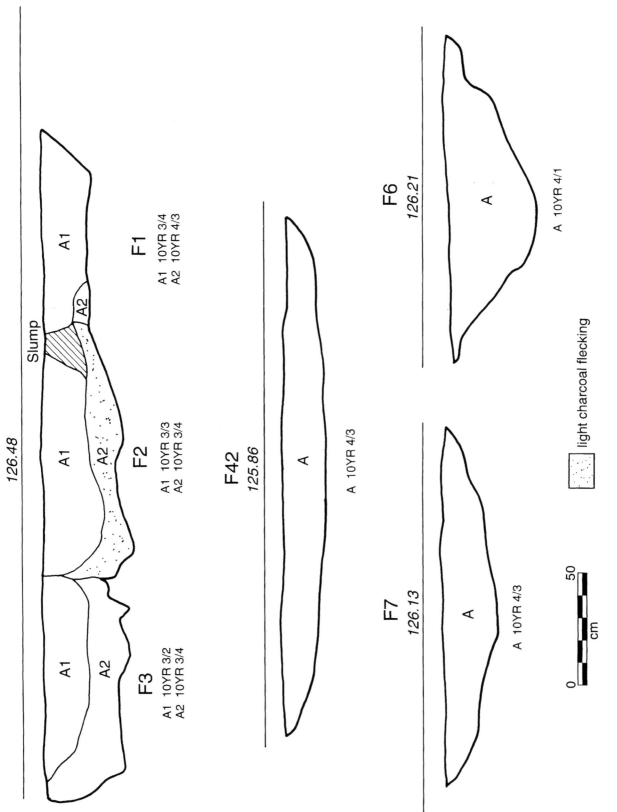

Figure 5.3. continued, Profiles of Open-Basin Cooking Pits

upon excavation proved to have no depth. Some cultural material was found in several of these features, as were small fragments of calcined bone. Charcoal flecks were also often present, but sometimes only small fragments of oxidized soil were visible. These features may represent the remaining basal portions of cooking pits or simply open or surficial hearths. It is perhaps significant that all five fire stains were found in the western portion of the occupation and were associated spatially with open-basin cooking pits.

Sunken Cooking Pits/Earth Ovens

Two features (Features 12 and 15) were classified as earth ovens or sunken cooking pits. Each feature consisted of an upper basin-shaped pit with a lower conical or cylindrical compartment or depression (Figure 5.4). The lower portions exhibited intense burning or charcoal lensing. These were the two deepest pits excavated, with Feature 12 measuring 53.5 cm and Feature 15 measuring 58 cm in depth. Curiously, only 50 g of cultural material was recovered from both pits combined. These appear to represent some type of specialized sunken cooker and perhaps were precursors of the deep earth oven facilities characteristic of the subsequent Late Woodland period in this area (Binford et al. 1970; Fortier et al. 1983:120–124; Lacampagne and Bentz 1988:83). Pits identical to these also have been identified at several Late Archaic sites in this area, including Missouri Pacific #2 (McElrath and Fortier 1983:27) and Dyroff/Levin (Emerson 1984:234). Both features at Dash Reeves were found in the western end of the occupation and appeared to be associated with the fire stains and open-basin cooking pits described above.

Cooking/Refuse Pits

Thirteen features were designated cooking/refuse pits. These include Features 8, 10, 20, 25, 26, 28, 32, 34, 36, 43, 47, 49, and 50 (Figure 5.5). These features were similar in size and depth (mean depth=23.2 cm) to the open-basin cooking pits but differed from the latter on the basis of their greater quantities and diversity of material remains. For example, the mean material weight per cooking/refuse pit, excluding limestone, is 580.5 g, compared with a mean weight of 41.6 g for open-basin cooking pits. In addition, the number of chert tools, pieces of debitage, and ceramics is significantly greater

for this feature category than for the open-basin cooking pit class.

Most of the pits uncovered in the eastern sector of the occupation were cooking/refuse pits. It is possible that more of the eastern pits contained greater amounts of material than pits in the western sector because material remains were densest in the eastern sector, i.e., the midden itself was thicker in that area. Since the preferred methods of refuse disposal at this site were scheduled dumping in creek swales and more generalized distribution of debris over the living surface (as opposed to disposal of trash in prepared pits), it is quite possible that the greater quantities of debris in the eastern cooking/refuse pits were fortuitous, i.e., the result of horizontal movement of materials from the midden into open pits. The primary function of these pits was probably similar to that proposed for the open-basin cooking pits. In that regard, the occurrence of burned limestone and clay in the pit fills was no doubt associated with cooking activities. Possibly, some of the ceramics found in these fills were also related to such activities.

Extended Hearths

Four features (Features 18, 46, 48, and 51) were placed in this category. This is a new feature type for the area, characterized by an elongated or extended, narrow basin or surficial stain, areas of intense burning, and the absence of cultural material (Table 5.2, Figure 5.6). These hearths were 2–3 m in length and varied in width from 40 to 76 cm. They varied in depth from 12 to 34 cm. With the exception of Feature 18, which was surficial and contained no fill, these hearths were all single zoned and basin shaped in profile. Three of the features (Features 46, 48, and 51) bracketed the creek midden area in the eastern portion of the occupation, while one, Feature 18, was located in the western sector. All except Feature 48 were oriented to the northwest; Feature 48 was oriented to the northeast. The significance of this pattern is unknown.

It is proposed that these features represent a specialized type of hearth. Their fills produced no faunal remains, and only wood charcoal was present, leaving no clue as to what was being processed in these facilities. Roasting large portions of meat on an extended spit or smoking fish on racks are two possibilities. In any case, such features appear to be unique to the Middle Wood-

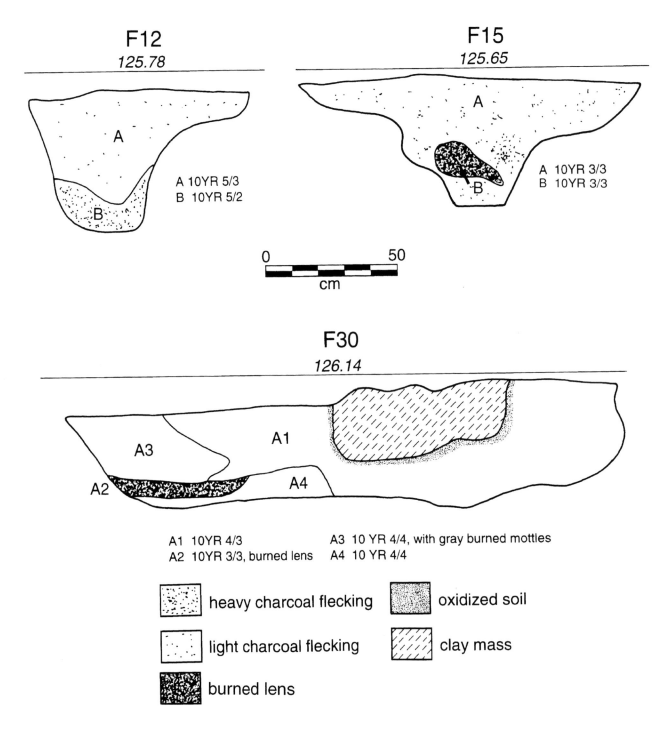

Figure 5.4. Profiles of Sunken Cooking Pits/Earth Ovens and Special Purpose Pit Feature 30

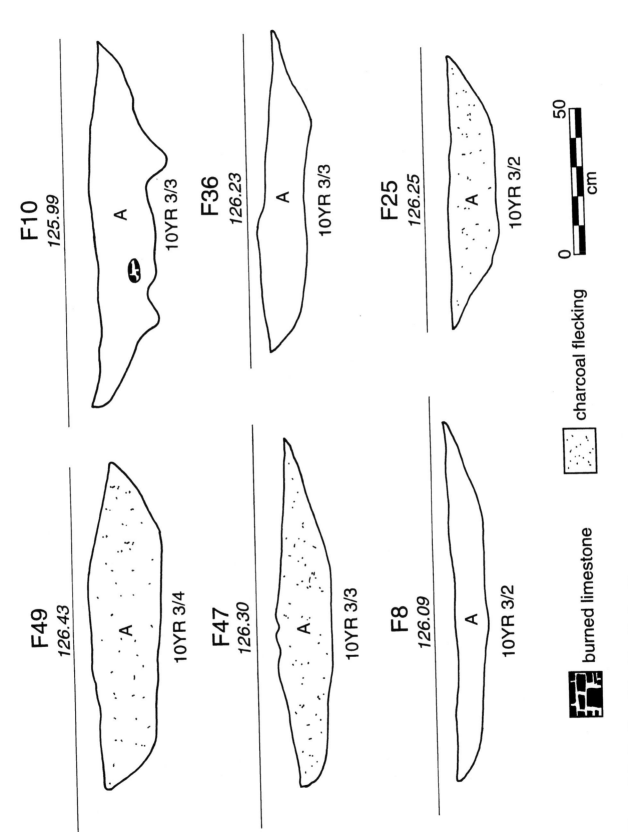

Figure 5.5. Profiles of Cooking/Refuse Pits

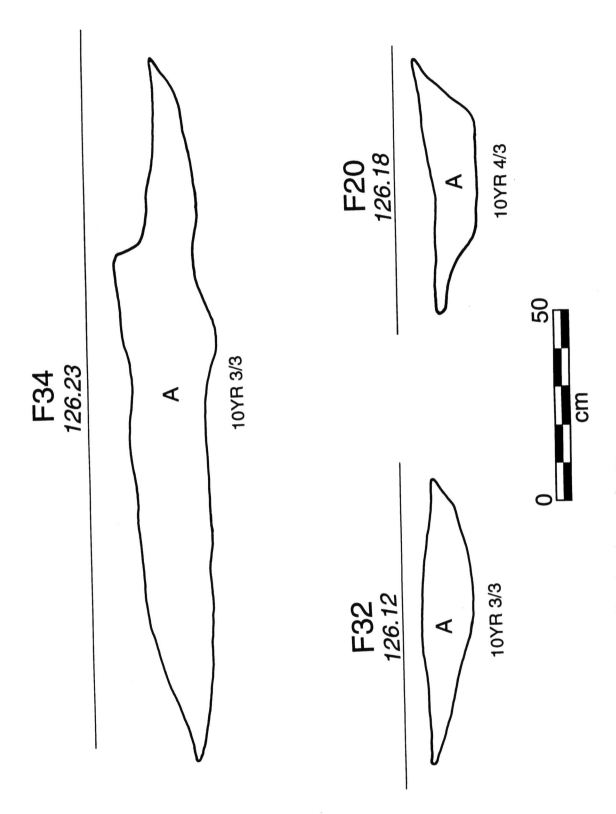

Figure 5.5. continued, Profiles of Cooking/Refuse Pits

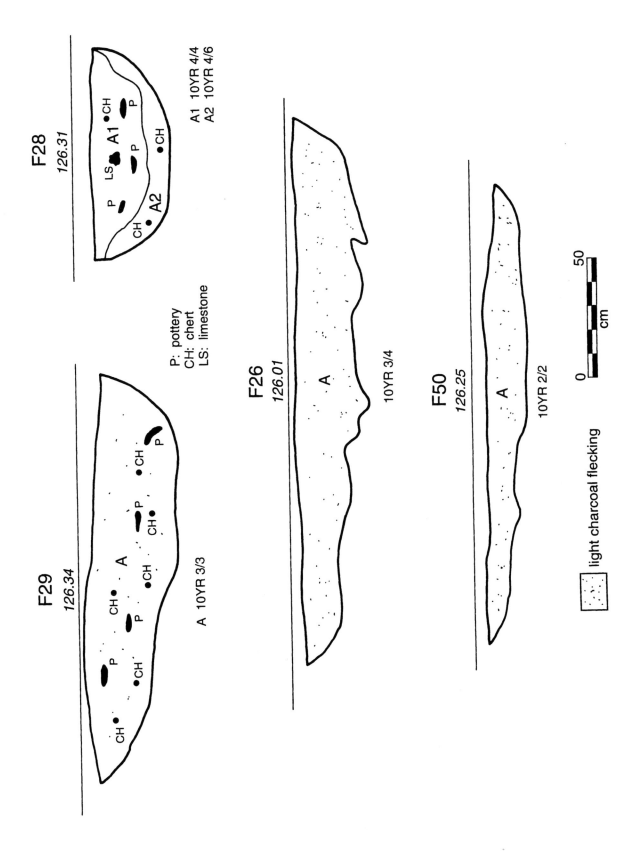

Figure 5.5. continued, Profiles of Cooking/Refuse Pits

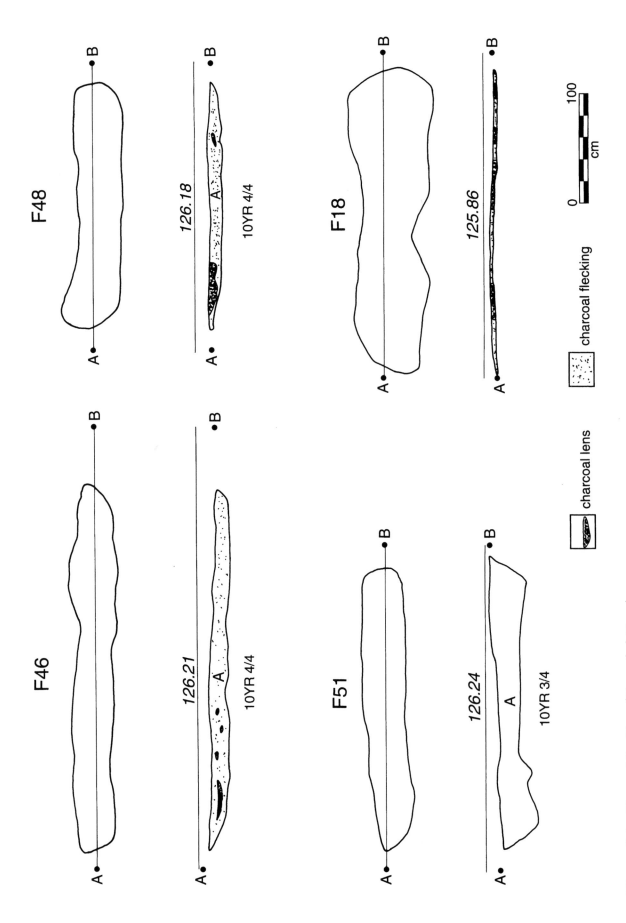

Figure 5.6. Plan and Profiles of Extended Hearths

Table 5.2. Attributes of Extended Hearths

Feature	Maximum Plan Length (cm)	Maximum Plan Width (cm)	Depth (cm)	Wall Orientation	Base Shape	Volume (dm³)	Material Wt (g)	N of Zones	Material Density (g/dm³)
18	276	76	surficial	–	–	–	0.0	1	0.00
46	326	46	18	cur	basin	104.7	2.4	1	0.02
48	223	44	12	cur	basin	46.83	21.5	1	0.46
51	254	40	34	outsl	convex	994.8	21.6	1	0.02

Key to wall orientation:
cur=curvilinear/curved
outsl=outslanted

land period and, to date, have not been recognized in any other contexts in the American Bottom.

Cache Pit

Feature 29 was defined as a cache pit. In most respects, it was similar to the cooking/refuse pits (see Figure 5.5). However, the occurrence of over 50 chert tools, both broken and complete, and extremely large amounts of chert debitage and ceramics suggests that this pit also functioned as a specialized refuse facility. Many of the larger pieces of chert recovered from this pit are a type of caramel-colored Ste. Genevieve red with white inclusions. It appears that finished tools, used and broken tools, and raw debitage (including every stage of production from cores to thinning flakes) of this chert type were intentionally deposited in this pit. The tools themselves represent a wide variety of formal types, including a complete hoe/spade, projectile points, a hammerstone, scrapers, knives, gravers, perforators, and gouges. Polished flakes and utilized flakes also are included (Plate 5.2). These tools are more thoroughly described in Chapter 8.

Feature 29 also contained burned limestone and clay as well as calcined deer and dog bone. Quite a number of unidentified calcined bones were recovered as well, indicating that this pit was utilized for cooking or roasting. The presence of burned dog bones is highly unusual and may indicate actual consumption of that animal. Although dog remains have been recovered from other Middle Woodland sites in Illinois (Cantwell 1981; Styles and Purdue 1986:518; Styles et al. 1985:425, 427, 440–445), the evidence for consumption is at best unclear. One of the deer bones recovered from this pit exhibits gnaw marks made by a carnivore, possibly a canine.

It is argued here that the material contained in Feature 29 represents a cache of artifacts and other materials quite possibly associated with one individual or perhaps a small kin group. This cache may represent a cleaning episode from a structure or, perhaps, an offering. A similar, although materially less diverse pit was identified at the Holding site (Fortier et al. 1989:84–87). Following Seeman's (1979a:39–46) analysis of Adena feasting pits in Ohio, it was argued that the Holding site example represented some kind of feasting or votive offering facility. The presence of a clay figurine, along with deer bone and shell, generally supported that argument. Unfortunately, except for the dog remains, no potentially ritual–related items were recovered from Feature 29. The artifacts instead appear to represent a more generalized inventory of refuse combined with perfectly usable tools. This strongly suggests that the material is debris from a cleaning episode that was deposited in an abandoned cooking pit.

Curiously absent from this deposit are unmodified blades, which are extremely common in almost all other contexts at the site. This may be significant in terms of determining whether or not this deposit was associated with an individual or a larger group. For example, in his analysis of Middle Woodland burial contexts in the Illinois River valley, Leigh has indicated that lamellar blades in such contexts are almost always associated with older females (1988:202–204). According to Leigh, "lamellar blades also probably provide the clearest correlation between grave goods, age, and sex of any of the types analyzed" (1988:204). Although Feature 29 was not a burial, it might represent personal items associated with a specific member of the Dash Reeves community, in this case a male, if Leigh's model is applicable. Perhaps his possessions were cleared from his

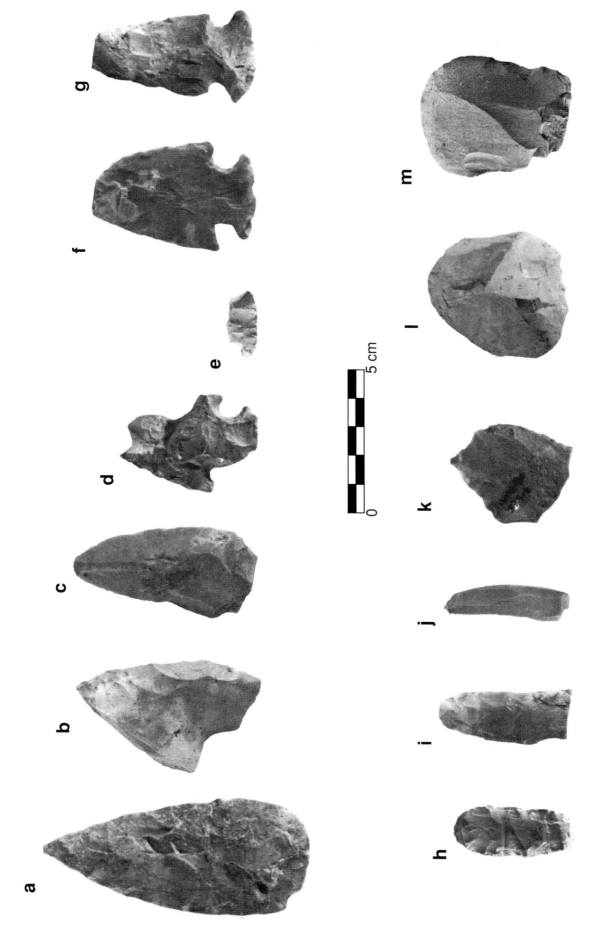

Plate 5.2. Lithics from Feature 29 Cache Pit: a, subtriangular knife; b, bifacial knife fragment; c, bifacial knife; d–g, hafted bifaces (all broken); h–i, bifacial knives; j, utilized blade; k, graver; l, ovate scraper; m, gouge

Plate 5.2. Lithics from Feature 29 Cache Pit, continued: n, chert hammerstone; o, gouge; p, igneous grinding stone; q, chert hoe

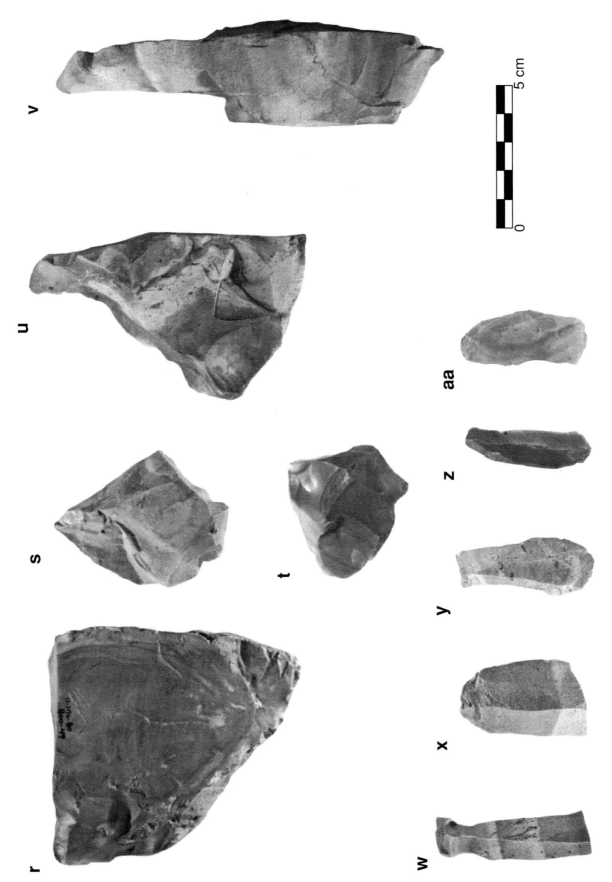

Plate 5.2. Lithics from Feature 29 Cache Pit, continued: r–v, chert cores; w–aa, nonutilized blades

work or personal space and deposited in the pit. It should be re-emphasized that the disposition of so many artifacts in one pit is highly unusual at this site, although caching of artifacts in general was not an uncommon phenomenon during the Middle Woodland period.

Other Special-Purpose Pits

In addition to the Feature 29 cache pit just described there were five other pits (Features 30 and 52–55) that appeared to have resulted from specialized activities not related to cooking. These pits were all located at the far west end of the exposed occupation (Figure 5.7). Feature 30 was the most unusual of these facilities in that it contained a large mass of burned clay in the central, uppermost portion of the pit (see Plate 7.16 and Figure 5.4). This mass was approximately 25 cm thick and nearly 60 cm in horizontal extent. The clay was exposed during shovel-scraping and the larger pit subsequently defined around the clay mass. The clay mass was fired, and oxidized soil was present along the base and edges. Charcoal flecking also occurred around the edges of the clay. It is apparent, therefore, that the mass was fired within the pit. The clay was not tempered and appears to have been derived from a light yellowish brown loessal deposit. No pebbles or sand grains were observed in the clay, suggesting that this mass had been refined in some manner. The clay was smoothed and did not exhibit heat cracking. Finally, a small amount of Middle Woodland cultural material was found around the clay and beneath it.

The function of this pit is conjectural. In all probability, the fired clay mass represented experimental potter's clay. Perhaps it was accidentally burned prior to its intended use, or perhaps it represented an intentional test firing of local clays that were not familiar to the potters at the site. It is interesting that temper was not added to the mass. Another possibility is that clays were ordinarily fired in pits like Feature 30 and utilized as a source of grog for temper. However, the area immediately around Feature 30 produced no evidence of pottery manufacturing activities. Fired masses of clay in pits are extremely uncommon in this area. I have observed only one other example, during the excavation of the Emergent Mississippian component at the Robert Schneider site in Madison County (Fortier 1985b:272–274). The function of that pit and clay mass was equally enigmatic.

Features 52–55 constituted a set of special-purpose pits. These features were contiguous units used as specialized refuse pits. They contained over 1,000 chert flakes and 14 chert tools, but very little else. Only one small piece of pottery, one large piece of schist, and a single large piece of unworked sandstone were recovered in addition to the chert. The majority of the chert flakes are small thinning/reduction flakes and were densely packed throughout the fills of the features. A variety of chert types are represented, including, significantly, a relatively high percentage of Cobden/Dongola, a southern Illinois-derived chert. This pit complex is interpreted as a depository for tool maintenance debitage that may have come from flaking or tool sharpening activities carried out in proximity to these pits. A number of triangular knives or possible preforms, possibly Manker projectile point preforms, were recovered from this area. It is conceivable that this area was the site of hafted biface manufacture. The fill of each of the pits in this complex exhibited burning, and many of the flakes are heat altered, possibly intentionally, as preforms were heat treated prior to final sharpening or forming.

Activity Area / Stain

In the far western portion of the occupation an irregular, dark stain was observed and designated Feature 11. The stain extended 9.12 m in a north-south direction and was 2.86 m at its widest point. Feature 10, a small cooking/refuse pit, was located at the far northern end of Feature 11. Feature 11 contained 30 cm of fill at its deepest point, but this tapered off dramatically from the center to the edges of the stained area.

Despite the fact that its edges were relatively sharp, this area of fill most likely represented a remnant portion of midden. The midden in this area of the site was extremely thin and was not observed in many of the excavation units. The Feature 11 remnant confirmed, in fact, that there had been a midden in this area but that most of it had been eroded, presumably downslope toward the west into the creek. It is also possible that the creek itself may have risen at various times and scoured out the midden. This area was draped by overbank deposit clays, indicative of such fluvial activity.

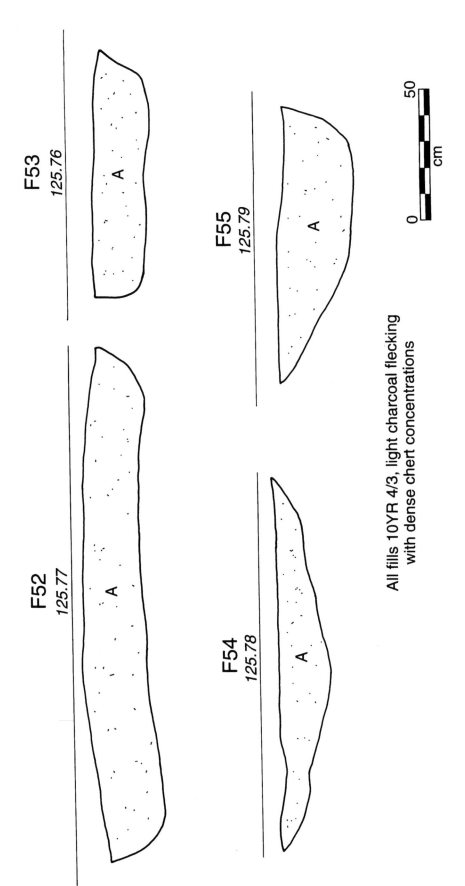

Figure 5.7. Profiles of Special–Purpose Pits: Features 52–55

Postmolds

Five postmolds were identified (Table 5.3; Figure 5.8). A sixth may have existed inside Feature 16 (a fire stain), but it was not assigned a number because of its questionable status. Two of the postmolds initially were assigned feature numbers (Features 9 and 17) in the field but subsequently were reclassified as Postmolds 4 and 5, respectively. Postmolds 1–5 were located in the south-central and westernmost portions of the exposed site area. All exhibited evidence of burning, and several contained pieces of burned limestone, which may have served as supports or props, similar to those described at the Middle Woodland occupation at Napoleon Hollow in the Illinois River valley (McGimsey and Wiant 1986:123–136).

All but Postmold 5 were directly associated with pit features. In all probability these postmolds represented the locations of special processing poles related to the cooking/roasting activities conducted in the pits. The burning evident in the postmolds was probably due to the proximity of the posts to pit fires. It is possible that such posts were utilized to hang food destined for cooking or smoking in the adjacent pits.

DISCUSSION

The feature pattern at Dash Reeves is unique in the American Bottom for the Middle Woodland period. Features form an arc that apparently coincides with the sinuosity of two creek beds, one active during the initial phases of occupation, and the other abandoned. The features lie mostly between the channel swales. Within the exposed site area the locations of most intense feature activity occur at the far western and far eastern ends. Hearths, cooking pits, and refuse pits dominate the assemblage, with several special-purpose pits present

in various areas of the occupation. No structures or large circular or oval stained areas, such as those observed at the Holding site (Fortier et al. 1989:58–72), were identified at Dash Reeves. Given the orientation of the arc of features and its association with the dark ring observed in the aerial photograph, it is argued that structures probably exist north of the excavation area. Feature density presumably is higher in that area as well, since surface refuse increases dramatically there (see Figure 3.5). Unfortunately, this proposition is untestable given recent non-highway related construction activities and landscaping in that area.

The features and their contents indicate that cooking and food preparation tasks were commonly undertaken in the excavated portion of the site. Considering the relatively small area of site opened, the number of recovered ceramic vessels, which probably were related directly to food preparation and serving activities, is remarkable. Moreover, nearly 85 percent of the pits and hearths produced calcined bone but very little in the way of wild or domesticated seeds. This suggests that most of the cooking in this area was focused on meat processing, with a probable emphasis on deer and fish, if the contents of Feature 8 are typical. Bone preservation was extremely poor, however, so the true diversity or spectrum of species exploited cannot be determined. Poor preservation probably resulted from a combination of open-air cooking or roasting methods, lengthy exposure of the site itself after its abandonment, and, possibly, bone grease extraction processes, which resulted in small pieces of splintered bone (see Chapter 10).

Open-basin cooking pits, specialized cooking pits, and fire stains occurred with greatest frequency in the western portion of the occupation. Generally, artifact densities were lighter in this area of the site, and tool types were not nearly as diverse in this area as they were elsewhere. It is possible that the eastern and western areas of the arc of features constituted two chrono-

Table 5.3. Postmold Attributes

PM	Maximum Diameter (cm)	Maximum Depth (cm)	Associated Feature	Base Shape	Evidence of Burning Materials	Comments
1	20	10.0	4	basin	burned limestone	–
2	30	13.5	12	basin	charcoal, calcified bone	–
3	22	8.5	23	basin	burned limestone	–
4	24	29.0	8	conical	burned clay, charcoal	originally designated Fea 19
5	17	18.0	–	conical	burned clay, charcoal	originally designated Fea 17

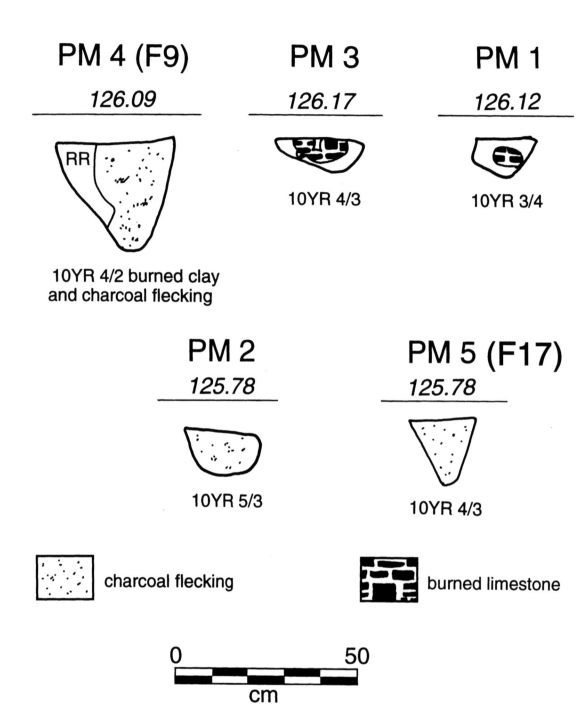

Figure 5.8. Postmold Profiles

logically separate occupations, but ceramically there is minimal evidence for this. There was a slightly higher incidence of Pike/Baehr and Crab Orchard types in the eastern area, but both types also occurred in the west. Moreover, from the standpoint of diagnostic lithics, including projectile point types, the two areas cannot be distinguished. Even chert type distributions are identical. Virtually every aspect of material culture analysis points to a single occupation.

In the following chapter the midden is described. It has been argued elsewhere (Fortier et al. 1989:28–36) that middens constitute an important feature type during the Middle Woodland time period. The Dash Reeves site provides evidence of several different types of midden developmental processes. As at other Middle Woodland sites where middens occur, the most significant part of the Dash Reeves artifact inventory is derived from midden contexts. For this reason alone, the formation of the midden deserves considerable attention.

6

FORMATIONAL PROCESSES AND MIDDEN CONTEXTS

One of the more conspicuous characteristics of Middle Woodland sites in the American Bottom is the refuse canopy that usually covers both pits and structures and, presumably, various living surfaces. Such middens vary in depth, depending on the duration of occupation, and developed as a result of generalized accretional processes or as products of locus-specific dumping activity, such as deposition into a creek or other specially designated areas. Although pits contain a certain amount of refuse as well, it is clear that the preferred method of refuse disposal during this period was not focused on pits but was more generalized. This kind of behavior is in stark contrast to the use of deep trash facilities in the subsequent Late Woodland period.

As a hallmark of the Middle Woodland period, middens warrant careful attention. Although the occurrence of Middle Woodland middens has long been recognized in the Midwest (Fecht 1961; Higgins 1990; Markman 1988:60–70; McGregor 1958), very few thorough analyses have been undertaken (see, however, Fortier et al. 1989; McGimsey and Wiant 1986:157–158; Stafford 1985). As alluded to above, there were essentially two kinds of formational processes at work, one involving a steady accumulation of debris upon a living surface, the other involving the transport of materials to a designated dumping area. In the latter case, creeks, swales, and terrace margins were used most commonly (Faulkner and McCollough 1974; Kellar 1979:101; Wiant and McGimsey 1986). This behavior is evident at the Dash Reeves site, where an abandoned creek swale was utilized as a dumping area. There is also evidence at Dash Reeves of a one-time dumping episode within an active creek that formed the southern limit of the occupation. These kinds of secondary disposal areas have been characterized by Schiffer (1976:129) as containing dense and diverse deposits of cultural materials, including a high percentage of broken, unusable artifacts. Schiffer later elaborated on processes of refuse disposal on house floors. Many of the same processes he described apply to selective midden dumps, including lateral cycling, scavenging, ritual deposition, and natural erosion (Schiffer 1985:24–30). In addition, at Dash Reeves "de facto refuse" also appears to be present within dump areas, as evidenced by pit features within and at the base of the primary creek dump (Features 32, 34, 36, and 37) and by the occurrence of complete and potentially usable artifacts in such deposits. "De facto refuse" refers to artifacts left behind as the result of activities conducted in the area of dumping. As a practical matter, separating de facto refuse from refuse brought in from other activity areas is nearly impossible. Within the creek midden at Dash Reeves both kinds of refuse occur side by side.

Secondary or tertiary movement of materials can occur within middens, although this is usually a characteristic of accretional middens. Movement can occur as a result of erosion or can be caused by periodic cleaning or sweeping of areas by a site's occupants. At the Holding site, which featured an accretional midden, there were several areas that contained pockets of denser refuse, possibly resulting from cleaning in and around structures or activity areas. At that site denser areas of midden accumulation often were not directly associated with major pit or household areas (Fortier et al. 1989:28–36).

It is unclear whether any secondary movement of material occurred within the accretional midden at Dash Reeves. This midden varied in thickness from 10–30 cm and sloped to the west, following the natural contour of the alluvial fan (Figure 6.1). It was densest, in terms of artifactual content, in the eastern and western portions of the occupation and thinnest in the central and southern areas. The actual depth of debris, however, as measured from the base of the plowzone, was relatively constant over the entire site. During excavation of the 4-x-4-m units, the depths and orientations of all diagnostic lithics and pottery were recorded. Artifacts found at the base of the midden were virtually always observed lying in horizontal positions, whereas materials above the base were found in horizontal, vertical, and oblique positions. It should be pointed out that this pattern was not duplicated in the main creek dump, where basal artifacts were oriented in all positions. The pattern within the accretional midden possibly indicates the presence of the original living surface at the base of the midden, with the subsequent development of the refuse stratum occurring in a haphazard fashion. Another possible explanation for the horizontally deposited materials at the base of the midden is that their orientations resulted from repeated trampling of a continuously utilized living surface on and above the basal portion of the midden. There were no differences observed, however, between the base and higher levels of the midden in the sizes of artifacts such as pottery sherds. This fact does not seem to support the trampling theory, as one would expect repeated trampling to result in smaller-sized debris fragments.

Another formational process at work within middens is vertical and lateral translocation of materials due to edaphic soil processes, e.g., drying and cracking, bioturbation, natural slumping, or water-related erosion. None of these factors offers a good explanation for the horizontal presentation of materials at the base of the accretional midden at Dash Reeves, for the consistent depth of materials in the midden, or for the regularity of the upper and lower boundaries of the midden fill. However, a faint transition zone underlying the base of the midden and measuring roughly 10–15 cm in depth was observed in virtually every profile at the site. This zone was darker than the subsoil beneath it but lighter than the midden above it. Although this zone generally contained few materials, diagnostic artifacts in vertical

and oblique positions were recorded, their orientations suggesting downward vertical translocation by the aforementioned natural processes. This zone is shown in Figure 6.1 but is combined with the midden in Figure 6.4 (see below).

The midden within the creek in the eastern portion of the occupation resulted not from accretional processes, but from selective dumping. This is indicated by the variable artifact density and diversity observed in the excavation units in this area. For example, Unit 9 produced over 11,000 g of material, while the contiguous Unit 14 produced only 675 g of material. Unit 9 also yielded 106 chert tools, while Unit 14 yielded only 11 tools. At its deepest point the midden extended over 45 cm below the base of the plowzone. Since it conformed to the slope of the creek swale, it sloped in depth, thinning considerably at the edges of the swale. It was much darker than the accretional midden, with Munsell colors of 10YR 3/1 and 2/1. Density of debris also varied widely depending on location, with the greatest density occurring at the north end of the exposed creek. Figures 6.2 and 6.3 depict the density of all materials as well as the density of ceramics recovered from individual excavation blocks at the site. The area of highest density clearly conforms to the creek swale and its associated midden. Figure 6.4 depicts two profiles of the creek midden and shows the gradual merging of this midden with the surrounding shallower accretional midden. Plate 6.1 gives several examples of both the creek and accretional midden, as seen in test and excavation unit profiles.

The creek midden extended approximately 30 m in a north-south direction within the right-of-way and was approximately 6 m wide. As has been mentioned, the swale actually extends for several hundred meters to the north-northwest, where it appears to form the northern and western limits of the site. At its southern end, however, the midden-filled swale terminated abruptly and feathered out within the right-of-way. The entire creek midden area within the right-of-way was excavated, but curiously, no bedded clays or laminae were encountered within the creek or at the base of the midden. It appears that the original creek depression had been partially, perhaps completely, filled at the southern end by natural erosional processes prior to the time of occupation. In fact, there is evidence that this swale was utilized for other purposes prior to its use as a dump. Four pit features (Features 32, 34, 36, and 37)

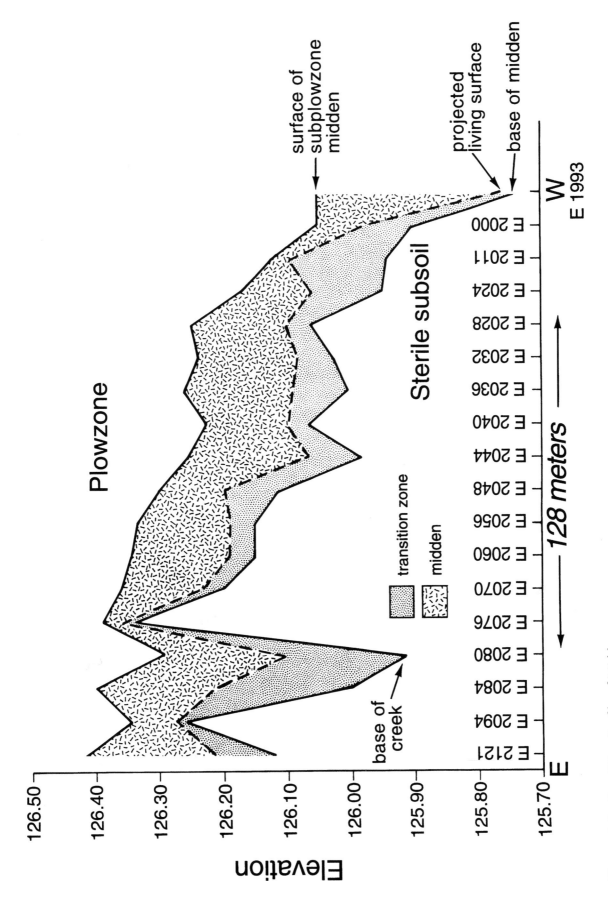

Figure 6.1. East–West Profile of Midden

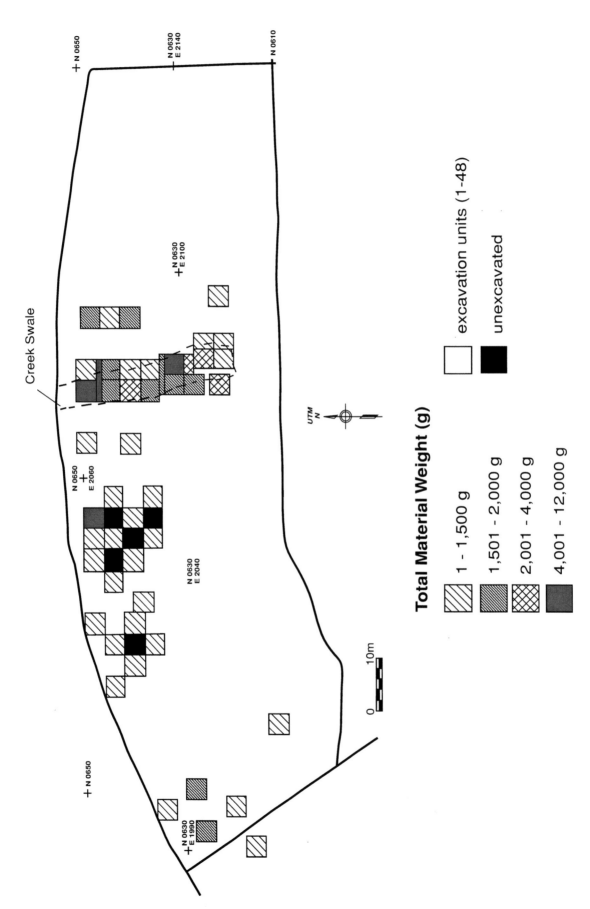

Figure 6.2. Distribution of All Cultural Materials by Weight

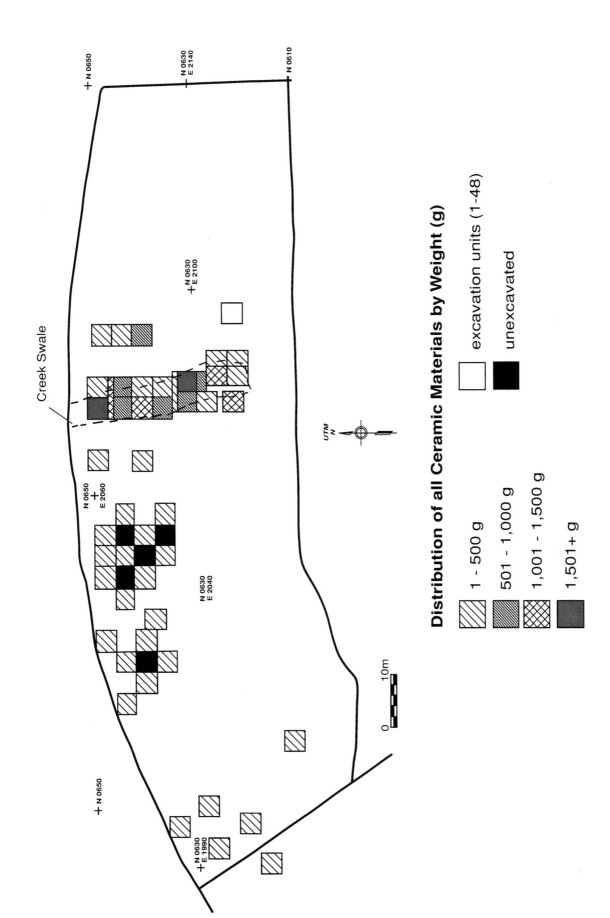

Figure 6.3. Distribution of All Ceramic Materials by Weight

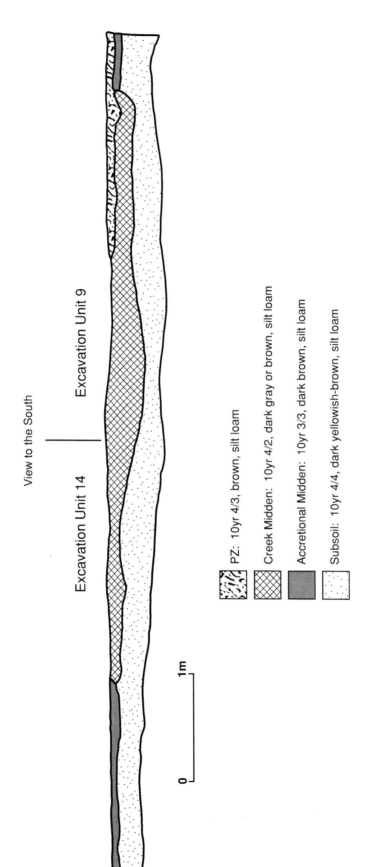

View to the South

Excavation Unit 14　　Excavation Unit 9

1m

0

PZ: 10yr 4/3, brown, silt loam

Creek Midden: 10yr 4/2, dark gray or brown, silt loam

Accretional Midden: 10yr 3/3, dark brown, silt loam

Subsoil: 10yr 4/4, dark yellowish-brown, silt loam

Figure 6.4. Profile of Creek and Accretional Midden in Excavation Units 9 and 14

Plate 6.1. Test Unit Midden Profiles: upper, north wall of Test Unit A (creek midden); lower, west wall of Test Unit E (accretional midden)

Plate 6.1. Test Unit Midden Profiles, continued: upper, west wall of Test Unit C (accretional midden); lower, west wall of Test Unit M (accretional midden)

were identified at the base of the midden. There is no direct evidence that the site's occupants themselves excavated this area to create a refuse facility or a moat, although the latter possibility may offer an explanation for the abrupt southern boundary of the swale.

Another more restricted dump was exposed accidentally during the excavation of a deep, geomorphological trench (Geo-Trench 1) along the southern limits of the right-of-way. It is believed that repeated episodes of selective dumping account for the refuse within the larger creek midden discussed above. Two interesting aspects of the dump episode exposed in Geo-Trench 1 are (1) the diversity of materials dumped, including carbonized wood remains, a deer carcass, pottery, and lithics, and (2) the fact that refuse was apparently thrown into an active creek, or at least an intermittently active creek. Contamination of a potential water resource so close to the occupation is surprising but perhaps not unusual, especially given the huge quantities of debris accumulating on the nearby living surface. It is clear that Middle Woodland peoples were less concerned about polluting their immediate aquatic surroundings with refuse than were Late Woodland people in this area, who systematically excavated deep pits to hold refuse and did not allow debris to accumulate on living surfaces to any appreciable degree.

All of the excavated midden contexts at Dash Reeves were characterized by their dark brown to black fill colors and homogeneous fine textures. This deposit resembled the fills encountered in prehistoric structure basins as well as natural A horizons in this area. Presumably, the dark color was derived from the deposition of organic materials in the refuse areas, particularly thatch or related plant remains. Carbonized plant remains, in fact, were present in the creek midden, albeit in surprisingly small amounts, but they were even less prevalent in the surrounding accretional midden. The creek midden fill was generally darker than the fill comprising the accretional midden, and this may be directly related to the greater amounts of plant remains, mostly uncarbonized, deposited in the creek midden. Essentially, the creek midden represented a large compost pile; its finer texture may have resulted from heavy bioturbation by earthworms and other insects attracted to the compost.

It is difficult to assess the contribution of bone to the general organic content of middens at this site. Very little bone was found in midden contexts, and most was

heavily calcined and fragmented. This contrasts with the deep middens known in the Illinois River valley, which contain large and well-preserved faunal assemblages (Styles et al. 1985). At Dash Reeves bone preservation was extremely poor in all contexts. This was probably due to the exposed nature of the site within a floodplain environment characterized by a fluctuating water table. The stream channel midden at the Smiling Dan site exhibited a similar pattern of low bone density, particularly when contrasted with pit contents at that site (Styles et al. 1985:406–412). This may reflect preservation factors, or it might indicate differential disposal patterns. In any case, it appears that plant remains, both carbonized and uncarbonized, played a more significant role in creating the color and texture of the Dash Reeves midden than did other organic constituents.

I have argued elsewhere (Fortier et al. 1989:35–36) that Middle Woodland middens should be regarded as a special feature type and are particularly important, since, where they occur, they produce the vast majority of a site's assemblage remains. At the Holding site nearly 70 percent of the diagnostic ceramics and lithics recovered were derived from midden contexts (Fortier et al. 1989:30). The situation is even more dramatic at Dash Reeves, where 90 percent of all material remains (by weight) were recovered from the midden. At such sites, simply removing middens to search for submidden features is clearly not only destructive but it also gives a completely false impression about the composition of the overall material culture of the site's occupants.

It should also be pointed out that not all Middle Woodland sites in the American Bottom have produced definable middens. At the Truck #7 site, for example, a thin veneer of material was encountered on an apparent living surface, but a specific midden zone or debris horizon was not observed (Fortier 1985a:178–181). The early Middle Woodland occupation at the Mund site also contained no midden, and in that case, there was virtually no distribution of material around features (Finney 1983). In both of these cases, however, the sites represent small, seasonal occupations. In the American Bottom, middens appear to be associated strictly with the larger, longer-lived settlements.

To summarize, both selective dumping and accretional factors were responsible for the Dash Reeves midden accumulations. The immediate impression one has at such sites is that the occupants paid scant attention to the accumulation of refuse in and around their living and activity areas. However, this may be a somewhat erroneous impression. The fact that selective dumping occurred on a regular basis, either in swales or active creeks, indicates that some areas of the occupation must have been periodically cleaned. Since no houses and no central community area were exposed at Dash Reeves, it is impossible to postulate exactly what areas of the occupation were maintained in this manner. The debris in specific excavation units within the creek midden represents a wide variety of artifact and debitage types. Both utilized and nonutilized artifacts were discarded in the midden. However, the density of particular artifact types varied considerably from excavation unit to unit. The variety of artifacts found in the midden suggests the cleaning up of general activity areas or household areas. We have already postulated that pit Feature 29 may have functioned as a specialized midden dump for one such household or even as a receptacle for the possessions of one individual. The dump in the active creek also appears to relate to a single activity or a restricted cleaning episode. From all of these examples it is clear that refuse discard patterns were more complex during the Middle Woodland period than previously believed. Future excavations at sites such as Dash Reeves need to be sensitive to the specific contexts of refuse and to the formational processes that produced them. The formation of a ringed midden at this site suggests a more orderly management of refuse than anticipated and highlights the importance of investigating nontraditional contexts in the vicinity of apparent living and activity areas.

7

CERAMIC ASSEMBLAGE

Thomas O. Maher

The ceramic assemblage derived from the various investigations of the Dash Reeves site includes 339 diagnostic and 6,164 body sherds, for a total of 36,229.3 g of identifiable pottery (Appendix B). There are also 5,847 fragments of pottery (2,768.8 g) that are too small for reliable identification and are designated "sherdlets." In addition, there are 1,911 fragments of burned clay or daub, weighing 15,307.1 g. This analysis focuses only on the ceramic sherds large enough to allow confident identification of certain basic characteristics, such as surface treatment and temper.

ANALYTICAL METHODS

The analytical methods used in the examination of the Dash Reeves ceramic assemblage are the same as those used to examine ceramics from the Holding site (Maher 1989:129–139). Body sherds provide only limited information. In this analysis body sherds were sorted into type-variety categories by excavation unit. Each group of body sherds was counted and weighed (to the nearest 0.1 g). As noted above, sherdlets (ceramic fragments under a gram in size) generally do not reveal the basic characteristics necessary to sort them into type-variety categories. These sherdlets provide no useful information to the analysis and, although tabulated for each surface collection or excavation unit, they are omitted from many summary tables.

Diagnostic ceramics are the analytical focus of this study. Diagnostics are arbitrarily defined as any rims or

obvious base sherds. Fourteen diagnostics in the assemblage are technically body sherds because they are rim fragments from which the lips are missing. On each of these, however, only the terminal lip is missing, and each retains enough characteristics to warrant its designation as a diagnostic. Every effort has been made to determine the minimum number of vessels in this collection by consistently searching for mends between the diagnostics.

The profile of each rim was drawn if the orientation could be determined with confidence. A select number of rim profiles have been illustrated for this report. Descriptive abbreviations and the presentation format for these profiles are given in Figure 7.1. Various quantitative and qualitative characteristics of each diagnostic were recorded on a data form and were subsequently entered into a computerized data base. Quantitative characteristics include the weight of each diagnostic to the nearest 0.1 g and an estimate of the rim orifice diameter using a standard rim arc board ruled in 2-cm increments. No rim diameter was recorded if the estimated proportion of the diameter represented by the individual rim sherd was less than 5 percent.

The body wall thickness of each diagnostic was measured using metric calipers. This characteristic was recorded only if some portion of the vessel wall was present at least 1 cm from the lip end point. This was done to avoid incorporating any upper rim or lip modifications that might affect the wall thickness. Three separate measurements were made if sufficient surface area was present.

Many rims consist of only the immediate lip area. In these situations, technically, no wall thickness measure-

Surface Treatment Abbreviations

BRS	Brushing
CM	Cordmarking
CWS	Cordwrapped Stick Impression
CHI	Crosshatched Incision
DI	Diagonal Incisions
DRS	Dentate Rocker Stamp
DS	Dentate Stamping
ER	Eroded
FI	Fabric Impression
HBRS	Horizontal Brushing
HCP	Hemiconical Punctation
ND	Indeterminate
I	Incisions
PDIN	Parallel/Diagonal Incisions
PL	Plain
PRS	Plain Rocker Stamped
R-BSLP	Reddish-Brown Slip
RP	Rectangular Punctation
SM	Smoothing
TP	Triangular Punctation
UDS	Unidentifiable Stamp
VDS	Vertical Dentate Stamp

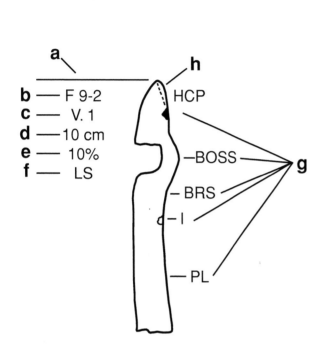

a	orientation line indicating interior
b	provenience (e.g., F 9-2 = feature 9, bag 2 or 9-2 = excavation unit 9, bag 2)
c	vessel number
d	orifice diameter
e	percent of orifice remaining
f	temper (LS = limestone)
g	surface treatment
h	lip impression

Figure 7.1. Rim Profile Template

ment is possible. A separate measurement (in mm) was made, therefore, of the wall thickness at or near (within 1 cm of) the lip end point. Again, where possible, the average of at least three separate measurements was recorded for the lip thickness. Unfortunately, this measurement is affected by upper rim modifications, such as embossed nodes, often rendering the value obtained unrepresentative of the vessel as a whole.

A measurement (in mm) was also taken from the lip end point to the center of any embossed nodes. This measurement was not included in past analyses of Middle Woodland ceramic assemblages in the American Bottom. Butler and Jefferies (1986:528) have suggested that in the Crab Orchard tradition embossed nodes were placed closer to the lip during late Middle Woodland times. It is unclear if this variable is chronologically sensitive in the American Bottom. Recording this information allows one to begin collecting data to test this possibility.

Several qualitative variables were recorded for each diagnostic. The form of the vessel was recorded if it could be determined from the rim. As in the Holding site assemblage, only simple jars and bowls are found in the Dash Reeves ceramic assemblage. The jars appear to be primarily subconoidal vessels with round bases and vertical to slightly outslanted walls. The assemblage contains bowls with both restricted and unrestricted orifices. This also resembles the Holding site assemblage. No bowl bases are found in the Dash Reeves assemblage.

The same temper categories were used in this analysis as in the Holding analysis. Again, the tempering material that macroscopically is most common was considered typical of a diagnostic's category. It appears, however, that mixtures of tempers are more common at Dash Reeves than at Holding.

If a distinct upper rim surface treatment was present on the diagnostic, it was recorded separately from the dominant body surface treatment. As in the Holding analysis, typological designation was not normally based upon the upper rim treatment. Only the Hopewell Cross Hatched and Hopewell Rocker Rim categories include diagnostic specimens carrying only these distinctive upper rim treatments (Maher 1989:173–176, 185–186). Any body surface modification was also noted for each diagnostic.

Some rims display a modification to their lips and upper walls known as a "ridge and channel." The

presence or absence of this characteristic was noted for each rim. The overall lip shape was also recorded for each rim. Modifications to the lip, such as notching or fabric impressions, are not common in this assemblage. Also recorded was the type of tool used to create notch impressions, as well as the location and orientation (in relation to the lip plane) of such impressions.

Finally, if possible, each diagnostic was assigned to a ceramic type-variety. The ceramic types and varieties defined during the Holding ceramic analysis are used in this study (Maher 1989:139–251). As in that study, the type-variety designation is based primarily on variations in temper and surface modification. Detailed descriptions of types and varieties are found in the Holding report and are not repeated here.

There are, however, two revisions to these ceramic categories. For the Holding assemblage I defined two ceramic types that were numerically dominant, Holding Cordmarked and Holding Plain, which were said to be related to Havana Cordmarked and Havana Plain. The Holding material, however, has thinner walls and a sandier paste than the latter two types, and it is characterized by round, unbeveled lips (Maher 1989:160–173). At the time of the Holding analysis, such differences appeared to warrant definition of separate American Bottom types. Since then, examination of ceramic assemblages from Meridian Hills (Williams et al. 1987), Little Hills (Lopinot 1990), Dash Reeves, and sites in the Illinois River valley have led me to doubt whether a distinction at the type level is necessary. There are distinct differences between the cordmarked and plain jars in the American Bottom versus the Illinois River valley, but they are variations on a basic theme. As Braun (1985) has pointed out, wall thickness seemed to decrease from Middle to Late Woodland times. The thinner walls of the cordmarked and plain jars at Holding may, therefore, reflect a general chronological trend in Middle Woodland utilitarian vessels in Illinois.

The sandy paste that characterizes the *Bottoms* variety of Holding Cordmarked and the *Collinsville* variety of Holding Plain, distinguishes this pottery from the grit-tempered Havana Cordmarked and Havana Plain of the Illinois River valley. It is, therefore, a useful spatial marker. In addition, the jars in the American Bottom are regularly notched on the lip exterior with cord-wrapped or plain dowels, whereas lip modification on Havana Cordmarked and Plain vessels is usually on the lip interior.

There undoubtedly are differences between the large cordmarked and plain jars found in the two regions, but the overwhelming impression is one of similarity. Surface treatment is identical; there are embossed nodes on both groups of vessels. In addition, the shape and size of these vessels are very similar. In this analysis, therefore, the type names Holding Cordmarked and Holding Plain have been dropped in preference for Havana Cordmarked and Havana Plain. The variety names *Bottoms* and *Collinsville* are retained to maintain the spatial differences that exist between cordmarked and plain pottery in the two regions. The descriptions of Holding Cordmarked, *var. Bottoms* and Holding Plain, *var. Collinsville* presented in the Holding report therefore apply in their entirety to the Havana Cordmarked, *var. Bottoms* and Havana Plain, *var. Collinsville* found in the Dash Reeves assemblage.

One common ceramic category appearing in the accompanying tables should be explained. "Indeterminate" is a category containing ceramics whose surface treatment cannot be determined but whose temper is obvious. This category provides only slightly more information than the "sherdlet" designation, but is useful when analyzing the proportions of different tempers present in the assemblage.

One analytical category used in this analysis but not in the Holding analysis is "Lip Fragments." This category includes very small portions of vessel lips that did not provide sufficient information to warrant the completion of a diagnostic form. They were counted, weighted, and usually categorized as "Indeterminate."

SURFACE COLLECTIONS

Historic Sites Survey

The first investigation of the Dash Reeves site to produce a substantial amount of pottery was completed by James Porter during the Historic Sites Survey of the early 1970s. That material is incorporated into the present analysis. Also included are a few sherds collected by Warren Wittry during the 1980 Fish Lake Survey (Wittry 1981). Tables 7.1 and 7.2 present inventories of ceramics recovered in these two early unsystematic surface collections. Pike Rocker Stamped, *var. Black*

Lane was the most common ceramic type recovered, making up 28.6 percent of the diagnostics and 33 percent of the body sherds by count. Second in frequency among the diagnostics identified to type are Fournie Plain, *var. Fournie* rims at 9.5 percent by count. *Fournie* body sherds, however, are much less common (1.9 percent). Pike Brushed, *var. Robinson* and Pike Rocker Stamped, *var. Calhoun* are common body sherds, each comprising 9.5 percent of the earlier collections. Not surprisingly, there are several "Indeterminate" rims and body sherds too small to categorize at the type level. Based upon the early surface collections, the Dash Reeves site was identified as Middle Woodland.

1987 Investigation

As previously mentioned, University of Illinois involvement in the mitigation of the Dash Reeves site began with a systematic surface collection and limited excavations in 1987. Although no pottery was recovered from the test excavations, some was found during the surface collection. Tables 7.3 and 7.4 list the diagnostics and body sherds retrieved during the 1987 season.

Unfortunately, this collection contains very few diagnostics. The three largest diagnostic sherds are the *Robinson* (18 g; Collection Blocks 1–20), *Black Lane* (16 g; #800-22), and Havana Plain, *var. Unspecified* (11.6 g; #800-44) rims. Among the body sherds (excluding sherdlets) *Black Lane* is again the most common, 15.8 percent by count and weight. *Fournie* follows at 13.9 percent by count, with *Robinson* (5.9 percent), Hopewell Plain (5 percent), and Pike Rocker Stamped, *var. Fairmount* (4.5 percent) making up most of the rest. Although there are more ceramic types represented in the 1987 surface collection, the kinds and proportions of types are very similar to earlier surface collections.

As is apparent in Table 7.4, systematic surface Collection Blocks 111 and 112 yielded the largest amounts and the widest diversity of ceramics. These units were much larger than the standard units used in the surface pick up. Most of the other blocks produced few identifiable sherds. In fact, only Blocks 28, 38, 40, and 50 yielded more than 20 g of pottery. While this pattern suggested areas of more productive deposits, there were no other obvious spatial differences in the distribution of pottery revealed by the 1987 surface collection.

Table 7.1. Diagnostic Ceramics* from Early Surface Collections

	N	Wt (g)
Historic Sites Survey		
Brangenburg Plain	1	14.1
Fournie Plain, *var. Fournie*	2	20.1
Fournie Plain, *var. Unspecified*	1	15.3
Havana Plain, *var. Unspecified*	1	9.1
Hopewell Cross Hatched, *var. Mississippi*	1	2.3
Indeterminate (grit)	1	4.4
Indeterminate (grog)	2	4.2
Indeterminate (limestone)	4	7.0
Montezuma Punctate, *var. Granite*	1	6.3
Pike Rocker Stamped, *var. Black Lane*	5	31.3
Pike Rocker Stamped, *var. Calhoun*	1	3.4
Total	20	117.5
Wittry Surface Collection		
Pike Rocker Stamped, *var. Black Lane*	1	51.7
Total	1	51.7

*In this and subsequent tables, "diagnostic ceramics" refers to vessel rim and base fragments.

Table 7.2. Body Sherds from Early Surface Collections

	N	Wt (g)
Historic Sites Survey		
Cordmarked (grog)	3	23.6
Cordmarked (limestone)	1	4.2
Cordmarked (no temper)	1	0.9
Crab Orchard Fabric Marked (grit)	2	29.2
Fournie Plain, *var. Fournie*	3	11.3
Hopewell Zoned Incised, *var. Cross*	1	1.0
Hopewell Zoned Stamped, *var. Casey*	3	19.4
Hopewell Zoned Stamped, *var. Unspecified*	1	4.7
Indeterminate (grit)	9	39.6
Indeterminate (grog)	18	42.3
Indeterminate (limestone)	4	10.8
Pike Brushed, *var. Pike*	6	22.7
Pike Brushed, *var. Robinson*	15	45.7
Pike Brushed, *var. Unspecified*	3	23.2
Pike Rocker Stamped, *var. Black Lane*	52	251
Pike Rocker Stamped, *var. Calhoun*	15	257
Pike Rocker Stamped, *var. Fairmount*	8	61.7
Pike Rocker Stamped, *var. Unspecified*	3	18.7
Sherdlets	6	5.4
Untyped	2	6.5
Total	156	879
Wittry Surface Collection		
Pike Rocker Stamped, *var. Fairmount*	1	3.2
Total	1	3.2

Table 7.3. Diagnostic Ceramics from the 1987 Surface Investigations

	N	Wt (g)
Collection Blocks 1-20		
Indeterminate (grog)	1	5.0
Pike Brushed, *var. Robinson*	1	18.0
Collection Block 4		
Indeterminate (grog)	1	1.1
General Surface Collection		
Indeterminate (grog)	1	7.4
Surface Piece Plots		
#800-22		
Pike Rocker Stamped, *var. Black Lane*	1	16.0
#800-41		
Pike Rocker Stamped, *var. Unspecified*	1	1.8
#800-42		
Hopewell Rocker Rim, *var. West*	1	1.9
#800-43		
Fournie Plain, *var. Fournie*	1	2.4
#800-44		
Havana Plain, *var. Unspecified*	1	11.6
#800-46		
Hopewell Cross Hatched, *var. Snyder*	1	2.9

Table 7.4. Body Sherds from 1987 Surface Investigations

	N	Wt (g)
General Surface Collection (700-6)		
Crab Orchard Fabric Marked (grit)	4	31.4
Fournie Plain, *var. Fournie*	14	66.2
Havana Plain, *var. Unspecified*	4	29.6
Hopewell Plain	1	3.3
Hopewell Zoned Incised, *var. Cross*	1	0.6
Hopewell Zoned Stamped, *var. Ferry*	1	10.4
Indeterminate (grit)	2	7.1
Indeterminate (grog)	19	42.5
Indeterminate (limestone)	5	14.1
Pike Brushed, *var. Robinson*	3	6.4
Pike Rocker Stamped, *var. Black Lane*	17	68.8
Pike Rocker Stamped, *var. Calhoun*	1	2.7
Pike Rocker Stamped, *var. Fairmount*	5	29.0
Sherdlets	15	11.4
Untyped	1	2.3
Total	93	325.8
Surface Piece Plot (800-38)		
Hopewell Zoned Stamped, *var. Unspecified*	1	8.7
Total	1	8.7
Systematic Surface Collection		
Collection Block 7		
Indeterminate (grit)	2	2.2
Sherdlets	1	0.1
Total	3	2.3

	N	Wt (g)
Collection Block 9		
Fournie Plain, *var. Fournie*	1	1.6
Total	1	1.6
Collection Block 16		
Indeterminate (limestone)	2	1.2
Pike Brushed, *var. Robinson*	1	1.0
Total	3	2.2
Collection Block 18		
Pike Rocker Stamped, *var. Black Lane*	1	2.7
Sherdlets	2	4.0
Total	3	6.7
Collection Block 19		
Havana Plain, *var. Collinsville*	2	2.6
Hopewell Cross Hatched, *var. Mississippi*	1	2.5
Sherdlets	5	5.6
Total	8	10.7
Indeterminate (grog)	1	2.5
Total	1	2.5
Collection Block 27		
Indeterminate (grog)	1	3.2
Pike Rocker Stamped, *var. Black Lane*	1	2.0
Total	2	5.2

Table 7.4. continued, Body Sherds from 1987 Surface Investigations

	N	Wt (g)
Collection Block 28		
Fournie Plain, var. *Fournie*	2	15.2
Pike Rocker Stamped, var. *Black Lane*	1	1.3
Pike Rocker Stamped, var. *Unspecified*	1	5.9
Sherdlets	3	1.3
Total	7	23.7
Collection Block 29		
Havana Plain, var. *Collinsville*	1	3.4
Pike Rocker Stamped, var. *Black Lane*	2	3.9
Sherdlets	3	1.7
Total	6	9.0
Collection Block 30		
Pike Rocker Stamped, var. *Black Lane*	1	1.2
Sherdlets	3	1.0
Total	4	2.2
Collection Block 35		
Cordmarked (no temper)	1	9.9
Indeterminate (grit)	1	2.7
Pike Rocker Stamped, var. *Black Lane*	1	0.5
Sherdlets	1	0.1
Total	4	13.2
Collection Block 36		
Pike Rocker Stamped, var. *Black Lane*	1	1.7
Total	1	1.7
Collection Block 37		
Indeterminate (grit)	1	7.6
Total	1	7.6
Collection Block 38		
Havana Plain, var. *Collinsville*	2	14.2
Hopewell Zoned Incised, var. *Hertzog*	1	3.4
Indeterminate (limestone)	1	0.7
Pike Rocker Stamped, var. *Unspecified*	1	0.3
Sherdlets	4	2.9
Total	9	21.5
Collection Block 39		
Crab Orchard Fabric Marked (grit)	1	4.3
Fournie Plain, var. *Fournie*	1	1.0
Indeterminate (grit)	1	3.5
Indeterminate (grog)	2	6.4
Sherdlets	6	2.7
Total	11	17.9
Collection Block 40		
Fournie Plain, var. *Fournie*	1	4.3
Hopewell Zoned Incised, var. *Cross*	1	0.8
Indeterminate (grit)	2	4.7
Indeterminate (grog)	1	2.1
Pike Brushed, var. *Robinson*	1	0.8
Pike Rocker Stamped, var. *Calhoun*	1	3.8
Sherdlets	6	5.7
Total	13	22.2

	N	Wt (g)
Collection Block 46		
Sherdlets	1	0.9
Total	1	0.9
Collection Block 47		
Sherdlets	4	5.4
Total	4	5.4
Collection Block 48		
Indeterminate (grit)	1	3.0
Total	1	3.0
Collection Block 49		
Pike Brushed, var. *Robinson*	1	3.0
Pike Rocker Stamped, var. *Unspecified*	1	5.4
Total	2	8.4
Collection Block 50		
Indeterminate (grog)	4	13.0
Indeterminate (limestone)	1	0.9
Pike Brushed, var. *Robinson*	1	1.8
Pike Rocker Stamped, var. *Black Lane*	1	1.7
Sherdlets	5	3.2
Total	12	20.6
Collection Block 55		
Sherdlets	1	1.8
Total	1	1.8
Collection Block 57		
Sherdlets	1	0.3
Total	1	0.3
Collection Block 58		
Sherdlets	1	3.1
Total	1	3.1
Collection Block 59		
Indeterminate (grog)	1	1.3
Pike Brushed, var. *Robinson*	1	0.8
Total	2	2.1
Collection Block 60		
Havana Plain, var. *Collinsville*	1	2.3
Pike Rocker Stamped, var. *Fairmount*	1	10.5
Sherdlets	4	3.2
Total	6	16.0
Collection Block 63		
Indeterminate (grog)	1	1.8
Total	1	1.8
Collection Block 64		
Indeterminate (limestone)	1	0.3
Total	1	0.3

Table 7.4. continued, Body Sherds from 1987 Surface Investigations

	N	Wt (g)
Collection Block 67		
Sherdlets	1	0.5
Total	1	0.5
Collection Block 69		
Indeterminate (grit)	1	6.4
Sherdlets	1	0.2
Total	2	6.6
Collection Block 70		
Pike Rocker Stamped, var. Fairmount	2	6.5
Sherdlets	3	2.8
Total	5	9.3
Collection Block 77		
Sherdlets	4	1.6
Total	4	1.6
Collection Block 80		
Sherdlets	1	0.2
Total	1	0.2
Plain (no temper)	1	3.4
Sherdlets	2	0.3
Total	3	3.7
Collection Block 88		
Havana Plain, var. Collinsville	1	2.3
Total	1	2.3
Collection Block 99		
Sherdlets	4	1.8
Total	4	1.8
Collection Block 100		
Pike Brushed, var. Robinson	1	0.6
Sherdlets	1	1.2
Total	2	1.8
Collection Block 106		
Indeterminate (grog)	1	1.6
Total	1	1.6
Collection Block 108		
Fournie Plain, var. Fournie	1	1.1
Total	1	1.1
Collection Block 109		
Indeterminate (grog)	1	3.8
Indeterminate (limestone)	1	5.2
Sherdlets	9	3.2
Total	11	12.2

	N	Wt (g)
Collection Block 111		
Fournie Plain, var. Fournie	3	10.0
Hopewell Plain	1	3.1
Indeterminate (grit)	3	9.5
Indeterminate (grog)	6	25.1
Indeterminate (limestone)	2	8.1
Pike Rocker Stamped, var. Black Lane	4	34.0
Pike Rocker Stamped, var. Calhoun	1	1.7
Sherdlets	16	7.4
Total	36	98.9
Collection Block 112		
Crab Orchard Fabric Marked (grit)	2	13.6
Fournie Plain, var. Fournie	5	30.0
Havana Plain, var. Unspecified	1	2.3
Hopewell Plain	8	16.2
Indeterminate (grog)	1	2.8
Indeterminate (limestone)	2	13.3
Pike Brushed, var. Pike	4	6.2
Pike Brushed, var. Robinson	3	21.1
Pike Rocker Stamped, var. Black Lane	2	5.2
Pike Rocker Stamped, var. Calhoun	3	11.7
Pike Rocker Stamped, var. Fairmount	1	6.5
Pike Rocker Stamped, var. Unspecified	1	2.2
Sherdlets	17	18.8
Untyped	1	28.6
Total	51	178.5

Tables 7.5 and 7.6 present the diagnostics and body sherds recovered from the 1990 investigation of the Dash Reeves site. The compositional patterns seen in the earlier surface collections were observed in the material derived from the 1990 excavations. Although the percentages are not the same, *Black Lane* is the most abundant ceramic type found in all three collections. *Robinson* is also common in all three collections.

The most noticeable difference with respect to diagnostics is that Hopewell Cross Hatched, *var. Mississippi* is found in moderate amounts in the 1990 collection, whereas it is absent in the 1987 collection and is represented by only one rim in the HSS collection. There is also a distinct difference in the proportion of *Fournie* occurring in each collection. It is common in the 1987 collection, while it is a minor type in both the 1990 and HSS collections.

Although the actual proportions differ in the three collections, the relative ranking of the types based on count or weight is very consistent. There is also a similarly wide diversity of ceramics present. It is not surprising that the 1990 season produced the larger number of different types. It was gratifying to find that the surface collections predicted the kinds and proportions of pottery that would be recovered in intensive excavation. Given this outcome, it is reasonable to consider all three collections in the ensuing detailed discussion of the most common ceramic types recovered at the Dash Reeves site.

ASSEMBLAGE CHARACTERISTICS

Tables 7.7–7.9 present all ceramics recovered from the Dash Reeves site in the possession of the University of Illinois. It should be noted that the percentages in Table 7.8 are based on all body sherds, excluding sherdlets.

In contrast to the Holding site (Maher 1989:270–271), the varieties *Bottoms* and *Collinsville* are found in very low percentages at the Dash Reeves site. At the Holding site *Bottoms* and *Collinsville* combine for 40 percent of the diagnostics and 51.1 percent of the body sherds. In the Dash Reeves collection these two types make up only 3 percent of the diagnostics and 5.1 percent of the body sherds by count.

Black Lane is the most common ceramic type in the Dash Reeves assemblage. In fact, Pike Rocker Stamped dominates the assemblage as a whole, with 30 percent by count and 39.3 percent by weight. This is in contrast to the Holding site, where *Black Lane* is the fourth most common diagnostic and the third most common body sherd category.

Pike Brushed is distinctly more common in the Dash Reeves assemblage than in the Holding ceramic assemblage. *Robinson* is the most numerous variety of this type, but *Pike* is also common. In fact, due to one large rim profile recovered from Geomorphological Trench 1, *Pike* makes up a disproportionately large percentage of the diagnostics by weight. Of all the pottery recovered, Pike Brushed makes up 13.9 percent by count and 17 percent by weight. This is in clear contrast to the 2–3 percent occurrence in the Holding assemblage.

Crab Orchard Fabric Marked is also more common in the Dash Reeves assemblage than in the Holding. The latter assemblage contains only five rims and 54 body sherds, whereas in the Dash Reeves collection there are 16 rims and 226 body sherds. Interestingly, Hopewell Cross Hatched, *var. Mississippi*, which makes up 17 percent of the diagnostics at Holding, makes up only 5 percent of the diagnostics at Dash Reeves. This also may reflect the small amount of Hopewell Zoned Stamped and Hopewell Zoned Incised ceramics found at Dash Reeves. Neither site yielded large amounts of these ceramic types, but in the Holding assemblage these two types combined make up 3.5 percent of the total, whereas they make up only 1.6 percent of all pottery in the Dash Reeves assemblage. If body sherds are excluded, limestone-tempered *Ferry* is more common at Dash Reeves than grog-tempered *Casey*, which is the most common variety of Hopewell Zoned Stamped at Holding. If, however, body sherds are combined with rims, *Casey* is also numerically dominant at Dash Reeves.

There are ceramic type-varieties that are not shared by the two assemblages. The Holding assemblage includes Black Sand Incised, Naples Stamped, and classic Illinois valley Havana Cordmarked and Plain sherds, none of which occur in the Dash Reeves collections. In the Dash Reeves assemblage there is some evidence of contamination from non–Middle Woodland sources. Much of the "cordmarked grog-tempered" and "cordmarked limestone-tempered" pottery listed in

Table 7.5. Diagnostic Ceramics from the 1990 Season, All Contexts

Type-Variety	N	N %	Wt (g)	Wt %
Baehr Zoned Brushed	3	0.97	51.8	0.85
Baehr Zoned Punctated	1	0.32	11.5	0.19
Brangenburg Plain	1	0.32	2.7	0.04
Cordmarked (grog)	1	0.32	22.7	0.37
Cordmarked (limestone)	1	0.32	10.9	0.18
Fournie Plain, *var. Fournie*	10	3.25	229.1	3.75
Havana Cordmarked, *var. Bottoms*	6	1.95	92.7	1.52
Havana Cordmarked, *var. Unspecified*	3	0.97	40.3	0.66
Havana Plain, *var. Collinsville*	4	1.30	45.2	0.74
Havana Plain, *var. Unspecified*	2	0.65	23.4	0.38
Hopewell Cross Hatched, *var. Illinois*	3	0.97	41.3	0.68
Hopewell Cross Hatched, *var. Mississippi*	16	5.19	109.5	1.79
Hopewell Cross Hatched, *var. Snyder*	1	0.32	5.9	0.10
Hopewell Cross Hatched, *var. Unspecified*	1	0.32	8.3	0.14
Hopewell Plain	4	1.30	13.2	0.22
Hopewell Rocker Rim, *var. West*	8	2.60	86.8	1.42
Hopewell Zoned Incised, *var. Cross*	3	0.97	46.3	0.76
Hopewell Zoned Incised, *var. Fulton*	1	0.32	11.2	0.18
Hopewell Zoned Red, *var. Unspecified*	1	0.32	10.8	0.18
Hopewell Zoned Stamped, *var. Casey*	3	0.97	139.0	2.28
Hopewell Zoned Stamped, *var. Ferry*	6	1.95	362.9	5.95
Hopewell Zoned Stamped, *var. Unspecified*	6	1.95	142.4	2.33
Indeterminate (grit)	14	4.55	144.1	2.36
Indeterminate (grit/grog)	1	0.32	9.9	0.16
Indeterminate (grit/limestone)	1	0.32	2.5	0.04
Indeterminate (grog)	37	12.01	254.1	4.16
Indeterminate (grog/limestone)	1	0.32	1.8	0.03
Indeterminate (limestone)	9	2.92	56.7	0.93
Indeterminate (no temper)	1	0.32	0.5	0.01
Montezuma Punctate, *var. Granite*	1	0.32	4.5	0.07
Montezuma Punctate, *var. Montezuma*	1	0.32	4.1	0.07
Pike Brushed, *var. Pike*	17	5.52	1,034.6	16.96
Pike Brushed, *var. Robinson*	18	5.84	333.0	5.46
Pike Brushed, *var. Unspecified*	4	1.30	125.0	2.05
Pike Rocker Stamped, *var. Black Lane*	55	17.86	1,181.6	19.36
Pike Rocker Stamped, *var. Calhoun*	17	5.52	386.5	6.33
Pike Rocker Stamped, *var. Fairmount*	8	2.60	183.0	3.00
Pike Rocker Stamped, *var. Unspecified*	6	1.95	96.2	1.58
Untyped	16	5.19	265.4	4.35
Total	308		6,101.9	

Table 7.6. Body Sherds from the 1990 Season, All Contexts

Type-Variety	N	N %	Wt (g)	Wt %
Baehr Zoned Brushed	18	0.31	116.8	0.41
Cordmarked (grog)	43	0.74	275.6	0.98
Cordmarked (limestone)	23	0.40	240.8	0.85
Cordmarked (no temper)	1	0.02	4.5	0.02
Crab Orchard Fabric Marked (grit)	196	3.37	1,658.3	5.87
Crab Orchard Fabric Marked (grog)	17	0.29	204.1	0.72
Crab Orchard Fabric Marked (limestone)	4	0.07	55.1	0.20
Fournie Plain, *var. Fournie*	314	5.40	1,252.2	4.43
Fournie Plain, *var. Unspecified*	2	0.03	7.4	0.03
Havana Cordmarked, *var. Bottoms*	173	2.98	1,698.6	6.02
Havana Cordmarked, *var. Unspecified*	3	0.05	29.3	0.10
Havana Cordwrapped Stick	1	0.02	2.9	0.01
Havana Plain, *var. Collinsville*	134	2.31	999.7	3.54
Havana Plain, *var. Unspecified*	8	0.14	44.6	0.16
Historic	6	0.10	47.9	0.17
Hopewell Cross Hatched, *var. Mississippi*	1	0.02	0.7	0.01
Hopewell Plain	149	2.56	556.6	1.97
Hopewell Zoned Incised, *var. Cross*	5	0.09	16.8	0.06
Hopewell Zoned Incised, *var. Fulton*	5	0.09	20.7	0.07
Hopewell Zoned Incised, *var. Hertzog*	2	0.03	19.9	0.07
Hopewell Zoned Incised, *var. Unspecified*	1	0.02	4.1	0.01
Hopewell Zoned Stamped, *var. Bluff*	1	0.02	19.8	0.07
Hopewell Zoned Stamped, *var. Casey*	26	0.45	105.6	0.37
Hopewell Zoned Stamped, *var. Ferry*	17	0.29	93.4	0.33
Hopewell Zoned Stamped, *var. Unspecified*	15	0.26	37.7	0.13
Indeterminate (grit)	573	9.86	1,528.6	5.41
Indeterminate (grit/grog)	1	0.02	9.8	0.03
Indeterminate (grog)	958	16.49	2,150.0	7.61
Indeterminate (grog/limestone)	6	0.10	26.2	0.09
Indeterminate (limestone)	537	9.24	994.1	3.52
Montezuma Punctate, *var. Granite*	2	0.03	8.8	0.03
Pike Brushed, *var. Pike*	271	4.66	1,273.4	4.51
Pike Brushed, *var. Robinson*	471	8.11	2,409.4	8.53
Pike Brushed, *var. Unspecified*	82	1.41	816.7	2.89
Pike Rocker Stamped, *var. Black Lane*	1,191	20.50	6,745.7	23.89
Pike Rocker Stamped, *var. Calhoun*	364	6.26	2,655.3	9.40
Pike Rocker Stamped, *var. Fairmount*	170	2.93	1,878.1	6.65
Pike Rocker Stamped, *var. Unspecified*	14	0.24	196.9	0.70
Plain (no temper)	2	0.03	3.5	0.01
Red Slip (limestone)	1	0.02	1.1	0.01
Untyped	3	0.05	26.9	0.10
Total	5,811		28,237.6	

Table 7.7. Diagnostic Ceramics, All Collections

Type-Variety	N	N %	Wt (g)	Wt %
Baehr Zoned Brushed	3	0.88	51.8	0.82
Baehr Zoned Punctated	1	0.29	11.5	0.18
Brangenburg Plain	2	0.59	16.8	0.27
Cordmarked (grog)	1	0.29	22.7	0.36
Cordmarked (limestone)	1	0.29	8.0	0.13
Crab Orchard Fabric Marked (grit)	1	0.29	10.9	0.17
Fournie Plain, *var. Fournie*	13	3.83	251.6	3.97
Fournie Plain, *var. Unspecified*	1	0.29	15.3	0.24
Havana Cordmarked, *var. Bottoms*	6	1.77	92.7	1.46
Havana Cordmarked, *var. Unspecified*	3	0.88	40.3	0.64
Havana Plain, *var. Collinsville*	4	1.18	45.2	0.71
Havana Plain, *var. Unspecified*	4	1.18	44.1	0.70
Hopewell Cross Hatched, *var. Illinois*	3	0.88	41.3	0.65
Hopewell Cross Hatched, *var. Mississippi*	17	5.01	111.8	1.76
Hopewell Cross Hatched, *var. Snyder*	2	0.59	8.8	0.14
Hopewell Cross Hatched, *var. Unspecified*	1	0.29	8.3	0.13
Hopewell Plain	4	1.18	13.2	0.21
Hopewell Rocker Rim, *var. West*	9	2.65	88.7	1.40
Hopewell Zoned Incised, *var. Cross*	3	0.88	46.3	0.73
Hopewell Zoned Incised, *var. Fulton*	1	0.29	11.2	0.18
Hopewell Zoned Red, *var. Unspecified*	1	0.29	10.8	0.17
Hopewell Zoned Stamped, *var. Casey*	3	0.88	139.0	2.19
Hopewell Zoned Stamped, *var. Ferry*	6	1.77	362.9	5.72
Hopewell Zoned Stamped, *var. Unspecified*	6	1.77	142.4	2.25
Indeterminate (grit)	15	4.42	148.5	2.34
Indeterminate (grit/grog)	1	0.29	9.9	0.16
Indeterminate (grit/limestone)	1	0.29	2.5	0.04
Indeterminate (grog)	42	12.39	271.8	4.29
Indeterminate (grog/limestone)	1	0.29	1.8	0.03
Indeterminate (limestone)	13	3.83	63.7	1.00
Indeterminate (no temper)	1	0.29	0.5	0.01
Montezuma Punctate, *var. Granite*	2	0.59	10.8	0.17
Montezuma Punctate, *var. Montezuma*	1	0.29	4.1	0.06
Pike Brushed, *var. Pike*	17	5.01	1,034.6	16.32
Pike Brushed, *var. Robinson*	19	5.60	351.0	5.54
Pike Brushed, *var. Unspecified*	4	1.18	125.0	1.97
Pike Rocker Stamped, *var. Black Lane*	62	18.29	1,280.6	20.20
Pike Rocker Stamped, *var. Calhoun*	18	5.31	389.9	6.15
Pike Rocker Stamped, *var. Fairmount*	8	2.36	183.0	2.89
Pike Rocker Stamped, *var. Unspecified*	7	2.06	98.0	1.55
Untyped	16	4.72	265.4	4.19
Total	339		6,339.2	

Table 7.8. Body Sherds, All Collections

Type-Variety	N	N %	Wt (g)	Wt %
Baehr Zoned Brushed	18	0.292	116.8	0.39
Cordmarked (grog)	46	0.746	299.2	1.00
Cordmarked (limestone)	24	0.389	245.0	0.82
Cordmarked (no temper)	3	0.049	15.3	0.05
Crab Orchard Fabric Marked (grit)	205	3.326	1,736.8	5.81
Crab Orchard Fabric Marked (grog)	17	0.276	204.1	0.68
Crab Orchard Fabric Marked (limestone)	4	0.065	55.1	0.18
Fournie Plain, *var. Fournie*	345	5.597	1,392.9	4.66
Fournie Plain, *var. Unspecified*	2	0.032	7.4	0.03
Havana Cordmarked, *var. Bottoms*	173	2.807	1,698.6	5.68
Havana Cordmarked, *var. Unspecified*	3	0.049	29.3	0.10
Havana Cordwrapped Stick	1	0.016	2.9	0.01
Havana Plain, *var. Collinsville*	141	2.287	1,024.5	3.43
Havana Plain, *var. Unspecified*	13	0.211	76.5	0.26
Historic	6	0.097	47.9	0.16
Hopewell Cross Hatched, *var. Mississippi*	2	0.032	3.2	0.01
Hopewell Plain	159	2.579	579.2	1.94
Hopewell Zoned Incised, *var. Cross*	8	0.130	19.2	0.06
Hopewell Zoned Incised, *var. Fulton*	5	0.081	20.7	0.07
Hopewell Zoned Incised, *var. Hertzog*	3	0.049	23.3	0.08
Hopewell Zoned Incised, *var. Unspecified*	1	0.016	4.1	0.01
Hopewell Zoned Stamped, *var. Bluff*	1	0.016	19.8	0.07
Hopewell Zoned Stamped, *var. Casey*	29	0.470	125.0	0.42
Hopewell Zoned Stamped, *var. Ferry*	18	0.292	103.8	0.35
Hopewell Zoned Stamped, *var. Unspecified*	17	0.276	51.1	0.17
Indeterminate (grit)	596	9.669	1,614.9	5.40
Indeterminate (grit/grog)	1	0.016	9.8	0.03
Indeterminate (grog)	1,015	16.467	2,298.4	7.69
Indeterminate (grog/limestone)	6	0.097	26.2	0.09
Indeterminate (limestone)	556	9.020	1,048.7	3.51
Montezuma Punctate, *var. Granite*	2	0.032	8.8	0.03
Pike Brushed, *var. Pike*	281	4.559	1,302.3	4.36
Pike Brushed, *var. Robinson*	498	8.079	2,490.6	8.33
Pike Brushed, *var. Unspecified*	85	1.379	839.9	2.81
Pike Rocker Stamped, *var. Black Lane*	1,275	20.685	7,119.5	23.82
Pike Rocker Stamped, *var. Calhoun*	385	6.246	2,932.1	9.81
Pike Rocker Stamped, *var. Fairmount*	188	3.050	1,995.5	6.68
Pike Rocker Stamped, *var. Unspecified*	21	0.341	229.4	0.77
Plain (no temper)	3	0.049	6.9	0.02
Red Slip (limestone)	1	0.016	1.1	0.00
Untyped	7	0.114	64.3	0.22
Total	6,164		29,890.1	

Table 7.9. Rim Fragments, All Collections

Type-Variety	N	N %	Wt (g)	Wt %
Indeterminate (grit)	11	14.0	20.5	11.0
Indeterminate (grog)	49	62.0	141.2	75.5
Indeterminate (grog/limestone)	2	2.5	2.8	1.5
Indeterminate (limestone)	14	18.0	20.4	10.9
Sherdlets	3	3.8	2.2	1.2
Total	79		87.1	

Tables 7.6 and 7.7 has much thinner walls than the average Middle Woodland cordmarked pottery. In addition, the combination of limestone or grog tempering with a cordmarked surface treatment is not typical of Middle Woodland ceramics. This notion, however, may have to be revised in view of the discovery of a substantial amount of grog-tempered, cordmarked pottery in the Cement Hollow phase occupation of the Little Hills site (Lopinot 1990) in Missouri.

The presence of limestone-tempered, cordmarked pottery and a few fragments of very thin-walled, limestone-tempered, red-slipped pottery suggests that there may be some minor contamination from later prehistoric occupations. The source of the contamination is probably the adjacent Emergent Mississippian Marge site, but there also may have been a very minor (perhaps only transitory) Late Woodland occupation in the area. No feature materials at Dash Reeves, however, can be attributed to anything other than the Middle Woodland occupation. [Senior author's note: I examined this material and believe it may be associated with a Middle Woodland type, Hopewell Red Filmed or Zoned Red, as defined by Griffin (1952:118). Seven Zoned Red body sherds were identified at the Holding site (Maher 1989:195–197), and others have been recovered from lower Illinois River Middle Woodland sites, e.g., Napoleon Hollow and Smiling Dan (Morgan 1985:200, 1986:379).]

The vessel form could be determined for only 163 of the rims. Not surprisingly, 150 of the rims are from jars, while only 13 are from bowls. Table 7.10 shows that, for the diagnostics, grog is the primary tempering material, with limestone and grit tempers next in frequency. This is very different from the pattern seen in the diagnostics from the Holding site. In that assemblage grit/sand is the dominant temper (43.5 percent by count), with grog second (39.5 percent), and limestone rather uncommon (4.6 percent) (Maher 1989:275).

Upper rim treatments in the Dash Reeves assemblage are similar to those seen in the Holding assemblage. Cross hatching is common in both assemblages (Table 7.11). At Dash Reeves, however, it is often not the classic "Hopewell Rim" treatment with underlying hemiconical punctations common in the Holding site material (Maher 1989:274). Cross hatching at Dash Reeves often lacks underlying punctations and some-

times overlaps a row of embossed nodes. A band of plain rocker stamping with and without underlying punctations is also a common upper rim treatment at Dash Reeves.

Like the Holding assemblage, round lips are the most common type of rim terminus at Dash Reeves (Table 7.12). There are very few of the heavily notched, scalloped-shaped lips common in the Holding collection. No doubt this is related to the very low amounts of *Bottoms* and *Collinsville* in the Dash Reeves collection. Ridge and channel rims, on the other hand, are more common in the Dash Reeves assemblage. Although only 22 percent of sherds have both a ridge and a channel, 36 percent have a ridge, a channel, or both. This probably is due to the presence of large amounts of Pike Rocker Stamped and Pike Brushed in this assemblage.

A few general conclusions can be drawn from characteristics of the ceramic assemblage as a whole. Although it shares many types with the Holding collection, the Dash Reeves assemblage is characterized by distinctly different proportions. Recently, the pit features at the Holding site have been seriated using the dominant ceramic types found at that site (Maher 1991). This has resulted in the identification of three different temporal occupations. Comparison of the Dash Reeves ceramic percentages to the results of that study indicate that the assemblage most closely resembles the Hill Lake occupation at Holding. In fact, the small amount of *Bottoms* and *Collinsville* and the numerical dominance of Pike Rocker Stamped and Pike Brushed suggest that the Middle Woodland occupation at Dash Reeves perhaps occurred during the middle to late Hill Lake phase. Confirmation of this hypothesis will require radiocarbon dates, but the ceramic assemblage does suggest that this is a late Middle Woodland occupation.

TYPE-VARIETY DESCRIPTIONS

Although all the ceramic types recovered at Dash Reeves cannot be described, the most common warrant some illustration. As with the Holding report, the following descriptions are based primarily on the diagnostics.

Table 7.10. Temper in Diagnostic Ceramics

Temper	N	%
Grog	171	50.4
Limestone	77	22.7
Grit	44	13.0
Grit/sand	19	5.6
Grog/limestone	10	3.0
Grit/grog	8	2.4
None observed	5	1.5
Grit/limestone	2	0.6
Grog/sand	2	0.6
Total	338	

Table 7.11. Upper Rim Treatments on Diagnostic Ceramics

Upper Rim Treatment	N	%
Cross hatching, no punctations	26	21.0
Cross hatching, underlying punctations	20	16.1
Plain rocker stamping	17	13.7
Rocker stamping, underlying punctations	10	8.1
Vertical incisions	9	7.3
Diagonal incisions, underlying punctations	8	6.5
Crescent punctations	8	6.5
Brushing/Combing	6	4.8
Dentate rocker stamping	5	4.0
Other	5	4.0
Hemiconical punctations	4	3.2
Other punctations	3	2.4
Dot-dash	2	1.6
Dentate stamp	1	0.8
Total	124	

Note: Omits diagnostic sherds with no identifiable separate upper rim treatment.

Table 7.12. Lip Shapes of Diagnostic Ceramics

Lip Shape	N	%
Round	152	44.8
Flat	104	30.7
Round, beveled to interior	37	10.9
Not identifiable	25	7.4
Flat, beveled to interior	7	2.1
Round, beveled to exterior	4	1.2
Round, beveled to interior and exterior	4	1.2
Flat, beveled to exterior	3	0.9
T-shaped (Brangenburg)	2	0.6
Scalloped	1	0.3
Total	339	

Crab Orchard Fabric Marked

The Crab Orchard Fabric Marked material in the collection is similar in temper and surface treatment to that found at Holding (Plates 7.1 and 7.2; Figure 7.2). This type commonly occurs in Middle Woodland assemblages in southern Illinois (Maxwell 1951; Winters 1963). The southern location of the Dash Reeves site in the American Bottom doubtless explains the higher proportion of this type compared with the Holding collection.

The mean rim diameter is 16.1 cm (S=2.17 cm; N=8), which is identical to the median value, producing a normal distribution (Figure 7.3). This is a somewhat smaller diameter than recorded for the two measurable Crab Orchard Fabric Marked rims recovered at Holding (20 cm and 26 cm). The average body wall thickness is 7.24 mm (S=1.13 mm; N=12), which is slightly smaller than the median value of 7.55 mm, indicating a slightly skewed distribution (Figure 7.4). This value is greater than that recorded for the Holding assemblage (mean=6.02 mm; S=1.74 mm). Lip thickness for the most part is the same as body wall thickness.

Embossed nodes are common on these ceramics. The average distance from lip edge to the center of a boss is 14.86 mm (S=4.46 mm; N=14). The median, however, is 14.1 mm, and one can see that the distribution is positively skewed due to one rim with a distance of 24.5 mm (Figure 7.5). In general, the Crab Orchard Fabric Marked rims have bosses significantly closer to the lip than most of the *Black Lane* rims.

Thirteen of the 16 rims are from jars and the rest are from vessels of indeterminate shape. Round lips are most common (43.8 percent), but flat lips (31 percent) also occur. Rims of this type are among the few in the Dash Reeves assemblage to have any lip modification. Seven are notched on the lip exterior with a cord-wrapped dowel, two are notched on the exterior with an unidentified tool (round in cross section), one has fabric impressions on the superior lip surface, and five appear to be unmodified.

Fournie Plain, var. Fournie

Fournie Plain is a common ceramic type in both the Holding and Dash Reeves ceramic assemblages (Plate 7.3). The mean rim diameter of *Fournie* vessels in the Dash Reeves collection is 16.8 cm (S=6.34 cm; N=8),

which is larger than that seen for the *Fournie* vessels in the Holding collection (mean=13.73 cm). The reason for this difference is one extreme value (29 cm) that has skewed the Dash Reeves distribution (Figure 7.3). In this situation the median value of 14 cm better represents most of the *Fournie* at Dash Reeves and is much closer to the average found at Holding.

The distribution of body thickness values is also somewhat skewed (Figure 7.4), with a mean of 7.19 mm (S=1.41 mm; N=9) but a median of 6.44 mm. Both measures, however, are larger than the average of 4.87 mm for the Holding site. *Fournie* vessels at Dash Reeves are somewhat thinner at the lip, with a mean of 6.58 mm (S=1.92 mm; N=13). The distribution, again, is not normal (Figure 7.6), with one extreme value (11.03 mm) strongly affecting the mean. The median value of 6.1 mm is perhaps a more accurate measure of central tendency in this instance. Bosses are not characteristic of *Fournie*. Only three rims in this collection have them, with lip-to-boss distances of 8, 12.1, and 20.5 mm.

Like the *Fournie* ceramics recovered at Holding, bowl shapes are common in the Dash Reeves material. Of the five rims from vessels whose shapes could be identified, three are from bowls and two are from jars. Considering that there are only 13 bowls in the entire assemblage, it is reasonable to conclude that they are often plain and grog tempered at this site. This is also true of the Holding collection.

Of the 13 *Fournie* rims, 69.2 percent have round lips, 15.4 percent have flat lips, and one has a round lip with an interior bevel. Most of these vessels do not have "ridge and channel" upper rim wall modifications. In this collection only two have a ridge and channel and a third has a possible internal ridge.

Havana Cordmarked, var. Bottoms

Bottoms is not a common type in the Dash Reeves collection, but it is included here for comparative purposes. Only three of the six rims are large enough to allow estimates of diameter. Values of 13, 14, and 16 cm produce a mean and median of approximately 14 cm, which is much smaller than the Holding average of 22.3 cm. Measurements of five rims produced an average body wall thickness of 6.19 mm (S=0.74 mm). The distribution is skewed by one extreme value (7.5 mm) (Figure 7.4), which explains why the median (5.8 mm) is smaller than the mean. Both measures are distinctly

Plate 7.1. Crab Orchard Fabric Marked Rims

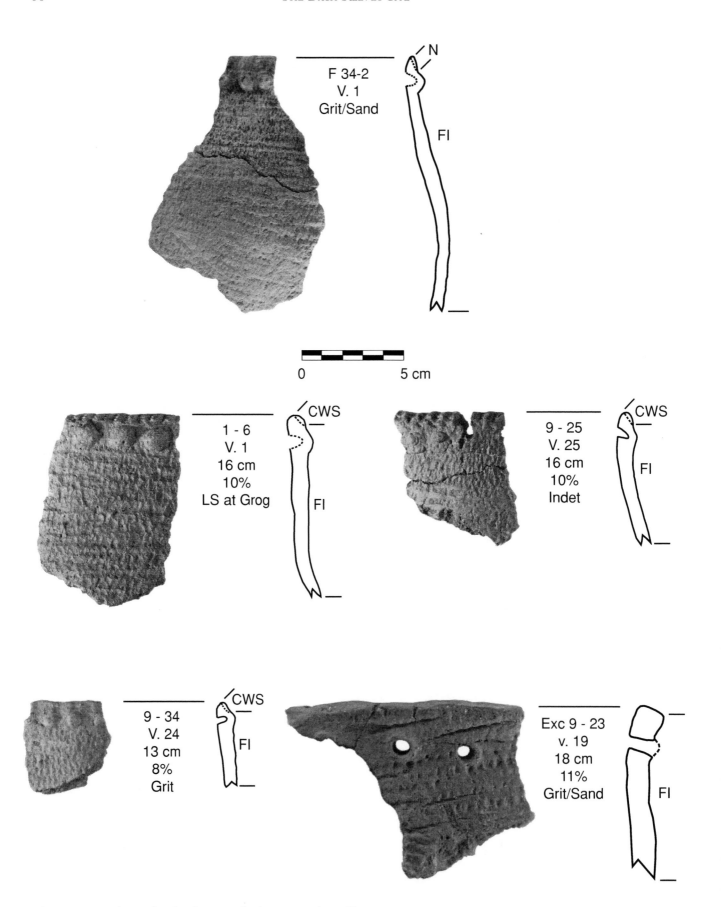

Plate 7.2. Crab Orchard Fabric Marked Rims and Profiles

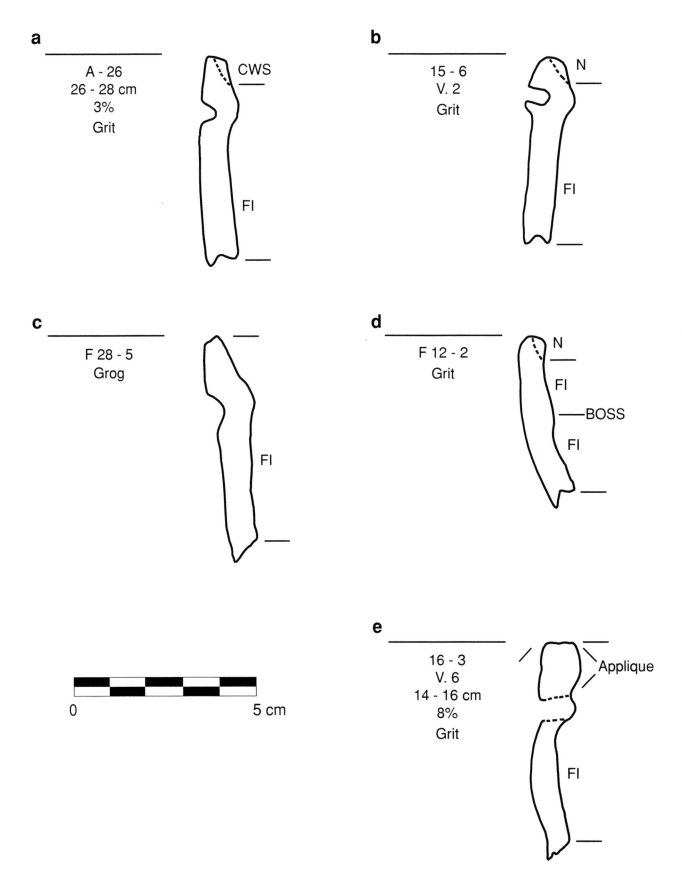

a

A - 26
26 - 28 cm
3%
Grit

CWS

FI

b

15 - 6
V. 2
Grit

N

FI

c

F 28 - 5
Grog

FI

d

F 12 - 2
Grit

N

FI

BOSS

FI

0   5 cm

e

16 - 3
V. 6
14 - 16 cm
8%
Grit

Applique

FI

Figure 7.2. Crab Orchard Fabric Marked Rim Profiles

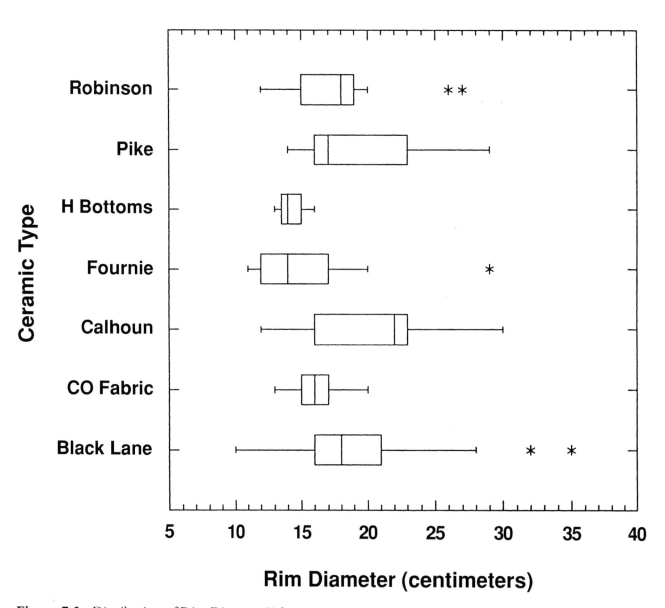

Figure 7.3. Distribution of Rim Diameter Values

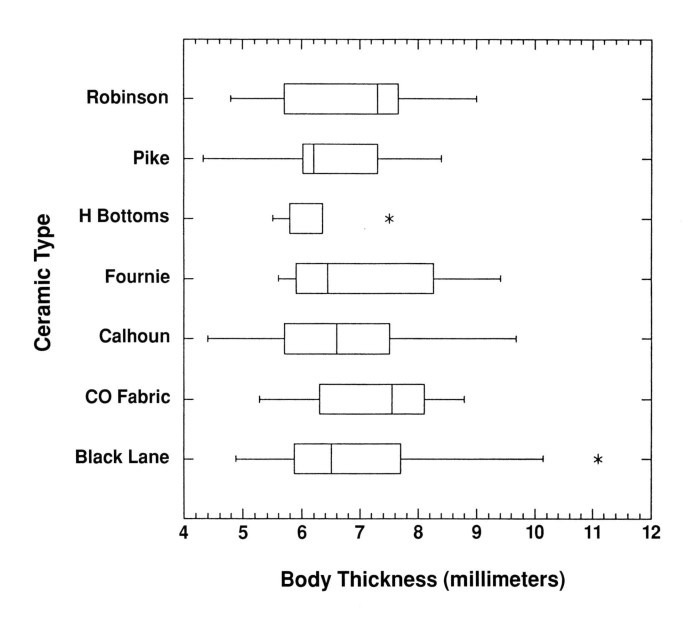

Figure 7.4. Distribution of Body Thickness Values

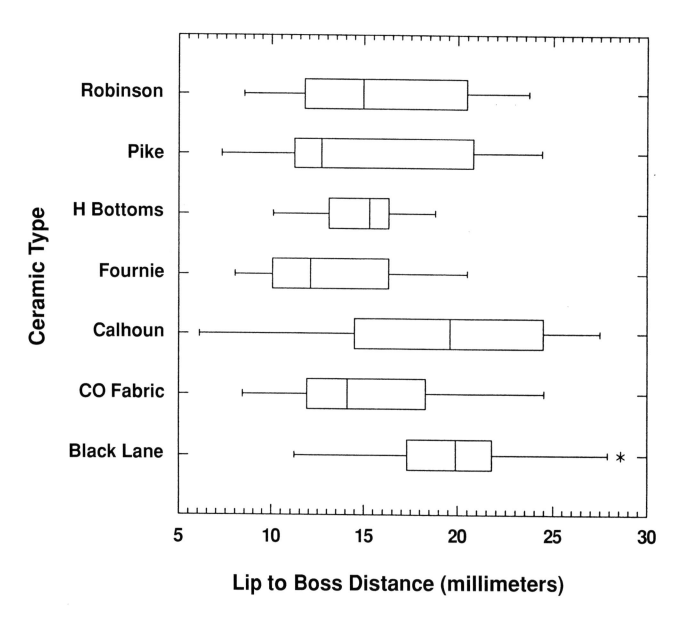

Figure 7.5. Distribution of Lip-to-Boss Distance Values

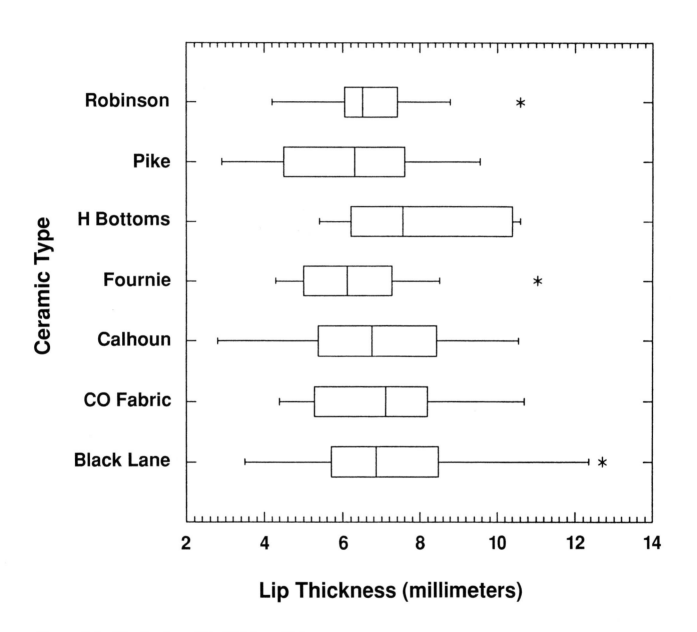

Figure 7.6. Distribution of Lip Thickness Values

900 - 48
V.1
30 - 34 cm
8%
grog

PL

0   5 cm

Plate 7.3. Fournie Plain, *var. Fournie* Rim and Profile

smaller than the Holding average of 7.5 mm. It is interesting that the mean wall thickness of the Havana Cordmarked, *var. Unspecified* in the Dash Reeves collection is smaller still (4.61 mm). It is distinctly possible that the pottery assigned to this category is actually Late Woodland or Emergent Mississippian in origin; its placement in the unspecified variety reflects its lack of typical *Bottoms* characteristics (e.g., thick walls).

Bottoms lip thickness is somewhat greater than wall thickness, with a mean of 7.95 mm (S=2.2 mm; N=6) and a median of 7.55 mm. The thicker measurement is possibly due to the presence of bosses near the lip on each of the vessels. The lip-to-boss distance mean is 14.82 mm (S=2.96 mm; N=6), with a median value of 15.3 mm. The distribution reveals a slight negative skewing, but it is not extreme.

The vessel form of one *Bottoms* rim could not be identified. The remaining five are all jars. Two of the rims have round lips, three are flat, and one is round with an interior bevel. None of the *Bottoms* rims have any ridging or channeling. Like the Crab Orchard Fabric Marked pottery in this collection, *Bottoms* lips are often notched. Three are notched on the exterior with

a cord-wrapped dowel. One is impressed with a cord-wrapped dowel on both the exterior and interior lip surfaces, and one is unmodified. In terms of lip shape, lip modification, and surface treatment, the *Bottoms* ceramics from Dash Reeves are similar to those from Holding. The Dash Reeves vessels, however, are generally thinner and have smaller orifices.

Hopewell Cross Hatched, var. Mississippi

Although the *Mississippi* variant is abundant (N=17) in the Dash Reeves collection, most sherds are small with few measurable characteristics (Plate 7.4 d–e; Figure 7.7). The mean diameter of the six measurable rims is 18 cm (S=2.53 cm), which is slightly larger than the average for the Holding site collection (16.83 cm). The mean body wall thickness is 5.78 mm (S=1.22 mm; N=6), and the average lip thickness is 5.83 mm (S=0.99 mm; N=13), neither of which is far from the Holding average of 5.81 mm for these attributes.

Only three rims are large enough to permit identification of vessel form; all are from jars. Five rims are missing the terminal lip surface, five are round, four are

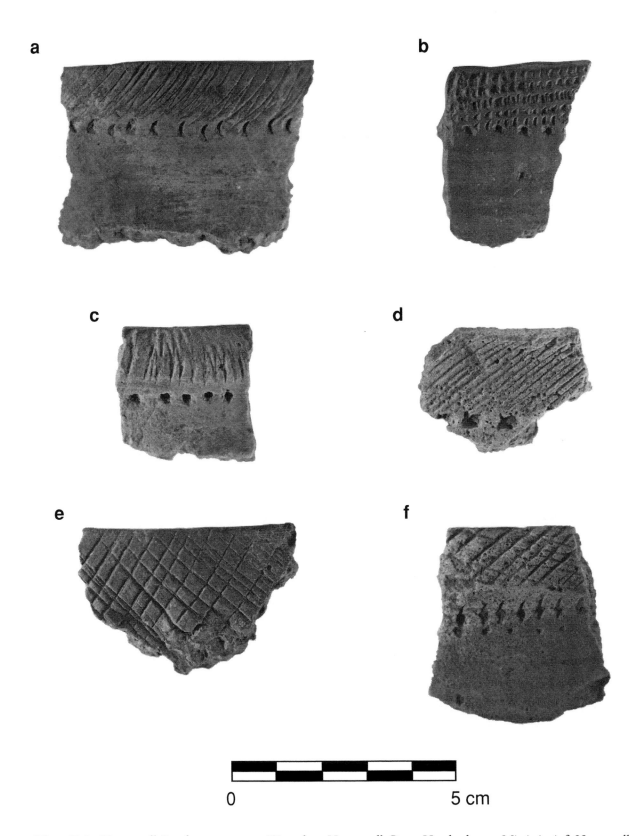

Plate 7.4. Hopewell Rocker: a–c, *var. West*; d–e, Hopewell Cross Hatched, *var. Mississippi*; f, Hopewell Cross Hatched, *var. Illinois* Rims

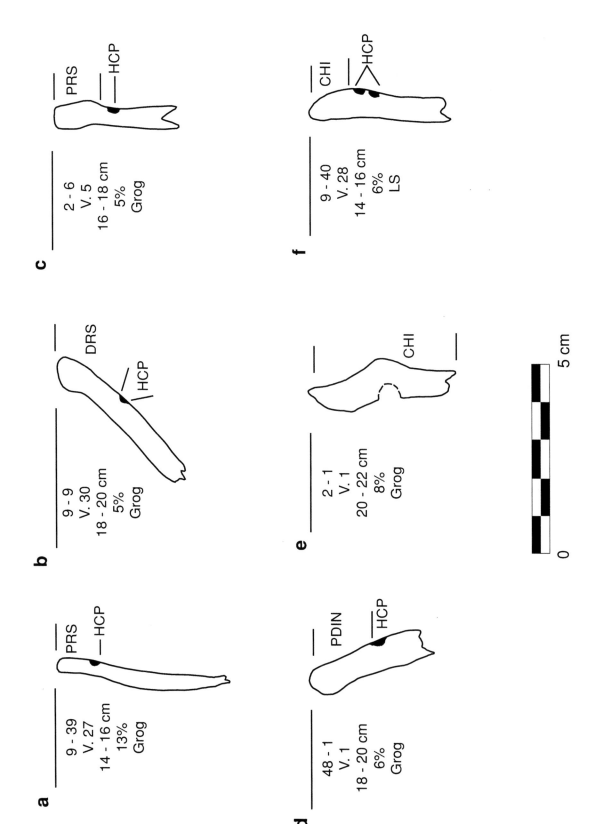

Figure 7.7. Hopewell Rocker (a–c) and Hopewell Cross Hatched (d–f) Rim Profiles

flat, and three are round with an interior bevel. Typically, *Mississippi* rims have a ridge and channel modification. In this collection 64.7 percent have a ridge, a channel, or both characteristics.

Hopewell Zoned Stamped, var. Ferry

Although there are more *Casey* body sherds, there are more *Ferry* diagnostics (N=6) (Plates 7.5 and 7.6; Figures 7.8 and 7.9). These two varieties of Hopewell Zoned Stamped differ only in their temper. General characteristics of *Ferry* also apply to *Casey*.

The mean rim diameter is 15.5 cm (S=3.11 cm; N=4), which is smaller than the diameter of either of the two *Ferry* rims recovered at Holding (18 and 19 cm). The average wall thickness is 6.09 mm (S=1.56 mm; N=6), compared with an average of 4.79 mm for the Holding site sherds. The mean thickness at the lip is 4.78 mm (S=1.35 mm).

Five of the six diagnostics can be identified as jar fragments. Three have cross-hatched or hatched incisions with underlying hemiconical punctations on the upper rim. One has fine rocker stamping with underlying punctations, and the other is brushed with no punctations on the upper rim. Five of the *Ferry* diagnostics have dentate rocker stamping as the zone filler, while one has plain rocker stamping.

Of these six diagnostics, three have flat lips, two are round, and one is missing the lip surface. Three have a ridge and a channel, two have neither characteristic, and the remaining sherd is missing that area of the rim. In general, both the *Ferry* and *Casey* sherds found in the Dash Reeves assemblage are similar to those found at Holding.

Pike Brushed, var. Pike

Pike is the limestone-tempered variety of Pike Brushed (Plate 7.7e–g; Figure 7.10). Dash Reeves *Pike* sherds have a mean rim diameter of 19.38 cm (S=5.15 mm; N=8), but the median value is 17 cm. This distribution (Figure 7.3) is strongly positively skewed by one extreme value (29 cm). The median in this instance is a more accurate measure of central tendency. It is also closer to the value for the one *Pike* rim in the Holding collection (12 cm).

The mean body wall thickness of 6.55 mm (S=1.25 mm; N=11) is slightly larger than the median value of 6.2 mm, producing only a somewhat negatively skewed distribution (Figure 7.4). Mean body wall thickness for Holding sherds of this type is 5.83 mm. The mean lip thickness is 6.26 mm (S=1.96 mm; N=17), which is the same as the median value (6.3 mm), indicating a reasonably normal distribution.

Bosses are found on 10 of the 17 *Pike* diagnostics. The mean distance from lip edge to boss is 14.69 mm (S=5.17 mm), but the median is 12.7 mm. This discrepancy is due to one extreme value of 24.4 mm (Figure 7.5) that strongly affects the mean. The median is a more accurate measure of central tendency for this skewed distribution.

Eight of the *Pike* rims are from jars, one is from a bowl, and the vessel form could not be determined confidently for the remaining eight diagnostics. Generally, *Pike* ceramics do not have upper rim treatments. Of the four in this collection that do have an upper rim treatment, three have brushing in a different orientation or application than the body treatment. One has crescent-shaped or fingernail punctations on the upper rim. Eight have both a ridge and a channel, and one has a channel but no ridge. A large rim portion of a Pike Brushed, *var. Pike* vessel was recovered from creek deposits in Geomorphological Trench 1 (Plate 7.8). Its surface is well burnished.

Pike Brushed, var. Robinson

Robinson is the grog-tempered counterpart of *Pike* and is a common type at Dash Reeves (Plate 7.7 a–d). The mean rim diameter for the Dash Reeves examples is 18.25 cm (S=4.45 cm; N=12) and the median value is 18 cm. Examination of the distribution (Figure 7.3) shows that there are two extreme values (26 cm and 27 cm), but the large number of rims with values around 18 cm prevents the extremes from excessively influencing the mean. Both the mean and the median are similar to the Holding assemblage values for this attribute (17.6 cm).

The mean body thickness of the *Robinson* sherds in the Dash Reeves collection is 6.77 mm (S=1.29 mm; N=15) and the median is 7.3 mm. Figure 7.4 suggests that this distribution is negatively skewed, but the difference between mean and median is not great. Both values are greater than the mean of 5.98 mm for the *Robinson* ceramics from the Holding site. The distribution of lip thickness values (Figure 7.6) shows that there

Plate 7.5. Hopewell Zoned Stamped, *var. Ferry*: a–c, rims; d, body sherd

Plate 7.6. Hopewell Zoned Stamped and Incised Rims: a–b, Hopewell Zoned Stamped, *var. Casey*; c, Hopewell Zoned Stamped, *var. Unspecified*; d–e, Hopewell Zoned Stamped, *var. Cross*

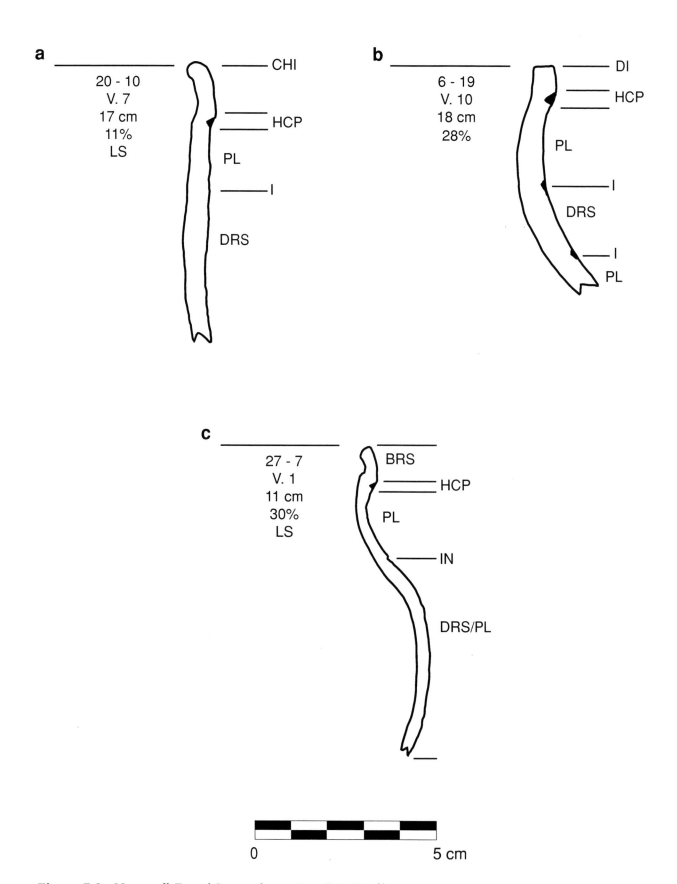

Figure 7.8. Hopewell Zoned Stamped, *var. Ferry* Rim Profiles

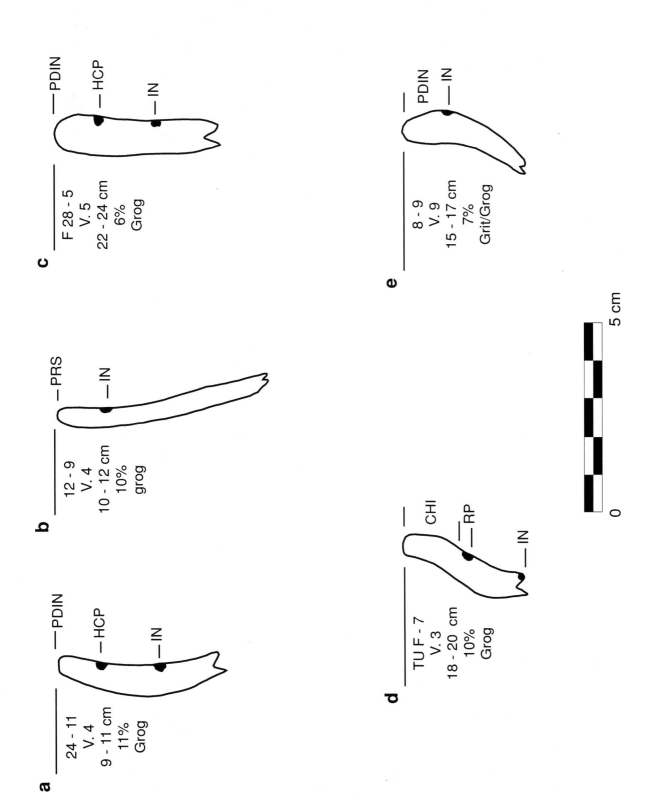

Figure 7.9. Hopewell Zoned Stamped (a–c) and Incised (d–e) Rim Profiles

Plate 7.7. Pike Brushed: a–d, *var. Robinson;* e–g, *var. Pike*

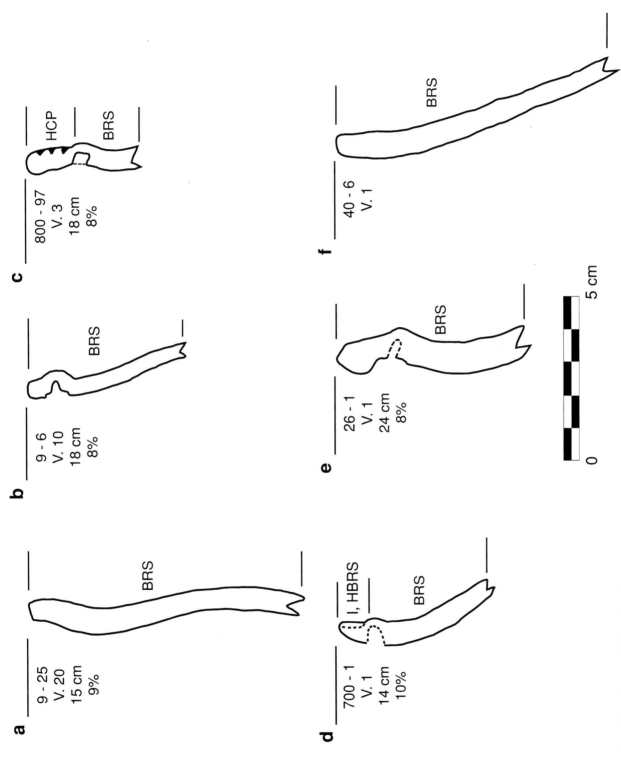

Figure 7.10. Pike Brushed Rim Profiles

800 - 64
V.1
22 cm
24%
LS

BRS

0   5 cm

Plate 7.8. Pike Brushed, *var. Pike* Rim from Geo-Trench 1

is one extreme value (10.6 mm) that contributes a mean of 6.73 mm (S=1.58 mm; N=19), greater than the median of 6.5 mm.

Sixteen of 19 *Robinson* diagnostics have bosses. The mean distance from boss to lip is 15.93 mm (S=4.97 mm) and the median is 14.95 mm. The slight positive skewing in this distribution is probably due to its bimodal nature. Most values are in the 10 to 15-mm range, but five are clustered in the 20 to 23-mm range.

Thirteen of the rims are from jars; the rest are too small to distinguish vessel form with confidence. Ten do not have a separate upper rim treatment. Of the nine that feature such treatment, two have vertical incising and two have dentate rocker stamping. There are also single examples of plain rocker stamping, brushing, fingernail punctations, hemiconical punctations, and cross-hatched incision without any underlying punctations.

Eleven of the *Robinson* diagnostics have round lips, five are flat, two are round with an internal bevel, and one is flat with an internal bevel. Nine of these rims have both an internal ridge and channel, two have only an internal channel, and eight have neither.

It should be noted that the four diagnostics and 85 body sherds in this assemblage categorized as Pike Brushed, *var. Unspecified* are so labeled because there is no grit-tempered variety of Pike Brushed. Although the

Dash Reeves examples constitute a small sample upon which to designate a new variety, these sherds are more numerous than in the Holding collection. If this combination of surface modification and temper continues to be consistently present in Middle Woodland contexts, a new variety name may become necessary. Only one *Unspecified* rim has a measurable diameter (20 cm), but the average body wall thickness (8.13 mm; S=2.28 mm; N=4) is markedly thicker than that of *Pike* or *Robinson* sherds at either Dash Reeves or Holding.

Pike Rocker Stamped, var. Black Lane

Black Lane is the single largest category of pottery in the Dash Reeves assemblage (Plates 7.9 and 7.10; Figure 7.11). Examples of this grog-tempered variety of Pike Rocker Stamped have a mean rim diameter of 18.97 cm (S=5.74 cm; N=33), with a median value of 18 cm. A plot of the distribution of rim diameter values (Figure 7.3) shows one extreme value (35 cm) that inflates the mean. The Dash Reeves mean is smaller than that for the Holding site (21.35 cm) but is markedly larger than the means of all the other major types at Dash Reeves except *Calhoun* and *Robinson*.

The mean wall thickness is 6.9 mm (S=1.45 mm; N=30) and the median is 6.5 mm. This is due to an extreme value (11.1 mm) (Figure 7.4), which causes

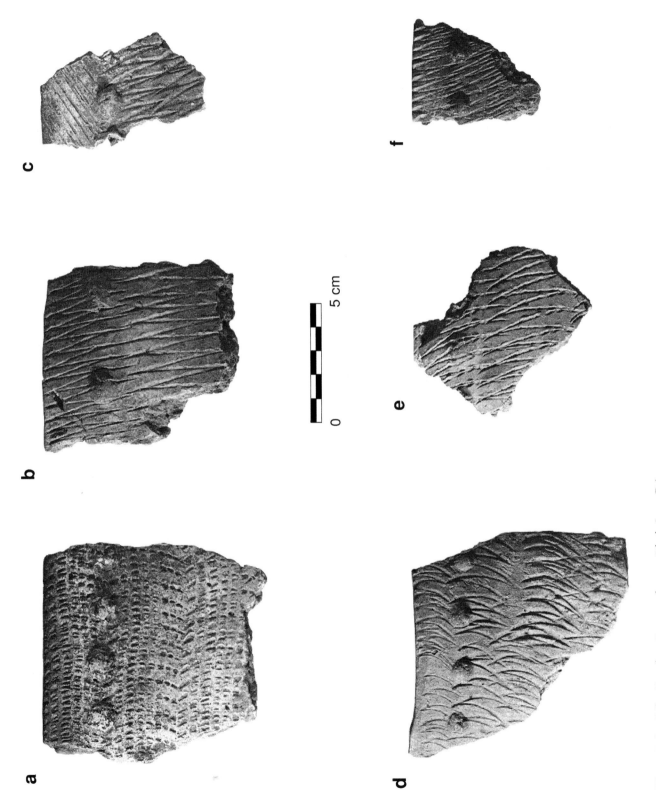

Plate 7.9. Pike Rocker Stamped, *var. Black Lane* Rims

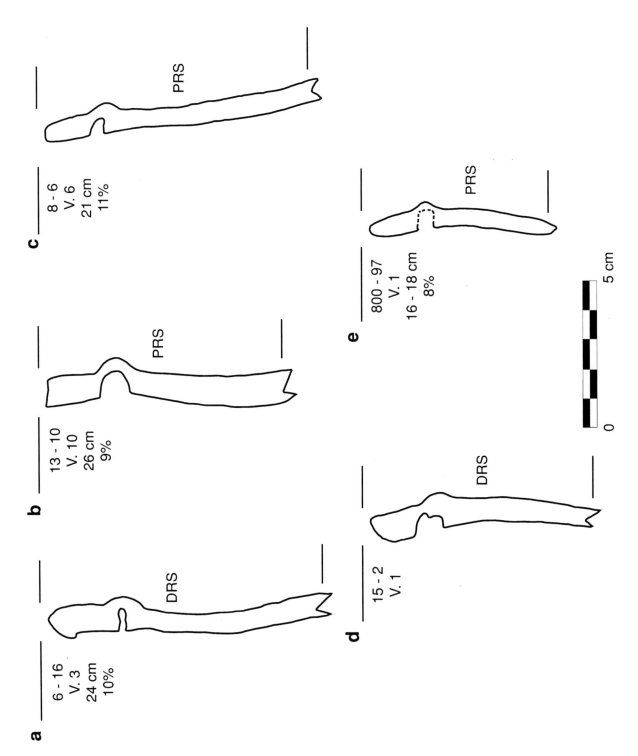

Figure 7.11. Pike Rocker Stamped, *var. Black Lane* Rim Profiles

9 - 27
V. 22
40 - 42 cm
9%
Grog

BOSS

PRS

0   5 cm

Plate 7.10. Pike Rocker Stamped, *var. Black Lane* Rim

some positive skewing of the distribution. Both measures of central tendency are close to the Holding site average of 6.59 mm. The mean lip thickness is 7.22 mm (S=2.16; N=56). This is larger than the median value of 6.85 mm because of the effect of one extreme value (12.7 mm) (Figure 7.6). In this particularly skewed distribution the median is probably the better measure of central tendency.

Forty-four of the *Black Lane* diagnostics have evidence of bosses, although only 35 allow a clear measurement of lip-to-boss distance. The mean for this measure is 19.8 mm (S=3.76 mm), which is slightly smaller than the median value of 19.9 mm. One extreme value (28.5 mm) does not seem to have unduly affected the mean (Figure 7.5). *Black Lane* rims have bosses significantly further from the lip than any of the other types except *Calhoun*.

Most of these rims could not be confidently assigned to a vessel form category. Twenty-eight are definitely jars, while only one is a bowl. Most (75.8 percent) do not have a separate upper rim treatment. Of those that do, nine have a band of plain rocker stamping. Three rims have a band of dentate rocker stamping, and three have cross-hatched incisions that overlap bosses.

It is interesting that 53.2 percent of these diagnostics are impressed with a plain rocker stamp, while 29 percent are dentate rocker stamped. This is in marked contrast to the Holding site collection, where dentate rocker stamping is more common (54.4 percent) than plain (45.7 percent). Although in the past the type of tool used to create the rocker stamping has not been considered spatially or temporally sensitive, it would be wise to record these characteristics in the future to test this assumption.

Twenty-seven *Black Lane* rims have round lips, 14 are round with an internal bevel, 14 are flat, two are flat with an internal bevel, and two are missing the lip. There are also single examples of a flat lip with an exterior bevel, a round lip with an exterior bevel, and a round lip with both an interior and exterior bevel. Just over half (51.6 percent) of the *Black Lane* diagnostics have a ridge, a channel, or both. Approximately 40.3 percent have neither attribute, and the remainder do not have enough upper rim remaining to make a confident identification.

Pike Rocker Stamped, *var. Calhoun*

Calhoun is the limestone-tempered variety of Pike Rocker Stamped (Plates 7.11 and 7.12b, c; Figure 7.12c). In the Dash Reeves collection the mean rim diameter is 20.2 cm (S=5.47 cm; N=10), with a median value of 22 cm. The distribution is somewhat skewed (Figure 7.3). Both the mean and the median are larger than for any of the other major types in this collection.

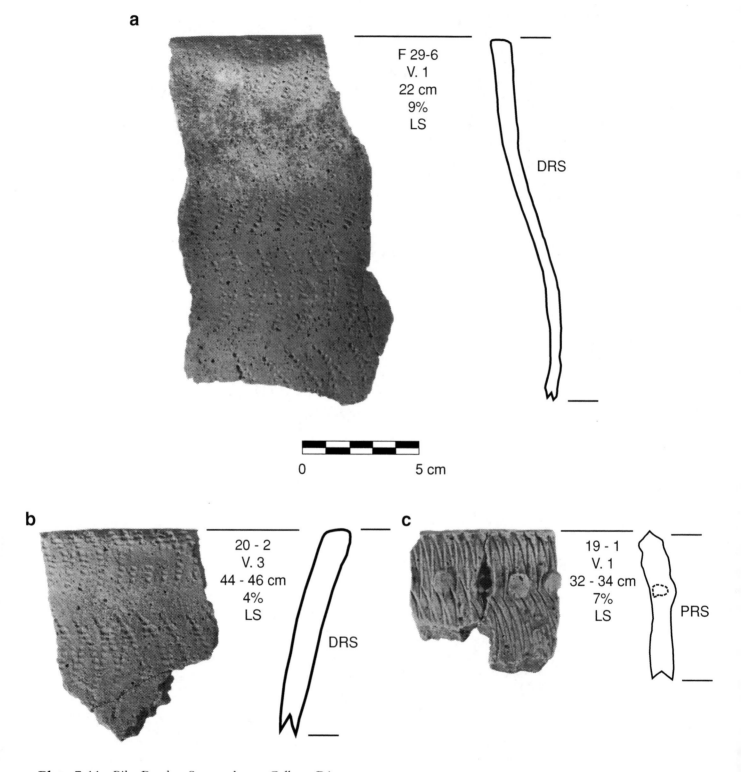

Plate 7.11. Pike Rocker Stamped, *var. Calhoun* Rims

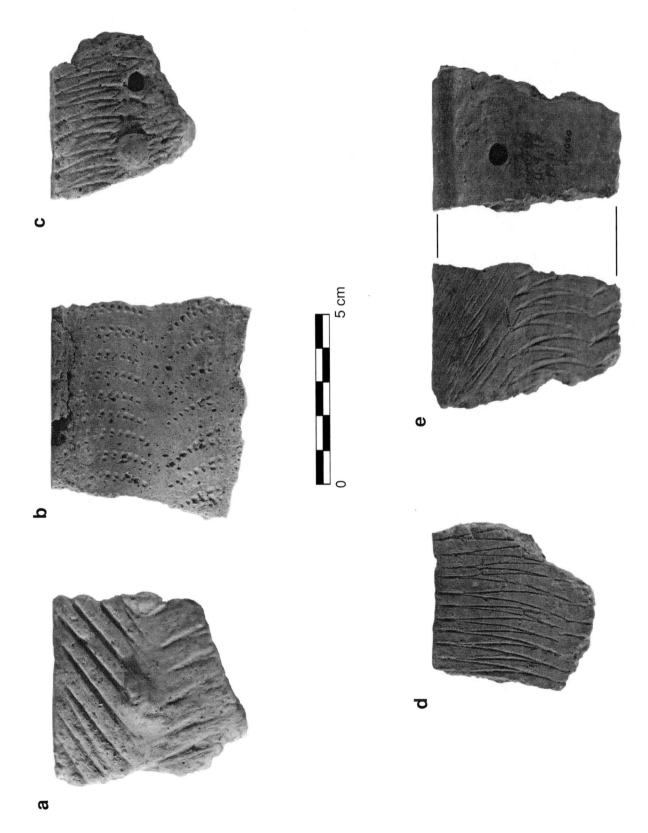

Plate 7.12. Pike Rocker Stamped Rims: a, *var. Fairmount*; b–c, *var. Calhoun*; d–e, *var. Black Lane*

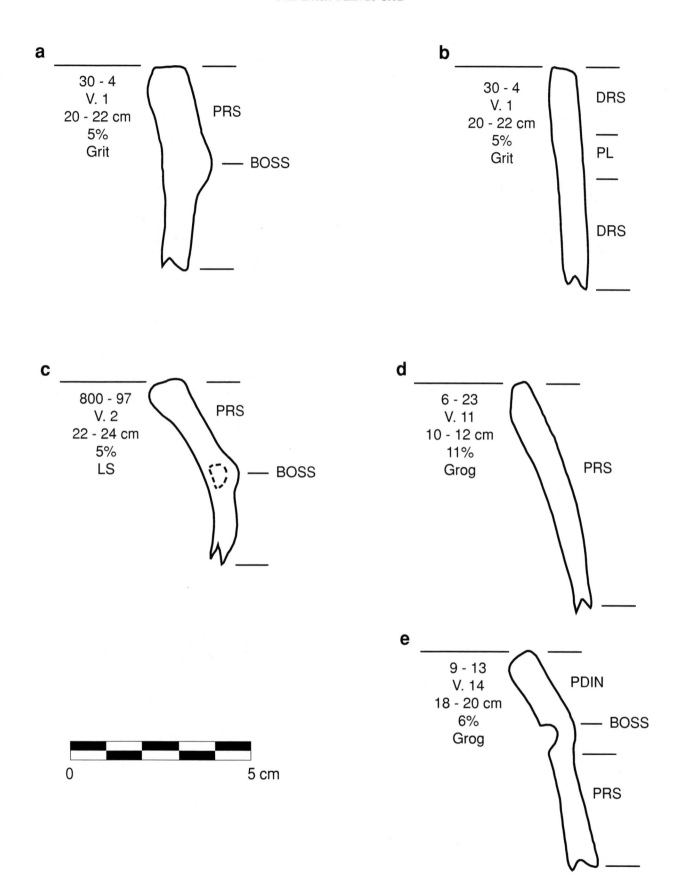

Figure 7.12. Pike Rocker Stamped Rim Profiles

They are also larger than the diameters of the two examples of this type from the Holding site (16 and 18 cm).

The mean body thickness is 6.69 mm (S=1.49 mm; N=13) and the median is 6.6 mm. This looks like a normal distribution (Figure 7.4). Mean body thickness for the Holding site sherds is (6.17 mm). The mean lip thickness is 7.03 mm (S=2.17; N=16), but the median value of 6.75 mm suggests that the distribution is slightly negatively skewed (Figure 7.6). The distance from lip edge to boss is also skewed (Figure 7.5), with a mean of 18.84 mm (S=7.22 mm; N=8) and a median of 19.6 mm. In fact, this distribution includes a wide range of values from 6.1 to 27.5 mm.

Ten of the *Calhoun* rims are from jars, while eight are too small to identify vessel form. Like *Black Lane*, most of these rims do not have an upper rim treatment. Of those that do, three have cross-hatched incisions with no underlying punctations, one has a band of plain rocker stamping, and another has dentate rocker stamping. Also like *Black Lane*, most of the *Calhoun* diagnostics are modified with plain rocker stamping (72.2 percent) rather than dentate rocker stamping (27.8 percent).

Nine of these diagnostics have round lips, seven have flat lips, one lip is round with an exterior bevel, and the surface of one lip is missing. Unlike *Black Lane*, most of the *Calhoun* diagnostics do not have an internal ridge or channel. Only two rims have both and a third has an internal ridge.

Miscellaneous Types

The Dash Reeves assemblage contains a number interesting but rare ceramic types, several of which are illustrated in Plate 7.13. The Hopewell Zoned Red sherd (Plate 7.13f) is the first rim of this type recovered in the American Bottom. Seven body sherds of this type were recovered at the Holding site. The Dash Reeves rim is a fragment of an unrestricted bowl with a diameter of 17 cm and body wall thickness of 6.63 mm. It is limestone tempered. An incision parallel to the lip separates the upper rim treatment from a lower zone that is covered in a red-brown slip. The lip is unmodified and flat with a slight interior bevel.

The upper rim treatment is distinctive and is similar to that seen on two Hopewell Zoned Stamped, *var. Unspecified* rims (Plate 7.13a, b), where broad, deep, discontinuous incisions are separated by rectilinear to hemiconical punctations. This upper rim treatment is similar to the "Dot-Dash" modification seen on Marksville Incised, *var. Marksville* and other rims in the Holding collection (Maher 1989:246, 253). The vessels on which this upper rim modification occurs are bowls, which is also the case in the Holding collection.

Brangenburg Plain is a rare Middle Woodland ceramic type in the American Bottom. Three rims with this type's distinctive "T-shaped" lip were found at Holding (Maher 1989:145), and another was found at the Meridian Hills site (Williams et al. 1987). Two examples occur in the Dash Reeves assemblage. The larger (Plate 7.13c) has a rim diameter of 16 cm and a wall thickness of 5.15 mm. It is tempered with grog and limestone, and the surface and lip are unmodified.

Only two Baehr Zoned Brushed body sherds were identified in the Holding site collection (Maher 1989:242–243). This type is more common in the Dash Reeves assemblage, with three diagnostics and 18 body sherds. A rim diameter measurement could be obtained on only one of the two largest diagnostics (12 cm) (Plate 7.13d, e). These two sherds represent thin-walled vessels (4.26 and 3.24 mm). One is tempered with grog and the other, limestone. Both are from small jars with curvilinear incisions defining decorative zones. One has only brushing as the zone filler. The other has two zones visible, one filled with brush marks and the other with small hemiconical punctations. It is possible that the Baehr Zoned Brushed and Baehr Zoned Punctated found at both Dash Reeves and Holding are sherds from a ceramic type that employs both zone fillers on the same vessel. Analysis of additional large fragments may allow combination of these two types into one.

Some sherds in the collection do not fit any of the established type-variety categories, yet they are large and distinctive enough not to be classified as "Indeterminate" or "Sherdlet." These sherds are labeled "Untyped." A few of the untyped diagnostics are illustrated in Plate 7.13 (i–l) in hopes that other researchers might recognize similarities to material in their regions.

One rim (Plate 7.13g) is cordmarked, grog tempered, and displays a series of cord-wrapped stick impressions on the superior lip. Exterior cordmarking is uneven and rough. A drill hole, perhaps a mend, is located just below the upper rim. This sherd is somewhat reminiscent of early Late Woodland Rosewood

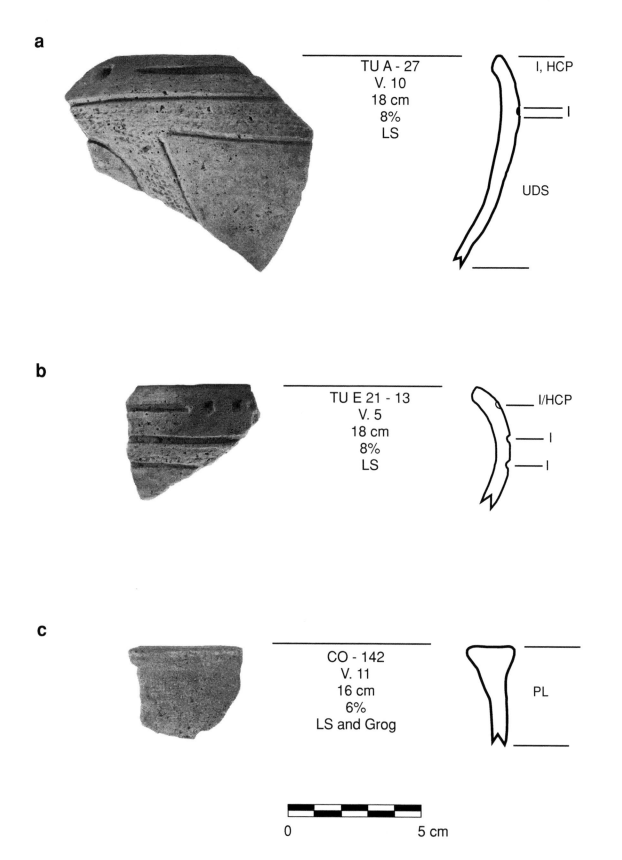

a

TU A - 27
V. 10
18 cm
8%
LS

I, HCP

I

UDS

b

TU E 21 - 13
V. 5
18 cm
8%
LS

I/HCP

I

I

c

CO - 142
V. 11
16 cm
6%
LS and Grog

PL

0   5 cm

Plate 7.13. Miscellaneous Ceramics: a–b, Hopewell Zoned Stamped, *var. Unspecified* (Marksville-like); c, Brangenburg Plain

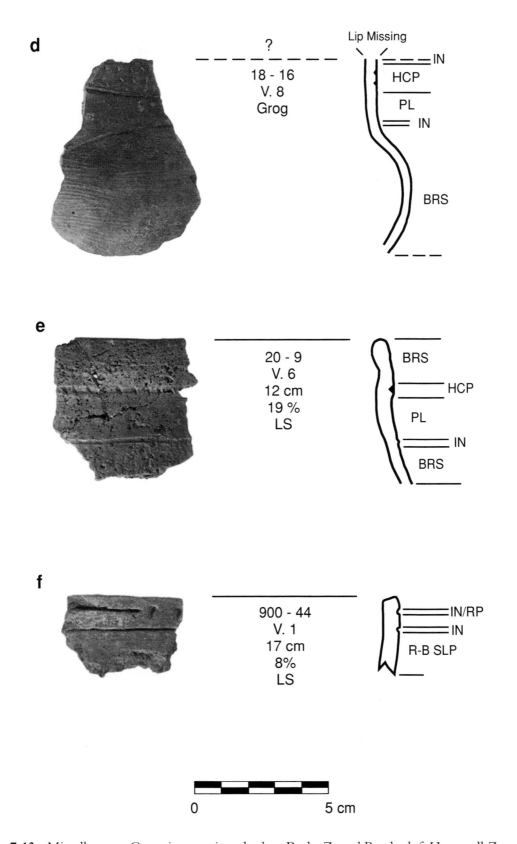

Plate 7.13. Miscellaneous Ceramics, continued: d–e, Baehr Zoned Brushed; f, Hopewell Zoned Red

Plate 7.13. Miscellaneous Ceramics, continued: g, Untyped Cordmarked; h, Baehr Zoned Punctated; i–l, Untyped

ceramics in the American Bottom except that superior lip treatment, observed on this sherd, is extremely uncommon for that period. The sherd was found deep in the creek midden and is unlikely to have been a later intrusion. It may represent a grog-tempered variant of Havana Cordmarked. It remains untyped in this analysis.

A possible Baehr Zoned Punctated vessel is illustrated in Plate 7.13h. It is dentate stamped along the upper rim and is unique in this collection. A thick-walled, plain-surfaced, bossed rim (Plate 7.13l) with exterior lip notches also could not be typed.

Unusual surface modifications include pairs of wedge-shaped punctations (Plate 7.13i), intersecting paired incisions placed over faint dentate stamping or punctations (Plate 7.13k), multiple parallel incisions in an indistinguishable design (Plate 7.13j), and a possible chevron design (on a small, grog-tempered ridge and channel rim). Another untyped and unique vessel is illustrated in Figure 7.13. Four parallel incised lines outline the upper rim. A single incised triangle is superimposed over the band of lines. The vessel has a deep, broad interior channel and is limestone tempered. It is probably some kind of Hopewell Zoned Incised type, but it is problematic enough to remain untyped. Given the ceramic diversity common in Illinois Middle Woodland assemblages, the presence of unique or untypable ceramics is not surprising.

CHRONOLOGY

As previously discussed, the initial excavation units at the Dash Reeves site measured 2 m square and were excavated in 10-cm levels. All soil was screened through 1/4-inch hardware cloth. This enables one to recover not only a sample of the small objects present on the site, but also to explore if there is any vertical segregation of the archaeological deposits. To explore the possibility of multiple prehistoric depositional events at the site, the ceramic contents of each level of each 2-m-square unit were examined and compared to identify any meaningful changes from the surface to the base of excavation.

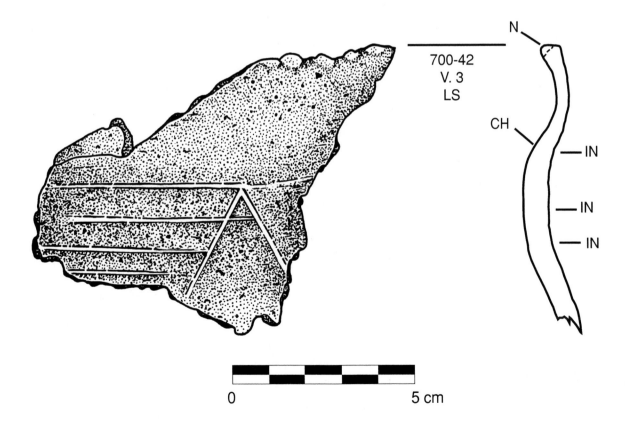

700-42
V. 3
LS

0   5 cm

Figure 7.13. Untyped Zoned Incised Vessel and Profile

Unfortunately, some of these small units produced little, if any, pottery. Units A, B, E, F, and G were the only 2-m squares that produced a pottery sample sufficiently large to allow meaningful comparisons. Examination of quantitative and qualitative variables by excavation level revealed no meaningful differences between the upper and lower levels in these units.

A recent seriation of the ceramics at the Holding site has revealed that Havana Cordmarked, *var. Bottoms*, Havana Plain, *var. Collinsville*, Pike Rocker Stamped (all varieties), and Pike Brushed (all varieties) show some temporal sensitivity during the Middle Woodland period in the American Bottom. The proportions per level of these types and of Crab Orchard Fabric Marked were studied for each 2-m square at Dash Reeves, but no convincing changes were apparent in the relative proportions of these types from the upper to the lower levels.

Figure 7.14 is a line plot of the percentage of each of these ceramic types of the total ceramics (excluding sherdlets) in each level of Test Unit A. Both diagnostics and body sherds were included in the computations. *Bottoms* and *Collinsville* counts were combined, as were all the varieties of Pike Rocker Stamped and Pike Brushed. In Test Unit A each level was 10 cm in depth, except Level 4, which was approximately 5 cm deep. Levels 1–4 were all contained by the plowzone, whereas Levels 5–8 were in the midden or "A" zone. Havana Cordmarked and Plain first occurred in Level 2 and increased until Level 4. Thereafter, the proportion per level remained the same through Level 7. These types (as well as Crab Orchard Fabric Marked) again increased by percentage (although not number) in Level 8. However, very little pottery occurred in that level (10 sherds). There was only one sherd of *Bottoms* and of Crab Orchard in Level 8. This points out the sensitivity of percentages to small sample sizes. Pike Rocker Stamped was the dominant type in each level.

Figure 7.15 is a similar graph for Test Unit G. In this unit Level 1 was a natural level comprising all the plowzone and was approximately 26 cm thick. In this unit there was no increase in Havana Cordmarked, Havana Plain, or Crab Orchard Fabric Marked in the lower levels. Pike Rocker Stamped was predominant throughout, and the amount of Pike Brushed was somewhat variable.

Figure 7.16 is a plot of the ceramic percentage per level in Excavation Unit 4. This unit was excavated in

10-cm levels, and none of the soil was screened. It is included here because of its location at the western edge of the site, which contrasts with the eastern location of the two units previously discussed. Level 1 of Excavation Unit 4 contained what remained of the plowzone after machine scraping and was about 12 cm in depth. No Crab Orchard Fabric Marked was recovered in this unit. There was no evidence of an increase in the Havana types in the lower levels. Pike Rocker Stamped and Pike Brushed were the most common types found in this unit. A very small amount of pottery in Level 6 produced very erratic changes in the relative percentages.

Braun (1985) has shown that jar wall thickness decreased through time from the Middle to Late Woodland period in several adjacent regions. To search for any changes in wall thickness in the Dash Reeves assemblage, a study was made of the diagnostics. Wall and lip thicknesses of diagnostics from the 2-m squares were compared to the elevations of each ceramic piece plot. When the piece-plotted diagnostics in Test Units A, B, E, F, and G (Figure 7.17) were combined they revealed a weak linear relationship between wall thickness and elevation (r=-0.32; N=12). To increase the sample size, another plot was constructed using all of the piece-plotted diagnostics at the site (Figure 7.18). This diagram indicates no meaningful relationship between depth in the archaeological deposits and vessel wall thickness. In fact, except for Test Units A, E, and G, most diagnostics were found between 126.1 and 126.4 m above sea level. Test Units A, E, and G penetrated some of the deepest deposits at the site, yet the presence of older Middle Woodland ceramics in their lowest levels is not obvious. Regardless, no evidence was uncovered elsewhere on the site to support any substantial vertical stratification of the archaeological deposits.

The lack of any clear vertical stratification of the ceramics suggests that these deposits were probably laid down during a single phase of Middle Woodland occupation. Whether the occupation was brief and intense, or small and long-term, cannot be deduced from this level of ceramic analysis. At the time of analysis, radiocarbon dates were not available from this site. Therefore, I utilized the results of the ceramic seriation of pit features at the Holding site (Maher 1991) to place the Dash Reeves assemblage in a temporal context. The very small amount of *Bottoms* and *Collinsville* and the numerical dominance of Pike Rocker Stamped

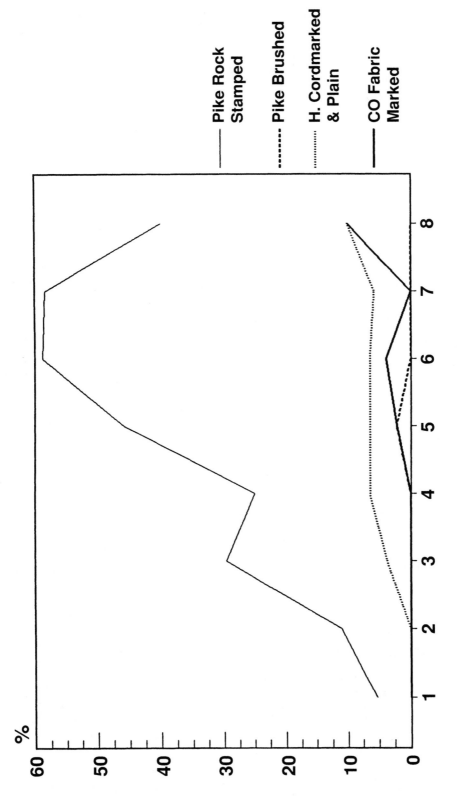

Figure 7.14. Ceramic Type Percentages by Level in Test Unit A

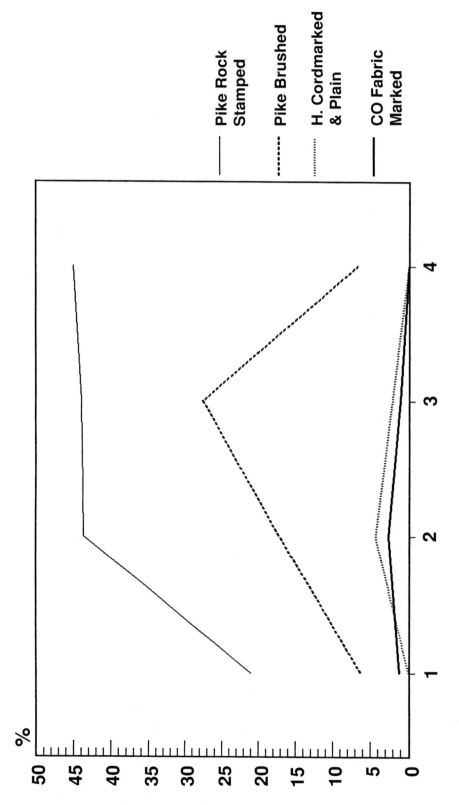

Figure 7.15. Ceramic Type Percentages by Level in Test Unit G

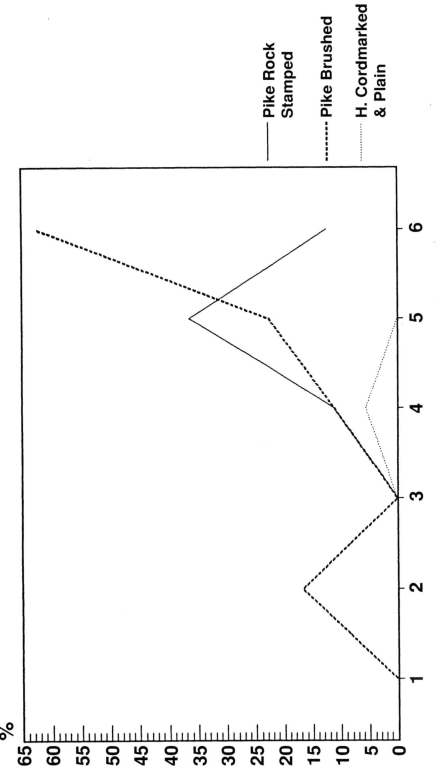

Figure 7.16. Ceramic Type Percentages by Level in Excavation Unit 4

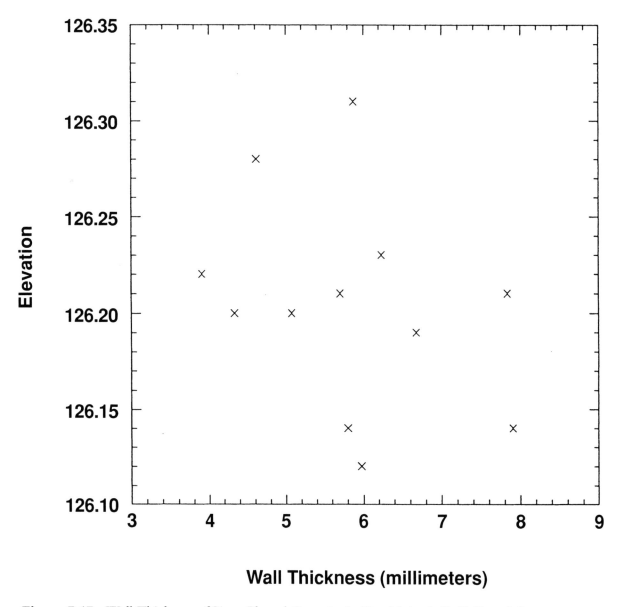

Figure 7.17. Wall Thickness of Piece-Plotted Ceramics in Test Units A, B, E, F, and G

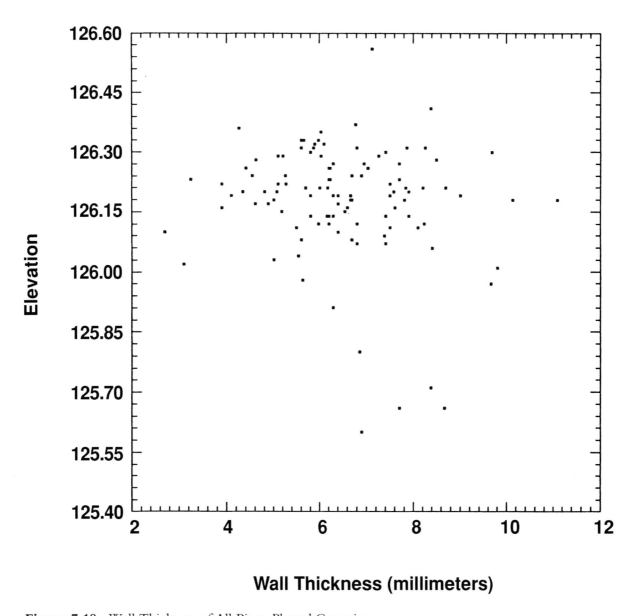

Figure 7.18. Wall Thickness of All Piece-Plotted Ceramics

and Pike Brushed suggest that the Dash Reeves archaeological deposits were generated during the Hill
Lake phase (A.D. 150–300) of the Middle Woodland
period. The presence of some Hopewell Zoned Stamped
and Hopewell Zoned Incised pottery at this site suggests
that the occupation is unlikely to have been at the
terminal end of the Middle Woodland sequence. The
radiocarbon dates from this site eventually confirmed
this conclusion (see Chapter 11).

CLAY OBJECTS

A few nonvessel clay objects are present in the Dash
Reeves collection. Two fragments of a ceramic ear
spool (Plate 7.14a–c) were recovered in Excavation
Units 9 and 23. Although these fragments could not be
refit, they are probably from the same spool. They are
very well made, created from untempered clay. The ear
spool is biconcave in cross section with an open center
producing a "donut" shape. Four perforations are obvious in the fragment from Excavation Unit 9 and two
in the fragment from Excavation Unit 23. These small
perforations penetrate the central axis of the spool from
the sides. They are not drill holes. The evidence of a
buildup of clay in an interior burr around these holes
suggests that small sticks or vegetable fibers were thrust
through the spool while the clay was still wet. All
surfaces of these fragments are very smooth and unmodified in any way. There are no other ear spools from
Middle Woodland contexts in the American Bottom.
Clay pulley ear spools are generally considered to be
Hopewell interaction artifacts (Seeman 1979b:335–
339), their stone and copper counterparts being particularly common in Ohio. Braun (1979:70) and Griffin et
al. (1970:96–97) have documented a number of spools
in mortuary contexts in the Illinois River valley, but
such artifacts rarely occur in midden or pit feature
contexts. McGimsey (1988:54, 61) reports a single
example from a disturbed pit context at the Haw Creek
site in the upper Spoon River valley in Knox County.
It appears to be virtually identical to the one recovered
from Dash Reeves.

A small (5.3 g) ovoid clay object was found in unit
18 (Plate 7.14d). It is plano-concave in cross section and

has an intentionally rounded end. It may be part of a
figurine, but no anthropomorphic characteristics can be
identified.

Another clay object recovered from Excavation
Unit 18 is undoubtedly part of a figurine, a human head
with most of the facial features present (Plate 7.15). This
object is tempered with fine sand and some larger pieces
of grit. It weighs 14.3 g. The hair of the individual
depicted appears to be drawn together above the fore-
head in a top knot. The eyes are formed by two lines that
intersect at the corners of the face, producing an angled,
closed-eye look. The nose is missing and may have been
removed accidentally during excavation. The mouth is
small, horizontal, and no teeth are visible. The ears are
distinct and are large in proportion to the rest of the
head. There appear to be ear spools projecting outward
perpendicular to the ears. Unfortunately, there are no
obvious details that would indicate whether they are the
same style as the ear spool fragments recovered at the
site.

No figurines of this style and detail have been
recovered from Middle Woodland contexts elsewhere
in the American Bottom. Very simple "Casper-the-
Ghost" figurine fragments were found at the Holding
site (Maher 1989:266–267), but they do not resemble
this example. This figurine is, however, very similar to
ceramic figurines illustrated by Griffin et al. (1970:Plates
73, 81–88). It particularly resembles the figurine recovered from Mound 8 of the Knight Mound Group. That
figurine has a front top knot, large ears, distinct ear
spools, and similar facial features (Griffin et al. 1970:Plate
73). Depicting a female, it was recovered with four
others from a burial context and is painted with red,
white, and black pigments (Griffin et al. 1970:71–76).
A Baehr Zoned Brushed vessel was also associated with
the burial.

The gender of the Dash Reeves figurine cannot be
determined. There is also no evidence of any pigments
on the Dash Reeves figurine. The similar facial characteristics and the similarity of the pottery associated with
the figurine in each case suggest that Dash Reeves and
the Knight site are culturally and chronologically similar. Griffin et al. (1970:87) place the Knight figurines in
an A.D. 100–300 time range, which agrees closely with
the temporal placement of the Dash Reeves site.

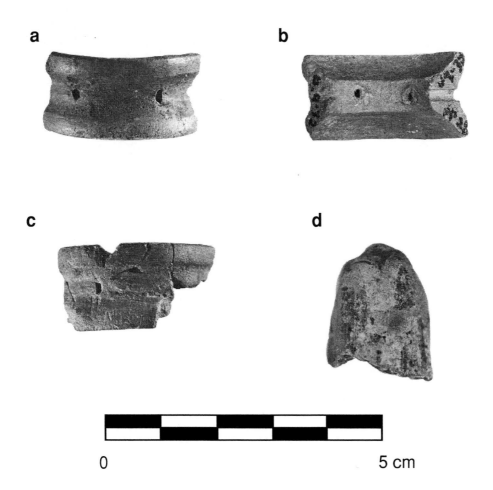

Plate 7.14. Clay Objects: a–b, exterior and interior views of clay ear spool (exc. Unit 9); c, exterior view of ear spool fragement (exc. Unit 23); d, clay figurine (?) fragment

Plate 7.15. Clay Figurine Head

DAUB AND BURNED CLAY

Daub and burned clay from each 1990 recovery unit were counted and weighed. Table 7.13 provides an inventory of this material by unit. During excavation an exceptionally large concentration of burned clay was found in the center of Feature 30 (Plate 7.16). This concentration was removed as a single unit. Later analysis in the lab revealed it to be both burned clay and soil matrix. Attempts to wash the soil from the clay mass were abandoned when they proved destructive to the clay, which began to rehydrate and dissolve. The weight shown in Table 7.13, therefore, refers to both the burned clay and adhering soil.

The small amount of pottery in Feature 30 (see Appendix A) is Middle Woodland. This clay mass, therefore, is associated with the prehistoric occupation of the site. The function of this feature is unknown, although it may have been a clay preparation pit for the potters or house builders at the site.

CONCLUSIONS

Ceramics in the surface collections and the excavated materials from the Dash Reeves site are all relatively similar. They suggest an occupation during which varieties of Pike Rocker Stamped were the most common ceramics in use. Less common in the assemblage are Pike Brushed and several other types, including classic Hopewell Zoned ceramics. There are very few Havana Cordmarked or Havana Plain ceramics in the collection and none of the ceramic types often associated with an early Middle Woodland occupation (Naples Stamped, Naples Ovoid Stamped, Sister Creeks Punctate, etc.). This indicates that the primary occupation at the site occurred during the Hill Lake phase, at the end of the Middle Woodland sequence.

The pottery types in the Dash Reeves collection are similar to the types found at the Holding site to the north, but as previously mentioned, the proportions are very different. The dominance of rocker-stamped ceramics at Dash Reeves is similar to that seen at the Truck #7 site, which is also a Hill Lake phase occupation (Fortier 1985a). Curiously, there are a substantial number of limestone-tempered ceramics at Dash Reeves.

Table 7.13. Daub and Burned Clay

Unit*	N	Wt (g)
A	171	76.4
B	13	6.8
E	190	141.8
F	78	54.3
G	485	316.3
J	22	20.0
K	3	1.4
L	8	5.1
M	2	0.4
U2	8	35.8
U3	1	0.3
U4	4	6.0
U5	30	44.3
U6	55	67.3
U7	4	3.6
U8	7	7.5
U9	116	333.1
U10	20	28.9
U11	12	19.5
U12	7	7.6
U13	12	41.2
U14	39	45.5
U15	6	12.1
U16	20	33.8
U18	50	65.2
U19	8	7.7
U20	19	14.9
U21	2	1.7
U23	2	2.3
U24	10	26.3
U26	7	11.7
U27	11	24.3
U30	3	4.1
U34	2	2.2
U38	9	6.0
U40	4	0.7
U41	13	48.1
U44	4	3.2
U45	4	3.3
U46	5	6.8
U48	1	2.3
F7	5	3.3
F8	22	14.9
F10	14	20.8
F11	4	4.7
F20	1	12.8
F25	7	9.4
F26	6	12.3
F28	22	36.5
F29	20	27.8
F30	201	13,457.8
F31	1	1.0
F32	2	3.0
F34	1	2.8
F36	7	7.1
F47	1	4.1
F49	1	0.7
F50	19	21.1
700s	66	41.7
800s	10	11.9
900s	34	73.6
Total	1,911	15,307.1

*A–M: test units
U: excavation units (1–48)
F: features
700s: surface, backdirt
800s: subplowzone piece plots
900s: machine excavation

Plate 7.16. Burned Clay Concentration in Feature 30

This is in contrast to the Holding, Truck #7, and Meridian Hills sites, where limestone is a rare tempering material. Limestone is abundant in the bluff remnant east of Dash Reeves, and perhaps its ease of accessibility resulted in its more common use.

Crab Orchard Fabric Marked pottery is found at Dash Reeves in larger amounts than at any other excavated Middle Woodland site in the American Bottom. This is probably due to the site's location in the southern part of the American Bottom. It also suggests that there was more interaction between inhabitants of Dash Reeves and Crab Orchard tradition groups in southern Illinois than was the case with sites in the central and northern part of this region.

A substantial amount of pottery was recovered from the Dash Reeves site. This material may represent a slow accumulation over the 150 years of the Hill Lake phase, but it also may reflect a more extensive and sedentary occupation focused outside the excavated right-of-way. Regardless, this is the largest ceramic collection from a Hill Lake phase context in the American Bottom. Excavations at the Dash Reeves site have substantially improved our understanding of the temporal duration and spatial distribution of the Middle Woodland cultural pattern in this region.

8

LITHIC ASSEMBLAGE

The size and diversity of the Dash Reeves lithic assemblage is impressive. It is the largest collection of lithic remains ever excavated from a Middle Woodland site in the American Bottom. This is sobering, considering the relatively small area of site actually excavated. The chert debitage alone totals over 48,700 items, including 2,165 unmodified blades and 729 cores. There are also over 1,000 formal chert tools, another 1,500 expedient chert tools, and 532 blade tools. In addition, there are over 300 polished flakes and over 150 nondiagnostic biface fragments. The chert assemblage alone weighs 140,228.8 g. The nonchert assemblage consists of over 3,500 items, including 142 tools, and weighs 121,377.2 g. The weight of lithic remains recovered from all contexts is 261,606 g, or approximately 576 lbs (Table 8.1).

Table 8.1. Lithic Assemblage Count & Weight Summary

	Count	Weight (g)
Chert debitage	48,743	117,097.3
Chert tools	3,611	23,131.5
Nonchert debris	3,367	86,364.9
Nonchert tools	142	35,012.5
Total	55,863	261,606.2

From the standpoint of mass quantities, the Dash Reeves lithic assemblage differs considerably from the Holding site lithic assemblage. The chert assemblage from the Holding site weighs 19,513 g (Williams 1989:319). By contrast, the Holding site nonchert assemblage weighs 209,681.9 g, almost twice that of the Dash Reeves nonchert assemblage. This is perhaps due to the fact that at Holding grinding tools were more common, not unexpected at a proposed horticultural settlement. Its smaller nonchert assemblage suggests that the Dash Reeves site was not *primarily* focused on horticultural activities but on chert tool manufacturing and other nonagricultural pursuits.

Analysis of the lithics from Dash Reeves is focused primarily on description of the chert and nonchert assemblages. The chert assemblage is considered first. The analysis includes a discussion of chert sources and procurement patterns as well as a description of the production sequence and knapping technology. This is followed by an analysis of the chert tools, including nonblade and blade tools. A discussion of the spatial distribution of chert tools and debitage at the site, as well as the place of this assemblage in American Bottom and regional contexts, follows. The chert analysis concludes with a consideration of the extensive blade industry identified at this site. General observations concerning the origins of blade technology in this area, the function of the industry, and the eventual disappearance of this technology are offered. Analysis of the nonchert assemblage is presented in the second half of this chapter.

THE CHERT ASSEMBLAGE

The chert assemblage from this site is both diverse and sizable. The chert debitage totals 48,743 items, weighing 117,097.3 g. In addition, there are 1,052 formal tools, 1,534 utilized flakes, 532 blade tools, 167 biface fragments, and 326 polished flakes, altogether weighing 23,131.5 g. With several exceptions, this assemblage is associated with the Middle Woodland period. In many respects it is typical of other Middle Woodland assemblages, but it does include a much higher percentage of blade tools than expected, and it contains a number of tool types not previously encountered at sites of this period in the area. Specifically, there is a tremendous variety of small flake and blade tools, including nearly 50 different formal, nonblade tool types (see Fortier 2000 for a detailed description of the "Middle Woodland small-tool tradition" in the American Bottom). It is clear that the Dash Reeves site functioned primarily as a major lithic procurement and blade production center, and secondarily as a substantial long-term settlement focused on a variety of activities. The diversity of tool types from this site strongly supports the latter notion. In short, Dash Reeves is a unique site offering insights into the technological world of Middle Woodland peoples in the American Bottom. The following sections document this technology from a number of vantage points.

CHERT RESOURCES AND PROCUREMENT PATTERNS

Over 40 different chert types are recognized in the assemblage. Such diversity is characteristic of the Middle Woodland time period, as is the selection of colorful cherts and of cherts not naturally occurring in the American Bottom. The cherts in the assemblage were identified by comparison with an extensive chert type collection housed at the University of Illinois. A system of identification, using numbers for specific chert types, was devised during the early 1980s by FAI-270 Project personnel (Emerson 1984; McElrath and Fortier 1983) and has been expanded over the years to account for additional chert types (Appendix C). Many locally available chert types had been recognized in the American Bottom long before the FAI-270 Project, and these were incorporated into the system (Fowke 1928; Ives 1975; Kelly 1984; Titterington 1938). Extraregional cherts also have long been recognized in the area, particularly those from southern Illinois, including Dongola, Cobden, Kaolin, Mill Creek, and Mansker (Fowke 1928:530–532; Gregg 1974; Porter 1974; Tho-

mas 1891:68; Whelpley 1915:137). While the identification of many chert types is relatively straightforward, their association with a specific source or quarry is not; moreover, approximately 3 percent of the chert debitage in the assemblage could not be identified as to type or source.

The counts and weights of debitage by chert type and provenience are presented in Table 8.2. Only 10 chert types account for nearly 85 percent of the debitage by weight. These include, in order of frequency, Ste. Genevieve red (Type 7), local coarse Salem cherts (Types 24 and 46), Old Blue (Type 11), Ste. Genevieve purple (Type 29), Salem creamy (Type 25), and white Burlington types (Types 1, 3, 6, and 69). Red Ste. Genevieve chert is the preferred chert at Dash Reeves, accounting for 48.4 percent of the debitage and also occurring as blades and formal tool types. The unusually high frequency of this chert is due to the proximity of a major Ste. Genevieve red chert outcrop, located approximately 1,500 m south of the site area at the outlet of Carr Creek into the Mississippi River floodplain. That outcrop is the only known major bedrock source of this chert in this area of the American Bottom and may be the single most important factor responsible for a clustering of Middle Woodland sites in the area. At the nearby Middle Woodland Truck #7 site, Ste. Genevieve red chert accounts for 21.3 percent of the chert by weight (Fortier 1985a:232). Other sites in the area also have a high percentage of this chert. Conversely, the Holding site, which is located approximately 50 km to the north, yielded only 8.4 percent of this chert by count (Williams 1989:323). The relative stratigraphic position of the Ste. Genevieve Formation in the Dash Reeves area and the potential occurrence of outcrops of other chert-bearing formations have been presented in Chapter 2 (Figure 2.5).

Although specific outcrops have not been identified, it is very likely that in addition to Ste. Genevieve red, sources of both Salem creamy and Ste. Genevieve purple occur in the same locality. These three types are closely associated at sites in the area. In fact, at the Truck #7 site Ste. Genevieve purple chert constitutes 58.3 percent of the recovered chert by weight (Fortier 1985a:234). Salem creamy chert is the third most abundant chert at that site, accounting for 13.7 percent by weight (Fortier 1985a:234). It is very likely that the latter chert actually comes from the Ste. Genevieve rather than the Salem Formation, since Salem cherts

Table 8.2. Summary of Chert Debitage by Raw Material Type and Provienence

	Features		Excavation Units		Test Units (A–N)		Machine Excavations (BPZ)		Surface (PZ)		Totals		
	N	Wt(g)	N	Wt(g)	N	Wt(g)	N	Wt(g)	N	Wt(g)	N	Wt(g)	% Wt
Ste. Genevieve Red (7)	1,736	2,776.4	6,762	14,453.9	5,382	4,619.0	1,088	9,113.5	5,805	25,700.6	20,773	56,663.4	48.4
Local Salem Coarse (24,46)	404	693.3	2,046	4,203.9	1,672	1,375.8	318	3,775.5	946	7,604.9	5,386	17,653.4	15.1
Burlington (1,3,6,69)	428	150.1	1,521	1,108.7	766	317.4	318	456.5	1,379	1,376.5	4,412	3,409.2	2.9
Old Blue (11)	538	501.3	859	2,094.5	399	557.7	411	2,775.7	1,113	4,656.3	3,320	10,585.5	9.0
Salem Creamy (25)	286	429.9	955	2,196.4	187	347.6	93	759.8	211	1,042.8	1,732	4,776.5	4.1
Ste. Genevieve Purple (29)	186	398.8	643	1,881.4	329	540.6	223	1,996.9	410	1,686.3	1,791	6,504.0	5.6
Fern Glen (10)	148	270.9	383	469.1	220	119.1	66	744.2	159	440.3	976	2,043.6	1.7
Salem Banded (34)	151	660.3	351	1,014.0	28	54.9	62	607.3	98	755.2	690	3,091.7	2.6
Salem (40)	66	75.0	137	357.6	44	41.3	18	162.0	41	88.1	306	724.0	0.6
Burlington/Salem (57)	8	1.2	93	88.5	46	10.5	35	17.9	22	12.5	204	130.6	0.1
Cobden/Dongola (13,12)	297	206.7	110	178.6	85	28.0	23	65.5	53	71.0	568	549.8	0.5
Mill Creek (9)	21	1.4	36	73.3	40	56.0	3	3.8	12	44.2	112	178.7	0.2
Kaolin (15)	32	22.1	43	49.0	18	7.5	13	10.7	15	25.4	121	114.7	0.2
Mansker (16)	40	165.4	71	250.2	5	10.2	11	1,093.9	31	54.4	158	1,574.1	1.3
Blair (36)	–	–	7	11.8	1	1.9	6	59.0	9	247.3	23	325.0	0.3
Grimes Hill (81)	30	26.9	122	84.1	22	13.9	36	51.2	124	208.5	334	384.6	0.3
Unknown (17)	1,181	182.8	3,169	1,585.3	1,523	539.2	160	746.9	482	566.2	6,515	3,620.4	3.1
Other	179	105.3	390	923.9	163	248.2	308	2,648.8	282	841.9	1,322	4,768.1	4.1
Total	5,731	6,667.8	17,698	31,024.2	10,930	8,888.8	3,192	25,089.1	11,192	45,422.4	48,743	117,097.3	

tend to be coarser and less lustrous in texture. Salem creamy, therefore, is grouped with the other Ste. Genevieve cherts in the Dash Reeves analysis and probably should be renamed at some future date, with the caveat that, as yet, a specific source has not been identified in the area. Old Blue chert is similar in texture and luster to the aforementioned Ste. Genevieve cherts and may be locally available as well. Although represented at Dash Reeves (9 percent of debitage by weight), it was not recognized at all at the Truck #7 site.

The second most frequent chert type (15.1 percent by weight) comprises several varieties of local coarse Salem chert. These cherts are nonlustrous, sometimes oolitic, and dull brown or gray in color. They were heavily utilized at Dash Reeves and appear at most sites in this area regardless of cultural affiliation, so in all probability, outcrops exist somewhere in the vicinity. A high percentage of thick gouges, hoes, and core scrapers are made from these cherts.

White Burlington cherts, including high-quality imports and local oolitic varieties, rank fourth in frequency but eighth in weight. Although Burlington chert naturally occurs in the site area, it is not high in quality. The higher-quality material originates mainly in the Crescent Hills quarry area, located south of St. Louis on the Missouri side of the Mississippi River. Generally, the higher-quality white cherts (Types 1, 6, and 69) appear in the form of finished tools or as blades at Dash Reeves. In contrast to the Holding site, where white chert comprises 68 percent of the chert assemblage (Williams 1989:321–323), Burlington cherts at Dash Reeves make up only 2.9 percent of the debitage. This is curious given the fact that Dash Reeves is actually closer to the Crescent Hills quarries than Holding is. High-quality white chert is also rare (N=8) at the Truck #7 site (Fortier 1985a:235). Local white cherts, on the other hand, are nearly as frequent at that site as the red Ste. Genevieve cherts. The Holding, Dash Reeves, and Truck #7 sites represent three different procurement patterns associated with this chert type. At this time no reasonable explanation can be offered for the observed differences.

A variety of other area cherts were procured at Dash Reeves, including Fern Glen (Type 10), local Salem banded (Type 34), Salem gray (Type 40), and a chert referred to as Type 57, which is derived from either the Burlington or Salem Formation. This is a white chert with large gray mottles. Together these other area cherts

comprise only 5 percent of the chert debitage at the site. Only a handful of tools appear to have been made from these cherts, with the notable exception of Salem banded varieties, which were preferred for gouges and core tools.

Seven exotic, or non-American Bottom, chert types were identified. These include six southern Illinois types (Mill Creek, Kaolin, Mansker, Cobden, Dongola, and Blair) and one (Grimes Hill) that originates at the far north end of the American Bottom and southern Illinois River valley. For the purpose of this analysis, Cobden and Dongola varieties have been combined. Together, exotic cherts make up 2.7 percent of the debitage assemblage by weight. Excluded from this figure are Mill Creek and Kaolin polished flakes. The low frequency of exotic chert at Dash Reeves contrasts with the Holding site, where just over 10 percent of the chert assemblage is exotic (Williams 1989:329). This is perhaps to be expected since the Holding site dates to that part of the Middle Woodland period when regional exchange was at its apex, while Dash Reeves postdates that time, the occupation there occurring when the collapse of interregional material exchanges was well underway.

A number of other local chert varieties also were identified, but these make up such a small percentage of the chert assemblage that they have been combined into a single "Other" category. In addition, there are a sizable number of unidentifiable chert pieces (6,515 items, weighing 3,620.4 g) that have been placed in a general "Unknown" category. Many of these items are either extremely small, heavily heat damaged, or simply unrecognizable as to type. Just over 7 percent of the assemblage by weight falls into these two categories.

Chert types can be organized arbitrarily into five groups to highlight procurement strategies at the site (Table 8.3). Only debitage is calculated here. The most prolific group includes all of the Ste. Genevieve cherts, including the red, purple, blue, and creamy varieties. These cherts constitute 67.1 percent of the cherts (by weight) recovered from the site. Next are the local, coarse Salem cherts, which comprise 18.3 percent of the chert assemblage. Unknown and other cherts make up 7.2 percent of the debitage. Burlington cherts, including white varieties, and Fern Glen varieties make up only 4.8 percent of the assemblage. This again contrasts with the Holding site, where Burlington chert comprises 68 percent of the chert assemblage. Finally, exotic

Table 8.3. Distribution of Chert Debitage from All Contexts by General Chert Groupings

General Chert Groupings	N	% N	Wt (g)	% Wt	Mean Wt per Item (g)
Local Ste. Genevieve cherts (red, purple, Old Blue, "Salem Creamy")	27,616	56.7	78,529	67.1	2.8
Local Salem cherts (Types 24, 34, 40, 46)	6,382	13.1	21,469	18.3	3.4
Burlington cherts (Types 1, 3, 6, 10, 69)	5,592	11.5	5,583	4.8	1.00
Exotic cherts (Dongola, Cobden, Kaolin, Mansker, Mill Creek, Blair, Grimes Hill)	1,316	2.7	3,127	2.7	2.4 ★
Unknown and other cherts	7,837	16.1	8,389	7.2	1.1
Total	48,743		117,097		

★ If a single Mansker core weighing 1,007 g is excluded, then the mean size of exotic chert items is 1.61 g.

cherts represent only 2.7 percent of the Dash Reeves chert debitage.

Also included in Table 8.3 is the mean size of items in each of the chert groupings. What mostly stands out is the greater mean size of items made of local Ste. Genevieve and Salem cherts. Cherts that are not local are nearly three times smaller by weight. Quite simply, it appears that nonlocal cherts were transported to the site in smaller format and probably were more completely utilized and reutilized than more readily available local cherts. The larger sizes of local chert items can be attributed to the fact that sources of these cherts lie within a 1 to 5-km radius of the site. This kind of local-nonlocal chert size selection procurement pattern is not surprising, but it has not previously been so well documented in the area.

TECHNOLOGICAL MANIPULATION OF CHERT

Two technological industries are distinguished at Dash Reeves. The production of lamellar blades clearly involves a process that differs significantly from the freehand or multidirectional techniques utilized to produce nonblade materials. While the blade industry at Dash Reeves is distinctive and impressive in size, it is a minority technology. The vast majority of the chert debitage recovered at this site is the product of nonblade techniques. Of the 729 cores identified in the assemblage, fewer than 25 percent are blade cores, and of these, only a handful are classic prismatic cores. Nevertheless, because blade technology is so unique and restricted in time in the Midwest, it requires special treatment and a separate discussion.

Nonblade Production Sequence

The manufacturing trajectories of numerous assemblages in the American Bottom have been examined in detail and have appeared in print in virtually every site report from the area, particularly in the FAI-270 Site Reports series. A variety of analytical approaches have been undertaken, but, in general, all have focused on defining the various stages and byproducts of production sequences leading to tool formation, tool maintenance, or modification of existing tools. It has been argued that such sequences can sometimes be temporally diagnostic and for this reason alone need to be documented at every site (Ahler and Vannest 1985; McElrath 1986; McElrath and Fortier 1983). In addition, it is clear that the issue of site function and occupational duration can also be approached through analysis of manufacturing sequence debitage (Emerson 1984:326).

Because of the size of the Dash Reeves debitage assemblage, a relatively straightforward descriptive approach was employed in the analysis, following the system devised by McElrath (McElrath and Fortier 1983:90–94), as modified from White (1953), Newcomer (1971), and Cook (1976). Initially, chert debitage was divided into seven categories, including cores, block fractures, primary decortication flakes, secondary decortication flakes, reduction flakes, thinning or sharpening flakes, and blades. Blades were separated and analyzed in a different manner.

Cores are characterized as larger pieces of modified chert with evidence of systematic flake removal. These were the stock materials brought to the site from the various quarry sources. Some of the cores from the site show very little evidence of on-site trimming, but most represent nearly exhausted stock material. There are a variety of core forms from the site, excluding blade cores, of course, but most can be characterized as multidirectional with multiple platforms. Some are plano-convex, but most are irregular, tabular, or blocky.

During the initial stage of reduction, primary and secondary decortication flakes are removed from the core stock material. In this analysis primary decortication flakes are 75 to 100 percent covered by cortex or rind on their dorsal surfaces. Secondary decortication flakes have less than 75 percent of the dorsal cortex remaining. Secondary decortication flakes are primary decortication flakes that have been trimmed or that derive from partially trimmed parent cores. Decortication flakes are often thick and irregular in shape.

Reduction flakes tend to be larger pieces of chert with no cortex but with specific flake attributes, such as pronounced platforms, bulbs of percussion, and hinge fractures. Most of the nonblade flake tools at the site are made on reduction flakes. The lateral edges of these flakes tend to be elongated and thus present ideal working edges. On many of the tools these edges exhibit secondary retouching.

Thinning or sharpening flakes are smaller flakes that are irregular or triangular in shape and are missing a number of attributes normally found on reduction flakes. These flakes are presumably derived from tool thinning or maintenance activities, but many may also represent shatter from various stages of primary reduction activity. Although recognized as resulting from separate technological activities, core rejuvenation flakes and bifacial thinning flakes were placed in this category and were not counted separately.

The final category of reduction debitage includes block fractures. Traditionally, such material has been combined with shatter flakes, and, in fact, most block fractures are shatter flakes. These are blocky and irregular pieces of chert with virtually no visible classic flake attributes. Unlike the other categories of reduction, these pieces are virtually never utilized. In fact, they are probably the only chert pieces in the Dash Reeves assemblage not evidencing utilization.

Table 8.4 presents the number and weight of all chert debitage by stage of production and provenience. Unmodified blades are included here also for comparative purposes. By count, thinning/sharpening flakes dominate the assemblage, accounting for 70.6 percent of debitage items. Sixty-five percent of the thinning/sharpening flakes were recovered from test and excavation units. There is a considerably higher percentage of such flakes in the test units (A–N) because those units were screened.

Table 8.4. Summary of Chert Debitage by Stage of Production and Provenience

	Features		Excavation Units		Test Units		Machine Excavation (BPZ)		Surface		Totals	
	N	Wt (g)	N	Wt (g)	N	Wt (g)	N	Wt (g)	N	Wt (g)	N	Wt (g)
Cores	40	2,164.2	119	4,694.0	19	1,007.8	169	12,057.6	382	22,405.8	729	42,329.4
Block fractures	112	595.0	1,315	8,878.1	419	2,302.6	366	4,796.8	880	7,396.6	3,092	23,969.1
Prim. decort. flakes	11	41.2	195	1,949.6	36	188.1	225	3,082.2	563	5,069.3	1,030	10,330.4
Second. decort. flakes	132	506.8	567	2,527.3	175	544.6	203	831.0	406	1,663.7	1,483	6,073.4
Reduction flakes	628	1,939.4	2,065	7,129.7	310	1,126.2	833	3,255.7	1,984	5,530.0	5,820	18,981.0
Thinning flakes	4,565	1,061.4	12,723	4,773.0	9,716	3,460.6	1,110	536.2	6,310	2,649.8	34,424	12,481.0
Blades	243	359.8	714	1,122.5	255	258.9	286	529.6	667	707.2	2,165	2,978.0
Total	5,731	6,667.8	17,698	31,074.2	10,930	8,888.8	3,192	25,089.1	11,192	45,422.4	48,743	117,142.3

Based on the number of cores, decortication flakes, and block fractures recovered from the site, it is clear that mechanical reduction of chert, presumably to make tools and modify existing tools, represented an important, if not *the* most important, activity at the site. The Dash Reeves occupation, in fact, is the most extensive Middle Woodland lithic production center known at this time in the American Bottom. This is highlighted, moreover, by the blade industry, which is described in the following section.

Blade Technology

A total of 2,165 unmodified blades, weighing 2,978 g, was identified in the chert assemblage. In addition, 532 modified blades were recovered. Approximately 180 blade cores were identified, but this number is somewhat deceptive since these are not all prismatic cores. Most of the blade cores are expended to the point of no return and have therefore lost many of their classic attributes. It should be pointed out that nearly 60 percent of the blades are not complete. Many are segments and many are represented by proximal ends only. For this reason, only 879 unmodified blades were measured and utilized in this study. It is very clear, however, that despite their not meeting the classic criterion for a blade, i.e., a flake that is more than twice as long as wide, these broken pieces were nonetheless produced by a blade technology and should be regarded as blades. Even unbroken blades often do not fit the expected length-width ratio criterion. As Sanger (1970:106) has aptly noted, "the traditional length/width definition of the Old World is unsuitable for New World purposes and should not be used. Assessment should be based on a combination of morphological and technological factors which distinguish blades from parallel-sided flakes." These attributes, as well as the overall technology of this industry, are described below.

Blade Cores. The literature on Middle Woodland blade core technology is extremely limited in the central Midwest. Most studies have focused primarily on the blades themselves rather than the parent core material. Moreover, blade cores are usually scarce at sites. While blade measurements and attributes were utilized in earlier studies, core attributes were rarely discussed except in general terms (Montet-White 1968:28; Pi-Sunyer 1965:60). Exceptions to this can be found in more recent studies by Greber et al. (1981), Reid

(1976), McNerney (1987), and Morrow (1987). Greber et al. (1981) defined nine core types associated with Hopewell in Ohio. Another important discussion of blade cores in the midcontinent region can be found in Patterson (1973), where blade cores of the Texas or Poverty Point-Gulf Coast Archaic blade and core industry were examined and categorized into six different types. A number of Gulf Coast core types are identical to those found at Dash Reeves, and at least some portion of Patterson's typology has been utilized in this analysis. It is interesting that this kind of variability is generally not mentioned for blade core traditions outside of the Midwest and Southeast regions.

Dash Reeves has produced a variety of blade core types, which are here designated prismatic, semiconical, cuboid, tabular, wedge, ball, multidirectional, and nucleated (Figure 8.1). Another Middle Woodland core type, not found at this site, is named tortoise. The only example of this type occurs at the Nochta site in the northern American Bottom (Higgins 1990:151). Each of these core types involves a slightly different method of detachment and/or preparation. The most common blade core types at Dash Reeves are the cuboid and semiconical forms. The least common types are ball and prismatic. The Dash Reeves core types are described below. Core attributes are illustrated in Figure 8.2.

Prismatic cores have a circular platform area with evidence of platform edge preparation but little evidence of secondary preparation on the remaining portion of the platform. They are tapered, usually to a point. Blade scars are present over the entire exposed area of the core, with the exception of the platform. Such cores yielded narrow, regular blades probably produced by a controlled punch technique. Montet-White has referred to this core technology as the "Fulton technique" (1968:28).

The Fulton technique is also associated with semiconical cores, which are very similar to prismatic cores except that the platform area is semicircular or crescent shaped and at least one-half or more of what might have been a fully prismatic core is missing. The backs and most of the lateral sides exhibit no blade scars. At Dash Reeves such cores tend to have cortical back sides. The blade scars tend to be more erratic and broader than on prismatic cores. Distal truncation is also more irregular, with multiple hinges often present. Some of the noncortically backed semiconical cores appear to represent broken prismatic cores or, possibly,

Prismatic   **Semi-Conical**   **Cuboid**   **Tabular**

Wedge   **Ball**   **Multi-Directional**

Nucleated   **Tortoise**

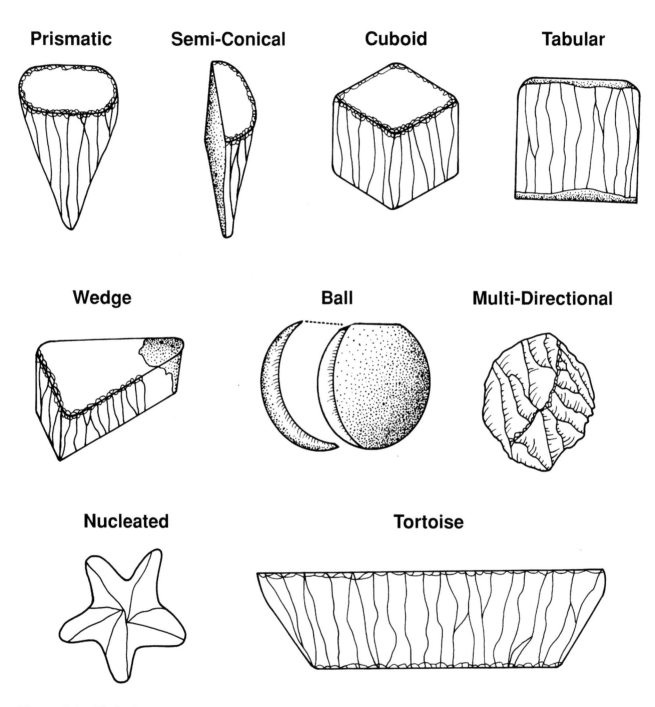

Figure 8.1. Blade Core Types

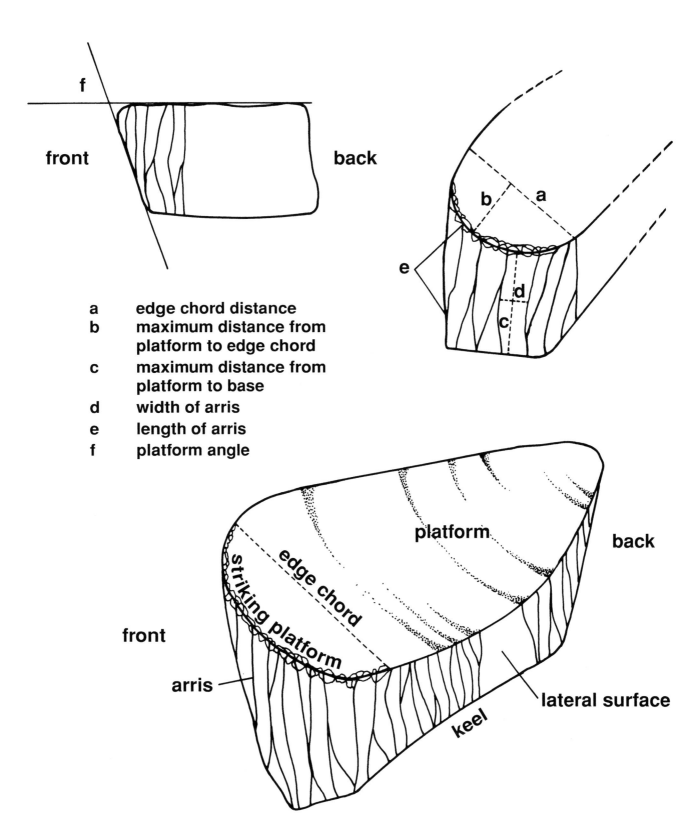

a   **edge chord distance**
b   **maximum distance from platform to edge chord**
c   **maximum distance from platform to base**
d   **width of arris**
e   **length of arris**
f   **platform angle**

Figure 8.2. Blade Core Attributes

segments of tortoise cores. Platform edge preparation is visible on all of these cores.

Cuboid cores are square to rectangular-sided cores with flat platforms. Platform edges are normally prepared, and there is more secondary flaking on the platform surface than on prismatic or semiconical cores. Blade scars tend to be broad and relatively short. Typically, one of the sides is not worked. In addition, many of these cores appear to have bidirectional platforms. Blade detachment may have alternated from both flat platforms. Edge preparation often occurs on both flat sides.

Tabular cores are similar to cuboid cores in shape, but the parameters of the detachment area are dictated by cortex, usually located perpendicular to the blade detachment scars. There is virtually no evidence for edge preparation, and, in most instances, it appears that percussion blows impacted directly on the cortex. As a result, the blade scars are often irregular. These cores are made almost exclusively on Old Blue (Type 11) tabular cherts. In fact, it is clear that the Old Blue source at Dash Reeves must have been tabular or seam-like, since the chert is most often bracketed by cortex. This area on the core is never more than 4–5 cm thick, so blades made from this material are always in the 2 to 3-cm length range. Many of the Old Blue blades from the site retain cortex on the proximal or distal end, although in some cases cortex was removed after detachment.

Wedge cores are made on blocky, rectangular pieces of chert and exhibit blade detachment on only one end. Cortex is often apparent on the back side of the platform area. There is evidence of platform preparation and sometimes secondary thinning of the lateral sides as well as the platform itself. Unlike semiconical cores, which have curved platforms, these cores have relatively straight or squared edges. Blade scars tend to be straight and regular.

There are only a few examples of ball chert cores, but they represent local American Bottom lithic sources. Most of the Dongola and Cobden chert blades from the site, however, appear to have been detached from spherical nodules or ball cherts. They are semilunate or curved and often have cortex on the proximal ends. In profile they are similar to outrepassé blades, which are distinguished by their curved distal truncations. Such forms characterize the so-called Cobden or Crab Orchard blade and core technology described by Montet-

White (1968:26–28), McNerney (1987), and Morrow (1987). Most probably, the Dash Reeves blades were produced somewhere in southern Illinois and imported to the site. There is little evidence that this core technique was used at Dash Reeves, except perhaps experimentally on local ball cherts.

Multidirectional blade cores represent attempts to produce expedient blades from multiple platforms and from multiple orientations. The flake scars are erratic and multidirectional. It is not clear what the intent was except perhaps to utilize any remaining potential in more formal, expended blade cores.

Nucleated cores are rare and probably represent slightly more formal multidirectional cores. They tend to be star-shaped and have broad, deeply indented oval to circular platforms. The final blade scars on these cores are extremely short and broad with uneven lateral edges. The platform angles are extremely sharp, i.e., less than 40°. Almost all of these cores are expended to the point of no return.

As previously mentioned, tortoise cores do not occur at Dash Reeves, but the prismatic and semiconical cores from the site resemble such forms. Tortoise cores, in fact, may represent the initial stage of blade detachment, the byproduct of final utilization being semiconical cores. The one intact example from the Nochta site (see above) contains a broad, flat, and somewhat ovate platform with edge preparation. The opposite side is also flat but exhibits no secondary preparation. Blade detachment occurred around the entire circumference, and blades were regularly spaced and all of a consistent length.

Despite the variety of core types at the site, the ultimate objective of this diverse technology was to produce blades. The blade core industry at Dash Reeves could even be called expedient, in the sense that multiple material sources were utilized and the technological format was less than formalized. Blades from the central Illinois River valley appear to have been made from only the best-quality cherts, i.e., imported white Burlington cherts (Cantwell 1980:148). This was not the case at Dash Reeves, where even coarse Salem cherts were utilized in blade production. Given the relatively short lengths of the blade scars on the Dash Reeves expended cores, it is also clear that the purpose of this industry was probably not the production of the kinds of elongated, specialized blades reported in the literature at nonhabitation sites (Griffin et al. 1970; Leigh et al. 1988:83; Pi-Sunyer 1965:78), an issue that will be examined in a subsequent section.

Blade core technology in the American Bottom appeared only during the Middle Woodland period, i.e., 50 B.C. to A.D. 300. In light of that, it is amazing to observe multiple blade core formats, especially at one site. Although occasional blade flakes are known from earlier time periods, there is essentially no precedent for the kind of technological diversity found at Dash Reeves. Even other sites in this area, such as Holding, do not produce this kind of variability (Williams 1989).

Because of the unique nature of the assemblage at the site, a sample of 36 blade cores was selected for detailed study. Because the sample size was so small, core types were not distinguished. Core selection was based on the occurrence of a complete set of nine measurable attributes. These included weight, length of edge chord, maximum distance of edge chord from platform edge, distance from platform edge to base, number of arrises, mean length of all arrises, mean width of all arrises, length-width ratio, and platform angle (see Figure 8.2). Platform measurements as well as blade scar attributes were tabulated, ultimately to be utilized for comparison with the blades themselves. Table 8.5 summarizes the results of this analysis.

There is very little comparative data on core dimensions from Illinois sites. Fourteen cores from the Snyders site were restudied by Greber et al. (1981) and compared with a limited sample from several Ohio sites. The cores are described as "haystack" (probably prismatic) and "hemisphere" (semiconical?) shaped. The width

and thickness measures used in that study are not comparable to those employed here, and attributes such as edge chord or arris length and width were not measured. Moreover, data in that study were grouped. Finally, inconsistent attribute terminology (e.g., the interchangeability of "length" and "height") also makes use of the Synders site data for comparison somewhat difficult. This highlights a general problem in the Midwest, namely, the lack of a common blade core type and attribute terminology.

However, some useful comparisons can be drawn between the Dash Reeves cores and those from the Snyders and Ohio valley sites. For example, platform angle averages 67.6° at Dash Reeves and about 70° at Snyders and, apparently, for the Ohio samples (Greber et al. 1981:19–20). However, as a comparative device, platform angle should be used with caution. The means mask important differences between the various core types. At Dash Reeves, for example, cuboid, wedge, and tabular cores have platform angles ranging from 70° to 90°, while many of the semiconical, prismatic, tortoise, and multidirectional cores may have angles as acute as 30°–40°. Moreover, a platform angle measurement represents only one moment in the life of a core. Most angles are considerably steeper or right-angled at the outset of blade detachment and gradually become more acute as detachment progresses. Eventually, the knapper either discards the core or prepares another platform surface. The larger the core assemblage from a site, the more likely it is that a full range of detachment histories will be represented. This is a significant issue when comparing blade industries within regions or

Table 8.5. Summary of Blade Core Attributes★

	A	B	C	D	E	F	G	H	I
Mean	32.3	3.17	2.7	2.9	5.6	2.2	0.8	2.8	67.6
Sd	15.6	0.60	0.9	0.6	2.6	0.4	0.1	0.7	15.7
Minimum	4.4	1.90	0.4	1.8	2.0	1.3	0.5	1.6	37.0
Maximum	66.0	4.70	4.5	4.4	13.0	2.8	1.1	4.9	109.0

★Based on a sample of 36
A: weight (g)
B: length of edge chord (cm)
C: maximum distance from edge chord to platform edge (cm)
D: maximum distance from platform edge to base (cm)
E: number of arrises
F: length of arrises (mean cm)
G: width of arrises (mean cm)
H: length-width arris ratio
I: platform angle

when comparing Midwest industries with Mesoamerican, Arctic, Northwest coast, Plateau, or earlier Archaic blade core technologies. Platform angle, in fact, along with length and width measures, is one of the most commonly used comparative attributes in discussions about the origins and regional relationships of the Hopewell blade and core technology (Ford et al. 1955:148; Greber et al. 1981). However, in order for this measurement to have comparative value, the individual cores being measured should be distinguished by type. The mean platform angle recorded for the Dash Reeves sample was obtained by measuring a variety of core types and, presumably, both initial and terminal-stage cores. Unfortunately, measurements of cores were taken early in the analysis, before an actual core typology was recognized. For this reason, the Dash Reeves figure should be used with caution. Other core attributes are considered in the following discussion of blades.

Blades. A total of 2,165 unmodified blades was recovered at the Dash Reeves site. Of this number, 1,286 (59.4 percent) are segments or fragments retaining few or no measurable attributes. The remaining 879 blades were selected for analysis. All minimally have intact proximal ends and arrises. However, only 512 blades exhibit a complete array of attributes (Table 8.6). Most commonly, distal ends are missing or severely broken. It is not known whether such damage occurred during manufacture or as a result of secondary factors, such as postdepositional trampling, plowing, or handling during excavation. Blades should be given extra care in the field since even the slightest contact with other artifacts in bags can produce breakage or false utilization scars.

Table 8.6. Distribution of Complete and Fragmented Unmodified Blades by Provenience

| | Complete | | Fragments | |
	N	%	N	%
Features	87	66.9	43	33.1
Exc. Units	195	65.9	101	34.1
Test Units	91	74.6	31	25.4
900s	63	49.6	64	50.4
700s	76	37.3	128	62.7
All	512	58.3	367	41.7

Although blades have received a great deal of attention in the literature, measured attributes have not been standardized, and there seems to be no agreement on what the most important attributes are, with the exception of length, width, and platform angle. Some studies have even combined unmodified blades with tools and, therefore, consider modification attributes important (Williams 1989). The importance of recording quantitative and qualitative attributes may not be readily apparent for a within-assemblage analysis, but such data should provide a means of comparing assemblages within regions or between regions. A variety of attributes were selected for this analysis with this in mind. A more thorough analysis of platform and arris attributes is presented here than is usual in the literature. In her study of the Holding site blades, Williams (1989:338) referred to flake scars on blades rather than arrises, as is more common in the Arctic and Europe (Sanger 1970). Focusing on these and other less recognized traits highlights the complexity of this blade industry and makes its eventual demise a hundred years later even more inexplicable.

As previously mentioned, blades were removed from the general debitage population, and a sample of 879 unmodified blades was selected for analysis. Eighteen qualitative and 14 quantitative attributes were utilized in this analysis. The qualitative attributes or coding system is presented in Appendix D. The quantitative attributes include length, width, thickness, weight, number of platform facets, number of arrises, width of all arrises, length of all arrises, platform angle, platform width, platform length, blade curvature index, blade length/width ratio, and blade thickness/width ratio. It is hoped that these measurements will prove useful for regional comparisons with other blade industries. A good discussion of the rationale for blade attribute measurement can be found in Reid (1976), and the reader is directed to that source. Most of the attributes used in this study are illustrated in Figure 8.3. Thickness was always measured just below the bulb of percussion at the proximal end. The blade curvature index measures the maximum distance from a plane linking the bulb to the distal end of the blade. This was accomplished on graph paper with the aid of a straight ruler. This measure provides information about blade detachment, particularly in terms of control of material. The higher this figure, the later in the production sequence a blade was detached. This measure may also

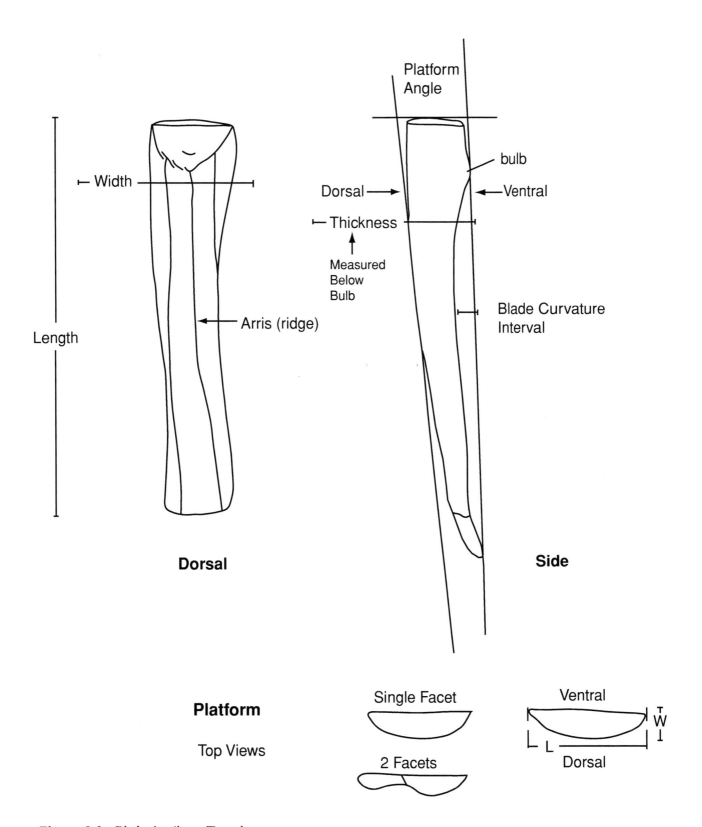

Figure 8.3. Blade Attribute Template

serve as a good comparative tool in distinguishing the Cobden and Fulton core techniques, since ball chert Cobden blades should be relatively more curved. Table 8.7 provides a summary of the quantitative attributes of unmodified blades.

The most commonly cited blade measurement is that of length (Table 8.8). In comparison with other assemblages, the Dash Reeves blades are small, averaging only 2.71 cm per blade. Holding blades measure 3.67 cm on average. My examination of 122 blades from the Twenhafel site in southern Illinois revealed a length measure of 3.57 cm (see also Hofman 1987). Blades from the McGraw site in Ohio average 3.96 cm

(Pi-Sunyer 1965:64; Prufer 1965); blades from Fisher-Gabert (Reid 1976:88) in the Big Bend area of the Missouri River are 4.03 cm; blades from the Trowbridge site near Kansas City range from 4.2 to 4.8 cm, depending on material type (Reid 1976:84). Finally, blades from the Snyders site in Illinois (Montet-White 1963:18–23) are 4.87 cm long on average. The length/width ratios of all except the Dash Reeves blades are approximately 3:1; the Dash Reeves blades average 2:1. There are several possible explanations for this difference. First, virtually all of the sites mentioned above date to the Hopewell period, to the apex of blade technology in the Midwest. Dash Reeves is later and may have been

Table 8.7. Unmodified Blade Quantitative Attributes

	Cases	Max.	Min.	Mean	SD
Blade length (cm)	879	7.18	0.72	2.71	1.02
Blade width (cm)	879	2.87	0.35	1.24	0.42
Blade thickness (cm)	879	1.22	0.07	0.31	0.14
Weight (g)	879	22.80	0.06	1.65	2.02
Arris count	874	4.00	0.00	1.42	0.59
Platform angle (degrees)	825	115.00	43.0	84.7	7.08
Platform width (cm)	813	1.34	0.01	0.17	0.12
Platform length (cm)	770	1.94	0.05	0.49	0.26
Blade index curvature	834	0.90	0.00	0.11	0.11
Max. width of arris (cm)	870	2.07	0.15	0.74	0.31
Min. width of arris (cm)	868	1.41	0.05	0.45	0.24
Intermediate arris width (1) (cm)	321	1.52	0.09	0.44	0.20
Intermediate arris width (2) (cm)	34	0.96	0.17	0.36	0.16
Max. length of arris (cm)	867	6.19	0.43	2.20	0.90
Min. length of arris (cm)	326	4.79	0.36	1.70	0.73
Intermediate length arris (1) (cm)	39	4.18	0.69	1.92	0.75
Intermediate length arris (2) (cm)	2	1.76	1.29	1.53	0.33
Blade length/width ratio	879	6.50	0.75	2.26	0.71
Blade thickness/width ratio	879	1.01	0.10	0.25	0.08

Table 8.8. Regional Comparison of Mean Unmodified Blade Lengths, Widths, and Thicknesses

	Mean Length (cm)	Mean Width (cm)	Mean Thickness (cm)	Length/Width Ratio
Dash Reeves	2.71	1.24	0.31	1:2.2
Snyders*	4.87	1.83	0.38	1:2.7
Holding	3.67	1.61	0.42	1:2.3
Twenhafel	3.57	1.69	0.38	1:2.1
McGraw	3.96	0.97	0.22	1:4.1
Trowbridge	4.22–4.80	1.39–1.73	0.34–0.50	1:2.4–1:2.8
Fisher-Gabert	4.03	1.35	0.33	1:3.0

*Figures from the Snyders site are based on Montet-White 1963; in a later study by Greber et al. (1981:510) mean length and width measures were listed as 4.74 cm and 1.7 cm, respectively.

experiencing some kind of technological downsizing of its blade industry, an industry that would disappear altogether a few centuries later. Alternatively, the short blade lengths at Dash Reeves may be due to the kinds of tabular, cortical cherts preferred at this site. In particular, the Old Blue and Ste. Genevieve cherts used here have a high percentage of cortex, which often brackets a relatively narrow band of usable chert. Table 8.9 presents length statistics by chert types for both modified and unmodified blades. This measure rarely exceeds 4–5 cm. The mean length of arrises on Dash Reeves blades is, in fact, only 2.2 cm, and the average distance from platform to base or keel only 2.9 cm (see Table 8.5). The utilized cherts from the other sites are generally of much higher quality, allowing much greater flexibility in terms of material potential and core shaping.

Blade width has been utilized to distinguish Ohio from Illinois blade industries (Pi-Sunyer 1965; Sanger 1970:111), with the Illinois blades generally being much broader and longer. In comparison with the six sites mentioned above (McGraw, Snyders, Holding, Trowbridge, Fisher-Gabert, and Twenhafel) the Dash Reeves blade widths (mean=1.24 cm) rank above McGraw (mean=0.97 cm) but are much narrower than the other non-Ohio examples, which range from 1.73 cm to 1.35 cm in width (Table 8.8). Interestingly, the length/width ratios observed on blades from Dash Reeves, Holding, and Twenhafel are virtually identical (i.e., ca. 1:2.2). The McGraw blades are significantly different, with a ratio of 1:4.1. The other ratios, which fall between the American Bottom and Ohio examples, are presented in Table 8.8. The McGraw blades are also significantly thinner than those found at other sites, averaging 0.22 cm.

The Dash Reeves blades are also unusual in terms of the relatively small number of flake scars or dorsal ridges (arrises) per blade. Arris number ranges from none to four, averaging 1.42 per blade (Table 8.7). Unfortunately, this attribute was not recorded at other sites, except indirectly through flake scars at the Holding site. About 65 percent of the blades at Holding appear to have three or more arrises, which is not surprising given the greater widths of the Holding blades and the fact that knappers there were not limited by the poorer-quality cherts utilized at Dash Reeves. It is apparent that even in the American Bottom there were subtle differences in blade technology, probably dependent mostly on material type but also perhaps on affiliation with the Hopewell period.

The distribution of blades by chert type and provenience is presented in Tables 8.10 and 8.11. The distribution generally follows the nonblade debitage selection strategy, with one important exception. Whereas local Salem cherts constitute 13 percent of the nonblade debitage (by count), Salem chert makes up only 6 percent of the blade assemblage. Otherwise, the blade assemblage is dominated by Ste. Genevieve cherts (72 percent by count). White Burlington cherts account for nearly 14 percent of the blades, a figure that closely matches that of the nonblade debitage distribution. Finally, there are slightly more exotic chert blades proportionally than exotic chert debitage, but this figure is still low (4.3 percent). In short, in terms of material selection for the blade industry, the Dash Reeves assemblage is clearly oriented toward local resources.

Significant variation in some blade attributes may be accounted for by the use of specific chert types (Table 8.12). For example, platform lengths increase significantly on blades made on local Salem as well as on nonlocal Cobden/Dongola cherts. This is probably due to the fact that these are not seam cherts, i.e., the potential blade lengths and widths are greater at the beginning of reduction. Conversely, the smaller length-width ratios observed on Burlington chert blades probably resulted from there being less material available at the outset of knapping.

Some form of heat alteration was recognized on 17.5 percent of the blades, with the highest percentage occurring on white Burlington cherts (Tables 8.13 and 8.14). Over 65 percent of the heat-alteration effects are in the form of color changes. These effects appear to be intentional, i.e., to modify white cherts into pinks. Heat alteration on red cherts appears most often in the form of potlid fractures, which seem to represent incidental damage from surface or pit fires.

Cortex (excluding platform cortex) occurs on 12.3 percent of all blades (Tables 8.15 and 8.16). Nearly 88 percent of these blades are made from Ste. Genevieve red, Old Blue, and "Salem Creamy" or fine cherts (Table 8.17). Platform cortex occurs on 8.2 percent of the blades, and, again, the aforementioned cherts comprise nearly 81 percent of these blades. It should be pointed out that platform cortex is almost always located on the ventral side. The dorsal side usually exhibits

Table 8.9. Length Comparison of Unmodified and Modified Blades by Chert Type

Chert Type	Unmodified Blades			Modified Blades		
	N	Mean (cm)	SD	N	Mean (cm)	SD
All chert types	879	2.71	1.02	552	2.94	1.08
Burlington (1,3)	93	2.47	0.87	73	2.42	0.92
Salem (25)	56	3.17	1.15	19	3.69	1.44
Ste. Genevieve Red (7)	446	2.63	0.97	300	2.97	1.02
Ste. Genevieve Purple (29)	26	2.98	1.22	5	3.04	0.77
Fern Glen (10)	16	2.12	0.65	8	3.72	1.30
Old Blue (11)	97	2.69	0.92	63	2.84	0.93
Cobden/Dongola (13/12)	21	3.22	1.00	65	2.52	0.99
Grimes Hill (81)	5	2.69	1.38	6	3.26	1.34
Salem (34)	17	3.40	1.40	11	3.17	0.89
Salem (24)	34	3.27	1.12	5	4.69	2.33

Table 8.10. Percentile Distribution of Unmodified Blade Chert Types

	A	B	C	D	E	F	G	H	I	J
Features	10.8	3.1	2.3	44.6	7.7	4.6	16.9	5.4	0.0	4.6
Exc. Units	7.4	1.7	1.7	50.0	14.2	1.3	17.6	2.7	0.3	2.7
Test Units	6.6	4.9	1.6	51.6	9.0	5.7	9.0	4.1	0.0	6.6
900s	10.9	5.5	1.6	41.4	14.1	3.9	10.2	7.0	1.6	3.1
700s	6.9	3.9	2.0	61.1	12.8	2.0	8.9	1.0	1.0	0.5
All	8.2	3.4	1.8	50.7	12.2	3.0	13.2	3.5	0.6	3.1

Chert Types
A: Burlington (1, 6, 69)
B: Burlington, oolitic (3)
C: Fern Glen (10)
D: Ste. Genevieve Red (7)
E: Old Blue (8, 11)
F: Ste. Genevieve Purple (29)
G: Local Salem (18, 24, 25, 34, 45, 36, 40, 46, 57)
H: Southern Illinois chert (9, 12, 13, 15)
I: Grimes Hill (81)
J: Unknown

Table 8.11. Distribution of Unmodified Blades by Chert Type Groupings

	N	%
Local Ste. Genevieve cherts (red, purple, Old Blue, "Salem Creamy," Olive)	635	72.2
Burlington cherts (1, 2, 3, 6,10, 57, 69)	121	13.8
Local Salem cherts (24, 34, 35, 40, 46)	54	6.1
Exotic cherts (Dongola, Mill Creek, Cobden, Kaolin, Mansker, Blair, Grimes Hill)	38	4.3
Unknown chert	31	3.5
Total	879	

Table 8.12. Comparison of Selected Unmodified Blade Attributes by Major Chert Type Groupings

Chert Types	$\bar{x}$ * Blade Length	SD	$\bar{x}$ * Blade Width	SD	$\bar{x}$ ** Platform Width	SD	$\bar{x}$ ** Platform Length	SD	$\bar{x}$ ** Platform Angle	SD	$\bar{x}$ * Length Width Ratio	SD
Ste. Genevieve Red (7)	2.97	1.04	1.21	0.42	0.16	0.11	0.47	0.23	84.8	7.11	2.54	0.73
Old Blue (11)	3.01	0.97	1.17	0.34	0.14	0.08	0.40	0.17	85.3	6.87	2.65	0.73
Burlington (1, 3, 69)	2.69	0.94	1.22	0.43	0.16	0.14	0.46	0.25	84.4	6.42	2.25	0.48
Local Salem (24, 25, 34)	3.55	1.15	1.52	0.44	0.22	0.13	0.60	0.35	82.9	8.04	2.36	0.52
Cobden/Dongola (13/12)	3.71	0.79	1.59	0.44	0.20	0.11	0.58	0.25	83.4	4.09	2.50	0.81

All length-width measures are given in centimeters; platform angles are degrees.
*Includes only complete blades.
**Includes all blades with available attributes.

Table 8.13. Distribution of Heat-Altered and Non-Heat-Altered Unmodified Blades

	Heat-Altered N	%	Non-Heat-Altered N	%
Features	22	16.9	108	83.1
Exc. Units	47	15.9	249	84.1
Test Units	24	19.7	98	80.3
900s	25	19.5	103	80.5
700s	36	17.7	167	82.3
All	154	17.5	725	82.5

Table 8.14. Heat-Altered Unmodified Blades by Chert Type

	N	%
Burlington (1, 3, 69)	56	36.4
Ste. Genevieve Red (7)	47	30.5
Local Salem (24, 25, 34, 35, 57)	24	15.6
Unknown (17)	10	6.5
Exotics (12, 15, 81)	6	3.8
Old Blue (11)	5	3.2
Others (8, 10, 29)	6	3.8
Total	154	

Table 8.15. Dorsal Cortex on Unmodified Blades by Provenience

	Present N	%	Absent N	%
Features	21	16.2	109	83.8
Exc. Units	51	17.2	245	82.8
Test Units	15	12.4	106	87.6
900s	10	7.8	118	92.2
700s	11	5.4	192	94.6
All	108	12.3	770	87.7

Table 8.16. Platform Cortex on Complete
Unmodified Blades by Provenience

	N	%	Total Sample
Features	10	11.5	87
Exc. Units	24	12.3	195
Test Units	9	9.9	91
900s	6	9.5	63
700s	2	2.6	76
All	51	10.0	512

Table 8.17. Dorsal and Platform Cortex
on Unmodified Blades by Chert Type

| | Dorsal Cortex | |
	N	%
Burlington (1)	2	1.8
Burlington (6)	1	0.9
Ste. Genevieve Red (7)	59	54.1
Ste. Genevieve Olive (8)	1	0.9
Old Blue (11)	23	21.1
Salem Coarse (24)	4	3.7
Salem Creamy (25)	13	11.9
Salem Gray (34)	1	0.9
Unknown (17)	3	2.7
Ste. Genevieve Purple (29)	2	1.8
Total	109	

| | Platform Cortex | |
	N	%
Burlington (1)	2	2.8
Burlington (3)	1	1.4
Ste. Genevieve Red (7)	27	37.5
Ste. Genevieve Olive (8)	1	1.4
Old Blue (11)	14	19.4
Dongola (12)	2	2.8
Salem Coarse (24)	7	9.7
Salem Creamy (25)	10	13.9
Unknown (17)	2	2.8
Ste. Genevieve Purple (29)	3	4.2
Salem Gray (34)	2	2.8
Salem Banded Gray (46)	1	1.4
Total	72	

evidence of modification and preparation, probably related to removal of platform area cortex. The intentional removal of cortex from seam cherts highlights the extra preparation needed to produce blades from such material and re-emphasizes the homegrown nature of this blade assemblage.

About 39 percent of blade platforms are elliptical in shape. The majority (54 percent), however, are either irregular or indeterminate. The remaining 4 percent are triangular or trapezoidal in cross section. Only 45 percent of the blades have intact platforms. This is partly due to secondary breakage, but most damage occurred because of platform preparation battering or trimming. Platform modification was observed on 42.2 percent of blades with visible platforms. Battering (21.1 percent) consists of stepping, crushing, and grinding, observed just below the platform edge. Trimming (21.1 percent) is evidenced by multiple vertical flake scars located between the platform edge and the reverse side of the bulb of percussion. Presumably, trimming involved a more careful or controlled process of platform preparation, perhaps resulting from soft-hammer techniques. Crushing and grinding probably occurred as a result of hard-hammer percussion. Curiously, the occurrence of battering or trimming is not dependent upon chert type, although in the case of exotic chert blades, there are slightly more battered platforms than trimmed ones. In addition, the local Salem chert blades tend to show almost no platform preparation. As a final note on platforms, only 2.8 percent of all blades in the assemblage are multifaceted. This suggests that once the initial platform was prepared, very little was done to that edge until it was time to rejuvenate the core. This indicates a high level of skill and confidence in terms of detachment consistency. It also suggests that this was not an experimental industry.

The distal shapes of blades were subdivided into three categories: pointed, flat, and broken. Flat-ended blades comprise 57 percent of the assemblage; pointed, 28.7 percent; and broken, 14 percent. The termination breaks also were recorded, with blades falling into the following categories: snapped (44.8 percent), feathered (36.3 percent), stepped (1.9 percent), hinged (10.7 percent), plunged (2.4 percent), and axial (3.9 percent) (Table 8.18). These are illustrated in Figure 8.4. Related to this are outrepassé blades, which constitute 6.4 percent of the blade assemblage at this site. Such blades normally are produced at the end of a core sequence when the platform angle becomes extremely acute. The relatively high percentage of this kind of blade indicates that this industry was successful in maximizing core resources and that long, straight blades were not necessarily the desired end products (i.e., presumably a large number of short blades would have been produced prior to the creation of outrepassé blades).

In summary, the Dash Reeves blade assemblage is quite complex from a technological standpoint. By comparison with other Middle Woodland industries in the Midwest, outside of Ohio, these blades are shorter, narrower, and thinner and are made from a diverse number of chert types, including local varieties that seem inferior to the cherts utilized elsewhere for this kind of technology. Of course, it is possible that better-quality blades also were produced at the Dash Reeves site, perhaps for exchange purposes, but the on-site evidence suggests otherwise. It is clear from the selection of seamed or tabular cherts, which could not have produced long blades, that smaller blades were actually the desired end products. The diverse array of small blade tools from the site supports this.

Table 8.18. Distribution of Terminal Break Types on Unmodified Blades

	Feathered (0)		Stepped (1)		Hinged (2)		Plunged (3)		Axial (4)		Snapped (5)	
	N	%	N	%	N	%	N	%	N	%	N	%
Features	53	40.8	3	2.3	12	9.2	0	0.0	5	3.8	57	43.8
Exc. Units	94	31.8	9	3.0	35	11.8	16	5.4	20	6.8	122	41.2
Test Units	52	42.6	2	1.6	19	15.6	4	3.3	5	4.1	40	32.8
900s	49	38.3	2	1.6	12	9.4	0	0.0	2	1.6	63	49.2
700s	71	35.0	1	0.5	16	7.9	1	0.5	2	1.0	112	55.2
All	319	36.3	17	1.9	94	10.7	21	2.4	34	3.9	394	44.8

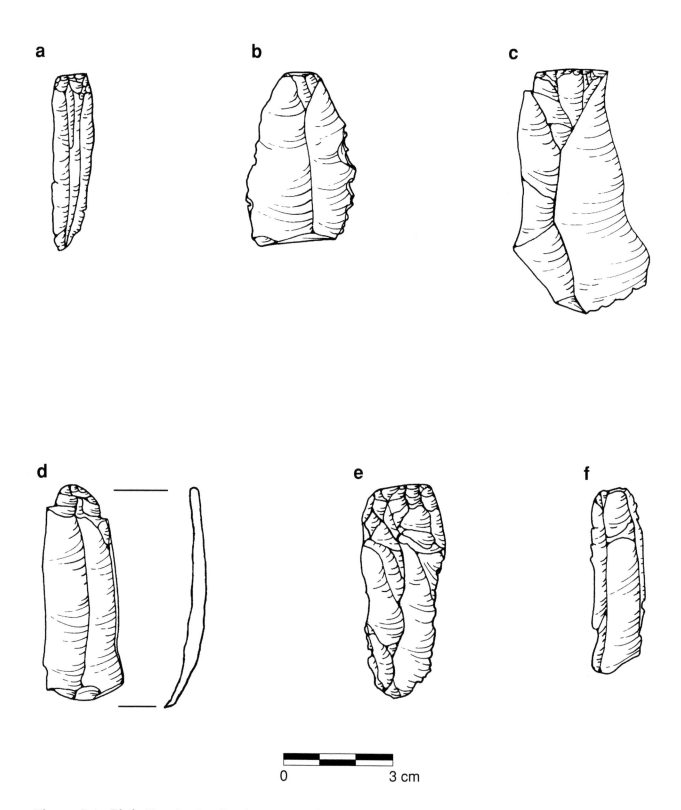

Figure 8.4. Blade Termination Break Types: a, feathered; b, snapped; c, hinged; d, plunging; e, crenulated; f, axial

CHERT TOOLS

Chert tools and fragments total 3,611 items and include 1,052 formal tools, 1,534 utilized flakes, 532 blade tools, 167 biface fragments, and 326 polished flakes. There are four different dichotomies recognized within this assemblage. They are **flake/core**, **blade/nonblade**, **biface/uniface,** and **micro/macro**. The latter distinction is perhaps the least useful, referring simply to big versus little tools having the same formal shape. There are, for example, micro- and macroperforators, drills, denticulates, spurs, and gravers in this assemblage. There are also flake and core scrapers, perforators, denticulates, and gravers, etc., as well as nonblade and blade versions of these tools. There is a microtool industry at the site, a core tool industry, a nonblade flake tool industry, and a blade tool industry. The tools produced by each overlap in form and, apparently, in function. This incredible diversity has no antecedents or inheritors in the American Bottom (Fortier 2000).

The distinction between form and function is a difficult problem and essentially is impossible to resolve without extensive microwear analyses. Certainly without such analysis even gross questions of hard versus soft material utilization cannot be addressed. Given the size of the assemblage and my inexperience with microwear analysis, microscopic examination of materials was not undertaken. The artifacts in this assemblage were assigned to formal categories first and later grouped into general, presumably functional, categories. In many cases the relationship between form and function is particularly close, as in the case of drills, perforators, and gravers. Likewise, it is improbable that hafted bifaces or so-called projectile points were used as drills. The formal and functional categories established here should be regarded as having only general applicability. The functional distinction between scraper and knife is particularly obscure, and the functional difference between core and flake scrapers is equally fuzzy. Nevertheless, it is hoped that the formal categories discussed below will have some comparative value, at least until more detailed microscopic analyses can be conducted on these artifacts. Chert tools are presented under three general headings: nonblade flake tools, nonblade core tools, and blade tools.

Nonblade Flake Tools

These tools include hafted bifaces, knives, scrapers, gravers, drills/perforators, denticulates, becs or spurs, utilized flakes, and polished flakes. Sixteen formal flake tool categories were recognized, but many of these categories represent subdivisions of more general types. For example, seven different categories of flake scraper were identified. These distinctions are highlighted in the major type descriptions that follow.

Hafted Bifaces. One hundred eighty-five hafted bifaces were recovered. Of these, three artifacts, including two Wanda points and a Matanzas point, are not associated temporally with the Middle Woodland occupation. These points are described in Chapter 12. The hafted biface category includes complete specimens as well as diagnostic bases lacking blades (Plate 8.1). This category does not include miscellaneous biface fragments (N=71; 230.3 g), nondiagnostic tips with partial midsections (N=57; 389.6 g), or nondiagnostic midsections lacking tips and bases (N=27; 155.9 g). Ten formal types were identified: Manker Corner Notched, Manker Stemmed, Gibson, Ansell, Burkett, Steuben, Clear Lake Side Notched, Snyders, Dickson/Waubesa, and Manker Side Notched. In addition, there are six Adena-like points and one Burkett/Adena-like point. Sixty-nine hafted bifaces were placed in an "Unknown" category, although all were presumed to be Middle Woodland in origin. While these examples are mostly bases, they do not fall into previously recognized types. A number of points are both corner and side notched and could not be placed into a type system. Table 8.19 presents a summary of attribute means for each of the 10 recognized types. Appendix E gives attributes for each of the artifacts, again organized by type. Figure 8.5 illustrates how and where the measurements were taken. Descriptions of the major types follow.

There are 22 Manker Corner Notched points or hafted bifaces (Plate 8.2; Figure 8.6a). These points have convex bases (Montet-White 1968:71–73). The blade is relatively broad at the shoulder, and the corner notches are also relatively broad. The base is often eared or flared slightly upward. The base form is somewhat similar to the Gibson type except that the latter points are significantly longer and have narrower blades and narrower, more acute corner notches.

0   3 cm

Plate 8.1. Hafted Biface Bases

Table 8.19. Summary of Mean Metric Attributes of Diagnostic Hafted Biface Types

	Manker Corner Notched			Manker Stemmed			Gibson			Ansell		
	N	Mean	SD	N	Mean	SD	N	Mean	SD	N	Mean	SD
Max. length (cm)	10	5.33	0.55	3	4.67	0.92	2	6.56	1.18	3	4.83	0.51
Blade length (cm)	12	3.95	0.55	3	3.38	0.76	4	4.97	1.03	3	3.52	0.28
Blade thickness (cm)	18	0.75	0.14	5	0.72	0.23	4	0.64	0.10	4	0.85	0.12
Shoulder width (cm)	19	3.36	0.36	5	3.15	0.42	4	3.34	0.11	2	3.10	0.13
Stem length (cm)	20	1.48	0.20	6	1.41	0.25	4	1.54	0.10	6	1.44	0.32
Stem width (cm)	22	1.87	0.19	6	1.73	0.23	4	1.83	0.23	6	1.69	0.23
Stem thickness (cm)	22	0.55	0.10	6	0.54	0.05	4	0.48	0.02	6	0.57	0.07
Base width (cm)	16	2.66	0.30	5	2.28	0.43	3	2.88	0.53	5	2.24	0.26
Left notch width (cm)	10	0.90	0.19	4	1.09	0.33	3	0.49	0.08	2	1.68	0.18
Right notch width (cm)	20	0.89	0.22	6	0.98	0.15	4	0.72	0.13	5	1.57	0.43
Left notch depth (cm)	10	0.73	0.11	4	0.68	0.21	3	0.74	0.07	2	0.53	0.04
Right notch depth (cm)	20	0.66	0.15	6	0.71	0.21	4	0.79	0.09	5	0.53	0.22
Left notch angle (deg)	12	49.00	19.00	4	49.00	18.4	3	64.30	8.33	2	69.00	32.53
Right notch angle (deg)	20	52.30	10.28	6	47.70	12.5	4	54.00	13.44	5	89.40	28.89
Weight (g)	19	12.30	3.81	6	9.98	3.50	4	13.50	3.41	6	10.07	4.55

	Burkett			Steuben			Clear Lake Side Notched			Snyders		
	N	Mean	SD	N	Mean	SD	N	Mean	SD	N	Mean	SD
Max. length (cm)	3	5.89	0.76	2	5.47	0.81	7	5.08	0.87	–	–	–
Blade length (cm)	3	3.74	0.89	2	4.05	1.17	8	3.85	0.90	–	–	–
Blade thickness (cm)	4	0.82	0.09	3	1.10	0.04	16	0.71	0.13	1	0.65	–
Shoulder width (cm)	4	3.22	0.60	1	2.81	–	12	2.98	0.29	1	3.84	–
Stem length (cm)	4	1.69	0.27	4	1.57	0.30	17	1.39	0.21	1	1.23	–
Stem width (cm)	4	1.99	0.13	3	1.63	0.18	17	1.81	0.16	1	2.11	–
Stem thickness (cm)	4	0.62	0.07	4	0.69	0.11	17	0.48	0.09	1	0.48	–
Base width (cm)	2	1.38	0.14	3	2.02	0.55	15	2.55	0.20	1	2.51	–
Left notch width (cm)	2	2.20	0.00	1	0.90	–	11	0.93	0.14	1	1.10	–
Right notch width (cm)	4	1.96	0.26	4	1.25	0.39	16	0.95	0.20	1	0.80	–
Left notch depth (cm)	2	0.65	0.07	1	0.30	–	11	0.51	0.09	1	0.70	–
Right notch depth (cm)	4	0.55	0.11	4	0.46	0.14	16	0.57	0.08	1	0.60	–
Left notch angle (deg)	1	10.00	–	1	39.00	–	11	71.90	7.92	1	34.00	–
Right notch angle (deg)	3	10.00	2.00	4	42.70	14.38	15	68.10	9.10	1	47.00	–
Weight (g)	5	13.76	3.55	4	11.28	6.04	18	8.94	3.33	1	7.20	–

	Dickson/ Waubesa			Manker Side Notched		
	N	Mean	SD	N	Mean	SD
Max. length (cm)	4	6.73	1.60	16	5.04	1.16
Blade length (cm)	4	4.73	1.33	16	3.49	1.03
Blade thickness (cm)	5	1.10	0.46	31	0.76	0.13
Shoulder width (cm)	5	3.15	0.32	25	3.01	0.32
Stem length (cm)	5	2.00	0.35	32	1.57	0.19
Stem width (cm)	5	2.27	0.17	31	1.79	0.21
Stem thickness (cm)	5	0.66	0.06	33	0.57	0.10
Base width (cm)	1	1.03	–	29	2.70	0.35
Left notch width (cm)	2	2.05	0.21	17	0.93	0.20
Right notch width (cm)	3	1.93	0.47	33	0.92	0.18
Left notch depth (cm)	2	0.55	0.21	17	0.61	0.10
Right notch depth (cm)	3	0.60	0.10	33	0.59	0.15
Left notch angle (deg)	1	13.00	–	17	73.10	9.13
Right notch angle (deg)	1	23.00	–	33	72.60	9.40
Weight (g)	5	17.06	6.61	33	10.36	3.91

WIDTHS

a   width of base
b   width of neck
c   width at shoulder
d   maximum width

LENGTHS

e   axial length
f   stem length
g   blade length

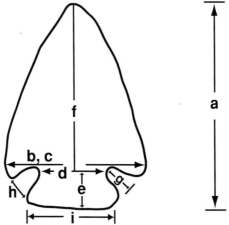

a   maximum length   e   stem length
b   maximum width   f   blade length
c   shoulder width   g   notch depth
d   neck width   h   notch width
                            i   base width

Figure 8.5. Hafted Biface Measurement Guide

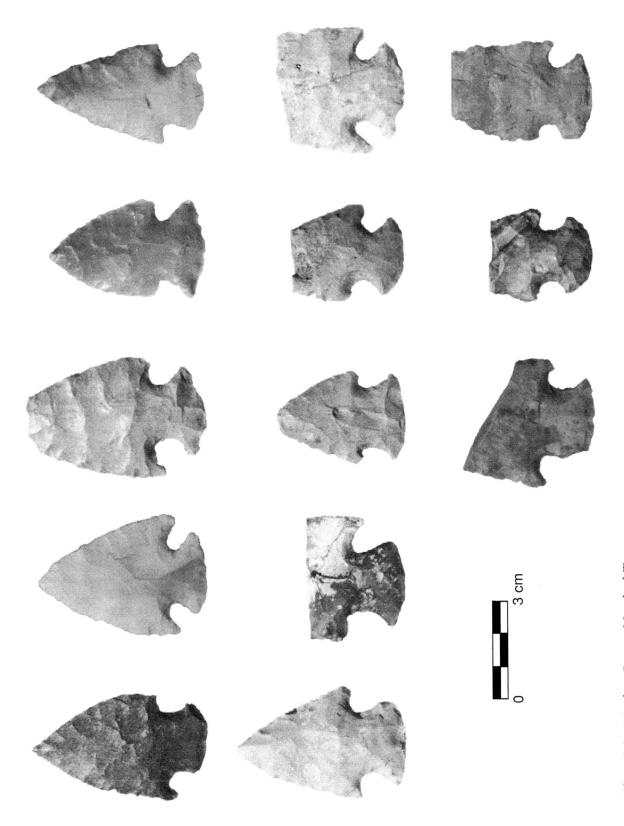

Plate 8.2. Manker Corner Notched Types

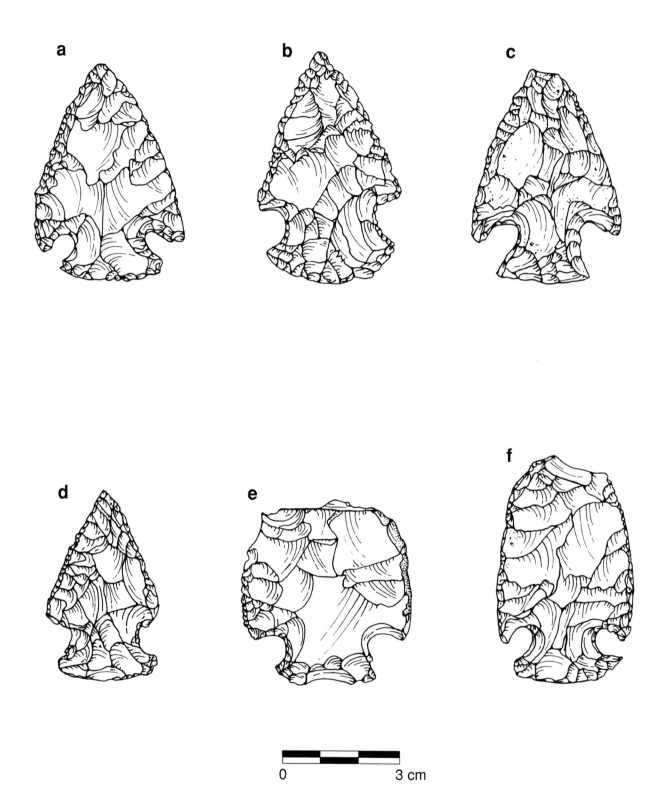

Figure 8.6. Hafted Biface Types: a, Manker Corner Notched; b, Manker Side Notched; c, Manker Stemmed; d, Clear Lake Side Notched; e, Snyders; f, Gibson

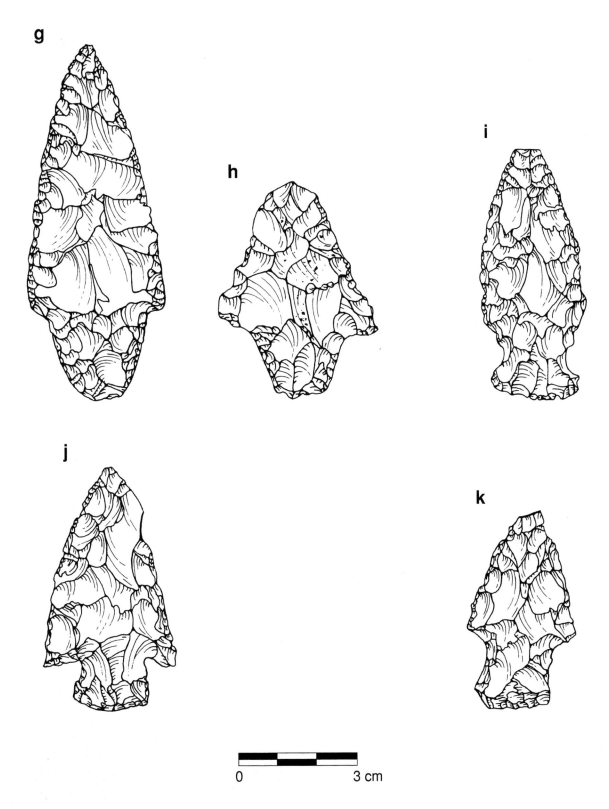

Figure 8.6. continued, g, Dickson/Waubesa; h, Burkett; i, Ansell; j, Adena Stemmed; k, Steuben

Six Manker Stemmed types were identified (Plate 8.3f–h; Figure 8.6c). These points are also corner notched but differ from Manker Corner Notched points in that their bases are straight or expanded. They are the shortest points in this assemblage, averaging 4.67 cm in length. Shoulder barbs are often rounded and not prominent (Montet-White 1968:73).

Four Gibson points were recognized (Scully 1951). These points are similar in shape to the Manker Corner Notched type, but are longer (Plate 8.4a–d). The average length of the Gibson points in the assemblage is 6.56 cm. Only the Dickson/Waubesa points in the assemblage are longer.

Clear Lake Side Notched points number 18 and are characterized by deep, broad lateral notches and straight bases (Plate 8.5; Figure 8.6d). This type was first defined by Montet-White (1968:81) based on materials recovered from the Clear Lake site in Illinois (Fowler 1952). The samples from Dash Reeves have relatively short and narrow stems. This point type has not been identified previously at American Bottom Middle Woodland sites (Williams 1989:354–358). It may prove to be a marker for the Hill Lake phase, but this remains to be documented.

Another side-notched form was identified for the first time at the Dash Reeves site and is introduced here as the type Manker Side Notched (Plate 8.6; Figure 8.6b). This type, represented by 33 examples, is closely related to the Clear Lake Side Notched type but differs from the latter in that it has a convex and slightly flared base. This is the most numerous point type at the site and, like the Clear Lake Side Notched type described above, may represent a Hill Lake phase marker.

Six Ansell points were recognized in this assemblage (Plate 8.4f–h; Figure 8.6i). These points are broadly side notched with inconspicuous shoulders and slightly convex and expanding bases (Montet-White 1968:75–81). Their overall form is fish tailed. In the American Bottom this point type is closely associated with the Hill Lake phase, and it persisted in the area well into the Late Woodland period, being particularly common during the Mund phase, i.e., A.D. 450–600 (Fortier et al.1983:252–259).

Four hafted bifaces were identified as Steuben points (Morse 1963). These points are closely related to the Ansell type except that Steubens have sharper notch angles at the haft and generally have straighter or more flared bases (Plate 8.3d, e; Figure 8.6k). Shoulders are

relatively narrow with inconspicuous tangs. The Steuben type persisted into the early Late Woodland period in this area and is also a marker for the Hill Lake phase.

Five Burkett points were recognized (Bell 1958:28; Montet-White 1968:65–67). These distinctive points have contracting, trapezoidal stems and triangular shoulders (Plate 8.7; Figure 8.6h). Bases are straight. They appear to represent variants of the Dickson/Waubesa contracting stem type.

There are five Dickson/Waubesa points in the assemblage (Baerreis 1953:155). These are long-bladed points with inconspicuous shoulders, contracting stems, and rounded bases (Plate 8.7a–d; Figure 8.6g). These points are generally associated with Early Woodland and early Middle Woodland peoples but may have been curated and utilized by mid-to-late Middle Woodland peoples as well. In the lower Illinois River valley these types are subsumed within the Belknap cluster, which includes the types Burkett, Waubesa, Florence, Mason, Dickson Broad Bladed, and Peisker/Goose Lake Diamonds (Farnsworth and Asch 1986:366).

A single Snyders point was recovered (Plate 8.4; Figure 8.6e). Snyders points are broad-bladed, short-stemmed, corner-notched points with curvate ends and expanding bases (Scully 1951). They probably functioned as hafted scrapers, since the end opposite the hafting element often exhibits signs of utilization. The type is generally associated with the early Middle Woodland period in this area, but as with the contracting stemmed varieties, Snyders points may have been curated by later peoples.

Within the hafted biface fragment category there are a number of artifacts with relatively intact blade portions that lack stems and bases. The stems are consistently snapped at the blade-stem juncture (Plate 8.8). The blades exhibit shallow basal or corner notching. The lateral edges of the blades are relatively straight and not curved, as is the case with the Manker and Snyders types. The blades are also generally broad shouldered. These fragments are tentatively categorized as Adena- or Mason-like. However, in some cases the blade size and shape resemble Norton or Gibson varieties.

A surprisingly high percentage (42.7 percent) of hafted bifaces from the site are made from Burlington cherts. This is curious, since Burlington chert comprises only 4.8 percent of the chert debitage from the site by weight and 11.5 percent by count. Conversely, Ste. Genevieve red chert, which dominates the chert debitage

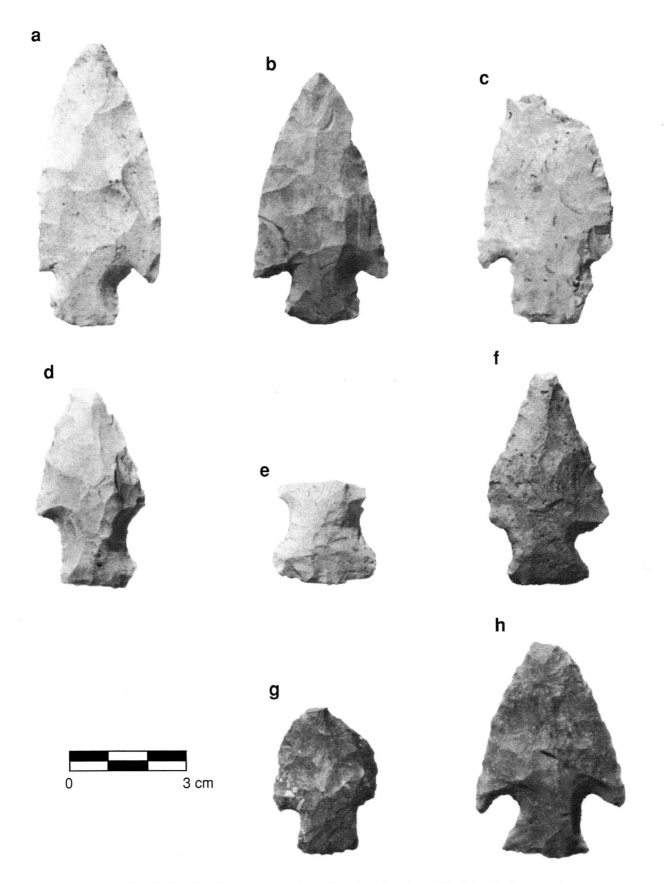

Plate 8.3. Selected Hafted Biface Types: a–c, Adena-like; d–e, Steuben; f–h, Manker Stemmed

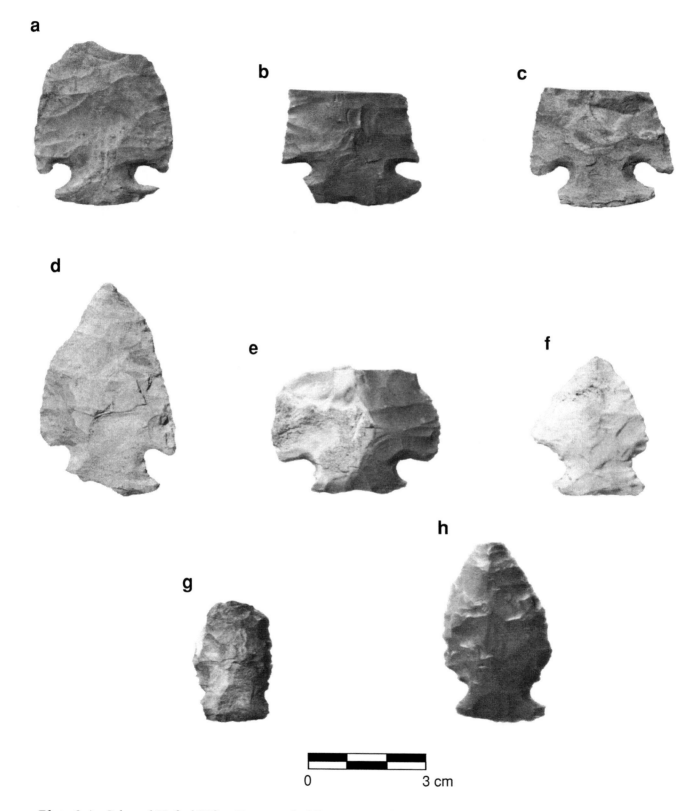

Plate 8.4. Selected Hafted Biface Types: a–d, Gibson; e, Snyders; f–h, Ansell

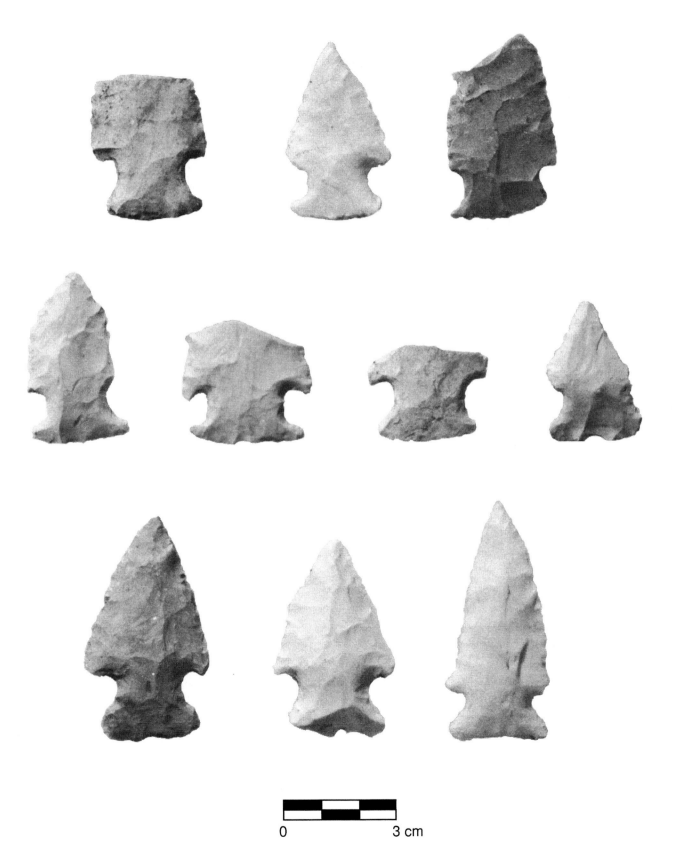

Plate 8.5. Clear Lake Side Notched Types

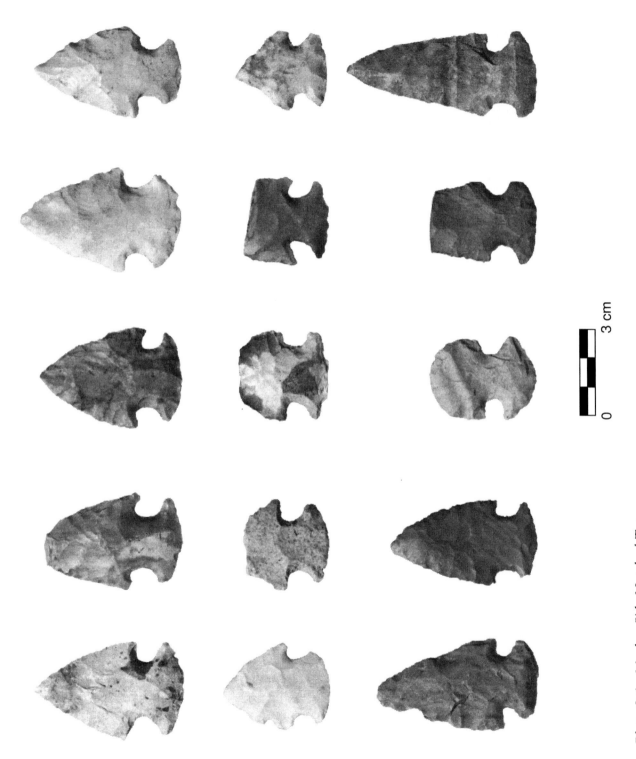

Plate 8.6. Manker Side Notched Types

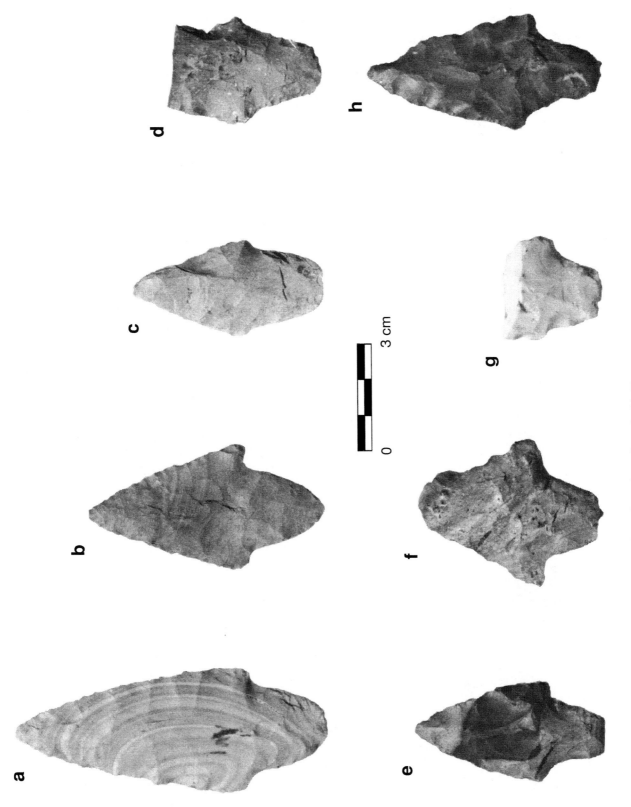

Plate 8.7. Waubesa Contracting Stemmed (a–d) and Burkett (e–h) Types

0   3 cm

Plate 8.8. Possible Adena-like Blade Portions

assemblage, comprises only 17.3 percent of the hafted biface assemblage. Moreover, exotic non-American Bottom cherts, which are relatively rare in the debitage, make up nearly 10 percent of the hafted bifaces. Nearly 65 percent of the hafted bifaces from the site are made from cherts that were not directly obtainable from the site environs. This suggests strongly that many of the hafted bifaces recovered at the site may have been imported.

The hafted biface assemblage represents the largest collection of Middle Woodland points recovered from an American Bottom site and certainly the largest and most diverse collection known from the Hill Lake phase. The point types generally typify middle to late Middle Woodland assemblages in this region. As expected, point types such as Snyders, Dickson/Waubesa, and Gibson, which typify the earlier phases of the Middle Woodland period, occur rarely at Dash Reeves (Fortier et al. 1989:557–558). Earlier types such as Norton or Mason do not occur at all. The appearance of Ansell and Steuben points would place this assemblage at the latter end of the Middle Woodland sequence in this area. The short, ovate Manker types recognized at the site may prove to be important

markers for the Hill Lake phase in this area, although larger variants are known from earlier phases as well. The general downsizing of many hafted biface types is an important but not well understood trend during the Middle Woodland period. The Dash Reeves assemblage should serve as a useful comparative framework for studying this trend.

Knives/Scrapers. Thirty-seven artifacts were placed in this category. These tools represent specialized cutting and scraping implements, characterized by utilization on one or both lateral edges, on the distal end, and sometimes on the proximal end. The distal end is usually pointed or beaked. Within this category there are five varieties. The largest group (N=20) consists of elongated bifacial knives/scrapers with utilization along both lateral edges and usually the distal end (Table 8.20; Plate 8.9; Figure 8.7a). In profile they range from flat to biconvex to plano-convex. Several of these artifacts resemble small Copena Triangular knives (Cambron 1958; Kneberg 1956) or Dupo knives (Kelly et al. 1987:319–321), although the latter have been exclusively associated with the Late Woodland period in this area.

Table 8.20. Elongated Bifacial Knives

Items	Length (cm)	Thickness (cm)	Wt (g)	Chert Type	Cross section
1	7.84	1.76	41.5	24	biconvex
2	5.59	1.61	27.1	11	plano-convex
3	2.22 ★	0.75	3.1	7	plano-convex
4	3.79 ★	0.79	6.5	13	flat
5	4.46	0.79	9.4	7	flat
6	6.21	0.96	15.0	10	biconvex
7	6.80	0.93	14.9	11	biconvex
8	6.39	1.08	13.6	3	plano-convex
9	6.34	1.08	18.5	24	plano-convex
10	4.71	1.28	13.1	24	plano-convex
11	6.01	1.40	24.9	3	irregular
12	3.46 ★	0.90	7.6	17	biconvex
13	2.32 ★	0.72	2.5	25	biconvex
14	1.97 ★	0.50	1.4	17	biconvex
15	2.20 ★	0.63	3.8	13	biconvex
16	2.71 ★	0.89	5.2	29	biconvex
17	2.13 ★	0.66	3.2	81	biconvex
18	4.29	1.06	10.2	11	biconvex
19	4.77	1.00	10.8	7	biconvex
20	2.75 ★	0.73	5.3	46	flat

*Incomplete

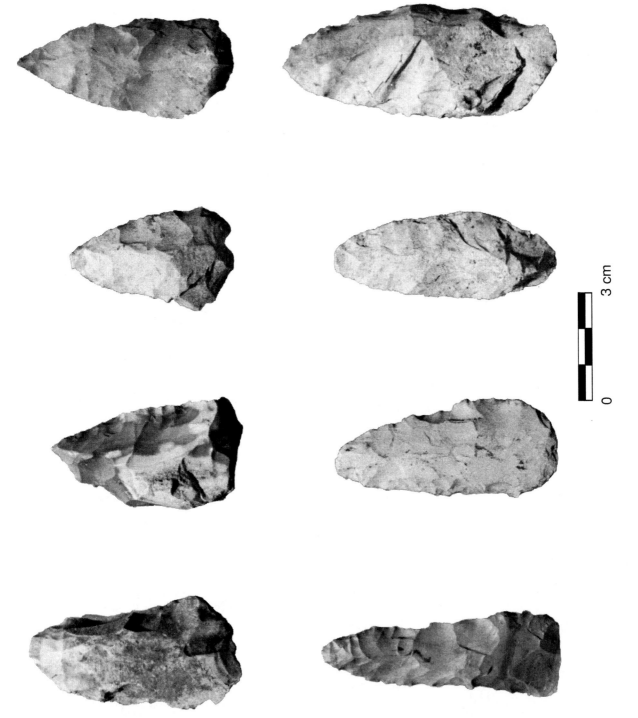

3 cm

0

Plate 8.9. Bifacial Knives

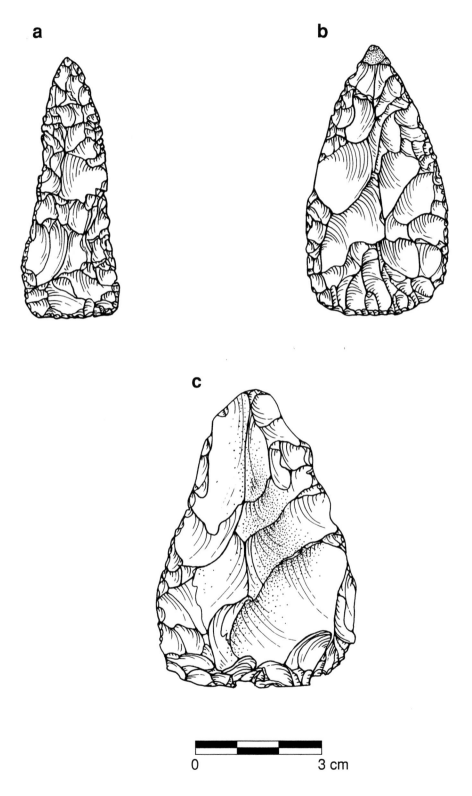

Figure 8.7. Unhafted Knives/Scrapers and Preform: a, knife; b, subtriangular knife/scraper; c, preform

The second variety (N=12) includes subtriangular bifacial knives/scrapers (Plate 8.10; Figure 8.7b). This distinctive type is identical in form to Montet-White's subtriangular preforms (1968:48–49); these ovate to triangular artifacts are not regarded here as preforms (Table 8.21). Evidence of utilization, sometimes gloss, occurs along the lateral and distal ends. These tools may have served as unhafted scrapers or knives.

The remaining varieties are represented by elongated unifacial knives/scrapers, subtriangular unifacial knives/scrapers, and three kinds of irregular-sided bifacial knives. The latter tools exhibit utilization along one lateral side and on the distal end. They are thick, irregularly flaked, and have relatively dull edges.

Preforms. There are seven preforms, weighing 413.2 g, in the collection (Plate 8.11; Figure 8.7c). These artifacts represent unfinished tools that were discarded during the process of manufacture. Although they are somewhat similar to the subtriangular bifacial knives described above, none exhibit any evidence of utilization. The dimensions are provided in Table 8.22. Considering the number of hafted bifaces and knives/scrapers at the site, it is curious that more preforms were not recovered. These artifacts, although triangular in shape, are only roughly formatted. Most have cortex. The basal width averages 5.1 cm, which is over twice the average of hafted bifaces.

Flake Scrapers. One hundred seventy-six flake scrapers, weighing 2,304.1 g, were recovered from the site. This category includes seven varieties: steeped (N=22),

end (N=5), bifacial (N=8), side (N=35), ovate (N=43), irregular (N=10), and multisided (N=53) (Figure 8.8). With the exception of the bifacial variety, all of these tools are unifacial and are distinguished from each other mainly on the basis of their utilization scar location. The varieties also are distinguished by the percentage of continuous edge use area, which ranges from 20 percent in the case of end scrapers to 100 percent in the case of ovate or steeped scrapers. These tools are distinguished from utilized flakes, which display less than 20 percent continuous edge use. Virtually all of these tools are made on large reduction flakes or, in some cases, primary or secondary decortication flakes.

The only variety that warrants further discussion is the steeped flake scraper. Steep edge retouch is a Middle Woodland phenomenon. It occurs on both flake and core tools from this period but is pronounced on several different types of flake scrapers. The best examples of steeped flake scrapers were found in a cache excavated at the nearby Go-Kart South/Truck #7 site (Fortier 1985a:255–271). The Dash Reeves scrapers are not as well made or as ovate as those found in the cache. Just over 70 percent of the steeply retouched scrapers from Dash Reeves are made from local Ste. Genevieve cherts. Those from Truck #7 are made on exotic Cobden/Dongola cherts and clearly were imported to that location. It was thought at the time of the Truck #7 excavation that this scraper type might have been a product of southern Illinois traditions, but it is clear now

Table 8.21. Subtriangular Bifacial Knives/Scrapers

Items	Length (cm)	Basal Width (cm)	Thickness (cm)	Wt (g)	Chert Type
1	9.58	4.24	1.75	60.1	24/34
2	8.13	3.64	1.08	29.0	1
3	7.08	4.32	1.72	51.3	10
4	7.59	4.35	1.29	34.2	10
5	7.16	3.58	1.85	35.6	7
6	6.88	3.75	1.13	27.6	7
7	6.10	3.56	1.98	18.9	1
8	5.64	4.01	0.77	13.9	3
9	6.81	3.89	1.05	27.4	1
10	5.32	3.39	1.98	20.0	7
11	9.86	4.09	1.04	39.5	16
12	★	★	0.90	23.7	7

★Incomplete

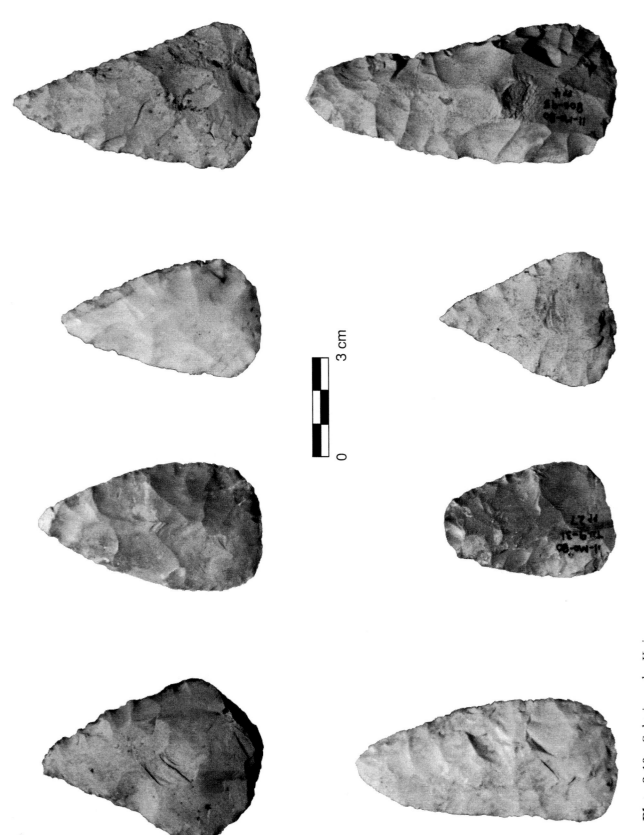

Plate 8.10. Subtriangular Knives

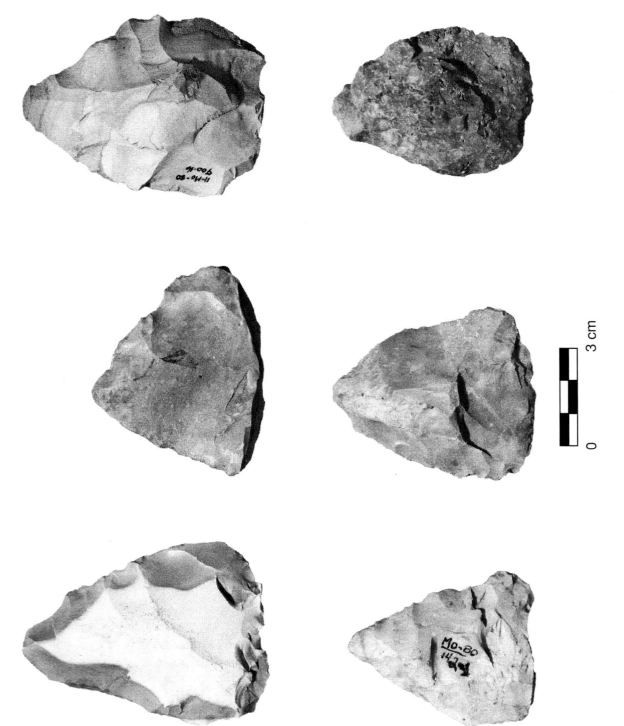

Plate 8.11. Preforms

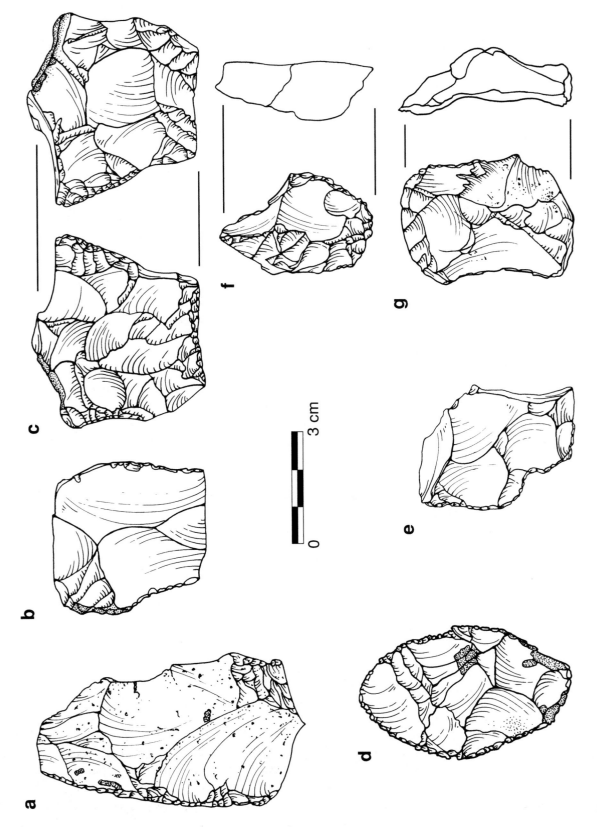

Figure 8.8. Flake Scraper Types: a, side; b, multisided; c, bifacial; d, ovate; e, irregular; f, steeped; g, end

Table 8.22. Preforms

Items	Length (cm)	Width (cm)	Thickness (cm)	Wt (g)	Chert type	Cross section
1	7.54	5.48	2.65	89.7	7	plano-convex
2	6.43	5.16	2.12	59.2	7	biconvex
3	5.66	3.95	1.96	40.2	29	plano-convex
4	5.85	4.63	1.44	39.8	10	plano-convex
5	5.60	6.38	1.95	69.6	7	irregular
6	7.74	5.40	2.10	76.6	11	biconvex
7	4.92 ★	4.38	1.75	38.1	7	irregular

★Broken

that production of this particular type was more widespread.

Flake Gravers. Forty-nine flake gravers, weighing 460.1 g, were recovered. These tools essentially represent truncated burins, with the truncation edge forming the worked area. Figure 8.9 gives examples of gravers made on flakes as well as on blades. The truncation edge often exhibits formal retouching. The bec end of the burin evidences use, usually restricted to one side. Presumably, these tools were used as multipurpose incisors or engravers. Possible uses include bone and wood engraving, ceramic decoration, bone splitting, or meat and hide working. It should be noted that the location of the burin blows on flake gravers at this site is not nearly as predictable or systematic as it is for gravers or burins made on blades. On flake gravers, this blow is often only one sided and appears almost unintentional and not well controlled. Conversely, many of the blade gravers exhibit prepared detachment notches, and burin blows on these tools were often two sided.

Flake Denticulates. Nine flake denticulates, weighing 141.7 g, were identified (Plate 8.12). These tools are characterized by a series of notches or indentations along one lateral side. Figure 8.10 shows examples of blade and flake denticulates. These tools possibly functioned as bone or wood whittlers. Their use as plant fiber shredders also has been proposed (Winters 1969:86).

Perforators. One hundred two perforators, weighing 347.1 g, were identified. Two types were recognized, one referred to simply as a flake perforator, the other as a keel-shaped perforator. Flake perforators, which number 75, are relatively flat, with an elongated, worked projection or element usually located at the distal end. Rounded ends are common, as is use wear along one or both edges. Occasionally, gloss was observed along the ends and main element. Keel-shaped

perforators, numbering 27, are made on ridged flakes with triangular cross sections. Use and sometimes retouch is observed on the highest dorsal flake ridge, usually located at one end of the flake. The flake comes to a point, which exhibits use wear. Both blade and flake perforators are illustrated in Figure 8.11. It is presumed that perforators were utilized to bore holes through hide, wood, bone, or shell, but this cannot be confirmed without microscopic use wear analysis.

Drills. There are 66 drills made on flakes, weighing 145.9 g. Three categories of flake drills were recognized: blunt end, classic, and needle (Figure 8.12). Blunt end drills comprise the largest group (N=46) and consist of flat flakes that have been purposely contracted at one end (Figure 8.13). Actually, the worked ends are usually triangular in shape, with use wear appearing on both lateral edges. The ends are rounded, appearing blunted, and often exhibit gloss. In this respect, they are unlike perforators, which have relatively sharp and pointed ends. So-called classic drills, of which there are 12, are rounded, elongated, thick flakes with use wear along the full extent of each lateral edge. The entire flake forms the use area. The end of the drill is rounded and exhibits gloss from use. The worked end appears blunted. Needle drills (N=8) are a form of microdrill made on short flake spalls (Figure 8.14). Some of these spalls actually may have come from blades, but because of their small size, this is unclear. All examples of this tool type are therefore presented here with the caveat that some may be blade tools. As the name implies, they are needle-like with use wear noticeable along the sides and on one end. The ends are pointed, although rounding from use was also observed. These tools average about 2–3 cm in length. Needle drills have not been well documented in the American Bottom. In other areas such tools have non-Middle Woodland associations, as

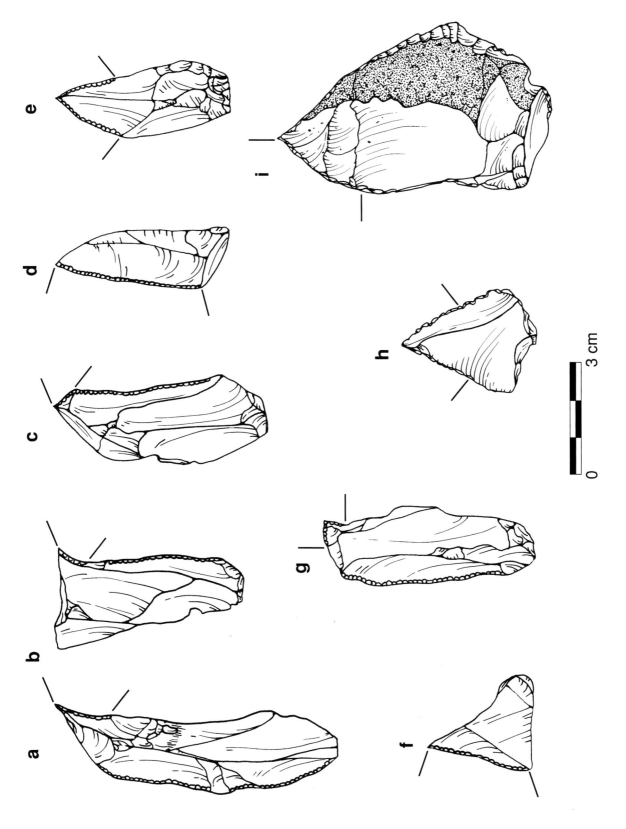

Figure 8.9. Gravers: a–g, on blades; h–i, on flakes

Plate 8.12. Flake Denticulates

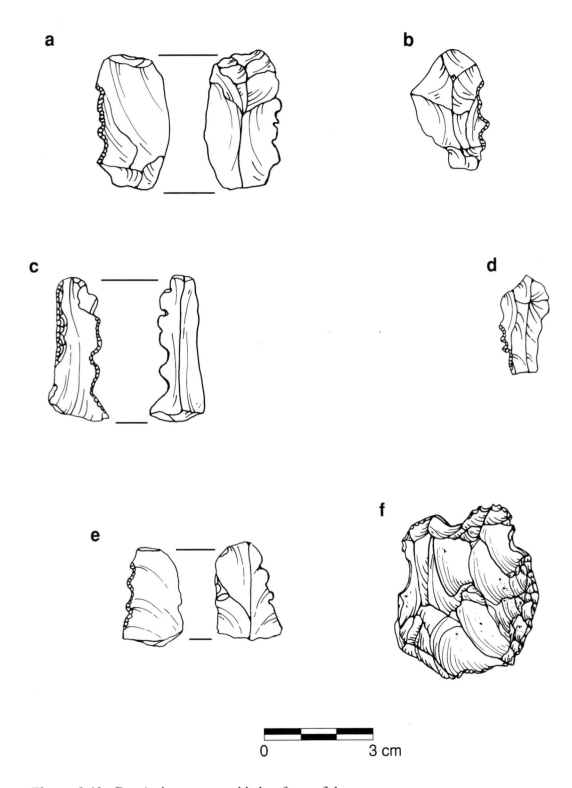

Figure 8.10. Denticulates: a–e, on blades; f, on a flake

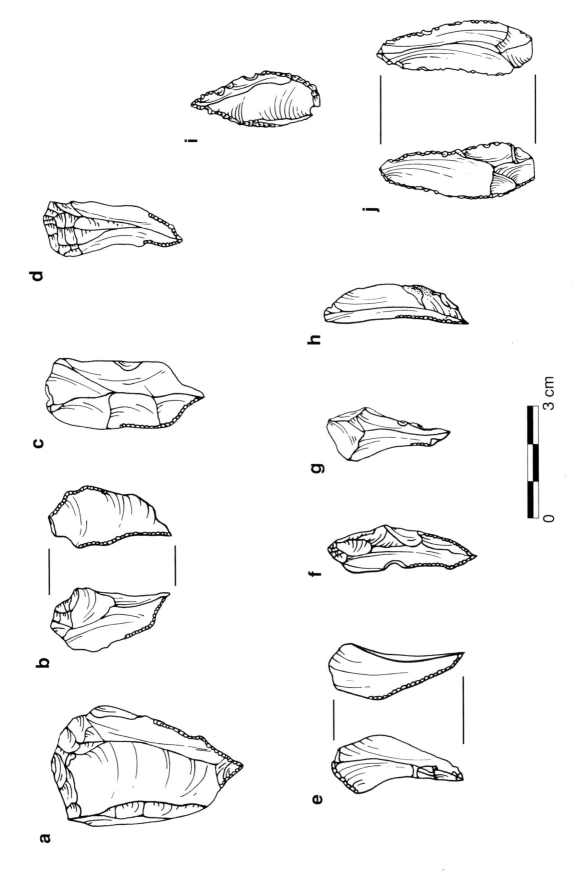

Figure 8.11. Perforators: a–d, short elements on blades; e–h, long elements on blades; i–j, on flakes

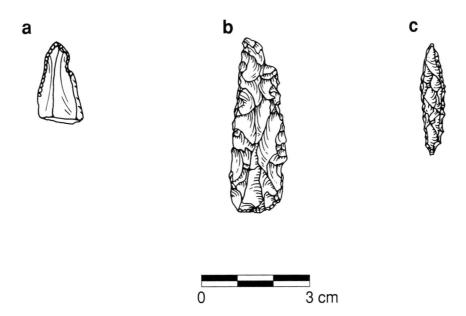

Figure 8.12. Drill Types: a, blunt end; b, classic; c, needle

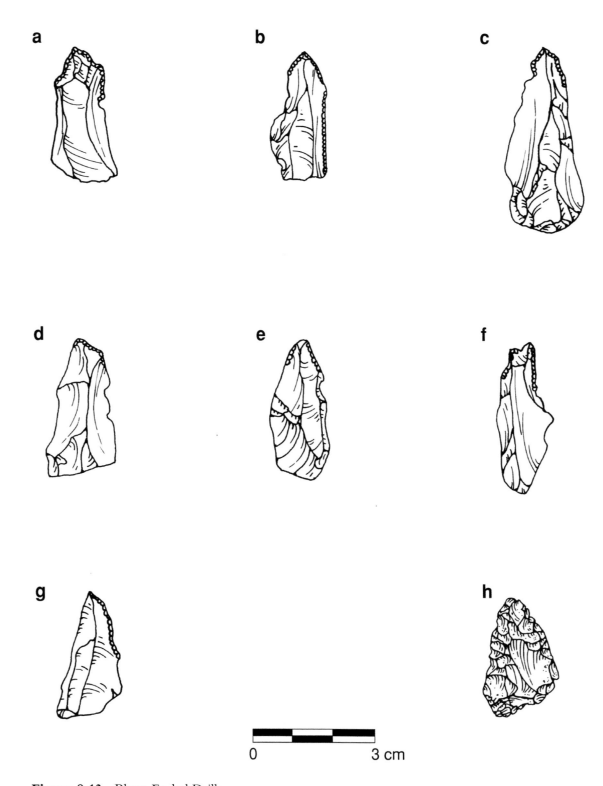

Figure 8.13. Blunt-Ended Drills

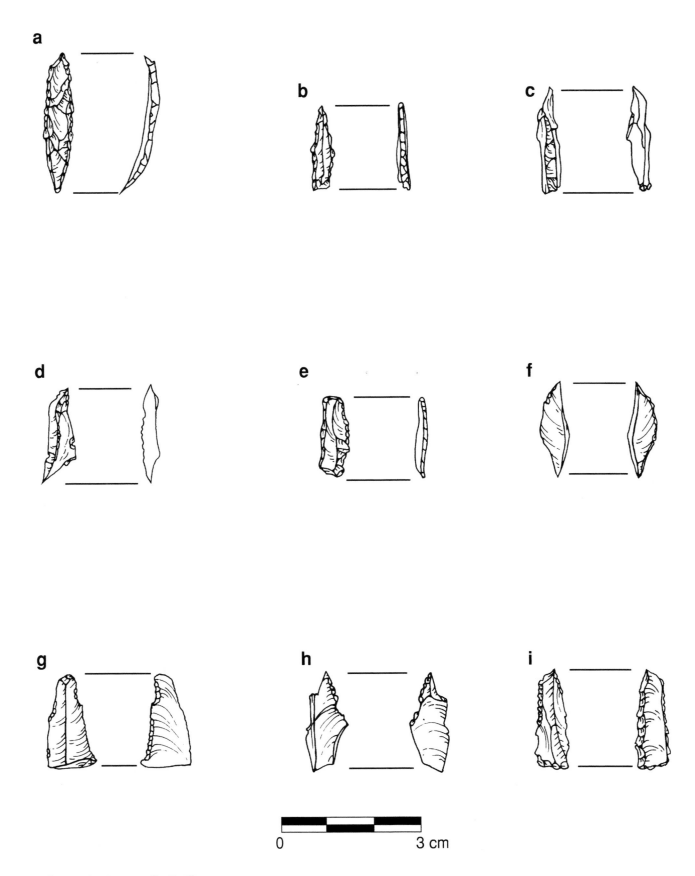

Figure 8.14. Needle Drills

for example, in the Late Archaic Poverty Point microtool industry, where they are known as perforators or simply as needles (Ford et al. 1955:141–142). There are several needle drills illustrated from the Holding site (Williams 1989:360), but they are clearly not common artifacts there nor is their function clear.

Becs or Spurs. Thirty-one becs or spurs, weighing 128.6 g, were identified (Figure 8.15). Both flake and core becs are included here since they presumably functioned in a similar manner. Two becs are made on cores, and one is made on a biface fragment; most are made on either secondary or primary decortication flakes. These tools are characterized by the occurrence of a single, small projection from the flake or core edge. Utilization is visible on the bec itself and sometimes 1–2 mm from the bec. The function of these tools is unknown, although their use as small engravers or punches is possible.

Utilized Flakes. The assemblage contains 1,534 utilized flakes, weighing 4,785 g. These informal tools are characterized by the presence of use wear or retouch on less than 20 percent of the flake edge. Use wear is discontinuous and often occurs in several places. Presumably, these artifacts represent expedient cutting tools with a short use life. The expedient nature of these tools is highlighted by the fact that they occur on a wide variety of chert types and production-stage debris. About 4 percent of the utilized flakes are exotic cherts such as Mill Creek, Cobden/Dongola, and Grimes Hill. Almost 40 percent are red Ste. Genevieve cherts. Just over 15 percent of the utilized flakes are white Burlington cherts.

Polished Flakes. Polished flakes number 326 and weigh 333.4 g. They are tool fragments produced by maintenance or use activities. The polish occurs as a result of digging or woodworking activities. In all probability the flakes come from hoes, adzes, gouges, or wedges; complete examples of these tools from the site exhibit gloss. Of the total polished flakes, 107 (32.8 percent) are Mill Creek chert. Nearly 20 percent are Burlington cherts, and 17 percent are local Salem cherts. Exotic cherts other that Mill Creek—especially Kaolin chert—comprise 4 percent of the polished flakes. Red Ste. Genevieve cherts make up only 8.3 percent of these tool fragments. The occurrence of so many Mill Creek polished flakes is puzzling, particularly since there are so few tools of this material at this site. Moreover, Mill Creek hoes have never been found in the American

Bottom on Middle Woodland sites, although they occur on Middle Woodland sites in southern Illinois. The most obvious possibility is that these flakes may not be Middle Woodland artifacts but the result of cultivation activities on Middle Woodland sites during the late Emergent Mississippian and Mississippian periods (Dale McElrath, personal communication 1998). Although this is certainly a possibility, it is argued here that such flakes are most likely associated with the Middle Woodland occupation. Of the 107 polished Mill Creek flakes at Dash Reeves, only 17 come from surface contexts. Ninety-seven flakes were found in feature or creek midden contexts. In fact, only two flakes came from non-creek midden contexts. Most were found in a very restricted area of the main creek midden. Such a restricted distribution is not indicative of generalized postoccupational cultivation but of selective dumping during the Middle Woodland occupation. It should be pointed out by way of comparison that the Holding site produced 101 polished Mill Creek flakes, 34 of which actually came from feature contexts (Williams 1989:373). Three Mill Creek excavating tool fragments also were recovered from that site. Middle Woodland hoes and polished hoe flakes have also been reported at Illinois River valley sites (Cantwell 1980; Farnsworth and Koski 1985; Wiant and McGimsey 1986), although normally those artifacts are not made of Mill Creek chert. The nature of the tools represented by the Dash Reeves Mill Creek polished flakes is unknown. In all probability these tools were not hoes but were smaller adze-like, gouge, or wedge implements used in woodworking. There are several Mill Creek gouge and wedge-like tools and tool fragments from the site, but only one, a wedge fragment recovered from the surface, exhibits any silica gloss.

Nonblade Core Tools

A wide range of tool types falls under this heading, including core scrapers, gouges, wedges, hammerstones, celts/hoes, adzes, chisels, gravers, perforators, denticulates, and miscellaneous edge tools. There are also a number of formal varieties within many of these general categories. These are discussed in the following sections.

Core Scrapers. There are 77 core scrapers, weighing 4,314.5 g, from the site. These are subdivided into six varieties: large, ovate disk scrapers (N=12), humpback

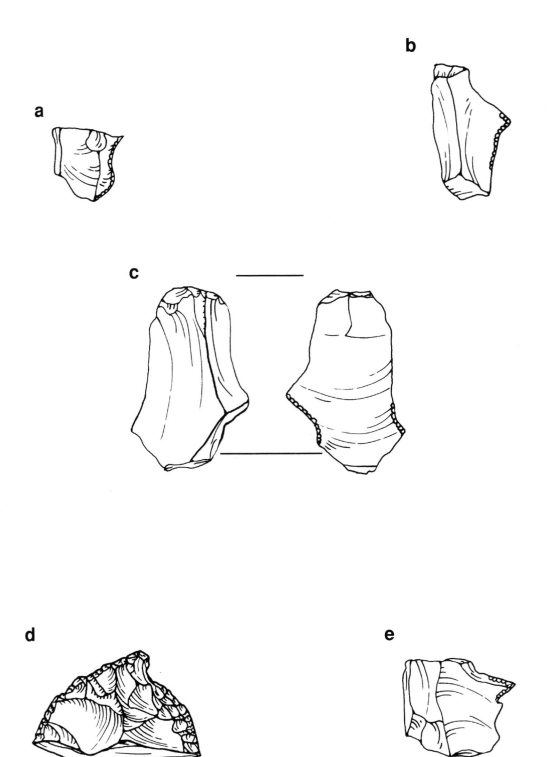

Figure 8.15. Becs/Spurs

scrapers (N=5), large side scrapers (N=8), large steeply retouched scrapers (N=20), small ovate disk scrapers (N=18), and large irregular core scrapers (N=14) (Figure 8.16). In order to qualify for this category, tools must exhibit a continuously retouched or utilized edge exceeding 20 percent of the total edge. Core tools with less than 20 percent use area were placed in the core edge tool category.

Large and small ovate disk scrapers are commonly associated with the Middle Woodland period in this area (Plates 8.13 and 8.14). These types constituted the majority of scrapers in the Go-Kart South/Truck #7 site cache (Fortier 1985a:255–271), although those scrapers were generally smaller and better made than the Dash Reeves examples. The Dash Reeves scrapers exhibit 70–100 percent edge use and have distinctive ovate forms, although not all of the tools of this variety are perfectly symmetrical. They are biconvex, plano-convex, or flat in cross section. Many exhibit gloss on one or the other side but not along the use edge. The mean length and width measurements of the larger scrapers are 6.37 cm and 5.13 cm, respectively. The smaller ovate disk scrapers are more symmetrical than the larger disk scrapers but are distinguished from the latter primarily on the basis of size. Their mean length and width measurements are 4.72 cm and 4.28 cm, respectively. Both sizes were made exclusively on local cherts, including red Ste. Genevieve varieties.

Humpback core scrapers are plano-convex cores with use wear covering 50–100 percent of the core edge (Plate 8.14). They tend to be elongate with evidence of heavy use on one or both ends. These scrapers are common at both Early and Middle Woodland sites in this area (Emerson et al. 1983:80–84) and at sites in the Illinois River valley (Cantwell 1980; Struever 1964), where they are called "Havana scrapers."

Eight scrapers were designated core side scrapers. These tools are characterized by a single, continuously worked lateral edge. In plan they are mostly irregular and sometimes curved or crescent shaped. They can either be large or small.

Steeply retouched core scrapers come in a variety of shapes and sizes but have in common a worked edge that is steeply retouched. They are similar to the steeply retouched flake scrapers described earlier. The function of steeply retouching the edge of a core tool was clearly to produce a sharper edge, but why this was not undertaken on all core scrapers is unclear.

The final category of core scraper consists of irregularly retouched or utilized edge tools. In these cases several areas of use are observed. These areas often follow the usable contours of a core. Such tools were probably expedient in nature and had short use lives. These irregular cores resemble core edge tools except that they are much larger and have multiple use areas.

Gouges. Thirty-six gouges, weighing 762.5 g, were recovered. Two varieties of gouges are recognized: thin, narrow-bit (N=17), and thick, broad-bit (N=19) artifacts (Plate 8.15). Both varieties are characterized by a beveled bit, which is ovate or spatulate in plan (Figure 8.17). When intact, the butt end tends to be squared or irregular. Silica gloss can occur on both varieties and is normally located on the convex side of the artifact. The thin, narrow gouges are generally flat in cross section, while the thicker, broader gouges are mostly plano-convex or biconvex in profile. The two varieties are distinguished on the basis of blade thickness and bit width. Blade thickness of thin gouges averages 0.94 cm and of thick gouges, 1.49 cm. Bit widths average 3.53 cm for thin, narrow gouges and 4.49 cm for thick, broad gouges. Presumably, these artifacts functioned as woodworking tools, but some could have been used as gardening tools. Relatively high-quality Burlington cherts, which are not that common at Dash Reeves, were preferred for both thin, narrow gouges (50 percent) and thick, broad gouges (41 percent). Other cherts utilized, in order of frequency, are coarse local Salem, Ste. Genevieve (Salem) creamy, and Ste. Genevieve red.

Wedges and Pièces Esquillées. Thirty-six tools, weighing 969.1 g, were placed in this category (Figure 8.17c–e). Wedges are subdivided into broad- and narrow-bit varieties. These tools are characterized by bipolar utilization, the bit end exhibiting retouch and utilization scars and the butt end evidencing battering. The narrow-bit specimens (N=14) have beveled, gouge-like ends, with usually no more than 3 cm of use area. These artifacts tend to be elongate with slightly curved to straight bit ends. The broad-bitted specimens (N=6) also have beveled bits, but the use area often exceeds 4–5 cm. Bit ends are straight, spatulate, or irregular. These artifacts tend to be made on coarse local Salem cherts and often have primary cortex covering 50 percent or more of the surface. Both wedge types are either biconvex or plano-convex in profile. Several of these artifacts have silica gloss on their convex sides.

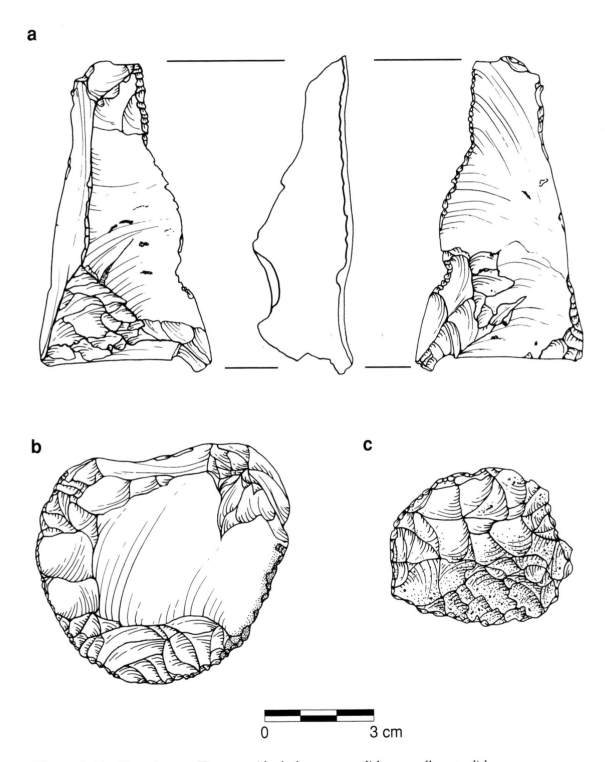

Figure 8.16. Core Scraper Types: a, side; b, large ovate disk; c, small ovate disk

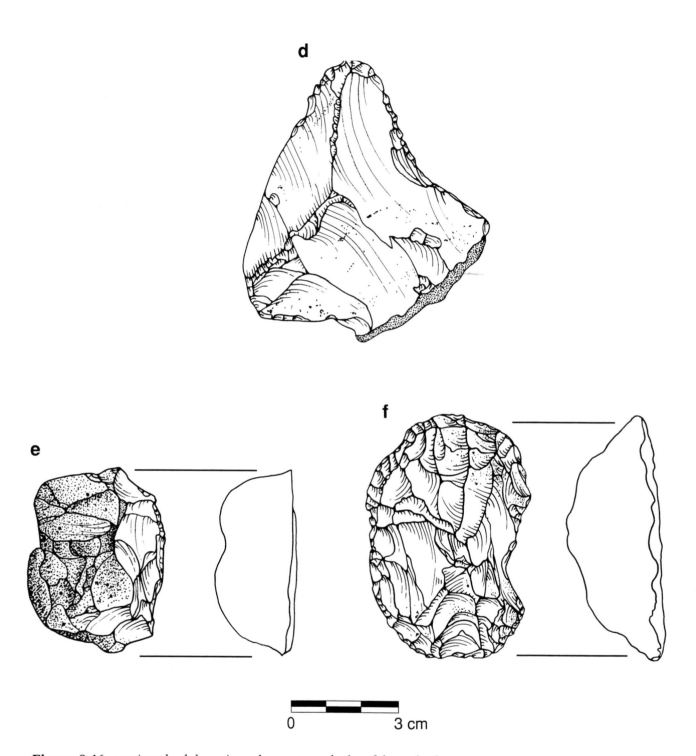

Figure 8.16. continued, d, large irregular; e, steeped edge; f, humpback

Plate 8.13. Large Disk Core Scrapers

Plate 8.14. Core Scrapers: upper, humpback variety; lower, small disk variety

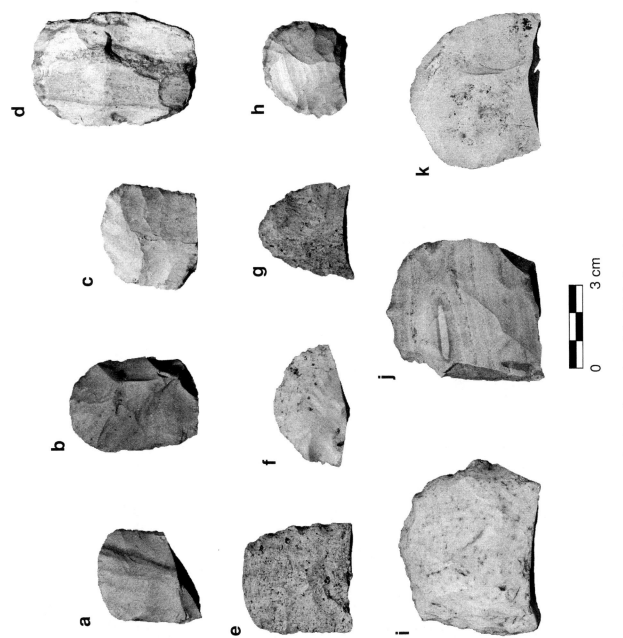

Plate 8.15. Chert Gouges: a–h, thin, flat variety; i–k, thick, broad variety

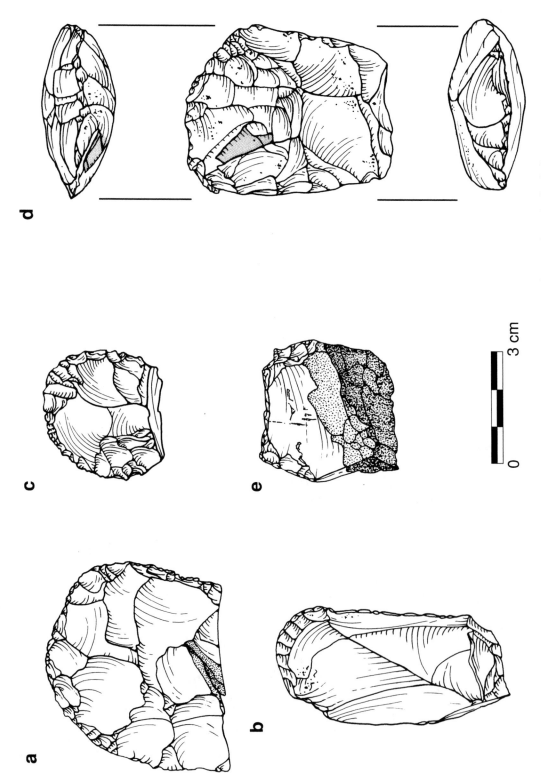

Figure 8.17. Gouges and Wedges: a, thick–bit gouge; b, thin–bit gouge; c, narrow–bit wedge; d, thick–bit wedge; e, *pièce esquillée*

Pièces esquillées (N=16) probably functioned as wedges but have slightly different formal traits. These artifacts are small (2–3 cm in diameter), square, and thick and exhibit battering or use wear on two to four sides. Some of the tools do not display battering and may not have functioned as wedges. It is generally assumed that these tools were used to split bone or wood.

Hammerstones. Nineteen chert hammerstones, weighing 2,181.4 g, were recovered from the site. These are round, ovate, or elongate chert cores exhibiting systematic pecking on one or more surfaces. Cortical areas are common, and some of the artifacts appear to represent small ball cherts. While the majority could not be identified as to chert type, there are several Ste. Genevieve red and two Burlington hammerstones. It is assumed that most chert hammerstones were utilized as hard-hammer percussion tools to make other artifacts, but some may have functioned as mauls or manos for plant-processing activities.

Chert Hoes. Three chert hoes, weighing 832.9 g, were identified (Plate 8.16). Two are complete; the third lacks both a bit and butt end. The two complete hoes have silica gloss over the bit ends, while the broken artifact lacks gloss. None of the hoes show any evidence of hafting, although in all probability such implements would have been hafted. The best-made hoe was recovered from Feature 29, the cache pit, and is made of high-quality Burlington chert (Type 1). It is 17.1 cm long, 7.94 cm wide near the bit, and 2.73 cm thick. It weighs 425.2 g. A thick silica gloss covers 25–40 percent of the worked end. The extreme end of the bit is rounded from use. It is plano-convex in profile.

The second complete hoe was found on the surface less than 10 m from pit Feature 29 (Figure 8.18). It is made of local tan Salem chert and weighs 303.6 g. It is 14.5 cm long, 7.3 cm wide at the bit, and 2.92 cm thick. It is plano-convex in profile, and silica gloss covers approximately 35 percent of the bit end on both sides. The bit end is also rounded from use, but several end flakes are missing, either from use or plow damage.

The broken hoe is made of poorer-quality Burlington chert. The hoe midsection shows evidence of heat alteration and heat cracking at one end and may have broken as a result of coming into contact with fire. The midsection measures 7.14 cm in length, 5.79 cm in width, and is 2.54 cm thick. It weighs 104.1 g. It is biconvex in profile. It was found on the surface approximately 50 m north of the other two hoes.

Hoes are not commonly found on Middle Woodland sites in this area, although polished excavating tools were found at Holding (Williams 1989:368–372) and a possible hoe/adze was found at the Truck #7 site (Fortier 1985a:248–249). At this time, the Dash Reeves examples are the best evidence for Middle Woodland hoe use in the area. As pointed out earlier, small Mill Creek hoes occur at southern Illinois sites dating to this period, and there is no reason to assume they are absent in the American Bottom, particularly at sites occupied when horticulture was emerging as an important subsistence pursuit.

Adzes. Four adzes, weighing 333.2 g, were identified. These tools are elongated to subtriangular-shaped, bifacial implements similar in most respects to hoes, but shorter and smaller and lacking gloss (Figure 8.19). They have relatively narrow bits with evidence of utilization on only one side. In profile they are plano-convex. Their length measurements range from 7.23 cm to 10.97 cm. Maximum widths, which range from 4.14 cm to 5.17 cm, always occur at the butt end. The absence of gloss on these artifacts is somewhat puzzling, since these tools are generally presumed to be woodworking implements. Similar artifacts were recovered from the Holding site (Williams 1989:368–369) and from other Middle Woodland contexts in Illinois (Stafford and Sant 1985:283–285), but in those cases gloss was observed. Perhaps the Dash Reeves adzes served other functions, such as bone shaving or even hide scraping. All of the Dash Reeves adzes are made of coarse local cherts.

Chisels. Five core chisels, weighing 315 g, were recovered. A sixth tool, weighing 198.8 g, is a combination chisel and denticulate and is regarded separately (Figure 8.20). Chisels are elongated artifacts made on blocky, tabular cores. The worked ends are tapered and usually very narrow, except in one case, where the worked end is nearly 10 cm in length. Use area normally does not exceed 15 percent. Utilization occurs on only one side. In profile these artifacts are triangular to blocky. No gloss was observed. Given that the use area is relatively restricted and very little if any secondary preparation was undertaken prior to use, these tools appear to represent an expedient class of woodworking artifacts.

Core Edge Tools and Fragments. There are 28 core edge tools, weighing 990.7 g, and 130 core edge tool fragments, weighing 2,217.6 g (Figure 8.21a). Core

Plate 8.16. Chert Hoes; upper, from Feature 29 cache pit; lower, from BPZ surface

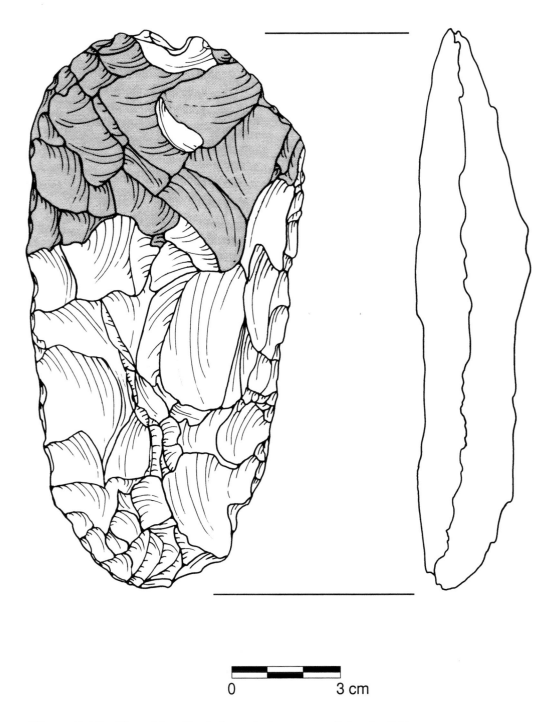

0   3 cm

Figure 8.18. Chert Hoe (shaded area is the extent of gloss/polish)

a

b

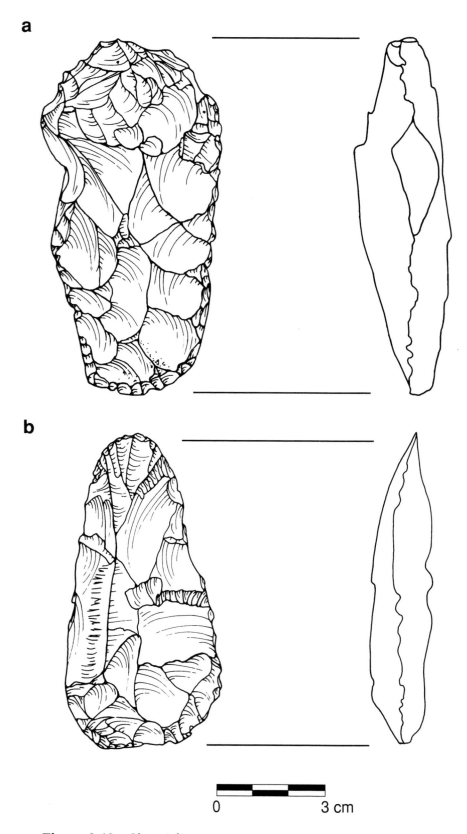

0   3 cm

Figure 8.19. Chert Adzes

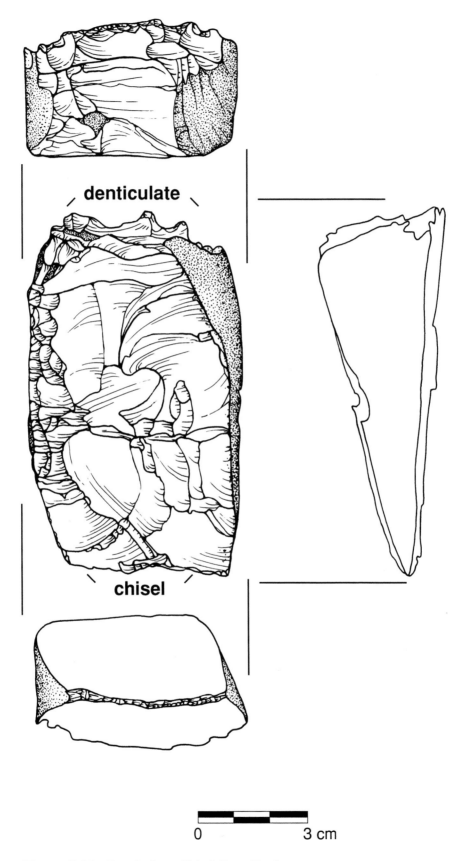

denticulate

chisel

0   3 cm

Figure 8.20. Denticulate-Chisel Core Tool

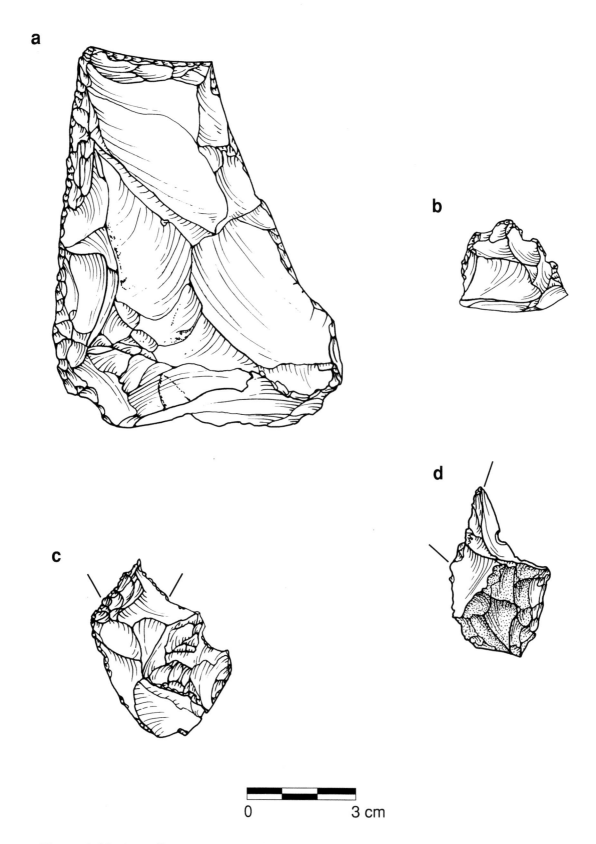

Figure 8.21. Miscellaneous Core Tool Types: a, edge tool; b, denticulate; c, graver; d, perforator

edge tools are defined as informal scraping, cleaving, and cutting implements exhibiting a worked edge area that ranges from 10 to 90 percent of the artifact. These artifacts are somewhat similar to the core scrapers described above except that their overall shape is less predictable and less formalized. During analysis, this tool category was subdivided into bifacial (N=5), straight-sided (N=2), curved to irregular-sided (N=4), flanged or end curved (N=7), and steeped (N=5) varieties. In addition, there are five core edge tools that are simply so much larger than the general core edge tool population that they were separated out. Core edge tool fragments represent portions of the various tool varieties mentioned above. Often, wear is present on less than 10 percent of the potential edge. Edge tools probably served a variety of functions including bone, wood, and hide working, as well as skinning and meat cutting. These tools occur on a wide variety of chert types but most commonly on local Ste. Genevieve red and Old Blue cherts.

Denticulates. Twenty-four core denticulates were recovered. They weigh 736.6 g. Fifteen of these are made of Ste. Genevieve red chert, five are Old Blue chert, and the remaining four are local Salem or St. Louis cherts (Figure 8.21b). These tools are characterized by a serrated edge produced by intentional notching. Utilization scars are visible within the notched areas as well as on the intervening spurs. As with their counterpart flake denticulates, the presumed function of these tools was for shredding plant or animal materials.

Gravers. Eighteen core gravers, weighing 513.4 g, were identified. All of the core gravers are made on Ste. Genevieve cherts (Types 7, 8, 11, and 29). Typically, these artifacts exhibit a triangular and peaked area of utilization (Figure 8.21c). Unlike on their flake counterparts, the worked area does not appear to have been produced intentionally by a classic burin blow, although evidence of an informal truncation blow is often present. Utilization scars and sometimes intentional retouch appear along the truncation scar up to the bec or point. These tools appear to represent precision cutting tools or engravers, possibly for bone splitting. It is impossible to determine whether these tools functioned in the same manner as flake gravers.

Perforators. There are 20 core perforators, weighing 218.6 g. These are similar in shape to flake perforators except that they are larger (Figure 8.21d). Characteristically, these tools have long utilized elements with wear along the lateral edges and tip of the element. All except four are made from Ste. Genevieve red or Old Blue cherts, a selection pattern similar to that observed for core gravers and denticulates. As with flake perforators, it is assumed that the primary function of these artifacts was to drill holes in hide or possibly bone or wood.

Blade Tools

There are 2,717 blades in the Dash Reeves lithic assemblage, of which 552 (20.3 percent) exhibit signs of utilization. It is entirely possible that under more intense microscopic examination more blades would evidence modification. On the other hand, some expedient uses might not have resulted in any use wear evidence at all. At the outset it was apparent that there was a wide range of blade tool forms in the assemblage, many of which mimicked nonblade tool categories. The following blade tool categories were recognized: drills, microdrills, end scrapers, side scrapers/knives, perforators, gravers, denticulates, spurs or becs, keel scrapers, expedient cutters, and hafted or notched cutters/scrapers. The frequency distribution of these tools is presented in Table 8.23. Given the variety of formal types, it is clear that blade tools at Dash Reeves served many functions,

Table 8.23. Formal Blade Tool Categories

	N	% by N	Comments
Expedient cutting tools	231	43.4	Use wear and/or retouch on one or more isolated lateral edges
Side scrapers	87	16.3	Continuous retouch on one lateral edge
Notched/hafted cutting tools	78	14.7	One or two opposed notches on lateral edge
Gravers	33	6.2	Use/retouch along burin truncation surface
Keel Scrapers/cutters	29	5.4	Use along one lateral edge of trapezoidal blade
Perforators	26	4.9	Use on one or both distal end edges, made on blades with partial burin blow at distal end
End Scrapers	21	3.9	Use/retouch on distal end of blade
Drills	15	2.8	Use on both lateral edges with tapered distal end
Denticulates	5	0.9	Series of utilized notched areas along one lateral edge
Spurs (bec)	5	0.9	Peaked spur on lateral edge with utilization above or below spur
Micro-drills/needles	2	0.4	Narrow, needle-like blade with utilization on both lateral edges
Total	532		

significantly, in most cases, duplicating many of the same functions performed by nonblade tools.

The most common blade tools (N=231; 43.4 percent) are expedient cutters/scrapers (Figure 8.22). These tools are essentially equivalent to utilized flakes and are characterized by the occurrence of edge wear or retouch on one or more isolated areas along the lateral edge of the blade. Usually, use is restricted to less than 10 percent of the blade. Like utilized flakes, these tools probably had short use lives.

Blade side scrapers/knives (N=87; 16.3 percent) are defined by the presence of continuous retouch along one lateral side (Figure 8.23). Use wear ranges from 25 to 50 percent of the edge area. In about 25 percent of these artifacts, use wear covers the entire lateral edge. These tools probably served as knives, but scraping functions cannot be discounted. Gloss and edge rounding were observed on about 10 percent of these artifacts.

Gravers made on blades are characterized by use/retouch along a burin truncation scar (see Figure 8.9). The end of the artifact is triangular in shape, and the very end exhibits use wear. A single truncation blow was made obliquely to the orientation of the arrises. Burinated gravers are typical artifacts in most blade industries, but these Middle Woodland tools are distinctive because of the single burin blow. It is believed that a small notch was made along the lateral side of the blade to prepare for the blow. This allowed for a well-controlled burin blow.

There are 78 blades in the Dash Reeves collection that have one or more notches (Figures 8.24 and 8.25). Some of these blades have opposing notches and appear to represent hafting elements rather than burin-blow preparations. Some single-notched blades also exhibit use or retouch, and it is not clear whether these tools were hafted or were in the process of being modified into burinated gravers. For this reason, all notched blades were separated out as a group rather than being placed in specific tool categories. They make up 14.7 percent of the modified blade assemblage. It is assumed that blade gravers functioned as microengraving or cutting tools.

There are 29 keel scrapers/cutters (5.4 percent of the assemblage). These are larger blades with triangular cross sections and continuous use wear along one lateral edge (Figure 8.26). They are similar to side scrapers/knives except that they are not made on flat blades. These tools probably functioned as knives or scrapers.

Blade end scrapers number 21 (3.9 percent) and are characterized by use wear or retouch on the distal end (Figure 8.27). One tool exhibits retouch on both the proximal and distal ends (Figure 8.27g). The ends are often intentionally curved. The function of such tools is unknown. The area of use is so small that the activity must have been very controlled and restricted. Bone or wood whittling or planing, or plant preparation, are possible functions.

Twenty-six blade perforators (4.9 percent) were recovered (see Figure 8.11). Like gravers, these tools were formed on blades after a burin blow was struck, usually near the distal end of the blade. The burin blow only extended across half of the blade width or less. Occasionally, multiple blows from opposite sides are apparent, producing the perforator element. Use wear and, sometimes, retouch were located on the elongated element, often on only one side, extending from the distal end. These delicate tools, like their nonblade counterparts, were apparently used to make small holes, perhaps in clothing, but possibly in shell or beads.

There are 15 drills (2.8 percent) made on blades and two microneedle drills (0.4 percent). The microneedle drills are made on extremely narrow and small blade spalls, with utilization occurring along both lateral edges (see Figure 8.14). These are probably the smallest and most delicate tools in the Dash Reeves assemblage and are unique to this time period. The other blade drills have tapered distal ends with utilization along both lateral sides. The end elements are broader than on perforators. These tools probably functioned in the same manner as the blade perforators, although their use was probably less controlled and would have produced a broader hole.

Five blade denticulates (0.9 percent) were identified. These tools, like their nonblade counterparts, are characterized by a series of small indentations along one lateral edge. Use wear is located both in and around the indentations. They were probably used to shred either plant or animal materials.

The final blade tool category consists of spurs or becs. There are five (0.9 percent). They are characterized by a single, small projection from the lateral edge of the blade. Use wear is located on the bec and sometimes around it. These tools probably represent some kind of microperforator or perhaps engraver.

A summary of the quantitative attributes of all modified blades is presented in Table 8.24. These data

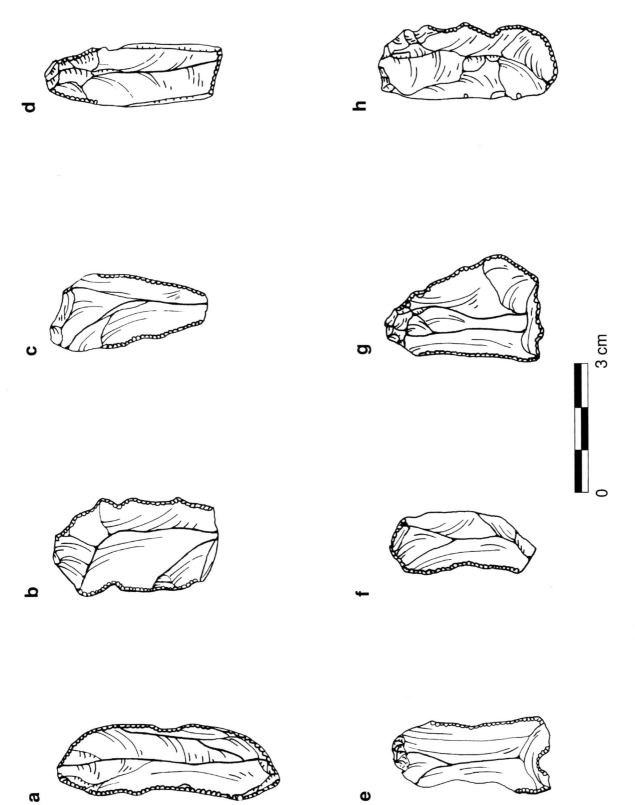

Figure 8.22. Expedient Blade Cutter/Scrapers

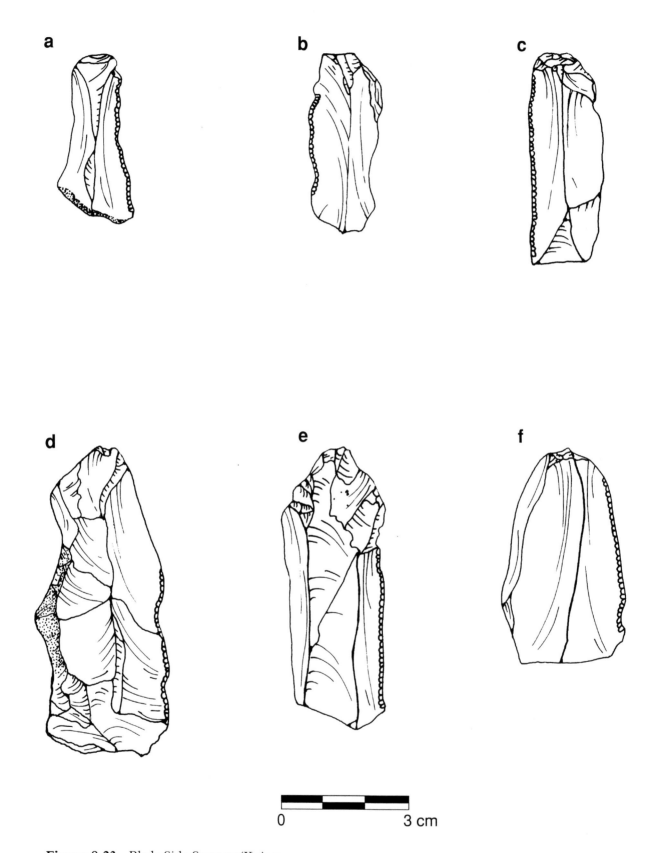

Figure 8.23. Blade Side Scrapers/Knives

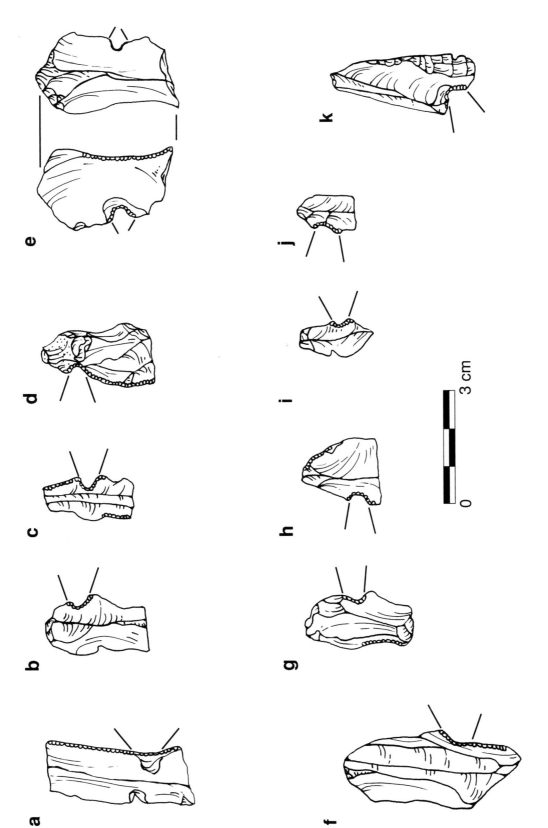

Figure 8.24. Unilaterally Notched Blades

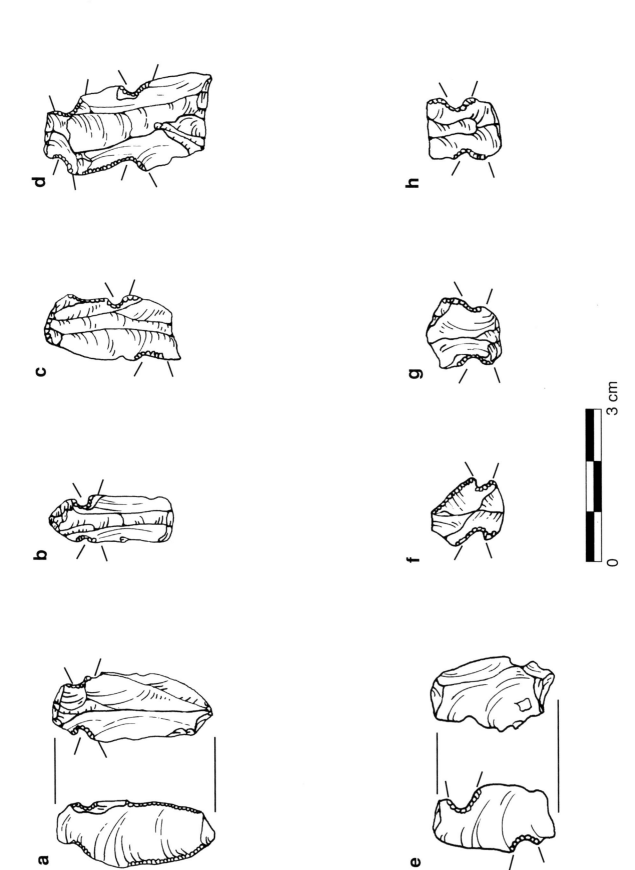

Figure 8.25. Bilaterally Notched Blades

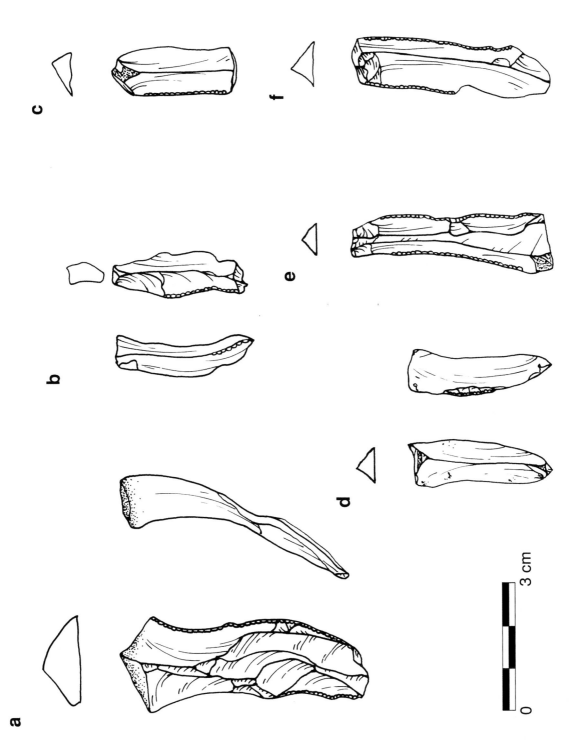

Figure 8.26. Blade Keel Scrapers/Cutters

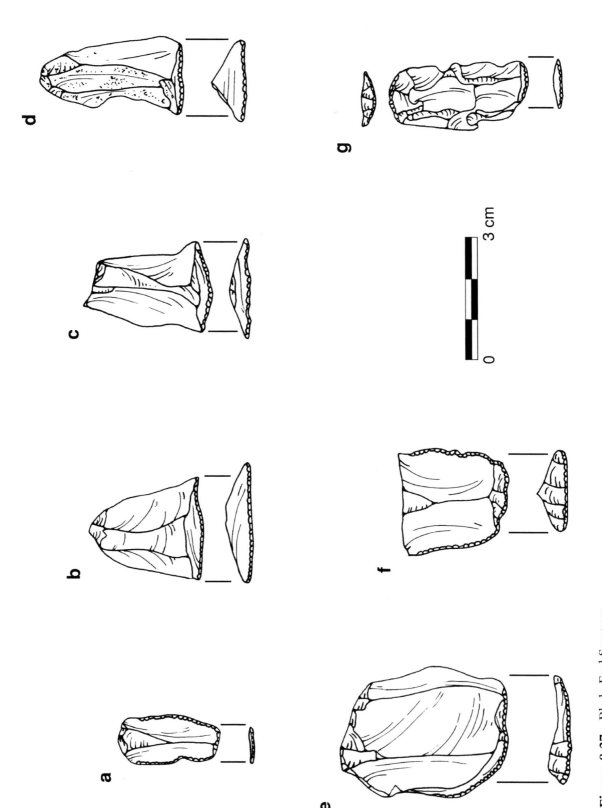

Figure 8.27. Blade End Scrapers

Table 8.24. Modified Blade Quantitative Attributes

	Cases	Max.	Min.	Mean	SD
Blade length (cm)	532	8.21	0.87	2.94	1.08
Blade width (cm)	532	3.20	0.48	1.49	0.44
Blade thickness (cm)	532	1.57	0.12	0.38	0.16
Weight (g)	532	34.90	0.10	2.58	2.79
Arris count	527	4.00	0.00	1.43	0.60
Platform angle (degree)	356	120.00	52.00	83.50	7.70
Platform width (cm)	360	1.46	0.03	0.21	0.17
Platform length (cm)	353	2.25	0.11	0.57	0.32
Blade curvature index	376	1.06	0.00	0.17	0.16
Max. width of arris	524	1.90	0.26	0.88	0.30
Min. width of arris	524	1.60	0.08	0.55	0.25
Intermediate arris width (1)	199	1.09	0.16	0.53	0.17
Intermediate arris width (2)	23	1.11	0.19	0.49	0.20
Max. length of arris	523	7.54	0.46	2.52	0.99
Min. length of arris	198	4.33	0.42	1.98	0.78
Intermediate length of arris (1)	25	4.10	0.75	2.12	0.97
Intermediate length of arris (2)	2	2.76	1.14	1.95	1.15
Blade length/width ratio	532	5.10	0.55	2.07	0.77
Blade thickness/width ratio	532	0.97	0.11	0.26	0.10

should be compared with the unmodified blade data provided in Table 8.7. The question raised here is whether certain blades were selected out from a general population of blades for tool use. A comparison of attributes suggests that this might have been the case. Blades used for tools tend to be longer, wider, thinner, and weigh more than their unmodified counterparts. They also tend to have broader and longer platforms, broader and longer arrises, and a shorter length/width ratio. What this suggests is that the first blades taken from cores, which would have been longer and broader and would have had larger platforms than subsequent blades, had a higher probability of becoming tools. Of course this does not mean that later, smaller blades were ignored as potential tools, particularly since microtools made on small blades occur in the Dash Reeves assemblage. It is not clear why modified and unmodified blades have nearly identical mean platform angles and similar platform angle ranges. In the scenario presented above, one would expect slightly more acutely angled unmodified blades since, in theory, platform angle would have decreased as the core was expended. This, however, may be a population problem, in the sense that a great many more blades were produced early in the sequence, which would naturally skew the platform angle means toward those on more steeply angled

blades. The hypothesis proposed by Webb (1982:52) that true blade tools in the Poverty Point assemblage were only those that were unaltered does not seem to apply to the Dash Reeves assemblage.

Modified and unmodified blade lengths appear to be inversely correlated to chert type (Figure 8.28). Modified blades of local cherts, such as Ste. Genevieve red and Old Blue, are, on the average, longer than unmodified blades of the same materials. The reverse is true for nonlocal cherts such as Cobden/Dongola or the higher-quality Burlington cherts, where unmodified blades are longer than their modified counterparts. This difference is probably due to the fact that blades made on less abundant nonlocal and higher-quality cherts tended to be conserved and reutilized over a longer period of time.

In terms of qualitative traits, there are a number of similarities between modified and unmodified blades. For example, there are no significant differences in chert type selection, with Ste. Genevieve red chert being the most popular for both modified (54.3 percent) and unmodified (50.7 percent) blades. Burlington cherts were utilized 11.7 percent of the time for unmodified blades and 15.8 percent for utilized blades. Exotic cherts such as Mill Creek, Kaolin, Mansker, Cobden/Dongola, Blair, and Grimes Hill together comprise 4.3 percent of

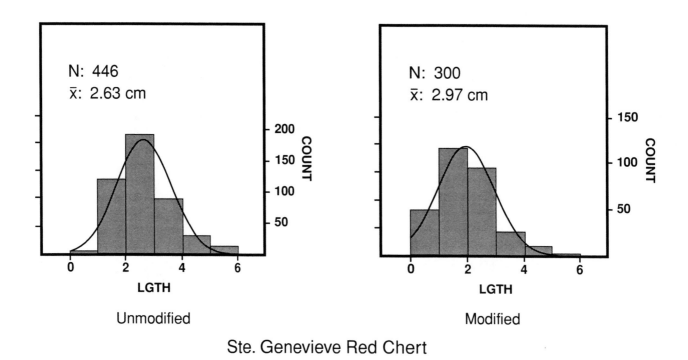

Ste. Genevieve Red Chert

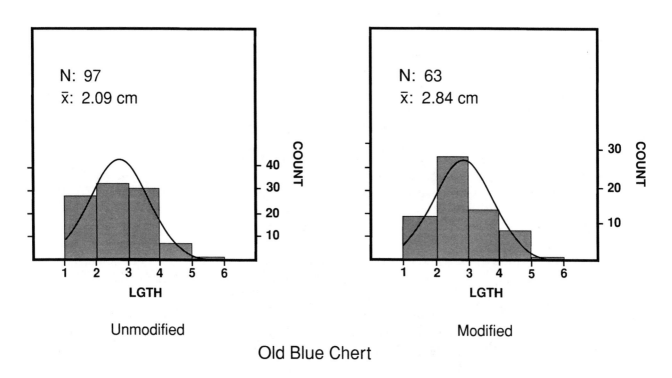

Old Blue Chert

Figure 8.28. Unmodified and Modified Blade Length (cm) Distribution by Chert Type

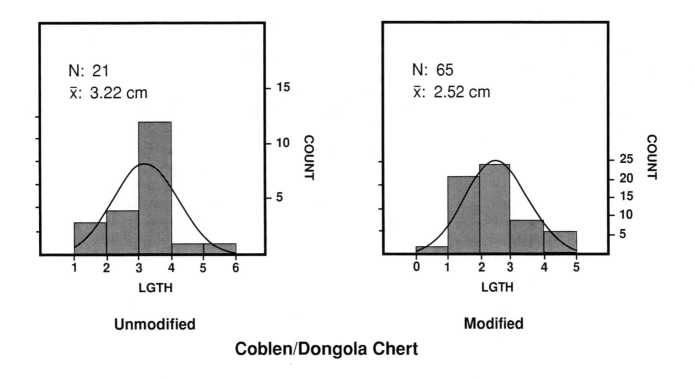

Coblen/Dongola Chert

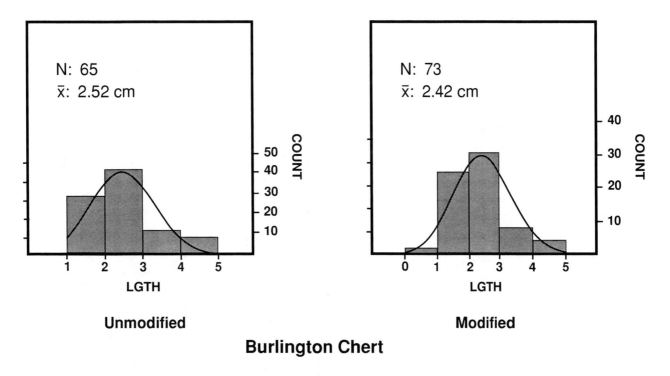

Burlington Chert

Figure 8.28. continued

the unmodified blades and 2.7 percent of the modified blades. Evidence of heat alteration occurs on 17.5 percent of the unmodified blades and on 20.3 percent of the modified blades. Likewise, termination break types and the presence of cortex on blades and blade platforms are virtually identical for the two groups.

The only significant difference in descriptive traits occurs in the area of platform modification and intactness. Of the 879 unmodified blades studied, 45.3 percent had intact platforms. Modified blades had only 19.6 percent of platforms intact. Moreover, 52.6 percent of unmodified blades displayed no platform modification, while only 27 percent of modified blades possessed no evidence of platform modification. The meaning of this is unclear, although it may provide indirect support for the idea that the first blades to be struck from cores were more apt to be modified. These first blades would probably have been detached from well-prepared platforms, while later blades would probably show less evidence of platform modification. The low percentage of intact platforms on modified blades also indicates that platforms were more often than not removed during the tool preparation process. Along with the notching of blades, intentional platform removal provides some insight into the complexity of the Dash Reeves blade industry.

The location of utilization on blades is much more regimented than it is for nonblade flake tools. Utilization was observed on the dorsal portion of the blade on all 552 modified blades. There are no instances where utilization or retouch was observed on only the ventral side. However, there are 100 blades with both dorsal and ventral utilization. The most common position of utilization on the dorsal side (7.2 percent) is along the right lateral edge (with the proximal end oriented upward and the dorsal side displayed) inclusive of the proximal, medial, and distal portions. The next most popular locations are the entire left lateral side (5.4 percent) and medial right side (5.4 percent). Only 0.7 percent of the modified blades have proximal end utilization, and only 2.9 percent have exclusively distal end utilization. The most popular location of ventral side utilization (1.8 percent) is on the medial portion of the right side (proximal side up, ventral face showing). In addition to the above positions, 78 other position combinations were recorded, although none occur on more than 4.5 percent of the modified blade assemblage.

SPATIAL DISTRIBUTION OF CHERT DEBITAGE AND TOOLS

Observations about the spatial distribution of the chert assemblage are necessarily guarded since only a portion of the Dash Reeves site was excavated. In addition, a relatively high percentage of material was recovered from the surface outside the excavation area and, thus, is only generally provenienced. Nevertheless, within the excavated portion of the site a number of interesting patterns provide insights into the nature of midden formation and suggest possible segregation of materials by type and, possibly, by social group.

The most intense concentration of chert debitage was found within the main creek midden (Figure 8.29). This material was not evenly distributed. Units not more than a meter apart contained widely disparate quantities and weights of chert. For example, Unit 9, at the north end of the excavated creek midden, produced more than 3,300 g of chert debitage and over 1,900 items, while adjacent Unit 8 contained only 318 items, weighing 840 g. At the south end of the excavated creek midden, Unit 5 yielded over 1,000 items, weighing nearly 1,700 g, while adjacent Unit 45 produced only 237 items, weighing 306 g. This kind of differential pattern was very common at the site. It clearly does not reflect generalized accretion but is the result of a selective process of disposal. This is supported by the fact that chert types were also unevenly distributed within the creek midden area. Old Blue chert, which virtually never exceeds 5 percent of the debitage by weight from most excavation units, comprises more than 20 percent of the debitage from Units 2 and 42 in the creek midden. This chert type also makes up 22–34 percent of the debitage from Units 25 and 31 in the central area of the site and from Units 3 and 39 in the western area of the site. In most of these cases, this chert type did not occur at all in adjacent units. Ste. Genevieve red chert makes up 29–89 percent of the debitage by weight, per unit, in the creek midden. White Burlington cherts, which never exceed 3 percent of the debitage from the creek midden units, comprise between 13 and 17 percent of the chert debitage in two western units.

Perhaps the most interesting distributional pattern pertains to nonlocal cherts, particularly those from southern Illinois (Mill Creek, Cobden/Dongola, Ka-

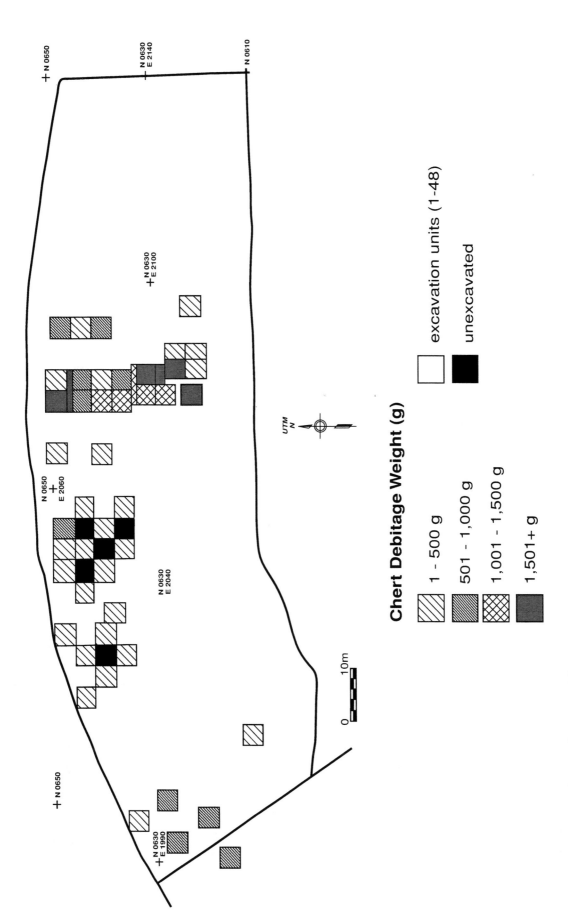

Figure 8.29. Chert Debitage Weight

olin, Blair, and Mansker). Although these cherts appear throughout the site area (Figure 8.30), they occur most frequently within an 8-x-10-m area in the south-central portion of the creek midden (in Units 6, 10, 11, 19, and 23). Of significance is the fact that the same area produced the highest quantities of nonlocal Crab Orchard pottery (Figure 8.31). This is the first clear example in the American Bottom of a southern Illinois artifact assemblage found in such a spatially retricted area. It is highly suggestive of an individual family or kin group from that area residing at the site and, further, may indicate that individual social groups had defined or allocated disposal areas within the settlement.

The distributional patterns with respect to manufacturing-stage debris are less clear. There appear to be two areas of intense disposal of thinning flakes, reduction flakes, and cores. These areas occur at the far north end and in the south-central portion of the creek midden. Cores are also closely associated with primary and secondary decortication flakes in those areas (Figure 8.32). There are also several thinning flake "hot spots" outside of the creek midden that may have resulted from specific maintenance activities in those areas (i.e., in Units 12, 26, and 27, in the north-central area of the site). Although lithic reduction may have occurred within the creek midden area, it seems more likely that debitage was transported there from other work areas. The lithic debris was so tightly packed in some of the midden units that periodic clean up of the full range of manufacturing debris probably occurred. It should be pointed out that unmodified lamellar blade debitage followed the same distributional pattern as the nonblade chert debitage, reaching its highest densities in Units 9 and 18, at the north end of the creek midden, and in Units 5, 6, 19, and 20, in the south-central portion of the midden (Figure 8.33). Blades made on nonlocal cherts also occurred in these two locations, and were particularly common in the same area that produced the southern Illinois materials mentioned above.

Twenty or more chert tools were recovered in nine excavation units. Most were located in the creek midden, where they occurred in some north-to-south contiguous units (Figure 8.34). Many of these tools are fragmentary, but complete examples also were found in the same contexts. Unit 9, in particular, produced a wide variety of tool types, including the highest numbers of drills, perforators, and gravers recovered at the site. Hafted biface distribution by specific type was

unpatterned, but two concentrations occurred in the Unit 9 area of the creek midden and in five contiguous units in the south-central creek midden (Units 5, 6, 10, 20, and 24). In this latter area, there was also a significant concentration of nondiagnostic biface tips, midsections, and polished flakes (Figure 8.35). Curiously, in the far western part of the site, an isolated unit (Unit 3) produced six biface fragments and two hafted bifaces. This is the highest total of biface fragments recovered from all units at the site.

TOOLS AND FUNCTION

Without microwear analysis, a precise determination of activities and tasks undertaken with specific chert tools is somewhat presumptuous. However, it is clear from the great diversity of formal types and from macrowear patterns that these tools were utilized for multiple purposes and that the Dash Reeves occupation was not focused on a single resource procurement or task pattern. While tool manufacturing was obviously of major importance at the site, the number and variety of tools utilized speaks to the diversity of activities carried out. It is not possible to determine specific activity areas in the excavated portions of the site or to define spatial clusters of functionally related tools because the artifacts were all essentially redeposited. Nevertheless, some general observations with respect to function are warranted.

An attempt was made to categorize chert tools, except blade tools, by function. Ten functional categories are presented in Table 8.25 with their corresponding tool types. The largest category is made up of what are termed expedient cutting tools and includes over 1,500 utilized flakes. Some artifacts in this category may have been used for scraping or incising rather than cutting, but only microwear analysis can determine this. Expedient cutting tools constitute 59 percent of the nonblade chert tool assemblage. It is clear that many blade tools also fall into this functional category; had they been included here, the general informal cutting category would have constituted over 70 percent of the chert tool assemblage at the site.

Other functional categories include scraping, drilling/perforating, combination cutting and scraping, incising, woodworking, large cutting, shredding, digging,

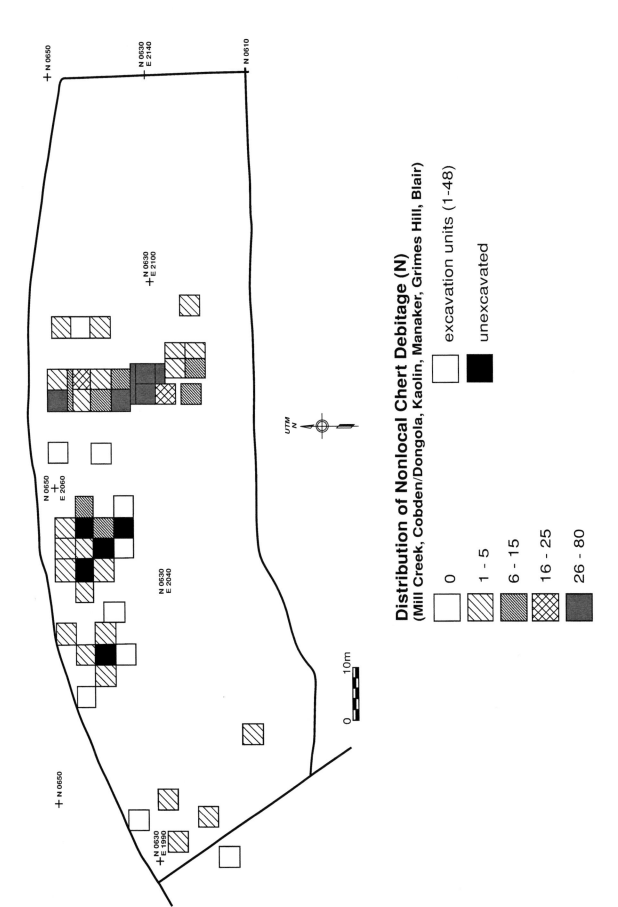

Figure 8.30. Distribution of Nonlocal Chert Debitage by Count

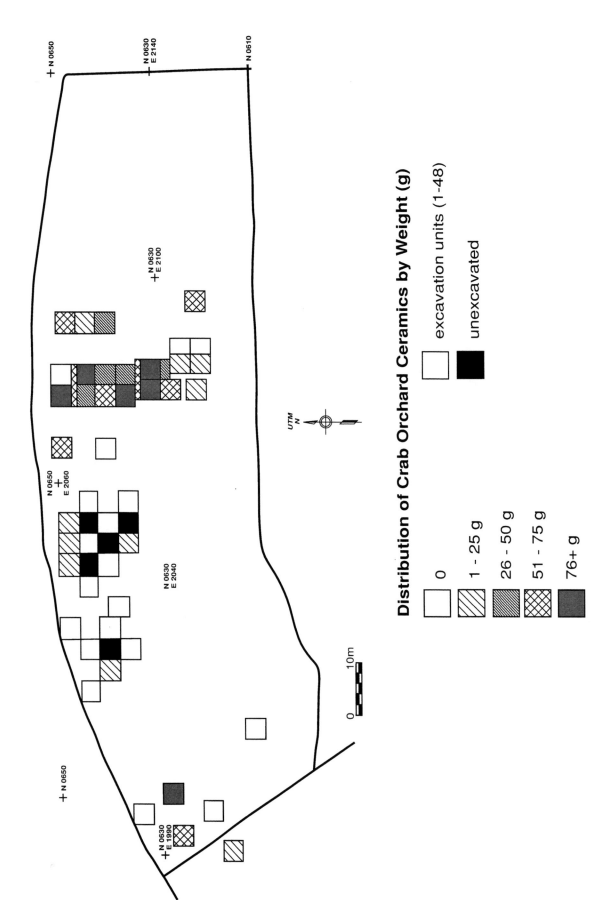

Figure 8.31. Distribution of Crab Orchard Rim and Body Sherds by Weight (g)

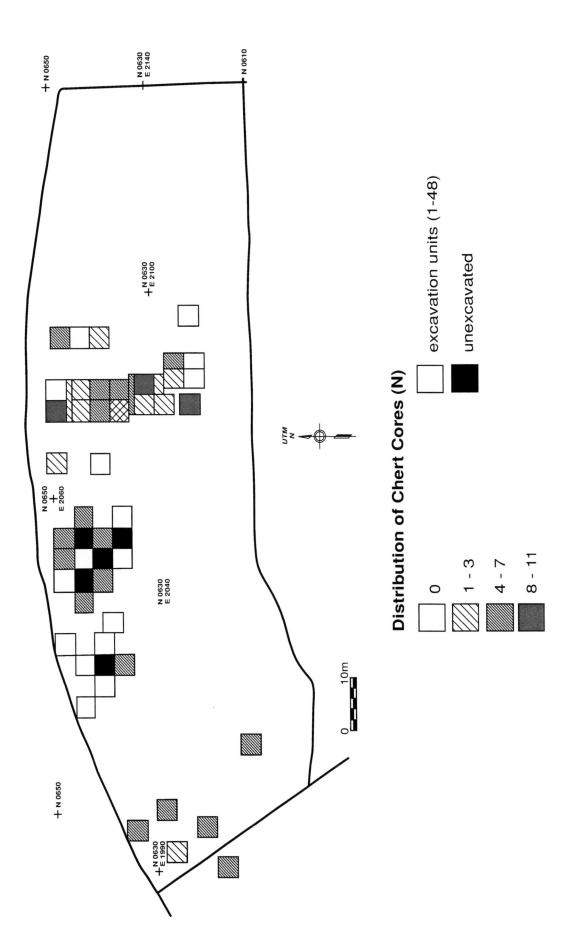

Figure 8.32. Distribution of Chert Cores by Count

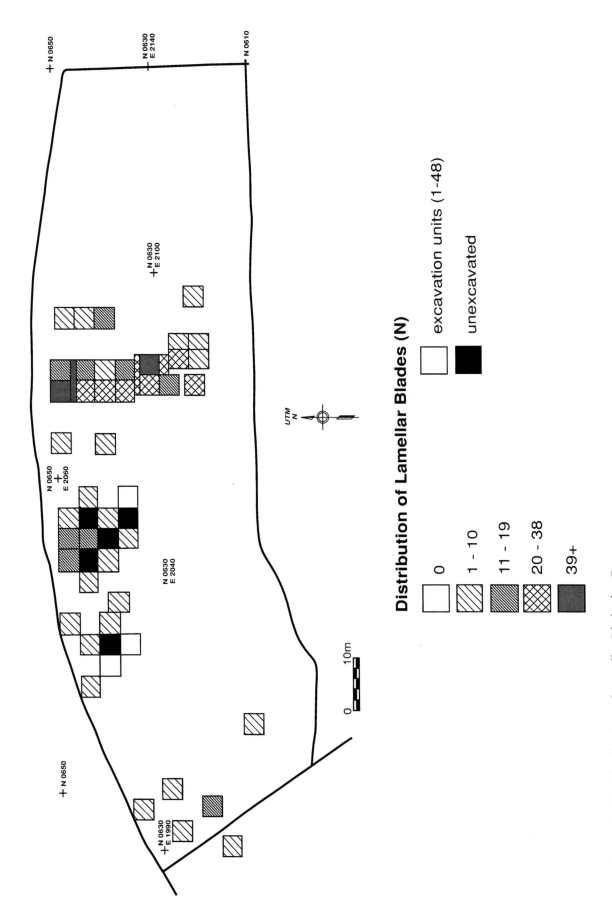

Figure 8.33. Distribution of Lamellar Blades by Count

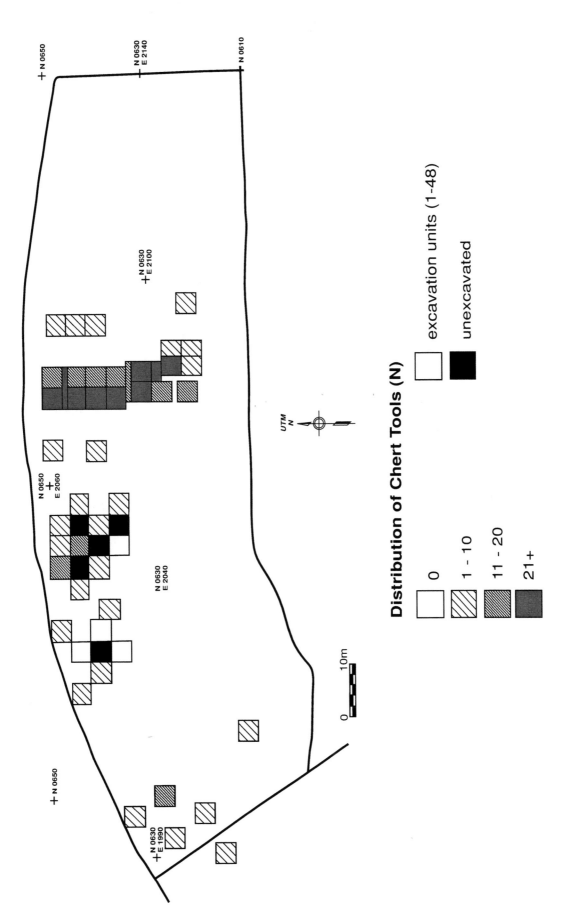

Figure 8.34. Distribution of Chert Tools

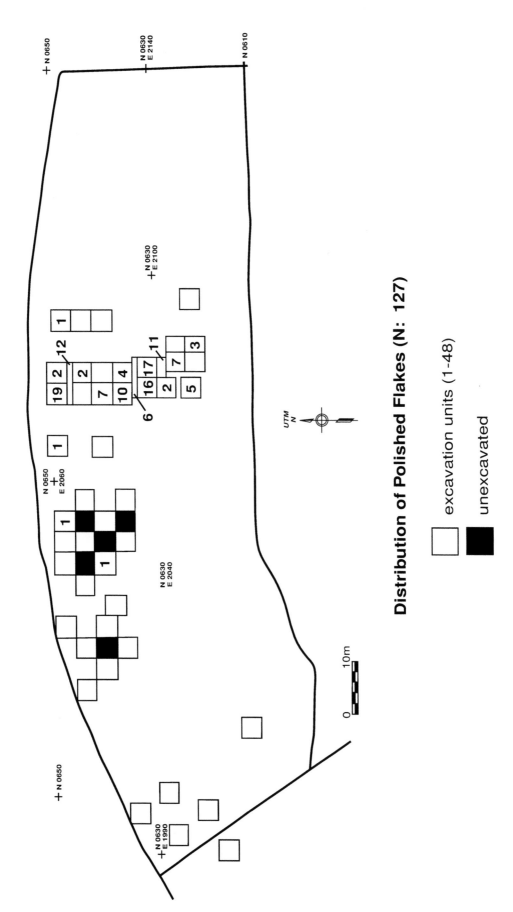

Figure 8.35. Distribution of Polished Flakes

Table 8.25. Nonblade Chert Tool Frequencies by Functional Categories*

Functional Categories	Tool Types	N	%
Expedient cutting tools	utilized flakes	1,534	59.3
Scraping tools	core scrapers, flake scrapers, core edge tools	409	15.8
Drilling/piercing tools	drills, perforators	185	7.2
Bifacial cutting/scraping tools	hafted bifaces	183	7.2
Incising tools	gravers, spurs	104	4.0
Woodworking tools	gouges, wedge, chisels	77	3.0
Large cutting tools	knives	37	1.4
Shredding tools	denticulates	36	1.4
Percussion tools	hammerstones	19	0.7
Digging tools	hoes	2	0.0 +
Total		2,586	100

*Excludes tips, midsections, and polished flakes

and percussion tools. The relative percentages of these types are presented in Table 8.25. Processing of meat products, i.e., meat cutting and hide scraping, appears to have been particularly significant at the site. Incising and drilling also appear to have been important, with 11 percent of the chert assemblage associated with such activities. It is not clear, however, exactly what materials were being incised or drilled. There is no evidence for bone or wood engraving, but these are possibilities, as is ceramic decoration. Bone, shell, or skin/hide drilling is also possible, but again, direct archaeological evidence is lacking. Woodworking tools, such as gouges, chisels, and wedges, and perhaps some of the adzes, make up a small percentage of the chert tool assemblage (3 percent); however, these are large tools that were probably used over and over again. Many exhibit gloss, battering, and end breakage, suggesting heavy woodworking activities, such as tree or bark removal, house construction, or, possibly, canoe construction.

It is clear that blades were not produced to perform one function. Apparently, they were not exclusively manufactured for ceremonial use but were used primarily for a variety of on-site tasks (see Yerkes 1994 for a detailed study of use wear on Ohio bladelets). I would not preclude the possibility that some artifacts may have been manufactured on site for the purpose of redistribution and exchange. The occurrence of red Ste. Genevieve blades at sites such as Holding in the northern American Bottom and Twenhafel in southern Illinois may evince interaction between Dash Reeves and those sites. The occurrence of Crab Orchard ceramics and southern Illinois cherts at Dash Reeves certainly supports some

level of interaction, if not potential exchange episodes. This assemblage includes blade drills, perforators, end scrapers, side scrapers/knives, denticulates, gravers, and tools that apparently functioned as expedient cutters. Although use wear is obvious on many of these tools, extensive use wear analysis needs to be undertaken to document the kinds of materials on which they were used. It is assumed that a variety of materials were involved. One might add that, given the elaborate hair styling observed on a number of figurines from this period, including one found at this site, it is very likely that some blade tools may have been utilized as razors. Tattooing, for which there is no direct evidence, also could have been accomplished with blades. It is perhaps significant to note that the blade tool industry appears to parallel the flake tool industry, at least in terms of the formal types recognized. Quite possibly, future wear studies will be able to distinguish exclusive functions for some of the blade tools, but at this time there is little to indicate that such exclusivity existed.

THE DASH REEVES BLADE INDUSTRY: REGIONAL PERSPECTIVES

No other aspect of lithic technology has so confounded midwestern archaeologists as has Middle Woodland blade manufacture. The origin of this technology, its apparently sudden disappearance, and questions of function continue to be major puzzles. Fundamental problems, such as the lack of a common terminology, obscure questions of regional comparison. Blades from midwestern sites have not been analyzed extensively. The few available studies focus on assemblages from widely separated regions and disparate types of sites. They generally do not address diachronic issues and pay minimal attention to archaeological context. The Dash Reeves materials represent only the second analyzed Middle Woodland blade industry from a site in the American Bottom (Williams 1989), so just how typical or unique this particular assemblage is remains to be seen.

There is no evidence for a Late Archaic, Poverty Point-like, blade technology in this area (Emerson 1984; McElrath and Fortier 1983; for discussions of Poverty Point blades, see Ford et al. 1955; Haag and Webb 1953; Johnson 1983; Webb 1982; Webb and Gibson 1981). In the American Bottom, blade industries first appeared during the Middle Woodland period. Isolated occurrences of blades have been reported in some pre-Middle Woodland contexts, but the artifacts in those cases appear to represent what might best be referred to as "pseudo-blades" or linear flakes (Sanger 1970:106). Other evidence of blade technology, such as blade cores, is never associated with these rare examples. True blades are almost always associated with so-called Hopewell assemblages or with the Holding phase (50 B.C.–A.D.150) (Fortier et al. 1989) but also occur in limited numbers in larger early Cement Hollow phase assemblages in this area, such as that from Petite Michele (which I am presently analyzing). In short, this unique technology suddenly appeared full-blown in the American Bottom, and it disappeared just as rapidly sometime at the end of the Holding phase or beginning of the Hill Lake phase (A.D. 150–300). This pattern appears to be regional or pan-midwestern in extent.

Given the fact that there are no precursory blade industries and no evidence of experimentation leading to this technology in the American Bottom, it is generally assumed that blade manufacture arrived as a specialized import from outside the Midwest. At various times in prehistory blade or microblade industries have developed in several areas of North and Central America (Parry 1994). Blade manufacture is closely associated with the first inhabitants of North America, and in that context is sometimes referred to as the

American Paleo-Arctic (Anderson 1970) and Plano microblade traditions. Over the course of several thousand years, these early blade industries gave rise to a number of regional traditions, such as the Northwest Microblade (Ackerman 1980; Mitchell 1968; Sanger 1968a), Plateau Microblade (Browman and Munsell 1969; Dumond 1962; Sanger 1968a), and Alberta High River Microblade (Sanger 1968b) traditions. Further evolution and diffusion of these technologies in North America resulted in such traditions as the Arctic Small Tool (Irving 1957; Nash 1969), Magic Mountain (in Colorado) (Patterson 1973), Texas Gulf and Poverty Point (Patterson 1973), and Dorset (Collins 1956; Taylor 1968) traditions. Of these, only the Dorset, Arctic Small Tool, and possibly later, unnamed variants of the Plateau or Northwest microblade traditions were contemporaneous with Hopewell blade industries. Although some researchers have found affinities between the Hopewell and Poverty Point blade traditions (Ford et al. 1955), the chronological discontinuity between the two is nearly half a millennium. It does not seem likely that such a technology would lie dormant for 500 years and then diffuse to another geographic region. It is clear that Hopewell blade technology did not merely evolve from a Poverty Point antecedent (see Montet-White 1968:28), nor, apparently, did it diffuse from the South to the Midwest. Moreover, the absence of extensive blade industries at Middle Woodland sites in the lower Mississippi River valley, and more generally in the South (John Walthall, personal communication 1997), argues against a southern origin for Hopewell blades. This would also suggest that Mesoamerican influences, at least via south-to-north diffusion, were relatively minor. Certainly the elaborate prismatic blade core technology of that area (Crabtree 1968; MacNeish et al. 1967) differs vastly from the Hopewell industries of the Midwest (particularly in Ohio and Illinois).

A possible relationship between midcontinental blade technology and the microblade tradition of the central and eastern Arctic Dorset culture has been proposed by several researchers (Ford et al. 1955:148–149; Patterson 1973), although some (Sanger 1970) suggest that such an affiliation is untenable. It has been argued that the Dorset blade industry was closely associated with wood carving or whittling (McGhee 1970:96), as manifested by numerous end-hafted blades. Many Hopewell blades exhibit evidence of hafting on the proximal end and may have functioned in a manner similar to the Dorset tools. However, that is conjecture and not a basis for confirming a Dorset-Hopewell relationship. Contact with the northern Boreal forests possibly could have occurred through Hopewellian-influenced cultures of southern Canada (e.g., Saugeen culture), but this link was probably weak. Although so-called Hopewell Interaction Sphere items occur in burial mound contexts in Ontario, blades are apparently absent (Spence et al. 1979).

Another possible source for Hopewell blade technology is the Interior Plateau region, specifically, the Yellowstone area. Although the Plateau blade traditions differ in many respects from Midwest Hopewell traditions (Sanger 1968a, 1969), particularly in techniques of platform and facial preparation and in the use of raw materials, there is a well-known connection between the Yellowstone area and the Midwest during Hopewell times: obsidian. Although not common at Middle Woodland sites in the Midwest, it does occur in the form of cores, blades, and finished tools. Virtually all of the smaller obsidian remains from Illinois sites are blades. Obsidian from three separate sites in the American Bottom has been specifically sourced to two locations: Obsidian Cliff, Wyoming (for material from the Holding and Nochta sites), and Bear Gulch, Idaho (for material from the Columbia Farms site) (Hughes and Fortier 1997). Obsidian and marine shell trade apparently was initiated and intensified throughout the Great Basin and Plateau between 1500 B.C. and A.D. 500, the period of the Reveille phase in central Nevada (Elston 1986:142). It is not uncommon to find Pacific coast shell beads in eastern Great Basin sites dating to this and subsequent periods (Hughes and Bennyhoff 1986:238–255). North-south and east-west exchanges occurred throughout prehistory and well into the Historic period. Technologies, ideas, and materials often moved through a series of transaction centers over vast areas of the West. It is not too farfetched to envision an interaction network during the Hopewell period extending up the Missouri River into the Plains and beyond. It should be pointed out that at least one researcher has hypothesized a Plateau or Northwest origin for the Texas Gulf and Poverty Point blade industries, although in those cases the route of diffusion was through Colorado (via the Magic Mountain tradition) and the southern Plains (Patterson 1973). I should also point out that that there is no direct evidence for any major prismatic blade industries in the Idaho-Wyoming area during Hopewell times (Richard Hughes,

personal communication 1996), so this proposed Midwest/Plateau blade technology-obsidian relationship remains hypothetical.

The occurrence of blade industries in the Midwest parallels the occurrence of obsidian, essentially following an east-west trajectory through the central portion of the region from Kansas City to eastern Ohio. As with most Hopewell objects, blades tend to be found at sites along major river arteries, especially the Missouri, Mississippi, and Ohio. It is along these major waterways that some of the most impressive Hopewell transaction centers occur; networks of associated settlements often are situated along secondary tributaries (Butler 1979; Johnson 1979; Kay 1980; Kellar 1979). Blade technology seems to have emerged within this context and diffused rapidly throughout the midcontinent. This technology almost certainly was imported, but because it is so distinctive and has so few affinities to other North or Central American blade technologies, it is apparent that it was rapidly modified within midwestern technological contexts. In this sense one can say that Hopewell blade industries resulted from both external and internal factors.

The blade technicians at Dash Reeves were not involved in experimentation but were working within a fully developed industrial tradition. They had probably long forgotten the source of their technology, accepting blade manufacture as an integral part of their daily lives, though perhaps as an activity with symbolic associations.

The eventual disappearance of this unique technology coincided with the general collapse of the Hopewell infrastructure. It is possible that blades had achieved symbolic importance and went the way of all other symbolically related artifacts and programs at the end of the Hopewell period. If so, the symbolic associations of the tools must have outweighed more technically mundane issues like the efficiency of blade tools and the large variety of tasks that blades had performed. The reasons for the collapse of Hopewell are beyond the scope of this discussion, and the Dash Reeves assemblage provides no clues as to why blade manufacture, an apparently successful technology, was abandoned. It is interesting that the nearby Hill Lake phase Truck #7 site, which probably postdates Dash Reeves by 50–100 years, has yielded no evidence of blade technology, although similar cherts were utilized and similar Middle Woodland nonblade artifacts continued to be manufactured (Fortier 1985a). This difference re-emphasizes the fact that blade technology in the American Bottom was associated with a relatively narrow range of Middle Woodland culture and that broader Middle Woodland cultural patterns did not disappear in this area with the collapse of symbolically embedded Hopewell inventories or programs.

THE NONCHERT ASSEMBLAGE

The nonchert assemblage consists of 3,509 items, weighing 121,377.2 g. Included in this figure are 142 tools and tool fragments. The assemblage is dominated by various kinds of grinding stones and hammerstones, but it also includes such artifacts as celts, pestles, and ground sandstone pieces. It is almost completely deficient in exotic or nonlocal materials. Nearly 95 percent of the raw materials in the assemblage were acquired from sources within the Palmer Creek locality, or within a 10 to 15-km radius of the site. The following sections outline the specific kinds of materials, worked and unworked, recovered from feature and nonfeature contexts at this site.

Nonchert Debris

Nonchert debris totals 3,367 items, weighing 86,364.9 g (Tables 8.26 and 8.27). A variety of raw materials are represented, including limestone, sandstone, rough rock/gravel, igneous rock, quartzite, gla-cial cobbles, schist, generic fire-cracked rock, quartz, limonite, hematite, ochre, and galena. Of all these materials, galena is the only one not available in the American Bottom. The derivation of schist and quartzite is unknown, but the materials probably occur in the local tills. Limestone, which constitutes the majority of recovered nonchert materials (62 percent by weight), outcrops 300–500 m east of the site.

No attempt was made to distinguish specific lithic types within the igneous rock or cobble categories, which include a variety of mafic-diabase rocks such as basalt, diabase, gabbro, and diorite, all of which can be acquired from nearby Palmer Creek. The diversity in these categories does not match that observed in the Holding site assemblage (Williams 1989:325–327), suggesting that the Dash Reeves inhabitants probably did not go far afield to procure these rocks. Of course, the Holding site, a horticultural hamlet that contained a tremendous diversity of archaeobotanical remains, produced nearly four to five times the number of grinding stones and cobble tools that Dash Reeves did, so the lack of diversity in rock types at Dash Reeves may simply reflect a functional difference between these two settlements.

As mentioned above, galena is the only exotic nonchert lithic resource recovered from the site. This material was probably imported from northern Illinois or southeast Missouri sources, but this cannot be verified, as the material has not been subjected to trace element analysis. Galena from the nearby Truck #7 site (Fortier 1985a) was analyzed by Walthall (1981), who

Table 8.26. Nonchert Debris from All Contexts

Material Type	N	Wt (g)	% by Wt
Limestone	1,983	53,901.8	62.4
Sandstone	920	19,492.6	22.6
Quartzite	69	4,485.9	5.2
Igneous rock	55	3,176.4	3.7
Cobbles	15	2,159.8	2.5
Rough rock/gravel	273	1,705.0	2.0
Schist	1	485.0	0.6
Quartz	6	460.1	0.5
Fire-cracked rock	27	256.1	0.3
Ochre	5	224.1	0.3
Galena	5	8.8	0.0 +
Hematite	6	6.6	0.0 +
Limonite	2	2.7	0.0 +
Total	3,367	86,364.9	

Table 8.27. Nonchert Debris by Provenience Units

	Surface		Machine Excavation		Test Units		Excavation Units		Postmolds	
	N	Wt (g)	N	Wt (g)	N	Wt (g)	N	Wt(g)	N	Wt (g)
Limestone	95	5,380.4	504	26,532.9	433	1,776.4	485	12,257.2	466	7,954.9
Sandstone	104	4,018.8	358	8,449.7	156	1,037.1	262	5,031.9	40	955.1
Rough rock/gravel	32	402.2	42	842.3	93	89.7	95	346.0	11	24.8
Cobbles	7	1,879.2	8	280.6	-	-	-	-	-	-
Igneous rock	5	462.9	14	1,969.4	5	22.0	30	720.8	1	1.3
FCR	9	80.0	4	97.4	9	6.6	4	36.8	1	35.3
Quartzite	8	633.1	32	2,445.2	11	492.3	15	844.9	3	70.4
Schist	-	-	-	-	-	-	-	-	1	485.0
Quartz	-	-	6	460.1	-	-	-	-	-	-
Limonite	-	-	1	0.7	-	-	1	2.0	-	-
Hematite	1	3.4	1	0.8	-	-	3	2.1	1	0.3
Ochre	-	-	-	-	2	102.5	2	82.1	1	39.5
Galena	-	-	-	-	2	2.6	3	6.2	-	-
Total	261	12,860.0	970	41,079.1	711	3,529.2	900	19,330.0	525	9,566.6

identified Potosi, Missouri, as the source of that material. No worked galena was recovered from Dash Reeves, although the smaller fragments may represent pieces from larger worked blocks. Presumably, galena was utilized as a pigment.

A small quantity of unworked hematite, limonite, and ochre also was recovered. Although sources can be found in local tills, a more probable source, especially for hard hematite, is located in Missouri, near the headwaters of the Meramec River, nearly 40 km west of the site (Kelly 1990:116). Interestingly enough, hard hematite, utilized as a red pigment, was not recovered at either the Holding or Truck #7 site.

The size of nonchert debitage is variable and is correlated with different site contexts. For example, items recovered from the surface and from machine-excavated contexts are nearly twice as large and heavy as remains from features or midden units (Table 8.27). The weight of limestone recovered from machine-excavated contexts is more than twice that of limestone from midden or excavation unit contexts, even though there are only 19 more pieces of limestone from the former than the latter. The mean weight of limestone from features is only 17 g, whereas the mean weight from machine-excavated contexts is 53 g. A similar pattern occurs with cobbles, igneous rock, and fire-cracked rock. Much, if not all of this material probably represents dispersed surficial hearths. Some must have been picked up occasionally and redeposited into the creek midden. Apparently, rocks were not utilized as pit

liners or as hearth material in pits, a pattern that was widespread during the Late Woodland period. Finally, the low mean weight of remains recovered from test units reflects the fact that these units were screened.

Nonchert Tools

One hundred forty-two nonchert tools and fragments, weighing 35,012.5 g, were recovered from combined contexts. An inventory of these remains is presented in Table 8.28. Tools are fashioned from igneous rock, schist, quartzite, sandstone, fossiliferous rock, and hematite. Various kinds of igneous rock far outweigh other nonchert material. It is presumed that the raw materials for virtually all of these tools were obtained from local till sources or outcrops. The one piece of worked fossiliferous rock probably came from a local limestone outcrop. In all probability over 90 percent of the raw materials for tools were transported to the site from less than a kilometer away. Nonchert artifact categories include grinding stones, hammerstones, pitted stones, combination grinding/hammer/pitted stones, pestles, axes/celts, worked sandstone, worked igneous rock, and worked hematite (Figure 8.36).

Grinding Stones. There are 27 complete grinding stones or manos and 21 fragments, weighing 16,470.9 g. These tools are characterized by the presence of one or more ground, flat surfaces. With the exception of one quartzite example, a variety of mafic-diabase igneous rocks, usually rounded to angular cobbles, were uti-

Table 8.28. Inventory of Nonchert Tools from All Contexts

	N	Wt (g)	% of Top 6 by Wt(g)
Igneous GS	26	11,884.5	33.9
Igneous GS frag.	21	4,586.4	13.1
Igneous HS	12	2,218.4	6.3
Igneous HS frag.	9	808.7	–
Igneous PS/GS	12	5,107.4	14.6
IgneousPS/GS frag.	2	813.4	–
Igneous PS	6	2,555.5	7.3
Igneous PS frag.	1	68.0	–
Igneous HS/GS	3	829.4	–
Igneous HS/GS frag.	1	587.6	–
Igneous HS/PS	1	166.3	–
Igneous pestle	1	270.5	–
Igneous pestle frag.	3	371.6	–
Worked igneous rock frag.	10	759.0	–
Igneous celt/axe	1	329.3	–
Igneous celt/axe frag.	1	298.0	–
Quartzite HS	1	136.3	–
Quartzite HS frag.	3	307.9	–
Quartzite GS	1	133.1	–
Schist HS/GS	1	445.2	–
Schist HS/GS frag.	1	214.7	–
Indet. HS frag.	1	133.5	–
Worked SS	10	1,035.5	3.0
Worked SS frag.	10	569.5	–
SS slot abrader	1	122.9	–
Worked fossiliferous rock	1	251.9	–
Worked hematite frag.	2	8.0	–
Total	142	35,012.5	78.2

Key:
GS=grinding stone
HS=hammerstone
SS=sandstone
PS=pitted stone

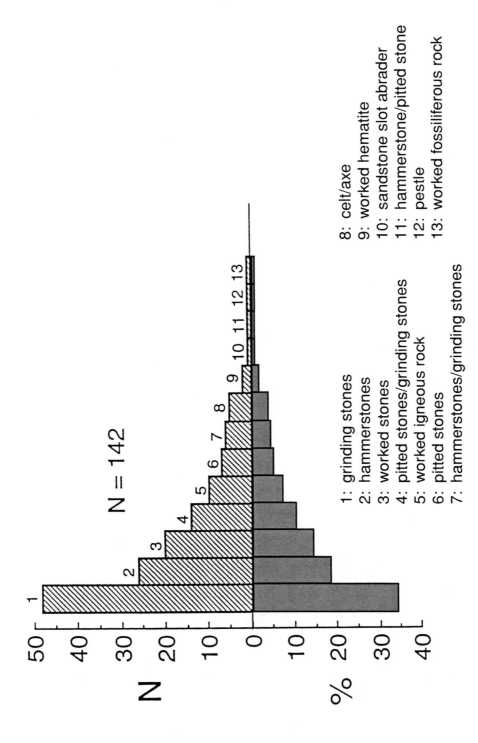

Figure 8.36. Distribution of Nonchert Tools

lized. It is widely presumed that such tools were used to grind plants, such as nuts, tubers, and seeds. It is interesting that so many fragments were found, suggesting some relatively heavy usage or percussion. Their use as anvil stones, therefore, cannot be discounted. The average weight of complete grinding stones is 445.1 g.

Hammerstones. Thirteen complete hammerstones and 13 fragments, weighing 3,604.8 g, were identified. The mean weight of complete hammerstones is 181.1 g. With the exception of one complete and three fragmentary quartzite specimens, hammerstones are made of igneous rocks in the form of small cobbles. These tools are characterized by the presence of a single, narrow, curvilinear, battered or pecked surface or, sometimes, by several discontinuously battered areas. These tools are hard- or direct-percussion implements utilized to manufacture chert tools. They are about two-thirds the size of the grinding stones described above.

Pitted Stones. There are six complete pitted stones and one pitted stone fragment, weighing 2,623.5 g. These artifacts, all made from igneous rock, are characterized by a pecked pit centrally located on a flat surface. These kinds of artifacts appear on sites in this area dating from the Archaic through the Late Woodland periods. Archaic and Late Woodland examples often have broad, bipolar pits with discoloration in and around them (Fortier 1984:152; Fortier et al. 1983:271). The interior pit surface is often smooth or ground. Pitted stones may have been utilized in plant processing, especially to break and pulverize nuts. Discoloration around the pits may be due to the adherence of nut oil to the fine-grained igneous rocks. Another suggested use for these artifacts is as anvils for chert reduction. Where so used, however, the pits are usually pecked and battered and generally are not discolored or ground (Ritchie 1929:9).

Both plant grinding stones and anvils were recognized by Meinkoth among the pitted stones at the Holding site (Williams 1989:388). At Dash Reeves virtually all of the pitted stones may have been used as anvils, as they exhibit heavy battering and lack discoloration. This is certainly consistent with the extensive lithic manufacturing activities at this site.

Combination Pitted/Grinding/Hammerstones. Seventeen complete and four fragmentary combination pitted/grinding/hammerstones, weighing 8,164 g, were identified. Igneous pitted/grinding stones (N=14) are most common and are characterized by one or more ground surfaces and the occurrence of one centrally located pecked pit, usually on one of the ground surfaces. Other combinations include igneous hammer/grinding stones (N=4), an igneous hammer/pitted stone, and two schist hammer/grinding stones. It is clear that individual igneous and metamorphic cobbles constituted expedient tools useful for a variety of tasks, including plant grinding and chert tool production.

Igneous Celt/Axes. One complete celt/axe and one fragment were recovered. The complete artifact weighs 329.3 g and is made of fine-grained dioritic basalt (Plate 8.17a). The bit end is bisymmetrically beveled, and the surfaces of both sides are ground. The edges along the side are coarse and unground. The tool is 9.48 cm long, has a maximum thickness of 3.01 cm, and is 6.08 cm wide at the haft end. There is no direct evidence for hafting, though the artifact may have broken below the conjectured haft area.

The second celt/axe, weighing 298 g, represents a nearly complete tool but is clearly broken at the haft end. It is made of a coarse-grained mafic-diabase rock (Plate 8.17b). It is ground on both surfaces and sides and is bisymmetrically beveled at the bit end. It measures 8.22 cm in length, 5.75 cm in width, and 3.44 cm in thickness. The broken haft end is chipped in several areas, including both sides.

Both artifacts appear to represent woodworking tools, perhaps utilized to fell trees or shape canoes. Their ground, flat surfaces and beveled bits distinguish them from unbitted pestles, which probably functioned as pulverizers.

Pestles. One complete pestle and three fragments, weighing 642.1 g, were identified (Plate 8.18). These are unground and made of coarse-grained igneous rock. They are cylindrical or conical and are distinguished by a biconvex or rounded bit end that exhibits heavy battering. The complete pestle displays battering along the edge at both ends. It is possible that this artifact also may have been utilized as a hammerstone. Two of the pestle fragments are relatively small and represent, in one case, the bit end, and in the other, the poll end. The three fragments are all conical or pear shaped, a type that, along with so-called bell-shaped pestles, is diagnostic of the Middle Woodland period in this area (see Williams 1989:397–399). Similar pestles were recovered from the Holding site, but in those cases, grinding is evident on all surfaces. The function of such tools is unknown although their use as manos is suspected.

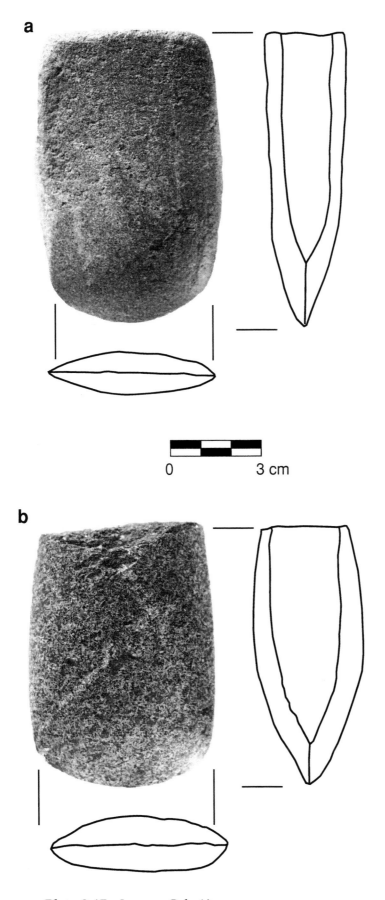

0   3 cm

Plate 8.17. Igneous Celts/Axes

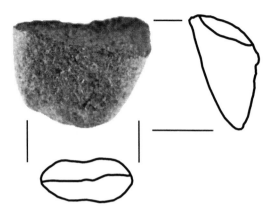

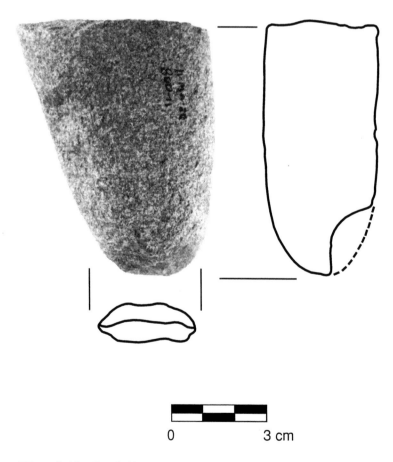

Plate 8.18. Pestle Fragments

According to several local collectors, quite a number of these tools have been recovered from the Dash Reeves site and currently reside in private collections or have been sold into antiquarian markets outside the state.

Worked Igneous Rock Fragments. Ten worked igneous rock fragments, weighing 759 g, were recovered. These fragments include ground rocks of various sizes, obviously pieces of larger tools. Considering the number of grinding stones and hammer stones from this site, it is somewhat surprising that such a disproportionately small number of worked igneous rock fragments were recovered. No explanation for this apparent discrepancy is offered.

Worked Sandstone. Ten complete worked sandstone tools and 10 fragments, weighing 1,605 g, were identified in a variety of site contexts. These artifacts are characterized by the presence of grinding on one or more surfaces. Grinding occurs on either flat or rounded surfaces and often covers an irregular area. Some of the larger complete tools may be small metates, but most of the pieces are generally too small to have functioned in this manner. Fragments, however, may have come from metates. Some of the more complete tools may have functioned as hand-held grinding stones or manos. Another possibility, especially for the smaller tools, is that they functioned as grinders utilized in the process of blade core platform preparation. As previously mentioned, ground and crushed surfaces occur just beneath the platforms on many of the blades and blade cores in this assemblage. Small sandstone tools would have been ideal for such platform preparation.

Sandstone Slot Abrader. One sandstone slot abrader, weighing 122.9 g, was recovered. Such tools probably functioned as bone or wood implement sharpeners or as files (Fortier 1984:160–162). The lone example from the site was found in the Feature 29 cache pit. It exhibits a single, broad, U-shaped groove that is ground and smoothed.

Worked Hematite. Two items, weighing 8 g, were identified as worked hematite. One of these fragments is a small, square piece of ground soft hematite. This was presumably utilized as a red pigment bar. The second item, weighing 7.3 g, is a broken drilled pendant (Figure 8.37). The edges have been ground and modified, and a drilled hole occurs at one end of the artifact. Rotary marks appear on both sides of the hole. The pendant is made of a hard, micaceous hematite, a variety not commonly encountered at sites in this area.

Worked Fossiliferous Rock. A single worked fossiliferous rock, weighing 251.9 g, was recovered. It is circular or disc-shaped, with a maximum diameter of 7.77 cm and a maximum thickness of 3.15 cm. There is a natural perforation through the center. The central portions of both flat, opposing surfaces exhibit grinding. It is possible that this artifact functioned as a mano or grinding stone.

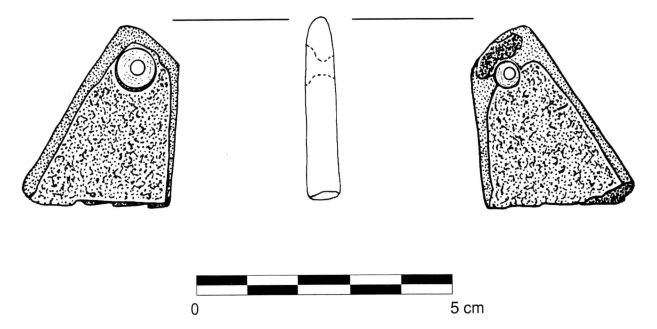

0   5 cm

Figure 8.37. Drilled Hematite Pendant

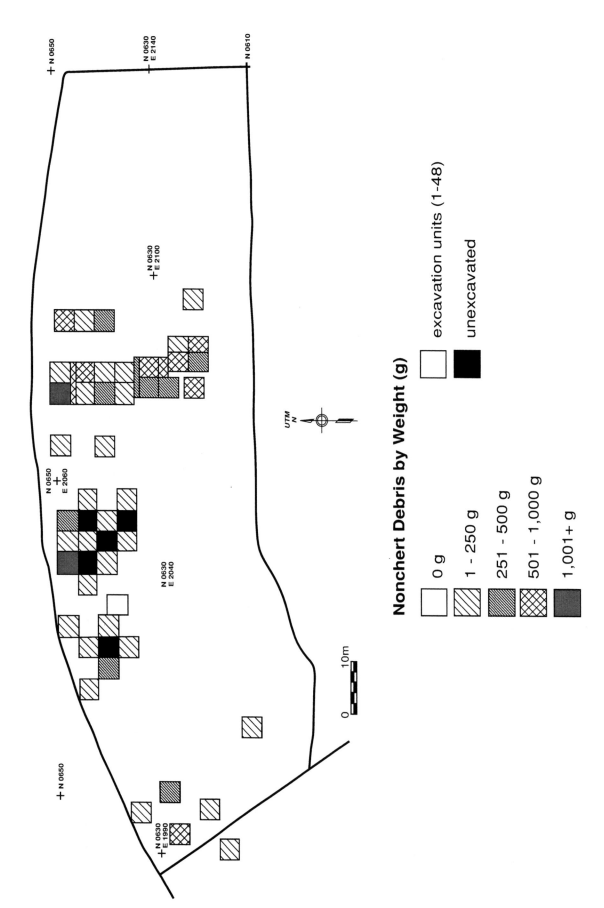

Figure 8.38. Distribution of Nonchert Debitage by Weight

DISTRIBUTION OF NONCHERT TOOLS

Seventy of the nonchert tools described in the above sections were found within the excavated portion of the right-of-way. The remaining 72 tools were recovered from the surface directly north and east of the excavation area. Of the 70 excavated tools, 49 came from just two areas: a 40-x-20-m area located within N UTM 0610–0650 and E UTM 2010–2030 (eastern concentration), and a 60-x-20-m area located within N UTM 0630–0650 and E UTM 2040–2100 (western concentration). The eastern concentration occurred just west of the creek midden. Grinding stones and fragments were particularly prevalent there, suggesting that this area may have served as some kind of specialized plant processing area. Interestingly, the eastern area was characterized by the lowest densities of chert debitage, tools, and features in the entire excavation area.

The nonchert tool total in the western concentration is somewhat inflated by the occurrence of five grinding/hammer/pitted stones in Feature 26 and a scatter of similar tools around Feature 10 and Excavation Unit 4. These tools may represent activities conducted in the immediate vicinities of these features or units. Aside from these materials, nonchert tools are relatively scarce in the western part of the excavated site area.

Only 7.7 percent (N=11) of the nonchert tools occurred in feature contexts, and, surprisingly, only 15.5 percent were recovered from excavation unit contexts. Hence, the vast majority of nonchert tools were retrieved from the surface and from generalized machine-excavated contexts in both plowzone and subplowzone levels. This essentially duplicates the pattern of recovery of unworked nonchert debris (Figure 8.38). The meaning of this is not entirely clear, although it is apparent that both nonchert tools and debris were not deposited secondarily into specific midden contexts, such as the creek, or in features, but apparently remained in the areas in which they were utilized. If accurate, this pattern, differs significantly from the pattern of chert tool and debris distribution, which appears to represent secondary deposition contexts.

9

THE ARCHAEOBOTANICAL ASSEMBLAGE

Mary Simon

INTRODUCTION

The results of analysis of plant remains from the Dash Reeves site are presented in this chapter. The site was a late Middle Woodland, Hill Lake phase, single-component occupation located at the bluff base in the southern American Bottom. Approximately 25 percent of the south edge of the site was investigated, resulting in the excavation of 53 features, two postmolds, and portions of two midden areas.

Analyses were designed to look at questions of both intrasite and intersite variation. Intrasite analysis focused on examining patterns of plant remains within the occupation area to identify specific activity areas and to determine associations of specific plant types with specific feature types. As would be expected with generalized secondary debris, no material type was found to be specifically associated with any feature type. However, the distribution of plant remains in features and midden areas differed from the distribution of other classes of remains, suggesting differential discard.

Dash Reeves produced a plant assemblage typical of Middle Woodland sites, composed almost entirely of wood charcoal, nutshell, and seeds. Subsistence remains indicate that site occupants exploited a variety of both wild and probable cultivated plant species. However, there is no evidence for cultivation of either maize or clearly domesticated indigenous plants, both of which have been identified in other Middle Woodland assemblages in the region. A comparison of middle and late Middle Woodland plant remains from the American Bottom reveals some intriguing variability that may be useful in supporting theories of population movements and/or contacts.

METHODS

Flotation samples from the Dash Reeves site were collected from pit features, postmolds, and midden units. The pit features were morphologically uniform, and consisted of shallow, basin-shaped depressions containing secondary fill deposits. At least one sample, usually from the second half excavated, was analyzed from all features identified.

Two types of midden deposit, a general, accretional sheet midden and a creek bed dump (designated the "creek midden"), also were sampled. At least one sample from each creek midden unit and samples from 20 percent of the sheet midden units were analyzed. In addition, samples from three test units, one located within and two adjacent to the creek midden, and samples from Geomorphic Trench 1 were analyzed. (Figure 9.1; see Figure 3.6 for the location of specific excavation and test units).

All samples were processed using a system of water flotation based on that developed for the Illinois Department of Transportation (Wagner 1976). After recording the dry volume, the sample was placed in a box lined with 40-mesh (0.42-mm²) screen and immersed in a tub of water. Hand agitation was used to disperse the sediments, and sodium hexametaphosphate was added as necessary to assist in deflocculation of clays. Materials that floated were skimmed off using a 40-mesh net. These materials constituted the light fraction and contained the bulk of the carbonized plant remains. Materials that did not float constituted the heavy fraction. Plant remains were essentially absent from this fraction, so it was not subjected to archaeobotanical analysis.

After drying, the light fraction was passed through a 2-mm mesh geologic screen, dividing the material into two size fractions (>2 mm and <2 mm). Both size fractions were examined under low (10X–30X) magnification. Items larger than 2 mm in size were sorted into general material categories and were counted and weighed by category. The <2-mm size fraction was scanned, and seed fragments and exotic or unusual items were removed and counted.

Identification was attempted for all items extracted from the small fraction and, with the exception of wood, for all items in the large fraction. Wood identifications for each sample were limited to 20 randomly selected pieces; all wood was identified in samples containing fewer than 20 pieces. Identifications of all material were made with the aid of standard texts (Core et al. 1979; Martin and Barkley 1961) and, ultimately, by comparison with modern reference material.

In addition to the flotation samples, a large number of organic material samples were hand-collected and bagged separately during site excavations. Hand-collected samples that were processed for radiocarbon dating were analyzed in a manner similar to the flotation samples; that is, materials were sorted by category, identified, weighed, and counted. The remaining samples were scanned under low magnification. For the most part, nutshell was identified and counted. If only a few pieces of wood were present, an attempt was made to identify all of them, and the number of pieces was counted. Several samples contained wood charcoal embedded in a clayey soil matrix. In these instances, an attempt was made to identify a sample of the wood, but total fragments could not be counted. For general comparative purposes, subjective observations of the character of the sample also were made.

RESULTS

One hundred fourteen samples having a combined volume of 868 liters were analyzed (Table 9.1). The assemblage consists almost entirely of nutshell, wood, and seeds (Table 9.2). Of these three categories, seeds are the most abundant and make up over one-half of all items identified. Wood charcoal pieces constitute about one-quarter of all items, and nutshell contributes only about 11 percent to the assemblage by count. Charred plant remains were recovered from features, sheet midden units, creek midden units (including the test units), and the geotrench. The quantities of materials and taxa diversities varied considerably among the different proveniences. A detailed material inventory is presented in Appendix F.

Nutshell

The nutshell assemblage is dominated by thick-shelled hickory residues, which constitute almost three-fourths of all nutshell by count (Table 9.2). In contrast, acorn, the second most common nutshell type, makes up only about 7 percent of the assemblage. Small amounts of hazelnut and black walnut also are present. A number of fragmented or eroded pieces could be identified only as belonging to the walnut family (Juglandaceae), which includes the genera *Carya* and *Juglans*. Based on the proportionate occurrences of identified thick-shelled hickory and black walnut, it is likely that most of these Juglandaceae pieces are thick-shelled hickory rather than walnut.

Nutshell was recovered from the geotrench, all test units, 14 of the creek midden units (77.7 percent), and 15 of the features (27.3 percent). Densities were highly variable, ranging from 0.04 fragments per liter in Test Unit A to 10.6 fragments per liter in Feature 8. Almost three-quarters of the nutshell (N=379; 74 percent) was

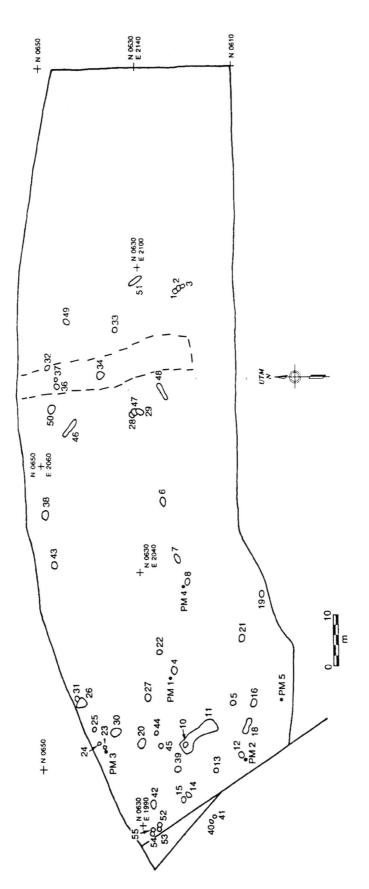

Figure 9.1. Distribution of Contexts Sampled for Floral Remains

Table 9.1. Summary of Results of Botanical Analyses

	Features and Postmolds	Sheet Midden	Creek Midden/ Test Units	Geotrench	Site Total
Total proveniences	55	7	20	1	83
Total samples	67	7	39	1	114
Volume (liters)	476	52	334	6	868
Nutshell count	379	0	134	1	514
Nutshell density (fragments/liter)	0.796	0.000	0.401	0.167	0.592
Wood count	874	7	238	32	1,151
Wood density (fragments/liter)	1.836	0.135	0.713	5.333	1.326
Seed count★	346	1	313	0	660
Seed density (fragments/liter)	0.727	0.019	0.937	0.000	0.760
Starchy seeds	128	0	203	0	331
Starchy density (fragments/liter)	0.269	0.000	0.608	0.000	0.381
Nut:wood ratio	0.434	0.000	0.563	0.031	0.447

★Less 1,948 purslane seeds from Feature 49

Table 9.2. Summary of Plant Remains From All Proveniences

Provenience	Features			Sheet Midden			Creek Midden Only			Test Units Only		
Total Liters	476			52			271			63		
	Total Count	Total Weight	Count Density	Total Count	Total Weight	Count Density	Total Count	Total Weight	Count Density	Total Count	Total Weight	Count Density
Nutshell Total	379	3.700	0.796	0	0.00	0.000	78	0.825	0.288	56	0.50	0.889
Carya sp. (hickory)	267	2.890	0.561	0	0.00	0.000	66	0.630	0.244	36	0.28	0.571
Corylus americana (hazelnut)	6	0.040	0.013	0	0.00	0.000	1	0.010	0.004	0	0.00	0.000
Juglandaceae (walnut family)	60	0.355	0.126	0	0.00	0.000	1	0.010	0.004	14	0.08	0.222
Juglans nigra (walnut)	6	0.200	0.013	0	0.00	0.000	5	0.140	0.018	5	0.13	0.079
Quercus sp. (acorn)	34	0.145	0.071	0	0.00	0.000	4	0.025	0.015	1	0.01	0.016
Unidentifiable	6	0.070	0.013	0	0.00	0.000	1	0.010	0.004	0	0.00	0.000
Wood Total	874	8.920	1.836	7	0.04	0.135	148	1.155	0.546	90	1.04	1.429
Carya sp. (hickory)	50	0.000	0.105	0	0.00	0.000	7	0.000	0.026	3	0.00	0.048
Fraxinus sp. (ash)	6	0.000	0.013	0	0.00	0.000	4	0.000	0.015	4	0.00	0.063
Juglans sp. (walnut)	11	0.000	0.023	0	0.00	0.000	0	0.000	0.000	0	0.00	0.000
Morus sp. (mulberry)	6	0.000	0.013	0	0.00	0.000	1	0.000	0.004	1	0.00	0.016
Plantanus sp. (sycamore)	3	0.000	0.006	0	0.00	0.000	0	0.000	0.000	0	0.00	0.000
Populus sp.	0	0.000	0.000	4	0.00	0.077	1	0.000	0.004	0	0.00	0.000
Prunus sp. (cherry)	0	0.000	0.000	0	0.00	0.000	0	0.000	0.000	0	0.00	0.000
Quercus sp. (oak)	32	0.000	0.067	0	0.00	0.000	3	0.000	0.011	5	0.00	0.079
Quercus sp. (red oak)	1	0.000	0.002	0	0.00	0.000	2	0.000	0.007	2	0.00	0.032
Quercus sp. (white oak)	1	0.000	0.002	0	0.00	0.000	0	0.000	0.000	2	0.00	0.032
Betulaceae (birch)	0	0.000	0.000	0	0.00	0.000	0	0.000	0.000	0	0.00	0.000
cf. Betulaceae sp. (birch)	1	0.000	0.002	0	0.00	0.000	2	0.000	0.007	0	0.00	0.000
Salicaceae (willow)	1	0.000	0.002	0	0.00	0.000	0	0.000	0.000	0	0.00	0.000
cf. *Ulmus rubus*	3	0.000	0.006	0	0.00	0.000	0	0.000	0.000	0	0.00	0.000
Ulmaceae (elm)	15	0.000	0.032	0	0.00	0.000	2	0.000	0.007	0	0.00	0.000
Total identified	130	0.000	0.273	4	0.00	0.077	22	0.000	0.081	17	0.00	0.270
Semi-ring porous	1	0.010	0.002	0	0.00	0.000	0	0.000	0.000	0	0.00	0.000
Diffuse porous	8	0.000	0.017	3	0.00	0.058	8	0.000	0.030	0	0.00	0.000
Ring porous	206	0.000	0.433	0	0.00	0.000	42	0.000	0.155	22	0.00	0.349
Unidentifiable	156	0.000	0.328	0	0.00	0.000	47	0.000	0.173	26	0.00	0.413
Identifications attempted	501	0.010	1.053	7	0.00	0.135	119	0.000	0.439	65	0.00	1.032
Bark	145	1.440	0.305	0	0.00	0.000	1	0.010	0.004	2	0.02	0.032
Total Seed	2,294	0.000	4.819	1	0.00	0.019	293	0.000	1.081	20	0.00	0.317
C. berlandieri (goosefoot)	33	0.000	0.069	0	0.00	0.000	10	0.000	0.037	3	0.00	0.048
P. caroliniana (maygrass)	39	0.000	0.082	0	0.00	0.000	178	0.000	0.657	4	0.00	0.063
P. erectum (erect knotweed)	56	0.000	0.118	0	0.00	0.000	0	0.000	0.000	2	0.00	0.032
H. pusillum (little barley)	0	0.000	0.000	0	0.00	0.000	0	0.000	0.000	6	0.00	0.095
Subtotal starchy cultigen	128	0.000	0.269	0	0.00	0.000	188	0.000	0.694	15	0.00	0.238
Amaranthus sp.	28	0.000	0.059	0	0.00	0.000	0	0.000	0.000	0	0.00	0.000
Chenopodium sp.	2	0.000	0.004	0	0.00	0.000	0	0.000	0.000	1	0.00	0.016
Compositae	1	0.000	0.002	0	0.00	0.000	0	0.000	0.000	0	0.00	0.000
Fabaceae sp. (bean)	1	0.000	0.002	0	0.00	0.000	0	0.000	0.000	0	0.00	0.000
Galium sp. (bedstraw)	1	0.000	0.002	0	0.00	0.000	2	0.000	0.007	0	0.00	0.000
Gramineae 6F	1	0.000	0.002	0	0.00	0.000	0	0.000	0.000	0	0.00	0.000
Gramineae sp. (grass)	5	0.000	0.011	0	0.00	0.000	0	0.000	0.000	0	0.00	0.000
Hordeum sp. (barley)	1	0.000	0.002	0	0.00	0.000	0	0.000	0.000	1	0.00	0.016
cf. *Hordeum* sp.	1	0.000	0.002	0	0.00	0.000	1	0.000	0.004	0	0.00	0.000
Panicum sp. (panic grass)	5	0.000	0.011	0	0.00	0.000	1	0.000	0.004	0	0.00	0.000
Polygonaceae sp. (knotweed)	17	0.000	0.036	1	0.00	0.019	2	0.000	0.007	0	0.00	0.000
Portulaca oleracea	1,952	0.000	4.101	0	0.00	0.000	0	0.000	0.000	0	0.00	0.000
Unknown	7	0.000	0.015	0	0.00	0.000	0	0.000	0.000	0	0.00	0.000
Subtotal other seed	2,022	0.000	4.248	1	0.00	0.019	6	0.000	0.022	2	0.00	0.032
Unidentifiable	131	0.000	0.275	0	0.00	0.000	99	0.000	0.365	3	0.00	0.048
Unidentifiable seed coat	13	0.000	0.027	0	0.00	0.000	0	0.000	0.000	0	0.00	0.000
Total Other	86	0.485	0.181	2	0.02	0.038	7	0.085	0.026	2	0.03	0.032
Fruit (?)	0	0.000	0.000	0	0.00	0.000	1	0.050	0.004	0	0.00	0.000
Monocot stem	1	0.000	0.002	1	0.01	0.019	0	0.000	0.000	0	0.00	0.000
Amorphous	85	0.485	0.179	1	0.01	0.019	6	0.035	0.022	2	0.03	0.032
Total-all	3,778	14.545	7.937	10	0.06	0.192	527	2.075	1.945	170	1.59	2.698

Table 9.2. continued, Summary of Plant Remains From All Proveniences

Provenience Total Liters	Test Units and Creek Midden Combined 334			Geotrench 6			TOTALS 868					
	Total Count	Total Weight	Count Density	Total Count	Total Weight	Count Density	Total Count	Total Weight	Count Density	Weight Density	Count Percent	Weight Percent
Nutshell Total	134	1.325	0.401	1	0.01	0.167	514	5.035	0.592	0.006	11.38%	27.06%
Carya sp. (hickory)	102	0.910	0.305	1	0.01	0.167	370	3.810	0.426	0.004	8.19%	20.47%
Corylus americana (hazelnut)	1	0.010	0.003	0	0	0.000	7	0.050	0.008	0.000	0.15%	0.27%
Juglandaceae (walnut family)	15	0.090	0.045	0	0	0.000	75	0.445	0.086	0.001	1.66%	2.39%
Juglans nigra (walnut)	10	0.270	0.030	0	0	0.000	16	0.470	0.018	0.001	0.35%	2.53%
Quercus sp. (acorn)	5	0.035	0.015	0	0	0.000	39	0.180	0.045	0.000	0.86%	0.97%
Unidentifiable	1	0.010	0.003	0	0	0.000	7	0.080	0.008	0.000	0.15%	0.43%
Wood Total	238	2.195	0.713	32	0.33	5.333	1,151	11.485	1.326	0.013	25.48%	61.71%
Carya sp. (hickory)	10	0.000	0.030	0	0	0.000	60	0.000	0.069	0.000	1.33%	0.00%
Fraxinus sp. (ash)	8	0.000	0.024	0	0	0.000	14	0.000	0.016	0.000	0.31%	0.00%
Juglans sp. (walnut)	0	0.000	0.000	0	0	0.000	11	0.000	0.013	0.000	0.24%	0.00%
Morus sp. (mulberry)	2	0.000	0.006	0	0	0.000	8	0.000	0.009	0.000	0.18%	0.00%
Plantanus sp. (sycamore)	0	0.000	0.000	1	0	0.167	4	0.000	0.005	0.000	0.09%	0.00%
Populus sp.	1	0.000	0.003	0	0	0.000	5	0.000	0.006	0.000	0.11%	0.00%
Prunus sp. (cherry)	0	0.000	0.000	0	0	0.000	0	0.000	0.000	0.000	0.00%	0.00%
Quercus sp. (oak)	8	0.000	0.024	4	0	0.667	44	0.000	0.051	0.000	0.97%	0.00%
Quercus sp. (red oak)	4	0.000	0.012	0	0	0.000	5	0.000	0.006	0.000	0.11%	0.00%
Quercus sp. (white oak)	2	0.000	0.006	0	0	0.000	3	0.000	0.003	0.000	0.07%	0.00%
Betulaceae (birch)	0	0.000	0.000	0	0	0.000	0	0.000	0.000	0.000	0.00%	0.00%
cf. Betulaceae sp. (birch)	2	0.000	0.006	0	0	0.000	3	0.000	0.003	0.000	0.07%	0.00%
Salicaceae (willow)	0	0.000	0.000	0	0	0.000	1	0.000	0.001	0.000	0.02%	0.00%
cf. *Ulmus rubus*	0	0.000	0.000	0	0	0.000	3	0.000	0.003	0.000	0.07%	0.00%
Ulmaceae (elm)	2	0.000	0.006	0	0	0.000	17	0.000	0.020	0.000	0.38%	0.00%
Total identified	39	0.000	0.117	5	0	0.833	178	0.000	0.205	0.000	3.94%	0.00%
Semi-ring porous	0	0.000	0.000	0	0	0.000	1	0.010	0.001	0.000	0.02%	0.05%
Diffuse porous	8	0.000	0.024	0	0	0.000	19	0.000	0.022	0.000	0.42%	0.00%
Ring porous	64	0.000	0.192	10	0	1.667	280	0.000	0.323	0.000	6.20%	0.00%
Unidentifiable	73	0.000	0.219	5	0	0.833	234	0.000	0.270	0.000	5.18%	0.00%
Identifications attempted	184	0.000	0.551	20	0	3.333	712	0.010	0.820	0.000	15.76%	0.05%
Bark	3	0.030	0.009	0	0	0.000	148	1.47	0.171	0.002	3.28%	7.90%
Total Seed	313	0.000	0.937	0	0	0.000	2,608	0.000	3.005	0.000	57.72%	0.00%
C. berlandieri (goosefoot)	13	0.000	0.039	0	0	0.000	46	0.000	0.053	0.000	1.02%	0.00%
P. caroliniana (maygrass)	182	0.000	0.545	0	0	0.000	221	0.000	0.255	0.000	4.89%	0.00%
P. erectum (erect knotweed)	2	0.000	0.006	0	0	0.000	58	0.000	0.067	0.000	1.28%	0.00%
H. pusillum (little barley)	6	0.000	0.018	0	0	0.000	6	0.000	0.007	0.000	0.13%	0.00%
Subtotal starchy cultigen	203	0.000	0.608	0	0	0.000	331	0.000	0.381	0.000	7.33%	0.00%
Amaranthus sp.	0	0.000	0.000	0	0	0.000	28	0.000	0.032	0.000	0.62%	0.00%
Chenopodium sp.	1	0.000	0.003	0	0	0.000	3	0.000	0.003	0.000	0.07%	0.00%
Compositae	0	0.000	0.000	0	0	0.000	1	0.000	0.001	0.000	0.02%	0.00%
Fabaceae sp. (bean)	0	0.000	0.000	0	0	0.000	1	0.000	0.001	0.000	0.02%	0.00%
Galium sp. (bedstraw)	2	0.000	0.006	0	0	0.000	3	0.000	0.003	0.000	0.07%	0.00%
Gramineae 6F	0	0.000	0.000	0	0	0.000	1	0.000	0.001	0.000	0.02%	0.00%
Gramineae sp. (grass)	0	0.000	0.000	0	0	0.000	5	0.000	0.006	0.000	0.11%	0.00%
Hordeum sp. (barley)	1	0.000	0.003	0	0	0.000	2	0.000	0.002	0.000	0.04%	0.00%
cf. *Hordeum* sp.	1	0.000	0.003	0	0	0.000	2	0.000	0.002	0.000	0.04%	0.00%
Panicum sp. (panic grass)	1	0.000	0.003	0	0	0.000	6	0.000	0.007	0.000	0.13%	0.00%
Polygonaceae sp. (knotweed)	2	0.000	0.006	0	0	0.000	20	0.000	0.023	0.000	0.44%	0.00%
Portulaca oleracea	0	0.000	0.000	0	0	0.000	1,952	0.000	2.249	0.000	43.20%	0.00%
Unknown	0	0.000	0.000	0	0	0.000	7	0.000	0.008	0.000	0.15%	0.00%
Subtotal other seed	8	0.000	0.024	0	0	0.000	2,031	0.000	2.340	0.000	44.95%	0.00%
Unidentifiable	102	0.000	0.305	0	0	0.000	233	0.000	0.268	0.000	5.16%	0.00%
Unidentifiable seed coat	0	0.000	0.000	0	0	0.000	13	0.000	0.015	0.000	0.29%	0.00%
Total Other	9	0.115	0.027	0	0	0.000	97	0.620	0.112	0.001	2.15%	3.33%
Fruit (?)	1	0.050	0.003	0	0	0.000	1	0.050	0.001	0.000	0.02%	0.27%
Monocot stem	0	0.000	0.000	0	0	0.000	2	0.010	0.002	0.000	0.04%	0.05%
Amorphous	8	0.065	0.024	0	0	0.000	94	0.560	0.108	0.001	2.08%	3.01%
Total-all	697	3.665	2.087	33	0.34	5.500	4,518	18.610	5.205	0.021	100.00%	100.00%

recovered from feature contexts, and over one-half of this total (N=223) was from Feature 8.

Wood

Wood charcoal comprises about one-quarter of all charred remains at the Dash Reeves site. Overall, wood charcoal fragments are small and poorly preserved; average weight of individual fragments is only 0.009 grams. The small size and poor preservation contributed to a lack of success in identification. Only 178 of the 712 pieces for which identification was attempted could be identified beyond the level of basic ring structure. The basic ring structure could be discerned on an additional 300 fragments, while 234 pieces examined could not be identified at all.

The wood charcoal assemblage is dominated by hickory, which makes up 33.7 percent of all identified fragments. Oak, including members of both the white oak and red oak groups, is the second most common wood type present. Together, oak and hickory comprise 62.9 percent of all wood identified from all proveniences. The three next most common taxa, elm, ash, and walnut, together contribute 25.2 percent to the assemblage total and make up the bulk of the remaining identified fragments. Mulberry, sycamore, birch, willow, and probable cottonwood also are represented.

Wood charcoal was highly ubiquitous. It was recovered from 80 percent of the features, 50 percent of the sheet midden units, 77.7 percent of the creek midden units, all test units, and the single geomorph trench sample. Densities were variable, ranging from 0.05 fragments per liter of fill in Excavation Unit 16 to 16.4 fragments per liter in Feature 16.

Asch and Asch (1986:497–498) have invoked the "firewood indifference hypothesis" to interpret wood charcoal assemblages from archaeological sites. This hypothesis posits that the nearest available deadwood was gathered to use as fuel for nonspecialized cooking and heating tasks. "Nonspecialized" can be inferred only for wood charcoal from secondary fill contexts. If this idea is valid, some level of congruence is expected between the archaeobotanical wood assemblage and the species composition of the nearby forests.

To test this hypothesis, the compositions of wood charcoal assemblages from the Dash Reeves site and other Middle Woodland sites in the region were compared to tree taxa data reported by Telford (1926) in his early twentieth-century forest survey (Table 9.3). Telford's model defines five forest types, among them, the mixed forests along secondary streams, which would have been present in the stream valleys cutting through the bluffs to the American Bottom, and upland mixed hardwoods, which would have characterized much of the bluff top per se. Although containing an inordinately large amount of hickory, the Dash Reeves site wood assemblage most closely approximates that of the secondary valley stream hardwood forest. This is not surprising, given the site's bluff base location near the mouth of Palmer Creek. Oak dominates all Middle Woodland assemblages other than that from Dash Reeves. However, except for the Truck #7 site, such secondary woods as elm, ash, Kentucky coffee tree or locust, and black walnut, are also relatively common. This holds true even for the upland Meridian Hills and Widman sites. Assuming that the Middle Woodland period forest composition approximated that presented by Telford, it appears that Middle Woodland occupants of both floodplain and upland sites exploited readily available wood at the bluff base and on bluff slopes and tops.

Seeds

By count, seeds are the most abundant plant class recovered, comprising 57.72 percent of all materials. No seeds were recovered from the geotrench, and only a single Polygonaceae seed was identified from the sheet midden units. Seeds were present in 77.22 percent of the creek midden units and 52.72 percent of the features.

About three-quarters of the seed assemblage consists of *Portulaca oleracea* (purslane) seeds (N=1,948) recovered from Feature 49. Excluding this group, seeds comprise just 25.68 percent of all materials. The relative contributions of features and creek midden units to the seed assemblage also are altered considerably when the Feature 49 purslane seeds are excluded. Including this mass, features yielded 87.96 percent of all seeds and the feature:creek midden seed ratio is 7.82; excluding it, features yielded only 52.42 percent of all seeds and the feature:creek midden seed ratio drops to 1.18. Because they represent such an anomalous occurrence, the seeds from Feature 49 are excluded from computations unless otherwise specified. This drops the total number of

Table 9.3. Comparison of Early Twentieth-Century Forest Composition and Middle Woodland Wood Assemblage Composition-Species as Percentage of Total

	Mixed Hardwoods of Main Streams (1)	Mixed Hardwoods of Secondary Streams (1)	Upland Mixed Hardwoods (oak and hickory less than 90%) North (1)	Upland Mixed Hardwoods (oak and Hickory less than 90%) South (1)	Oak and Hickory (more than 90%) (1)	Dash Reeves Site	Mund Site-Cement Hollow Phase (N=344) (2)	Widman Site-Cement Hollow Phase (N=64) (3)	Meridian Hills Site-Holding Phase (N=414) (4)	Holding Site-Holding Phase 7 (N=768) (5)	Truck 7 Site-Hill Lake Phase 8 (N=543) (6)
Maple-all	22.80	18.50	9.99	2.54	0.11	0.00	0.87	0.00	7.00	0.91	2.95
Elm	14.00	9.80	9.18	1.98	1.03	1.69	0.00	0.00	0.00	0.00	0.00
Ulmaceae	15.40	9.80	10.14	2.04	1.03	9.55	11.34	0.00	25.60	22.27	3.87
Ash	11.00	16.90	3.31	1.73	0.34	7.87	4.07	15.63	3.40	10.68	2.58
Hickory	5.50	4.10	7.24	16.12	9.18	33.71	0.29	29.69	18.80	11.98	10.31
Oak-all	24.60	30.80	58.32	0.00	88.29	29.22	31.10	39.06	34.80	31.12	48.07
Cottonwood	4.80	0.00	0.00	0.00	0.00	2.81	0.00	0.00	0.00	0.00	0.00
Salicaceae	7.40	0.30	0.00	0.00	0.00	0.56	0.00	0.00	0.00	0.00	2.39
River birch	3.40	0.00	0.00	0.00	0.00	1.69	0.00	0.00	0.00	0.00	0.37
Basswood	1.20	2.40	4.91	0.02	0.00	0.00	0.29	0.00	0.00	0.00	1.29
Black walnut	1.10	5.10	2.14	0.65	0.14	6.18	4.07	3.13	2.90	4.30	0.74
Sycamore	0.70	4.20	0.08	0.40	0.11	2.25	0.00	0.00	1.20	1.95	0.00
Honey locust	0.70	0.60	0.26	0.01	0.00	0.00	5.81	0.00	0.00	0.91	0.00
Ky coffee tree	0.00	0.10	0.39	0.00	0.00	0.00	0.29	0.00	0.00	0.00	0.00
Gymno/Gled	0.70	0.70	0.65	0.07	–	0.00	5.81	9.38	3.10	10.94	3.31
Mulberry	0.00	0.00	0.16	0.08	0.08	4.49	11.92	0.00	0.00	0.00	1.10
Buckeye	0.00	0.00	0.08	0.00	0.00	0.00	0.00	0.00	0.00	0.00	0.18
Pecan	0.80	0.00	0.00	0.00	0.00	0.00	0.00	0.00	3.10	0.65	4.97
Dogwood	0.00	0.00	0.00	0.00	0.00	0.00	0.00	0.00	0.00	0.78	0.00
Redbud	0.00	0.00	0.00	0.00	0.00	0.00	0.00	0.00	0.00	2.34	0.00
Persimmon	0.00	0.00	0.00	0.00	0.00	0.00	17.44	3.13	0.00	1.17	3.87
Grape vine	0.00	0.00	0.00	0.00	0.00	0.00	1.16	0.00	0.00	0.00	0.00
Unknown	0.00	0.00	0.00	0.00	0.00	0.00	5.52	0.00	0.00	0.00	14.00

N=Number of identified wood fragments in assemblage

1. Telford 1926
2. Johannessen 1983
3. Wolforth et al. 1993
4. Kathryn Parker, personal communication 1994
5. Parker 1989
6. Johannessen 1985

seeds recovered to 660, of which, 246 (37 percent) could not be identified.

Starchy Grains

Almost precisely half (N=331; 50.15 percent) of the total of 660 seeds belong to the starchy seed group: *Chenopodium berlandieri* (goosefoot), *Polygonum erectum* (erect knotweed), *Phalaris caroliniana* (maygrass), and *Hordeum pusillum* (little barley). Further, starchy seeds comprise 80 percent of all identified seeds (N=414). Starchy seeds are both abundant and ubiquitous in site assemblages dating from the Middle Woodland period and later in Illinois. Based on one or more criteria of temporal patterning, site or feature ubiquity, mutual association, presence in locations outside the plant's natural range, and abundance in archaeological contexts, all are presumed, minimally, to have been cultigens. *Chenopodium* is unique to this group in that it was ultimately domesticated, as reflected in changes in seed morphology through time. These changes involved increased seed viability and loss of dormancy-regulating mechanisms and are expressed by a thinning (and, ultimately, a loss) of the seed coat and by the development of a truncated margin to accommodate an increased perisperm size.

The most abundant starchy grain in the Dash Reeves site assemblage is maygrass, which constitutes 67 percent of the starchy seed group. Maygrass was recovered from test units, creek midden units, and features; however, the majority of the seeds (N=168; 76 percent of all) were recovered from Excavation Unit 9 in the creek midden.

As evidenced by its frequent occurrence in the archaeological record, maygrass was widely used across prehistoric southeastern North America (Cowan 1978; Yarnell and Black 1985). Its presence in fecal samples from Salts Cave, Kentucky, further provides direct evidence for its use as food (Yarnell 1969). Maygrass is extremely common in Middle Woodland site assemblages from the American Bottom (Table 9.4). It is also abundant in the Smiling Dan site assemblage from west-central Illinois (D. Asch and N. Asch 1985) and has been found as far north as Jo Daviess County, Illinois (Parker 1986).

Erect knotweed is the second most common starchy seed identified in the Dash Reeves assemblage, comprising 17.52 percent of all starchy seeds. This low

occurrence level is consistent with other Middle Woodland sites in the American Bottom region, where erect knotweed occurs erratically (Table 9.4). It was present in only three features at the Dash Reeves site.

Seed coat morphology could be determined for 21 erect knotweed specimens. Almost three-quarters exhibit striate punticulate coats, while the remainder have smooth coats. In modern collections of erect knotweed achenes, it was found that the former morph dominates material collected in the late summer, while the smoother, longer form predominates in collections of later-maturing achenes made in November (N. Asch and D. Asch 1985:144). Both forms are typically found at lower Illinois River valley sites (N. Asch and D. Asch 1985:139, 141). Both forms are also present in the assemblage from the nearby Marge site (Simon 1996). Achene sizes are small for both morphs in the Dash Reeves site materials (Figure 9.2), for the most part falling at the lower end of dimensions reported for the Newbridge site in the lower Illinois River valley (N. Asch and D. Asch 1985: Figure 4.3) and the Marge site in the American Bottom (Simon 1996:Figure 14.1).

Chenopodium is not abundant in the Dash Reeves site assemblage. The 46 seeds recovered comprise just 14 percent of the starchy grains and 11.11 percent of the identified seeds. *Chenopodium* was recovered from two creek midden units and eight features. As noted above, archaeological *Chenopodium* seeds can exhibit morphological changes that reflect domestication. In the American Bottom region, the earliest domesticated *Chenopodium* identified to date is from the Sponemann component (ca. 750–800 A.D.) at the Sponemann site (Parker 1991). Subsets of *Chenopodium* seeds from Emergent Mississippian components at the Robinsons Lake and Sampson Bluff sites also exhibit characteristics indicative of their derivation from domesticated plants.

The majority (N=28; 61 percent) of *Chenopodium* seeds from the Dash Reeves site are small and exhibit the clearly reticulate, thick seed coats and convex margins typical of seeds from wild plants. The seven seeds that appear to have slightly thinner, smoother coats are burst, lack embryos, and have obliterated seed margins. Seed coat morphology could not be determined for the remaining 11 specimens. Diameters were recorded for a subset of 15 seeds, among them, 11 thick-coated and four burst specimens (Table 9.5). Diameters parallel to the radicle range from 0.95 to 1.35 mm, with the diameters for the burst (potentially domesticated) speci-

Table 9.4. Starchy Seeds from Middle Woodland Sites in the American Bottom

Site	Total Number of Starchy Seeds	Total Identified Seeds	Starchy Seeds as a Percent of Identified Seeds	C. berlandieri			P. caroliniana			P. erectum			H. pusillum		
				Count	Percent of Starchy Seeds	Ubiquity	Count	Percent of Starchy Seeds	Ubiquity	Count	Percent of Starchy Seeds	Ubiquity	Count	Percent of Starchy Seeds	Ubiquity
Mund[1]	105	242	43.39%	8	7.62%	22.22%	96	91.43%	33.33%	–	0.00%	0.00%	1	0.95%	5.56%
Widman[2]	16	23	69.57%	15	93.75%	57.14%	1	6.25%	14.30%	–	0.00%	0.00%	0	0.00%	0.00%
Meridian Hills#[3]	5,122	5,590	91.63%	1,085	21.18%	23.08%	2,315	45.20%	28.21%	1,719	33.56%	23.08%	3	0.06%	5.13%
Holding##[4]	2,748	4,797	57.29%	240	8.73%	37.82%	2,372	86.32%	64.71%	86	3.13%	17.65%	50	1.82%	17.65%
Truck 7[5]	313	436	71.79%	193	61.66%	58.33%	116	37.06%	25.00%	4	1.28%	25.00%	0	0.00%	0.00%
Dash Reeves*–All	331	2,362	14.01%	46	13.90%	13.10%	221	66.77%	20.24%	58	17.52%	4.76%	6	1.81%	2.38%
All excluding Feature 49	331	414	79.95%	46	13.90%	13.10%	221	66.77%	20.24%	58	17.52%	4.76%	6	1.81%	2.38%
Features	128	2,150	5.95%	33	25.78%	14.55%	39	30.47%	14.55%	56	43.75%	5.45%	0	0.00%	0.00%
Features excluding F-49	128	202	63.37%	33	25.78%	14.55%	39	30.47%	14.55%	56	43.75%	5.45%	0	0.00%	0.00%
Creek midden	188	194	96.91%	13	6.91%	14.29%	182	96.81%	42.86%	2	1.06%	4.76%	6	3.19%	9.52%

1 Johannessen 1983:Table 21
2 Wolforth et al. 1990:Table 7
3 Williams et al. 1987; Kathryn Parker, personal communication 1994
4 Parker 1989:Table 83
5 Johannessen 1985:Table 78
*Calculations include 1,948 *Portulaca* seeds from Feature 49

#Excluding 2 seed masses, starchy seeds comprise 78.4 percent of identified seeds
Excluding 2 seed masses, starchy seeds comprise 80.45 percent of identified seeds

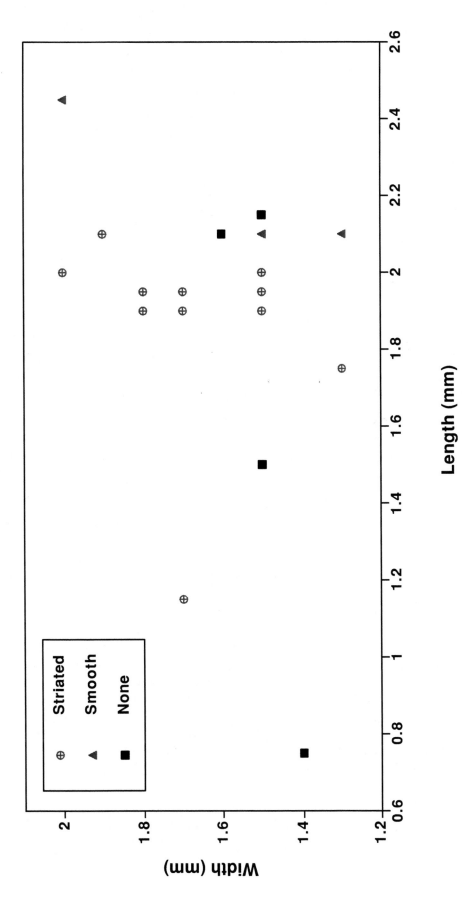

Figure 9.2.   Comparative Measurement of Three *Polygonum erectum* Morphs

Table 9.5. *Chenopodium berlandieri* Measurements

Feature	Specimen	Dimension Perpendicular to Break (mm)	Dimension Parallel to Break (mm)	Seed Coat Morphology
25	1	1.10	0.95	burst; thin, smooth (?)
	2	1.10	0.95	burst; thin, smooth (?)
32	3	1.10	0.80	burst; thin, smooth (?)
	4	1.30	1.25	burst; thin, smooth (?)
15	5	1.25	1.10	thick, reticulate
	6	1.25	1.20	thick, reticulate
36	7	1.20	1.20	thick, reticulate
	8	1.40	1.20	thick, reticulate
50	9	1.40	1.35	thick, reticulate
	10	1.25	1.20	thick, reticulate
	11	1.25	1.20	thick, reticulate
	12	1.20	1.20	thick, reticulate
EU 9	13	1.50	1.30	thick, reticulate
	14	1.20	1.00	thick, reticulate
EU 44	15	0.85	1.00	thick, reticulate radical emerging
Average		1.25	1.14	

mens falling mainly at the lower end of this range. Smith (1986:129) has noted that diameter is probably not a good indicator of *Chenopodium* domestication, as the overlapping ranges of these two samples suggest.

The final member of the starchy seed group, little barley, is represented by only six specimens, all of which are from Test Units A and E in the creek midden. Little barley is almost invariably the least common of the starchy seeds recovered from Middle Woodland sites in the American Bottom region (Table 9.4). It is more common in lower Illinois River valley sites of this period, but even there it only rarely approaches the other three starchy seeds in ubiquity or abundance. Quantitatively, it is best represented by the 2,040 caryopses recovered from the Smiling Dan site in the lower Illinois River valley (D. Asch and N. Asch 1985).

Other Seeds

Excluding the 1,948 purslane seeds from Feature 49, only 83 nonstarchy seeds were identified (20 percent of the identified seed assemblage). Excluding seed masses, similar percentages of nonstarchy seeds are present in other middle Middle Woodland and late Middle Woodland assemblages from the region (Table 9.4).

This group contains probable economic noncultigens, fortuitous weedy inclusions, and seeds that could not be identified to a level permitting their assignment to a specific category. Among the latter are three specimens of *Chenopodium* that are not intact enough to assign to a species, but which may be *C. berlandieri*, and four grass seeds designated *Hordeum* that resemble *Hordeum pusillum*, but could not be confirmed as such. In contrast, the 20 seeds identified as Polygonaceae are clearly not *P. erectum* but represent probable fortuitous occurrences of a different species.

The economic noncultigen class contains *Amaranthus* sp. and panic grass, both of which are recovered regularly, if in small numbers, from archaeological sites in the region. Additionally, cultivated amaranth has been recovered from Mississippian component rockshelters in Arkansas (Fritz 1984). Cultivated amaranth has not been identified from any American Bottom area site; however, given its potential both as a pot herb and as a bearer of edible seeds, it is unlikely that the plant was overlooked by prehistoric occupants of the region.

Panic grass grains have been recovered in low quantities from Middle Woodland components at the Mund (Johannessen 1983), Meridian Hills (Kathryn Parker, personal communication 1994), and Truck #7 (Johannessen 1985) sites. In addition, the Holding site yielded 1,762 grains, including a mass of 1,743 from a single feature (Parker 1989). The abundance and ubiquity of these seeds suggest at least occasional use of the plant, whether for subsistence (Parker 1991) or technological purposes (N. Asch and D. Asch 1985).

The significance of the large mass of purslane seeds from Feature 49 is problematic. This is not the only occurrence of this taxon at the site; four additional seeds were recovered from a single Feature 29 sample. Two seeds also were reported from the Middle Woodland Holding site (Parker 1989), and purslane has been recovered infrequently from later components in the region (e.g., ICT 2 site [Lopinot 1991]; Marge site [Simon 1995]). Although Mohlenbrock (1986) lists *Portulaca oleracea* as a European native that has been naturalized in waste areas across the state, its increasing identification in the archaeological record provides one line of evidence that the plant is in fact native.

DISTRIBUTION OF PLANT REMAINS

Nutshell, wood, and seeds were not evenly distributed among the various proveniences at the Dash Reeves site (Figure 9.3). The low density of plant remains in the sheet midden may reflect both the smaller number of samples obtained from this context and the high level of postdepositional attrition postulated for a shallow midden surrounded by features. It is likely that this area originally accumulated less debris than other contexts, since even the two sheet midden units from the western site area, where features were densest, yielded negligible remains. The geomorph trench also yielded quantitatively little material, although the wood density, at 5.33 fragments per liter of fill, was relatively high for the site. This unit also contained an unusually large number of deer bones, lithic debris, and remains of one large ceramic vessel.

In most cases, plant densities were highest in feature and creek midden contexts. Excluding the 1,948 purslane seeds from Feature 49, seed densities for both the features and the creek midden units were very similar. However, wood and nutshell densities were approximately twice as high in the features as in the creek midden. This contrasts with the pattern of distribution

of ceramics, larger faunal elements, and lithic remains, all of which were more abundant in the creek midden than in the features. Fortier (this volume) has suggested that the creek area was used as an intentional garbage dumping ground.

The different distributional patterns apparent between the plant remains and other materials may be due in part to the nature of the garbage itself. Most plant remains would not have posed the physical hazard that broken pottery, large broken skeletal elements, or chert flakes would and, therefore, would not have required as careful disposal. The main class of plant remains that would have posed a physical hazard is nutshell. However, use of the nutshells for fuel, in addition to satisfying a resource need, would have solved the disposal problem in that case. Apparently, disposal of charred plant residues in the creek midden did occur, as witnessed by the concentration of maygrass and other plant residues in the northwesternmost creek units. However, such intentional disposal of plant garbage does not seem to have been the rule. Of course, as far as archaeobotanical remains are concerned, our record is limited to charred materials; noncharred byproducts of day-to-day plant use may well have been disposed of in the creek midden and we simply have no record of it.

Plant densities were calculated for each of the 10 feature types recognized (Figure 9.4; Table 9.6). Overall, the cooking/refuse pits had the highest material densities at 7.47 fragments per liter (again, the 1,948 purslane seeds from Feature 49 are excluded from consideration). Six of the 10 individual features with the highest count per liter values were cooking/refuse pits. Nutshells were particularly abundant in this feature type; of seven features with greater than one fragment of nutshell per liter, six were cooking/refuse pits. Nutshell densities in cooking/refuse Features 8 and 10 were 10.62 and 9.429 fragments per liter of fill, respectively. These values are over five times higher than the next highest calculated value.

Although numerically most abundant in the cooking/refuse pits, wood fragment densities by feature type clearly varied because of strong skewing by individual feature values and small sample sizes. Earth ovens yielded a very high wood density of 4.75 fragments per liter. However, only two features of this type were identified, and most of the wood was recovered from only one of them; with 14.33 wood fragments per liter, Feature 12 contained the second greatest density of any

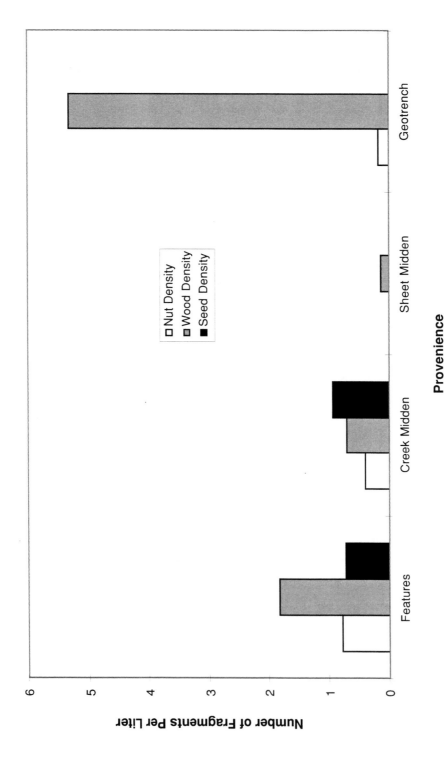

Figure 9.3. Average Densities of Plant Classes by Provenience

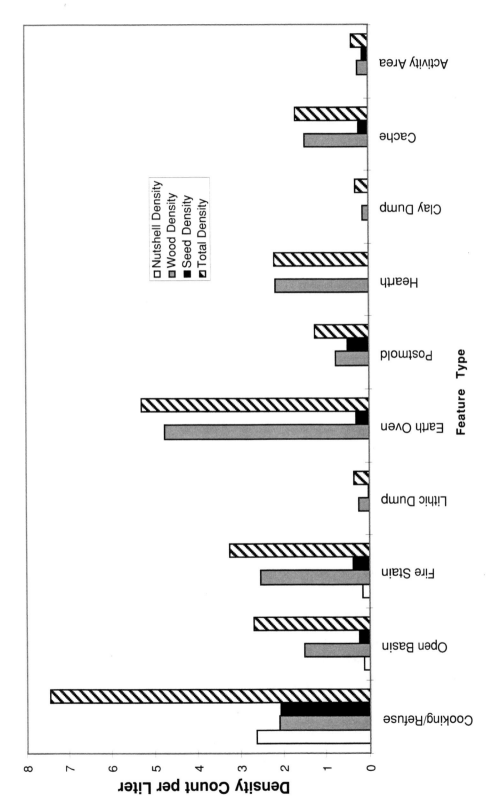

Figure 9.4. Material Densities for Nutshell, Wood, and Seeds by Feature Type

Table 9.6.   Feature Types Sampled for Plant Remains

Feature Type	Count	Feature Numbers
Open basin	22	1,2,3,4,5,6,7,19,21,22,23,24,27,31,33,37,38, 41,42,44,45,56
Cooking/refuse	13	8,10,20,25,26,28,32,34,36,43,47,49,50
Fire stain	5	13,14,16,39,40
Earth oven	2	12,15
Hearth	4	18,46,48,51
Postmold	2	PM 4 and 5
Lithic dump (in pits)	4	52,53,54*,55
Cache	1	29
Clay dump	1	30
Activity stain	1	11
Total	55	

*Feature 54 contained no plant remains

feature at the site. In contrast, the other earth oven, Feature 15, yielded only 0.6 fragments of wood per liter. Similarly, fire stain and hearth densities were skewed by single-feature contributions, fire stains by Feature 16, which yielded 16.4 wood fragments per liter, and hearths by Feature 46, which yielded six fragments per liter. Aside from the aberrant features, wood fragment densities from the remaining hearth and fire stain features are, in fact, on a par with densities from other feature types.

Seeds also were most strongly associated with the cooking/refuse pits. Even excluding the 1,948 purslane seeds from Feature 49, this feature type yielded 2.1 seeds per liter, four times the density of the next densest type.

Seeds also exhibited an interesting spatial distributional pattern. The three features with the highest seed densities, Features 36, 49, and 50 (all of which are cooking/refuse features), were located near one another in the northeastern part of the area excavated (Figure 9.1). These three features also contained 55.5 percent of all the starchy seeds recovered from features. Two of the three features with the second highest seed densities (Features 32 and 37) also were located in this area. In addition, a single concentration of seeds was found in Feature 8 in the south-central site area. This feature alone yielded 22 percent of all starchy seeds from features. It is possible that starchy seed processing took place in these two locations.

MIDDLE WOODLAND PLANT USE

In the foregoing discussion, numerous comparisons were made between Dash Reeves site materials and materials from other Middle Woodland sites in the American Bottom region. Perhaps the most significant pattern exhibited by these remains during the period is increasing utilization of starchy seeds at the apparent expense of other food resources, particularly nut crops. Traditionally, this pattern has been assessed using a number of quantitative measures, notably nut:wood ratio and the percentage of starchy seeds in the total seed assemblage (e.g., Johannessen 1984, 1988). Application of these ratios to the Middle Woodland data sets examined here results in the delineation of patterns that are in accordance with those previously identified for the region (Johannessen 1984, 1988). Both a slight increase through time in starchy seed quantities relative to other seeds (Figure 9.5) and a decrease in the nut:wood ratio, reflecting decreasing nut use (Figure 9.6), are demonstrated. Assuming wood as a constant, the seed:wood ratio was also calculated for comparative purposes (Figure 9.7). The resulting ratios are less conclusive but also show a gradual, if slight, increase through time. All seed statistics were calculated excluding any seed masses, defined as more than 1,000 of any given seed taxon from a single sample. The very presence of these starchy seed masses at two Middle Woodland sites, Holding and Meridian Hills, is significant in and of itself and further underscores the importance of such resources.

The data from these Middle Woodland sites is of interest not only in terms of how it fits into established long-term temporal patterns, but also in the variation exhibited by the individual sites when compared one to another. Interestingly, much of this variation seems to be associated with chronological positioning, with major differences between sites seen in the middle Middle Woodland period Holding phase, concurrent with the Hopewell manifestation in the American Bottom region. It is also worth noting that, to date, these middle Middle Woodland sites appear to be spatially restricted to the northern American Bottom, while earlier sites are distributed across the area and later Middle Woodland sites are situated to the south.

Perhaps the most outstanding variability exhibited by the middle Middle Woodland sites is in the composition of nutshell assemblages. The Hill Creek phase Dash Reeves site in a sense continues the pattern established during the Late Archaic and Early Woodland periods of thick-shelled hickory dominance. However, the large Holding phase assemblages at the Meridian Hills and Holding sites, the single Holding phase sample from the Nochta site, and the small, three-feature Holding phase component at the Willoughby site display interesting deviations from this generalization (Figure 9.8). With allocation, the nutshell assemblage from the Holding site is dominated by hazelnut, while black walnut is the most abundant type of nutshell from the Meridian Hills site, from the Willoughby site, and in the single Nochta site feature. Unfortunately, be-

cause of limited excavations, we cannot be sure that the samples from the latter two sites are entirely representative. However, the samples we do have are clearly distinct from most samples from early Middle Woodland Cement Hollow phase and late Middle Woodland Hill Lake phase sites, in that they are not dominated by thick-shelled hickory.

By way of comparison, in west-central Illinois and the lower Illinois River area, hazelnut is a common component of assemblages from Middle Woodland sites, often equaling or exceeding thick-shelled hickory in abundance. This pattern is consistent regardless of geographic location, occurring both at sites located in the uplands, where hazelnut would be expected to be a relatively common resource (e.g., Massey and Archie sites), and at sites located in what would appear to be less favorable habitats near the Illinois River bottom (e.g., Napoleon Hollow site). It also holds true regardless of duration of occupation. The year-round occupation at the Smiling Dan site yielded nearly as high a percentage of hazelnut as did the short-term occupation at the Massey site.

Hazelnut was also noted as the dominant constituent in the Middle Woodland component at the Eilers site, located in the uplands near the Sangamon River. In contrast, subsequent components at this and the nearby Griffie site were dominated by thick-shelled hickory (King and Roper 1976). The high incidence of hazelnut in the Middle Woodland component at the Eilers site is attributed to natural abundance in this ecotonal area, though this abundance declined with subsequent climatic changes (King and Roper 1976:147–149). D. Asch and N. Asch (1985:352–353), however, discount climatic variation as adequate to account for the utilization level evident in west-central Illinois site assemblages. Rather, they favor a theory that posits anthropogenically induced modification of the landscape by fire. Such intentionally set fires would have served as "a deliberate tool of landscape management" (D. Asch and N. Asch 1985:353) and opened the forest canopy, increasing the availability not only of hazelnuts, which favor an edge or ecotonal habitat, but also of hickory and oak masts. This theory is supported by the wood charcoal assemblage from the Smiling Dan site, which reflects gathering in an oak-hickory forest rather than in the mixed deciduous forest that was apparently present in the vicinity during the early nineteenth century (D. Asch and N. Asch 1985).

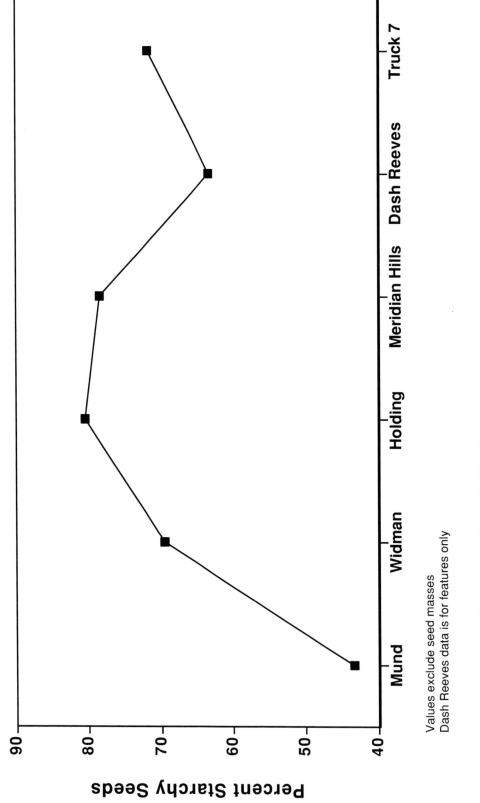

Values exclude seed masses
Dash Reeves data is for features only

Figure 9.5.   Starchy Seeds as Percentage of Identified Seeds

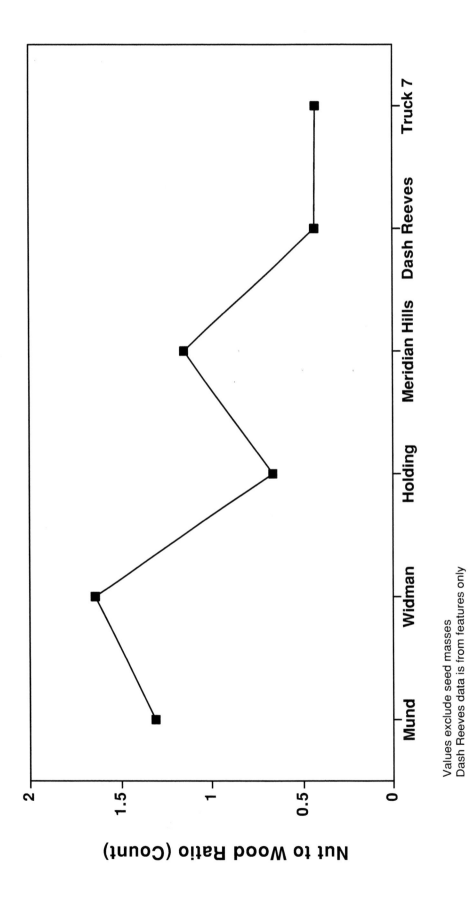

Values exclude seed masses
Dash Reeves data is from features only

Figure 9.6. Middle Woodland Nut-to-Wood Ratios

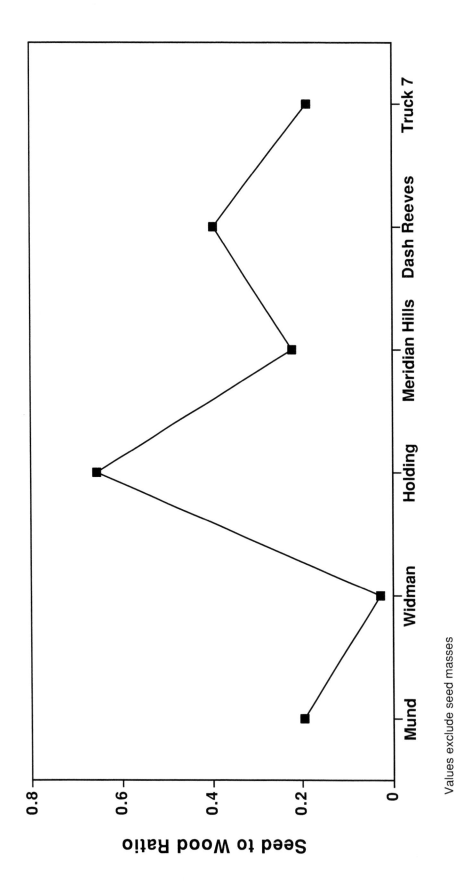

Values exclude seed masses

Figure 9.7. Middle Woodland Seed-to-Wood Ratios

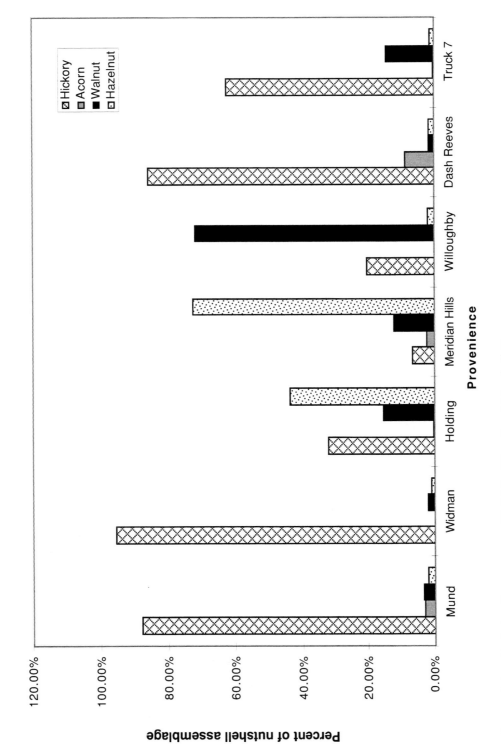

Figure 9.8. Relative Percentages of Middle Woodland Nutshell Taxa

The American Bottom data for the Middle Wood-land period does not demonstrate as consistent a pattern of hazelnut dependence as does the lower Illinois River valley material. However, it does indicate a clear short-term fluctuation in nut preference during middle Middle Woodland times. It seems unlikely the relatively high incidence of hazelnut or walnut at some American Bottom sites is simply a function of natural as opposed to anthropogenic availability. Certainly, such abundance is not reflected in the archaeobotanical records from earlier or later sites in the region. A recent summary study has shown that hazelnut is the dominant nutshell type in only three of 78 components in the American Bottom (Parker and Simon 1994). The three sites are Holding and two limited-activity upland loci. In addition to Meridian Hills, Willoughby, and perhaps Nochta, walnut dominates assemblages from three other sites, two of which are Mississippian and one of which is Late Archaic. All are in the floodplain. If the abundance of hazelnut and black walnut in Holding phase site assemblages reflects natural abundance, it indicates an unusually limited temporal phenomenon. It is possible that restricted intentional encouragement or propagation of hazelnut shrubs was occurring, resulting in the development of "microhabitats." If this were the case, cultural selection would ultimately be responsible for creating the observed pattern.

Site type and function may be relevant to understanding distributional patterns of Middle Woodland archaeobotanical remains. It is possible, for example, that the assemblages from the Meridian Hills and Holding sites reflect longer-term occupations than those represented at other Middle Woodland sites. Consequently, a more representative sample of all plants utilized would be expected (Parker 1989:449). Certainly, with the exception of the Nochta site, the Middle Woodland component of which remains essentially undisturbed and unexcavated, these two sites seem to be either the longest occupied or least specialized of the Middle Woodland sites considered here. Again, however, one must ask why, if hazelnut and black walnut were so readily available, they were being exploited so heavily at one time and essentially ignored or used only lightly at other times.

Finally, as always, sampling bias must be acknowledged. One issue that must be considered is the presence of large concentrations of a given nutshell taxon in a single feature. As pointed out in the earlier discussion of seed remains, these concentrations tend to bias the data. Since material is not uniformly distributed among features at most sites, what is meant by "concentration" must be stated explicitly. In a recent paper, concentrations of 1,000 or more seeds of a single taxon were subjectively designated "masses" and excluded from general quantitative analyses (Parker and Simon 1994). There are only two Middle Woodland sites, Mund and Meridian Hills, with features yielding nutshell of a single taxon in such quantities. Exclusion of these masses does not significantly alter the nutshell pattern, except in one interesting instance. After exclusion and subsequent allocation, the Meridian Hills assemblage is dominated by hazelnut rather than black walnut, with black walnut falling to second in abundance. In contrast, the Mund site is still clearly dominated by thick-shelled hickory. Exclusion of nutshell masses serves only to emphasize the importance of hazelnut in the Holding phase assemblage.

The nutshell pattern evident for Middle Woodland sites appears to be a real, behavioral phenomenon, reflecting changing cultural preferences and activities. Evidence provided by other artifact classes, most notably ceramics, indicates that there was a great deal of contact, if not actual population movement, between the lower Illinois River valley and the American Bottom at this time (Andrew Fortier, personal communication 1995). A preference for hazelnut, which was widely available in the former area during the Middle Woodland period, may have been transported to the American Bottom as the result of such contacts/movements. Hazelnut would certainly have been available, if not so readily as thick-shelled hickory, to populations in the American Bottom floodplain. Increased difficulty in procurement would have been offset by perceived desirability.

This period may also mark the initial prehistoric use of fire as a management tool in the American Bottom. Such practices may be reflected in the wood charcoal record, which shows a shift to oak-hickory in the later part of the Middle Woodland period. Compared to other species, both oaks and hickories are relatively fire tolerant; their "delay" in showing up as dominant constituents of archaeological wood assemblages may reflect a time lag in clearing large forested tracts. As noted above, this clearing not only would have increased the edge areas for hazelnut growth, but also, ultimately, all nut masts, including hickory. It is further possible that the dominance of oak and hickory in subsequent archaeological records reflects management of woodlands by fire.

Finally, we may perhaps be remiss in attributing only subsistence functions to these remains. For example, black walnut husks and shells render a dark brown, relatively colorfast dye (Adrosko 1971). The disproportionate occurrence of black walnut during the Holding phase may be due in part to use of this resource for a dye by a people that, in other respects, were very color conscious (Fortier 1992).

Plant assemblages from Late Archaic and Early Woodland sites indicate that these populations engaged in some level of cultivation. Maygrass, which does not naturally occur in this region, has been recovered from several of these earlier sites, as has cucurbit rind, although whether or not the latter actually represents a cultivated plant or use of an indigenous species is still open to question. Further, there is early evidence for use of the weedy annuals *Chenopodium* and erect knotweed. Thus, the knowledge of plant husbandry and at least some of the technology needed to implement cultivation were in place prior to the middle Middle Woodland period.

Nonetheless, it was not until the late Middle Woodland period that cultivated plants became truly significant. Notably, maygrass remains increased substantially, reflecting intensification of use. *Chenopodium* and erect knotweed also occurred with increasing frequency; however, in the American Bottom, we have not yet identified domesticated *Chenopodium* from this time. Finally, the recent recovery of small amounts of maize from the Holding site and of tobacco from the Meridian Hills site further underscores the fact that plant husbandry was part of the economic system, although in some aspects perhaps still on an experimental basis and not exclusively for subsistence purposes.

SUMMARY AND CONCLUSION

Plant remains from the Dash Reeves site conform to the predicted patterns of Middle Woodland plant use established by previously studied data sets. Three general trends characterize this period compared with earlier periods: an increase in the use of starchy seeds, a decrease in the use of nut crops, and a shift in wood

utilization patterns. In the Dash Reeves site assemblage, starchy seeds constitute almost 80 percent of all seeds recovered from any context (excluding Feature 49, with its mass of purslane seeds). The predominance of maygrass is also typical for sites of this period. The assemblage is characterized by a low nut:wood ratio of 0.43. Further, quantities of nutshell are relatively low, as indicated by the nutshell density of 7.96 fragments per 10 liters. This is in accordance with contemporary sites in the region and is lower than densities from many Archaic and Early Woodland sites. Finally, the wood charcoal assemblage, while leaning toward an emphasis on oak and hickory, also contains a fair amount of secondary wood types. In this respect, it is somewhat transitional between earlier assemblages that contain larger amounts of the so-called bottomland taxa and later assemblages that reflect a selection for oak and hickory. Middle and Late Woodland nutshell and wood patterns may be closely related, reflecting alteration of the landscape brought about by changing resource desirability and landscape management via fire. Further, the increased importance of the starchy seeds was probably at least to some extent at the expense of the nut crops. Studies of seed morphology suggest that the starchy grains from the Dash Reeves site were not from clearly domesticated plants.

Distributional studies of the Dash Reeves site materials indicate that plant residues probably had a different disposal trajectory than other types of materials. Remains from all plant classes were much more abundant in feature contexts than in the creek midden contexts, despite the fact that the reverse is true for both lithic debitage and ceramics. Plant remains degrade rapidly and pose less of a hazard than other material classes. Further, if most parts of the plant were used, there simply may have been quantitatively little waste produced. Differential disposal remains only a premise and must be tested with data from additional sites. Certainly the need to consider other contexts of deposition is underscored.

Some interesting anomalies and temporal patterns are apparent in Middle Woodland plant remains from individual sites in the American Bottom. The primary anomaly noted is the seeming shift in nut crop preference during the Holding phase from thick-shelled hickory to hazelnut and black walnut. Hazelnut was preferred by populations in the lower Illinois River valley at this time. The increase in these two nut types in the American Bottom may not have been solely due to changing subsistence preferences but to additional cultural factors, for example, the need for dark dyes that can be obtained from the black walnut husk and shell. Another anomaly is the recovery of both maize and tobacco from only Holding phase Middle Woodland contexts. The dramatic increase in starchy seeds further suggests that the Holding phase was a time of major change in the economic system. However, to date, maize has not been found in any subsequent component in the American Bottom until the Sponemann phase (ca. 750 A.D.). Starchy seeds, on the other hand, remained an important component of the economic system in post-Holding times.

10

FAUNAL REMAINS

Douglas J. Brewer and John T. Penman

The 1990 excavations at Dash Reeves produced over 4,660 vertebrate remains. The faunal assemblage presented here also includes one burned, large, mammal long bone fragment (deer-sized) found on the surface in 1971. This collection primarily represents food remains. The shaft of a mammal long bone from Test Unit E is the only utilized bone artifact recovered. This tool is fragmentary, and its function cannot be determined.

METHODS

Soil excavated from each 2-x-2-m test unit was sifted through 1/4-inch screen, and at least one 10-liter soil sample was taken from each 10-cm level in every test unit for flotation. Soil samples were taken from the 53 features as well. The heavy fraction from floats was processed through 1/16-inch (approximately 1.6-mm) mesh screen. Unidentified bone recovered from the test units is enumerated here to indicate relative horizontal concentrations. Unidentified bone from the 48 excavation units is similarly presented. Soil from the excavation units was not screened, however, and the bone sample recovered from those units may be biased toward larger fragments. General comparisons between excavation units in the sheet midden and those in the creek midden may be helpful in determining relative bone concentrations (Table 10.1).

The authority utilized herein for fish systematics is Bailey et al. (1991). Nomenclature for amphibians and reptiles is from Smith (1961). The American Ornithologists' Union *Checklist* (A.O.U. 1983) is the reference for birds. Hoffmeister (1989) is the source for mammal terminology. Douglas J. Brewer (University of Illinois Museum of Natural History) identified most of the elements in the faunal assemblage utilizing the comparative collection in the Department of Anthropology at the University of Illinois, Urbana. John Penman made additional identifications utilizing the collections at the Illinois State Museum, assisted by Karli White of that institution. Andrew C. Fortier conducted the fish scale analysis.

RESULTS

Bone was present in 39 of the 48 excavation units. A single fragment of tooth enamel was found in Excavation Unit 1, and only one bone was recovered from each of Excavation Units 32 and 48, located in the sheet midden. Excavation Units 13 and 15 were the only creek midden units where bone was absent (see Table 10.1). Bone was found in 45 of the features (Table 10.2) and was recovered from all test units except K, L, and N (Table 10.3).

Remains of amphibians, reptiles, fish, birds, and mammals are present in the assemblage. Reptiles, fish, and mammals identified to a taxonomic level beyond class represent 2 percent of the total assemblage.

Table 10.1. Unidentified Bone from Excavation Units

Unit Number	Excavation NISP			Flotation NISP		
	calcined	*burned*	*unburned*	*calcined*	*burned*	*unburned*
Creek Midden						
2	17	0	0	0	0	0
5	5	0	1	0	1	3
6	45	0	0	18	0	0
7	0	0	0	0	0	3
8	0	0	5	39	0	0
9	39	64	11	86	4	7
10	0	0	13	13	0	2
11	0	0	0	6	0	10
14	0	0	0	2	0	5
16	0	0	0	4	0	0
18	38	0	0	0	0	0
19	10	0	0	1	0	0
20	2	0	0	40	0	0
24	0	0	2	2	0	0
43	2	0	0	56	0	3
44	1	0	0	46	0	13
45	1	0	13	7	0	16
Creek Midden Total	160	64	45	320	5	62
Sheet Midden						
3	0	0	3	0	0	0
4	0	0	1	22	0	0
12	18	0	0	12	0	0
21	0	0	0	0	0	2
22	0	0	0	10	0	0
23	0	0	0	8	0	0
25	0	0	0	11	0	0
26	0	0	2	26	0	0
27	0	0	0	0	18	2
29	0	0	0	8	0	0
30	5	0	1	19	0	0
31	0	0	0	15	0	0
32	0	0	0	1	0	0
35	2	0	0	0	0	0
36	0	0	0	0	8	0
37	1	0	2	4	0	0
38	1	5	0	0	0	9
39	0	0	0	21	0	0
40	9	0	0	4	0	0
41	1	0	0	0	0	0
42	1	0	1	3	0	0
48	0	0	1	0	0	0
Sheet Midden Total	38	5	11	164	26	13

Table 10.2. Unidentified Bone from Features

Feature Number	Excavation NISP			Flotation NISP		
	calcined	burned	unburned	calcined	burned	unburned
2	0	0	0	22	4	0
5	0	0	0	59	1	3
6	5	0	0	0	0	0
8	30	0	5	336	0	0
10	51	37	0	34	0	14
11	15	0	0	24	0	0
12	4	0	0	27	0	0
13	18	0	0	12	0	0
14	0	0	0	19	0	5
15	0	0	0	0	0	7
18	0	0	0	71	0	0
19	0	0	0	0	0	24
20	0	0	0	82	0	0
21	0	0	0	7	0	0
22	0	0	0	29	0	0
23	0	0	0	8	1	0
24	0	0	0	10	24	0
25	0	0	0	3	0	0
26	27	0	13	54	0	1
28	14	0	0	16	0	0
29	0	0	0	19	0	0
31	0	0	0	4	0	0
32	2	0	0	30	3	0
33	0	0	0	0	0	1
34	1	0	0	3	0	0
35 & 38	0	0	0	0	6	2
36	11	1	0	0	0	16
37	0	0	0	26	0	0
38	0	0	0	2	0	0
40	0	0	0	33	0	40
41	0	0	0	12	0	0
42	0	0	0	27	0	0
43	0	0	0	44	0	3
44	3	0	0	13	0	0
45	0	0	0	11	0	8
47	0	0	0	1	0	0
49	0	0	0	10	1	0
50	0	0	0	48	3	0
52	2	0	6	29	0	7
53	3	0	0	161	0	0
54	5	0	0	77	0	0
55	0	0	0	61	0	0
56	0	0	0	6	0	0
PM 4	0	0	0	0	0	14
PM 5	0	0	0	20	0	0
Feature Total	191	38	24	1,450	43	145

Table 10.3. Unidentified Bone from All Contexts

Provenience and/ or Description	Excavation NISP			Flotation NISP		
	calcined	burned	unburned	calcined	burned	unburned
Features	191	38	24	1,450	43	145
Excavation Units						
Creek Midden	160	64	45	320	5	62
Sheet Midden						
Sheet Midden	38	5	11	164	26	13
Total	198	69	56	484	31	75
Geotrench One	0	0	0	4	0	0
Test Units						
A	22	0	0	41	1	4
B	5	0	4	0	0	0
C	0	0	0	0	0	1
D	1	0	0	0	0	0
E	182	3	1	88	0	0
F	111	1	0	45	0	3
G	152	2	175	92	0	85
H	0	0	0	1	0	0
J	0	0	0	0	0	2
M	1	0	1	0	0	0
Total	474	6	181	267	1	95
Unidentified Mammal	150	8	460	0	0	0
Medium Mammal	4	0	1	0	0	0
Large Mammal	69	3	14	0	0	2
Total	223	11	475	0	0	2
Site Total	1,086	124	736	2,205	75	317

Amphibians and Reptiles

The single frog or toad element is from a flotation sample taken from Level 2 of Geotrench 2. This bone, along with the remains of a colubrid snake in Feature 7, possibly represent intrusive modern individuals. A calcined snake vertebra was recovered from Feature 50.

Turtle shell was recovered from Features 10 and 47. There are 12 fragments of turtle carapace or plastron in the assemblage. Nine of these fragments are calcined, and three are burned.

Fish

The majority (86 percent) of the fish bones are unburned (N=24), and only four (14 percent) are calcined. Fish remains, including scales, were recovered from Features 8, 26, and 45. No fish scales were present in any of the excavation unit samples. The fish scales are included in the Number of Identified Specimens (NISP) in the tabulation of identified fauna (Table 10.4).

The inhabitants of the Dash Reeves site apparently exploited a variety of nearby aquatic habitats. Gar (*Lepisosteus* sp.) and bowfin (*Amia calva*), for example, can be found at varying depths in a number of different habitats. Clear, swift water is the preferred environment of rock bass (*Ambloplites rupestris*) (Tomelleri and Eberle 1990).

Birds

Only three bones could be identified as bird. Based on size, one appears to be from a passerine (small perching bird), and one burned element is from a larger, duck-sized bird. Bird bones are from Test Units F and G and a float sample from Excavation Unit 45.

Mammals

Although the vast majority of the bones from the site are too fragmentary for reliable placement in classes, approximately 15 percent are identifiable as mammal bone (N=711). "Small," "medium," and "large" mammals are represented. The small category includes animals the size of mice, voles, and other similar-sized rodents. Medium mammals equate in size to canids, woodchucks, raccoons, etc. Large mammals are represented by deer-sized species.

Mammals identifiable to at least the generic level include raccoon (*Procyon lotor*), canid (*Canis* sp.), and white-tailed deer (*Odocoileus virginianus*). A possible woodchuck (cf. *Marmota monax*) also was identified. The majority of the raccoon remains (from Test Units E and G) are burned, suggesting that this species may have been consumed by the site's inhabitants. The single canid element (a toe bone from Test Unit F) is not diagnostic to species. However, the presence of dog (*C. familiaris*) at the site is suggested indirectly by gnaw marks on three deer bones (from Geotrench 2, Feature 29, and the subplowzone midden).

White-tailed deer bone was found in Features 10, 29, and 52. The minimum number of individuals (MNI) is based on five scapulae from Geotrench 1, which produced the greatest quantity (35 percent of NISP) and variety of deer bone. The presence of cervical and lumbar vertebrae and the high proportion of smaller toe elements (14 percent of NISP) indicate that complete deer carcasses were brought to the site.

DISCUSSION

Flotation produced the majority (65 percent) of the bone recovered from excavation units, and bone from float samples accounts for 86 percent of the faunal remains from features (Table 10.3). By contrast, 64 percent of the bone from test units was recovered by hand excavation. The collection is skewed toward larger fragments in the excavation units, which produced 72 percent of the large mammal bone. The recovery of only large items from unscreened units obviously resulted in high frequencies of large mammal bone and under-representation of smaller, less obvious bone from those proveniences. However, the quantity of large mammal bone in some excavation units may be a function of actual spatial distribution rather than a bias in collecting technique, since 54 of the 88 large mammal bones were recovered from the A horizon in the top level of Excavation Unit 5.

Rodent gnaw marks are present on one unidentified mammal bone found in the midden below the plowzone. This element and three deer bones gnawed by carnivores are the only evidence of postmortem alterations by animals.

Deer is represented by five individuals. There possibly are two snakes. In general, only single individuals are represented in the case of remains identifiable (or potentially identifiable) to the species level. Considering that a single deer provides approximately 45 kg of usable meat (White 1953), the five deer from Dash Reeves would have provided over 200 kg of meat. Usable meat from fish (see Theler 1987), reptiles, and other mammals (White 1953) totals 40 kg.

While the calculated meat weights may not be useful for reliably reconstructing available protein amounts or estimating site population, they indicate the relative importance of deer in the diet. Hunters probably exploited upland areas in the immediate vicinity of Dash Reeves for deer and other mammals.

There is some slight evidence, both indirect and direct, in the faunal assemblage pointing to occupation of the site during specific seasons. For example, growth rings on two rock bass scales from Feature 26 indicate a late summer to early autumn period of capture. The scarcity of turtles in the assemblage and the complete absence of mussels may indicate occupation during late fall through winter, when such resources would have been unavailable.

The poor preservation of the faunal remains from excavation units and features may be largely due to the cooking methods employed by the prehistoric inhabitants of Dash Reeves. Seventy-one percent of the bone in the assemblage is calcined, and 4 percent is burned. The remainder of the bone is not heat altered. The proportions are similar in the large mammal category (Table 10.3), where 78 percent of the bone is calcined, 3 percent is burned, and 18 percent is unaltered.

The Dash Reeves faunal assemblage is similar to other American Bottom Middle Woodland assemblages in its modest size (Kelly 1989:465) and limited diversity. Due to the sizes of the assemblages, only cautious comparisons can be made between Dash Reeves and other American Bottom sites. Other sites, listed in chronological order, each with its total bone count, are: Mund (10,867) (Cross 1983), Holding (7,939) (Kelly 1989:465), and Truck #7 (1,061) (Fortier 1985a:271–273). The Middle Woodland sample from the Nochta site (11-Ms-128) is excluded from this discussion, as no faunal remains have been identified beyond the class level and analysis is incomplete (see Higgins 1990).

Dash Reeves and Truck #7 (11-Mo-200) were contemporary and represent terminal Middle Woodland occupations in the American Bottom. Truck #7, a Hill Lake phase site, yielded a floral assemblage indicating occupation during the autumn and perhaps the winter (Fortier 1985a; Fortier et al. 1989:565–566). Comparisons between Dash Reeves and Truck #7 are difficult due to the nature of the faunal collection at the latter site. The Truck #7 collection is less than a quarter the size of the Dash Reeves assemblage. Deer is predominant (34 percent) in the Truck #7 assemblage. A snake bone and five fish elements account for 1 percent of the total and are the only other bones identifiable to the class level or higher (see Tables 10.3 and 10.4). The meager faunal assemblage at Truck #7 is attributed to highly acid soils unfavorable to bone preservation (Fortier 1985a:277).

Only 12 percent of the unidentified bone at Truck #7 is unburned. As noted above, 25 percent of the bone from Dash Reeves is not heat altered. Calcined bone was not differentiated from burned bone in the Truck #7 assemblage.

High quantities of heat-altered bone were found at other Middle Woodland sites predating Truck #7 and Dash Reeves. The faunal assemblage at the incipient Middle Woodland Cement Hollow phase Mund site is twice the size of the Dash Reeves collection. As was the case at Truck #7, Mund was an autumn occupation. Mammal bone represents 8 percent of the total Mund fauna, and mussels are not present in the assemblage (Fortier et al. 1983). Ninety-one percent of the bone from Mund is unidentified. Burned or calcined specimens account for 94 percent of the unidentified total.

The faunal assemblage from the Holding (Hopewell) phase Holding site (11-Ms-118) contrasts with the three foregoing sites. At Holding, 20 different vertebrate genera were identified from a collection of 7,939 bones. The collection includes mussel shell fragments, which represent 3 percent of the total NISP (Kelly 1989). Evidence of dwellings, extensive midden deposits, and

a variety of floral remains indicate that Holding was occupied year-round, perhaps for as long as a decade (obviously longer if Cement Hollow and Hill Lake phase occupations are included) (Fortier et al. 1989:562). Presumably, more diverse activities were undertaken there than at sites occupied only seasonally. In spite of its apparently greater diversity, the Holding faunal assemblage contains a large amount of heat-altered bone. Kelly (1989:477) notes that bone at the Holding site is highly calcined. In the unidentified bone from the midden blocks, which represents 43 percent of the site total, 75 percent is calcined/burned and 25 percent is unaltered.

In attempting to reconstruct the type of food processing undertaken at Dash Reeves, analogy is drawn from Fort White Earth in Alberta. Historic accounts contemporary with the Fort White Earth occupation show the importance of bone grease production in that region. After marrow extraction, bone was boiled in water and the grease skimmed from the surface. Grease or bone butter was used for cooking or in producing a desirable form of pemmican (Hurlburt 1977:18–21). Bones were either splintered or crushed into "comminuted" bone before boiling to produce optimum results (Leechman 1951). Fresh artiodactyl bone is inherently greasy, and reduction to a comminuted state may have been unnecessary after marrow extraction but prior to boiling. The comminuted bones from Fort White Earth are slivers less than 2 cm in length. Long bone shafts, ribs, scapulae, and condyles were intentionally crushed. Comminuted bone at Fort White Earth comprises 15 percent of the total bone; 14 percent of comminuted bone is unburned, 24 percent is burned, and 62 percent is calcined (Hurlburt 1977:17). Hurlburt (1977:97) records heat-alteration to the large mammal long bones, ribs, and scapulae. This group of elements (N=5,627) is 74 percent of the site total and is characterized by quite different burned/unburned proportions than found in the comminuted bone. In the large mammal category, 72 percent is unburned, 16 percent is calcined, and only 12 percent is burned. These two apparently differing data sets may reflect the same activity, namely the production of bone grease. The comminuted bone may have resulted from crushing to optimize the removal of grease during boiling. Once accomplished, the comminuted bone, along with waste water, could have doused the fire. Since crushing artiodactyl bone was unnecessary, the splintered shafts of many large mammal long

Table 10.4. Identified Fauna

Taxon	Common Name	Excavation	Features
Fish (bones and scales)			
Class Osteichthyes	bony fishes	19	0
Lepisosteus sp.	gar	1	0
Amia calva	bowfin	1	0
Family Cyprinidae	minnow family	1	0
Family Catostomidae	sucker family	0	3
Family Centrarchidae	sunfish family	3	1
Ambloplites rupestris	rock bass	1	2
Total		26	6
Amphibians			
Class Amphibia	amphibians	0	0
Order Anura	frogs, toads, treefrogs	1	0
Total		1	0
Reptiles			
Class Reptilia	reptiles	1	0
Order Testudines	turtles	9	3
Order Squamata	snakes and lizards	-	-
Suborder Serpentes	snakes	6	0
Family Colubridae	nonpoisonous snakes	0	6
Total		16	9
Birds			
Class Aves	birds	2	0
Order Passeriformes	passerine birds	1	0
Total		3	0
Mammals			
Class Mammalia	mammals	586	125
Order Rodentia	rodents	4	0
cf. *Marmota monax*	woodchuck	1	0
Order Carnivora	carnivores	-	-
Canis sp.	dog, coyote, wolf	0	1
Procyon lotor	raccoon	3	0
Order Artiodactyla	even-toed ungulates	-	-
Odocoileus virginianus	white-tailed deer	50	8
Total		644	134

bones may simply have been boiled to release oil or bone butter.

The unidentified bone at Dash Reeves may be comminuted and shows greater heat-alteration than the Fort White Earth assemblage. The heat-altered percentages for large mammal at Dash Reeves (78 percent calcined, 3 percent burned) approximate those for unburned bone and differ greatly from the large mammal percentages at Fort White Earth. For all unidentified mammal bone, the Dash Reeves proportions of 31 percent calcined, 2 percent burned, and 67 percent unburned (Table 10.3) are similar to those for the large mammal group at Fort White Earth. This may indicate that meat at Dash Reeves was primarily prepared by boiling and that grease extraction may have been undertaken as well.

The 4,660 bones from Dash Reeves may be more representative of Middle Woodland subsistence during the Hill Lake phase than the small assemblage from Truck #7. The fauna from both sites apparently reflect food procurement activities from late summer extending into fall and possibly the winter. The paucity of turtles and the absence of mussels may be due to their scarce availability during these seasons. While the vari-

ety in fish species is unremarkable, rather diverse exploitation is indicated. Gar and bowfin may have been taken
within 400 m of the site at Hill Lake marsh or from the
reaches of the Mississippi River that lie within 2 km of
the site. Rock bass and similar species were probably
captured from Palmer Creek, directly adjacent to the
site. The mammalian fauna indicate hunting throughout the area, extending from the bluff line above Dash
Reeves to the water's edge. The number of deer in
relation to other fauna illustrates the importance of this
large game animal to the Middle Woodland diet.

The large quantity of fragmentary, calcined bone at
Dash Reeves and other Middle Woodland sites may be
indicative of grease processing, perhaps from late summer into the winter. Processing the bone for the grease
may well explain the paucity of species represented at
Mund, Truck #7, and Dash Reeves, as identifiable
elements of a diverse faunal array were crushed beyond
recognition.

11

RADIOCARBON DATES

Prior to this project only four dates had been obtained from Hill Lake phase contexts in the American Bottom, all from the Truck #7 site (Fortier 1985a:272). Although these dates essentially confirmed the anticipated range for this phase, it was felt that additional dates were needed from other sites. Seven samples from the Dash Reeves site were submitted to the Illinois State Geological Survey for conventional radiocarbon dating. Four additional samples were submitted to the Arizona AMS (accelerator mass spectrometry) Facility at the University of Arizona. These two sets of dates are discussed separately below.

CONVENTIONAL RADIOCARBON DATES

Seven charcoal samples were submitted for radiocarbon analysis at the Illinois State Geological Survey (ISGS) radiocarbon laboratory in Urbana. These samples were processed by Dr. Chao-li Jack Liu under the overall supervision of Dennis Coleman. Prior to submission, samples were identified by Mary Simon at the University of Illinois. An attempt was made to sample a variety of Middle Woodland contexts, including features. Based on the Middle Woodland cultural material recovered from these contexts, the dates were expected to fall within the Hill Lake phase.

Samples from four features (Features 8, 18, 29, and 50), two midden units (Excavation Unit 4 and a combined sample from Excavation Units 9 and 20 and Test Units E and G), and a creek refuse dump discovered in Geomorphological Trench 2 were selected for submission. Although carbonized material was relatively ubiquitous throughout the occupation, it was sparsely distributed. Because of this, all but one sample were made up of multiple wood or nutshell species. The results of the radiocarbon assays are presented in Table 11.1. The dates are presented in both uncalibrated and calibrated formats (Stuiver and Reimer 1993). The individual samples are discussed below, followed by a brief discussion of the significance and relevance of these dates to the Middle Woodland sequence in this area.

The sample from Feature 8, which was a shallow (16-cm-deep), single-zoned, cooking/refuse pit in the south-central portion of the occupation, consisted of carbonized nutshell, including hickory, walnut, hazelnut, and acorn. Hill Lake phase ceramics, chert flakes, and calcined bone also were recovered from this context. The date of this sample is 1870±70 radiocarbon years B.P., or A.D. 80 (uncorrected) (ISGS-2358). This date is earlier than expected. The ceramics from Feature 8 include Pike Rocker Stamped and Brushed, but also a single red-slipped, limestone-tempered body sherd. Red slipping occurred during the Holding phase, but is virtually unknown from Hill Lake phase contexts. Maher (this report) has suggested that this sherd may represent contamination from a late Emergent Mississippian period occupation in this area. However, it is possible that the Feature 8 pit and the red-slipped sherd are associated with an earlier Middle Woodland component at the site. The calibrated mean date for this sample is A.D. 135.

Table 11.1. Conventional Radiocarbon Dates from the Middle Woodland Occupation

Provenience	ISGS#	Carbonized Sample Material	Sample wt (g)	Radiocarbon Years (B.P.)	δPDB 13 C%	Uncalibrated Calendrical Dates	Calibrated Calendrical Dates (one sigma*)
Feature 29	2257	Wood (mixed)	4.21	1890 ± 80	−26.0	A.D. 60	A.D. 59 (125) 235
Feature 8	2358	Nutshell (mixed)	5.13	1870 ± 70	−25.2	A.D. 80	A.D. 75 (135) 240
Feature 18	2256	Wood (black walnut)	6.32	1840 ± 100	−25.2	A.D. 110	A.D. 75 (215) 329
Feature 50	2362	Nutshell (mixed)	3.03	1660 ± 80	−25.3	A.D. 290	A.D. 264 (412) 532
Test Units E and G	2360	Wood (mixed)	4.19	1780 ± 70	−27.1	A.D. 170	A.D. 145 (249) 375
Exc. Units 9 and 20	-	-	-	-	-	-	-
Exc. Unit 4	2258	Wood (mixed)	4.05	1760 ± 80	−25.7	A.D. 190	A.D. 214 (256, 296, 319) 398
Geo. Trench 2 (creek dump)	2260	Wood (mixed)	6.48	1710 ± 90	−25.1	A.D. 240	A.D. 239 (347, 360, 374) 428

*Based on the high-precision bidecadal calibration curve of Stuiver and Reimer (1993).
Calendar dates represent the minimum-intercept-maximum range of the calibrated radiocarbon assay.

The sample from Feature 18 consisted of black walnut wood charcoal. Feature 18 was a shallow extended hearth containing no cultural materials. It was situated in the western occupation area and was sampled as a representative of the extended hearth feature class, which at the time of submission, was of questionable cultural affiliation. Dating was intended to determine the association of this new feature type with the Middle Woodland occupation. A date of 1840±100 radiocarbon years B.P., or A.D. 110 (uncorrected) (ISGS-2256), was obtained, confirming this feature's Middle Woodland age. Like the date from Feature 8, it is earlier than expected, but, again, this may indicate the occurrence of a Holding phase component at the site. The calibrated mean date for this sample is A.D. 215.

The sample from Feature 29 came from a unique, 41-cm-deep cache pit containing many diagnostic Hill Lake phase rim and body sherds as well as diagnostic lithics. The pit was located in the eastern occupation area just 10 m west of the creek midden. The sample consisted of oak, hickory, and pecan wood charcoal. A date of 1890±80 radiocarbon years B.P., or A.D. 60 (uncorrected) (ISGS-2257), was obtained, placing this feature well within the Holding phase. Based on the pottery, this date appears to be too early. The calibrated mean date for this sample is A.D. 125.

The final pit feature sample originated from Feature 50, a shallow (19.5-cm-deep), basin-shaped cooking/refuse pit, located approximately 5 m west of the creek midden in the eastern occupation area. The sample consisted of carbonized black walnut, hickory, hazelnut, and acorn nutshell. Brushed and rocker-stamped sherds as well as a single cross-hatched rim were recovered and suggest a Hill Lake phase affiliation. A date of 1660±80 radiocarbon years B.P., or A.D. 290 (uncor-

rected) (ISGS-2362), was obtained, which places this pit in the middle to late portion of the Hill Lake phase. The calibrated mean date for this sample is A.D. 412.

Two samples were selected from midden contexts, one from the far western end of the occupation, the other from the eastern portion, from within the creek midden. Remarkably, the dates obtained are virtually identical. The western sample was taken from Excavation Unit 4, between elevations 125.79 and 125.59 amsl. Diagnostic brushed and rocker-stamped sherds were recovered from this 4-x-4-m unit. The sample consisted of a mixed assortment of oak, elm, walnut, sycamore, and maple wood charcoal. The date from this sample is 1760±80 radiocarbon years B.P., or A.D. 190 (uncorrected) (ISGS-2258). This fits into the early range of the Hill Lake phase. The calibrated mean date for this sample fell at three intercepts, A.D. 256, 296, and 319.

The second or eastern midden sample came from multiple contexts within the creek midden. Although carbonized plant remains were found in almost every unit excavated in this midden, a suitably sized sample could only be obtained by combining samples. The samples were taken from Excavation Units 9 and 20 and from Test Units E and G. Units E, G, and 9 were nearly contiguous and were located at the northern end of the exposed midden. Unit 20 was located at the southern end of the exposed midden. The sample consisted of oak, hickory, ash, walnut, and mulberry wood charcoal. The date from this mixed sample is 1780±70 radiocarbon years B.P., or A.D. 170 (uncorrected) (ISGS-2360), which dates the creek deposits to the beginning of the Hill Lake phase. A wide variety of diagnostic pottery and lithics were recovered from all units in this area, but especially from Excavation Unit 9. Both

Holding and Hill Lake phase ceramic types were identified. The calibrated mean date for this sample is A.D. 249.

The final radiocarbon sample was recovered from the base of a paleochannel skirting the southern limit of the site. At a depth of 1.5–1.8 m below the present surface (124.46–124.16 amsl), a deposit of pottery, chert, deer bone, and carbonized wood was identified during the excavation of Geotrench 2. This deposit was restricted in area and appeared to represent a single-episode dump (see Chapter 6). The cultural material was found within laminated clays and pebbles at the base of the then-active creek. It was hoped that the carbonized remains would date the Middle Woodland occupation located just north of the creek. The date from the sample, which consisted of carbonized ash, walnut, elm, oak, and maple woods, is 1710±90 radiocarbon years B.P., or A.D. 240 (uncorrected) (ISGS-2260), which places this dumping episode well within the expected Hill Lake phase range. The calibrated mean dates for this sample are A.D. 347, 360, and 374.

Four of the seven uncorrected radiocarbon dates fit the expected range of the Hill Lake phase (i.e., A.D. 150–300), but three dates fall within the latter portion of the preceding Holding phase (i.e., 50 B.C.–A.D. 150). Given the overall nature of the ceramic assemblage and the scarcity of Hopewell artifacts and exotic remains normally associated with the Holding phase, the earlier dates are somewhat surprising. It should be pointed out that our knowledge of what kinds of materials should occur in any given Middle Woodland phase component is still fuzzy, based on an extremely limited settlement and material inventory sample. Moreover, it is clear that several forms of ceramic decoration are not restricted to a specific phase. For example, rocker stamping and brushing, while hallmarks of the Hill Lake phase, also occurred in the preceding Holding phase. The same can be said of cross-hatching and bossing. These and other decorative attributes appear to form classic battleship curves of popularity within the Middle Woodland period. On the other hand, some traits found in two phases did not occur in the third phase. Brushing, for example, occurred in the middle Middle Woodland Holding and late Middle Woodland Hill Lake phases, but not in the early Middle Woodland Cement Hollow phase. Thick-walled, sand-tempered, cordmarked jars appeared in the Cement Hollow and Holding phases, but not in the Hill Lake phase. These

trends have not been documented formally in the American Bottom, although Maher (1991) attempted an intrasite seriation at Holding with some degree of success and broadened this in his dissertation to include other sites in the American Bottom, including Dash Reeves (Maher 1996). The reader is directed to that source for an in-depth analysis (primarily ceramic) of the Middle Woodland sequence in this area and for Maher's proposal to subdivide the Holding phase, a step that I think deserves further consideration at some future date.

The conventional dates seem to fall into two distinct groups. Following Spaulding (1958) and Hall (1981:383–414) the B.P. dates were grouped with their standard errors to test for significance of difference. The F-statistic calculated for this group of dates is 1.07 (df=6), essentially indicating that the two-group distinction is not statistically valid. However, because the dates cover a relatively narrow range of time, with standard errors ranging from 70 to 100 years, it is questionable whether it is even possible to statistically split this group of dates. The overlap in standard error range is apparent in Figure 11.1 and seems to suggest that the majority of dates fall within the expected Hill Lake phase range.

The most glaring discrepancy pertains to the 230-year difference between dates on Feature 29 and Feature 50, pits that contained virtually identical types of pottery, lithics, and archaeobotanical remains and that were located only 18 m apart. Perhaps the difference represents normal probability error; that is, there is a 33 percent chance that one of these dates falls outside of the calculated range (see Hall 1981:383–386). A classic example of this was demonstrated at the Truck #7 site, where material from a single burned post (PM31) was dated to A.D. 160 and A.D. 445 (Fortier 1985a:271–272). This resulted either from a laboratory error or an error of statistical probability. Another possibility is that both the inner and outer parts of the post were dated. The apparent discrepancy in dates, which theoretically should have been bunched more tightly at Dash Reeves, may simply reflect, therefore, a normal statistical run of dates. In short, the more dates one obtains from an occupation, the greater the likelihood that statistical probability will create so-called outliers.

Based on ceramics, it is conceivable that two occupations, one dating to the Holding and one to the Hill Lake phase, occurred at the site. The clay figurine, clay ear spool(s), and red-slipped sherd from Feature 8 are

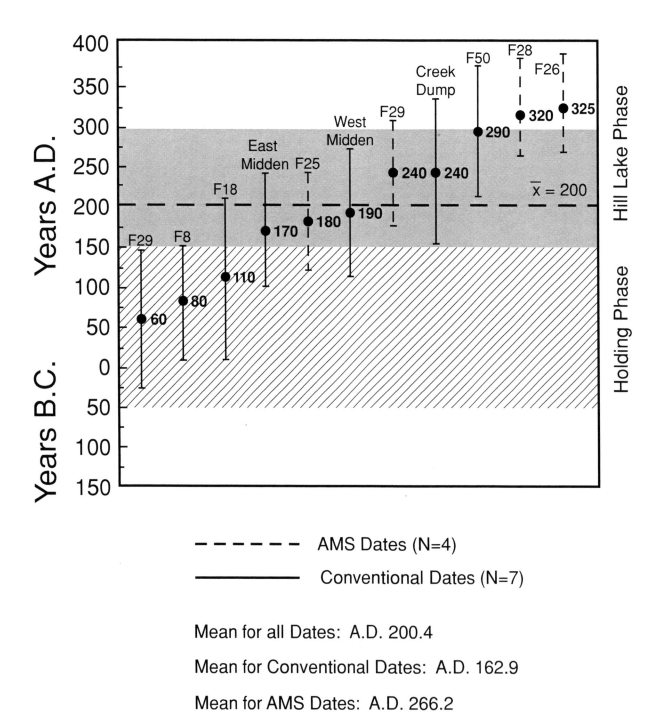

Figure 11.1. Uncalibrated Conventional and AMS Radiocarbon Dates from Dash Reeves

Table 11.2. University of Arizona AMS Dates on Carbonized Nutshell (*Carya* sp.)

Provenience	AMS Lab No.	Sample size (mg)	Years (B.P)	Uncalibrated Calendrical Dates	Calibrated Calendrical Dates (one sigma)*
Feature 25	A-13199	13.5	1770 ± 60	A.D. 180	A.D. 134 (245) 340
Feature 26	A-13207	16.4	1625 ± 60	A.D. 325	A.D. 348 (417) 532
Feature 28	A-13185	10.0	1630 ± 60	A.D. 320	A.D. 344 (414) 531
Feature 29	A-13186	15.0	1710 ± 65	A.D. 240	A.D. 235 (263, 276, 339) 410

*Stuiver and Reimer 1993.

essentially Hopewell or Holding phase artifacts. Many of the cross-hatched, rocker-stamped rims from this site would fit easily within a Holding phase assemblage. However, the overwhelming character of the ceramic assemblage points to a Hill Lake phase occupation. It is perhaps significant to compare the uncorrected conventional mean dates from the Holding and Dash Reeves site, which are A.D. 70 and A.D. 163, respectively (see Fortier et al. 1989:485). Based on their respective material assemblages, these are the dates one would expect from these sites. Comparing means at this level is clearly not statistically relevant. On the other hand, the dates do complement the material assemblages, at least as we expect them to appear at this time. The fact that all of the dates from Dash Reeves, except that from Feature 29, occur within or overlap the Hill Lake phase is important. Overall, the seven dates indicate an occupation that was initiated at the beginning of the Hill Lake phase and may have extended to the middle or even latter portions of this phase.

AMS Dates

In addition to the seven dates discussed above, four samples from Dash Reeves were submitted to the Arizona AMS Facility at the University of Arizona. This was supported by a National Science Foundation grant (SBR-9321825) as part of Thomas Maher's dissertation research on the Middle Woodland period in the American Bottom. I am indebted to Maher for sharing these dates and allowing their publication in this report. They are significant dates, since they confirm the placement of the Dash Reeves assemblage within the Hill Lake phase. Furthermore, they cast some doubt on the accuracy of the Feature 29 radiocarbon date discussed above. These new

dates are summarized in Table 11.2 and are incorporated into Figure 11.1.

Four pit features were selected by Maher for AMS dating. In three cases (Features 25, 26, and 28), feature selection was based on the types of diagnostic ceramics recovered from the pits. Because the initial radiocarbon date from that feature seemed too early, a fourth sample was submitted from Feature 29. In fact, the Feature 29 AMS date of A.D. 240 (uncorrected) appears much more in line with the ceramic assemblage from that pit. The other AMS dates of A.D. 180, 320, and 325 (uncorrected) (see Table 12.2), also fall within the expected Hill Lake phase limits.

The calibrated ranges for the four AMS dates and seven conventional radiocarbon dates are presented in Table 11.1. The calibration is based on the Stuiver and Reimer 3.03c (1993) calibration program. When the dates were first received, they were calibrated using an earlier program developed by the same laboratory (Stuiver and Pearson 1986; Stuiver and Reimer 1986). The 1993 calibration resulted in dates more recent by eight to 89 years. No attempt is made here to account for the calibrated sequence of Middle Woodland dates from this area. At one sigma there is a nearly 175 to 200-year range of dates and the means are approximately 50–125 years later for calibrated dates than for uncorrected calendar dates. At this time there is no point in revising the sequence, which is still in sync with the observed ceramic sequence, unless the entire prehistoric sequence is revised using a single calibrated system of dates. I am skeptical that calibration of all Middle Woodland dates will alter the actual sequence within the Middle Woodland period, or the relative positioning of Early, Middle, and Late Woodland cultures in this area. It may, however, open or consolidate some existing gaps in the sequence, and that may prove to be significant.

12

MISCELLANEOUS COMPONENT MATERIALS

A relatively small amount of material recovered from the Dash Reeves site is unrelated to the Middle Woodland component. This material includes a variety of Historic artifacts, several Late Woodland/Mississippian projectile points, a Late Archaic projectile point, and several possible prehistoric, non-Middle Woodland sherds. As previously discussed, it is possible that some of the Mill Creek polished flakes recovered from the surface are associated with Mississippian farming practices in the site area. I suspect, however, that the vast majority of these flakes are associated with the Middle Woodland occupation.

NON-MIDDLE WOODLAND PROJECTILE POINTS

During machine scraping of Geomorphological Trench 4, a Matanzas-like projectile point was recovered from a buried paleosol, (Figure 12.1a). This point probably dates to the Late Archaic period, ca. 3000–2200 B.C., and may be indirectly associated with the Falling Springs occupation identified at the Marge site, approximately 300 m east of Dash Reeves (Fortier 1996). The point is broadly side notched, with a straight base and relatively broad shoulders. The base is slightly expanding. The artifact is made of local Salem chert (Type 34) and is not heat treated. The dimensions are given in Table 12.1.

A Wanda point and a Koster-like point were recovered from the surface just north of the excavation area

(Figure 12.1b, c). The Wanda point is broadly side notched, with a straight base, and is made on a small flake of unheated white Burlington chert (Type 1). The Koster-like point is deeply side notched, with a straight stem and expanding base. It is made of heated Burlington chert (Type 69) and is bifacially worked on both lateral edges and the base. Both points have broken tips. Presumably, they represent Arron points. Similar points, lacking basal retouch and having unilateral retouch, asymmetrical, curved edges, and rectangular basal cross sections, probably represent drills or perforators (Dimitry Nuzhni, Ukrainian Archaeological Institute, Kiev, personal communication 1994). The dimensions of both points are given in Table 12.1.

NON-MIDDLE WOODLAND CERAMICS

A small number of sherds in the collection are untyped but do not appear to date to the Middle Woodland period. These are described in Chapter 7 and are only briefly mentioned here. They are from thin-walled, cordmarked vessels with cordwrapped-stick impressions on the superior lip. They probably date to the Late Woodland period. All were found in the midden. The only other possible ceramic contaminant at the site is a red-slipped, limestone-tempered sherd recovered from Feature 8. As discussed elsewhere, such ceramics are normally associated with late Emergent Mississippian and early Mississippian occupations in this

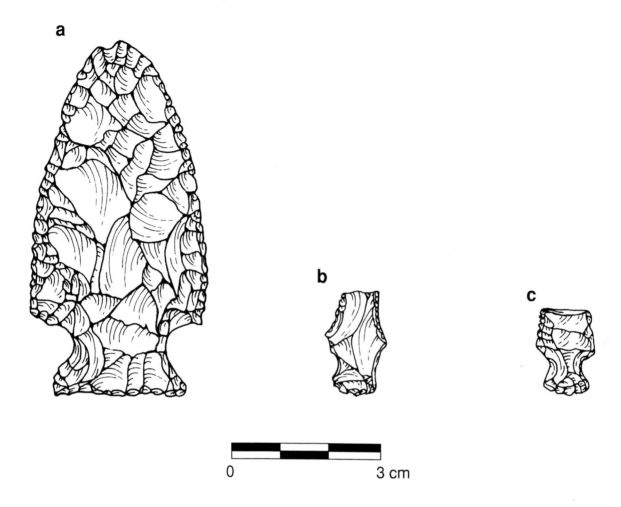

Figure 12.1. Miscellaneous Non-Middle Woodland Projectile Points: a, Matanzas; b, Wanda; c, Koster

Table 12.1. Non–Middle Woodland Projectile Point Attributes

	Matanzas	Wanda	Koster
Provenience	Geomorph Trench 4	Surface, PZ	Surface, PZ
Chert type	34	1	69
Weight (g)	21.9	0.9	0.6
Haft	side notched	side notched	side notched
Stem shape	expanding	straight	expanding
Heat treatment	no	no	yes
Maximum length (cm)	6.77	⋆	⋆
Stem length (cm)	1.30	0.73	0.69
Shoulder width (cm)	3.35	1.10	1.06
Base width (cm)	2.61	0.72	0.79
Neck width (cm)	1.75	0.84	0.49
Base treatment	thinned	retouched	retouched
Blade thickness (cm)	0.77	0.25	0.21
Stem thickness (cm)	0.67	0.41	0.31

⋆Not taken, tips broken

Table 12.2. Historic Materials

Iron	N
Corroded frag.	11
Concretions	9
Cut nails	5
Railroad spike	1
Nut/washer	1
Staple	1
Total	28

Ceramics	N
Ironstone/Hotelware (undercorded)	3
Salt-glazed stoneware (interior unglazed)	2
Salt-glazed stoneware (Albany slipped interior)	1
Whiteware	2
Redware	1
Red-transfer-printed whiteware	2
Total	11

Glass	N
Clear, flat	6
Clear, bottle	7
Amber bottle	1
Light green bottle	1
Total	15

Munitions	N
Shotgun shells (20-gauge)	5
Winchester Center-Fire (20-gauge)	2
.22-caliber bullet (short)	1
Lead ball (14.5 mm)	1
Lead musket ball	1
Total	10

Miscellaneous	N
Dry cell battery carbon pole	1
Clinker	1
Welder's rod	1
Total*	3

*Cinder (n=1,234; wt=576.8 g) is not included in this listing.

area, but they also occur in some Middle Woodland assemblages (Maher 1989:195).

HISTORIC MATERIALS

With the exception of cinders, the Historic materials from this site were all recovered from the plowzone. Joseph Phillippe of the University of Illinois undertook the analysis of this material. Because they were deemed to be mostly modern materials of dubious cultural significance, they were simply identified and tabulated. These artifacts are listed in Table 12.2. Most of the artifacts are fragments of modern bottles, pieces of corroded iron, iron concretions, cinder from the nearby railroad line, and modern shotgun shells. There is a small amount of stoneware (salt glazed), undecorated ironstone (Hotel Ware), redware, and whiteware, including two small pieces of red transfer print. A kaolin pipe fragment, lead ball (.28 caliber, 14.5 mm, 13.4 g), and a flattened musket ball (12.8 g) also were recovered. Although almost impossible to ascertain, the age of the musket ball and possibly the pipe fragment may be

eighteenth century, the period of the earliest Euro-American settlements in the area. The musket ball could also be modern.

Most of the Historic artifacts recovered from the site can be attributed to recent farming and hunting practices and to operation of a nearby railroad line. It is not clear how some of the older ceramic ware was deposited. There are no known Historic settlements or homesteads located in the site area itself, although several homesteads are identified in the Palmer Creek locality on early documents (Phillippe 1993). Eighteenth-century and modern artifacts were recovered from the nearby Marge site. Possibly some of the Dash Reeves material emanated from that site through plow drag or erosional processes.

13

INTERPRETATION

The Middle Woodland period in the American Bottom is no longer the unknown archaeological entity it was 20 years ago. A number of sites have been excavated and reported over the past two decades (Finney 1983; Fortier 1985a; Fortier et al. 1989; Fortier and Ghosh 2000; Higgins 1990; Williams 1993). Many aspects of this period, such as the chronological sequence, subsistence patterning, and material culture format, are slowly coming into focus, especially with the addition of assemblages from good feature contexts and an increasing battery of radiocarbon dates supporting these contexts. Yet, there is much missing in the archaeological record in this area, and our level of understanding is still immature at best. The Dash Reeves site represents the latest addition to the Middle Woodland family in the American Bottom and contributes a tremendous amount of new information about the middle to later portions of the period. The following discussion is aimed at highlighting some of the more important aspects of this site, including temporal placement, site function, subsistence, technology, and material contexts. An attempt is made to place this occupation within regional contexts and discuss its significance within the frameworks of broader Middle Woodland studies in the area.

CHRONOLOGICAL AND CULTURAL AFFILIATION

The Middle Woodland period is subdivided into three temporal phases, from earliest to latest, Cement Hollow (150–50 B.C.), Holding (50 B.C.–A.D. 150),

and Hill Lake (A.D. 150–300). These phases were defined on the basis of diagnostic artifacts and supporting uncorrected radiocarbon dates (see Maher 1996 for proposed revisions of this sequence). A good description of these phases and their diagnostic artifacts can be found in the Holding site report (Fortier et al. 1989:555–579). The boundaries between these phases are not always clear-cut, especially when sites with small assemblages are involved. Many Middle Woodland artifact types are time transgressive, as are some ceramic attributes. A number of changes in artifact format appear to represent real discontinuities in the cultural continuum, or sudden additions or subtractions (Fortier 2001). Blade technology, for example, appeared dramatically and without precedent during the Holding phase and by the end of the Middle Woodland period had disappeared just as dramatically. The Dash Reeves site contains the highest number of blades ever recovered from a Hill Lake phase occupation, but the nearby Truck #7 occupation, dating to the same phase, produced no blades at all. Is this a function of time or of site function?

The radiocarbon dates from the Dash Reeves site indicate that the occupation fell mostly in the Hill Lake phase. The uncorrected AMS dates from Arizona (mean=A.D. 266) place the occupation at the latter end of the phase, in some cases in the early Late Woodland period. Meanwhile, the conventional uncorrected ISGS radiocarbon dates (mean=A.D. 163) indicate that the occupation fell within the early part of the Hill Lake phase, perhaps even overlapping the preceding Holding phase (see Chapter 11). The expected date of occupation, therefore, is sometime between A.D. 150 and A.D. 300. The radiocarbon dates are generally consistent with the material assemblage, especially the ceramics, which clearly fall within the expected range of variation for the Hill Lake phase. The occurrence of a high percentage of Pike Rocker Stamped and Baehr Brushed ceramics strongly supports the Hill Lake phase affiliation. In addition, the diversity of decorative attributes and the number of so-called Hopewell ceramic types do not approach the levels observed at the Holding site, which dates primarily to the preceding Holding phase. There are, however, some Hopewell ceramics and exotics in the Dash Reeves assemblage, such as the clay ear spool and the figurine, enough to perhaps suggest that some part of the occupation dates to the Holding-Hill Lake phase boundary.

The predominance of smaller Manker and Clear Lake type projectile points and the scarcity of earlier contracting-stemmed, Snyders, Norton, and Gibson types also indicate a Hill Lake phase affiliation for the Dash Reeves occupation. It is possible that some other lithic tools in the assemblage will prove to be temporally sensitive. There are many tool types at the site that do not occur in either the Holding phase or other Hill Lake contexts in this area, but this may reflect the small size of the excavated sample to date or the diversity of activities at any given site.

The occurrence of a blade industry at the site is somewhat surprising, since previous excavations had produced blades only from Holding phase contexts. Apparently, this technology persisted for some time into the Hill Lake phase, although one might speculate that it became increasingly focused at fewer and fewer sites. Sites like Dash Reeves may have served as specialized areal centers for blade manufacture. This conjecture, of course, remains to be tested.

Another lithic trait diagnostic of the Hill Lake phase is the general scarcity of exotic lithic materials and extralocal cherts. Exotic cherts often comprise 10 percent of the chert materials on Holding phase sites. At Dash Reeves and other Hill Lake sites in the area this percentage drops to 1–2 percent. Generally, this pattern is thought to represent a decline in Hopewell Interaction Sphere exchanges and a corresponding shift to local resource use during the period A.D. 150–300, a pattern that persisted into the subsequent Late Woodland period of this area.

An interesting question regarding cultural affiliation at this site is related to the occurrence of Crab Orchard pottery and southern Illinois cherts, which are often found in closely associated contexts. This strongly suggests the presence of southern Illinois Middle Woodland people at the site. Evidence of Crab Orchard culture in the American Bottom has been recognized previously (Maher 1989:146–148) but usually has been attributed to long-range trade. The Dash Reeves evidence appears to indicate an actual on-site intrusion of southern Illinois people in the American Bottom. A major Crab Orchard presence also has been identified at the Middle Woodland Archie and Massey homesteads in western Illinois (Farnsworth and Koski 1985). It is not possible to determine whether there was an isolated Crab Orchard occupation at Dash Reeves or an intermingling of both Crab Orchard and American Bottom groups. The latter situation is better supported by the archaeology, as both groups used precisely the same trash depot in the creek. The appearance of fabric-impressed pottery is associated primarily with the Holding and Hill Lake phases in the American Bottom and is another trait that did not persist into the Late Woodland period in this area.

COMMUNITY CONFIGURATION, FUNCTION, AND DURATION

As defined by a series of surface collections, the Dash Reeves site occupies an area of roughly 30,000 m². The main portion of the Middle Woodland settlement appears to have been encircled by channels and channel scars, with the community occupying a roughly oval area within these natural boundaries. The paleochannel on the north and east was utilized as a dump and was completely filled in with refuse at the time of site abandonment, if not earlier. Middle Woodland sites with ring middens have not been documented previously in the American Bottom, but the use of on-site creek swales for refuse deposition has been observed at Middle Woodland sites in the Illinois River valley (Stafford and Sant 1985:95–112; Wiant and McGimsey 1986).

Because it was not included within the area of proposed highway construction, the central portion of the occupation was not investigated. Excavations were focused on the southwestern area of the site, which probably represented less than 25 percent of the entire occupation. The 53 features uncovered in the excavated portion of the site were mostly located along the inner edges of several paleochannels. Because of the size and diversity of the material assemblage and the overall size of the occupation, it is presumed that dwellings or structures were erected at this site. The most likely location for these dwellings was in the center of the occupation, beyond the limits of the excavation area. The refuse deposited in the creek swales probably originated elsewhere on the site, possibly in activity areas in and around the presumed central dwellings. According to this scenario, the community would have included a central living area ringed by small hearths and cooking pits located on the edges of the paleochannels, which in turn served as the community's refuse receptacles. A few isolated features may have existed outside the limits of this contained area.

It is not possible to assign a single function to the Dash Reeves settlement. The artifact assemblage suggests that a variety of tasks and activities were undertaken in and around the site. Among these tasks were the production of stone tools, cooking, food processing, hide scraping, ceramic production (?), woodworking, nut collecting, and gardening. The archaeobotanical and faunal assemblages are not diverse, and, in fact, are small compared to sites such as Holding, which appears to have functioned primarily as a horticultural hamlet. The ceramic assemblage at Dash Reeves is relatively small as well. The general scarcity of ceramics recovered from the initial surface surveys was striking and was confirmed during subsurface excavations. Given the huge lithic debitage and tool inventory recovered from this site, it is proposed that *primary* activities included the procurement of lithic raw materials and the manufacture of tools. The settlement was strategically located to take advantage of sources of red Ste. Genevieve chert, which can be acquired from outcrops less than 2 km from the site. Red chert outcrops are extremely rare in the American Bottom, and this material may have been especially prized by Middle Woodland peoples in the area, particularly for blade manufacture.

Dash Reeves represented a major lithic production center, not only for blades, but also for a variety of other tools, including projectile points. It is possible that many of the other activities evidenced in the tool, ceramic, feature, and subsistence assemblages merely supported the primary activities of stone extraction and tool production. The disposition of the final products of these activities can only be suggested. The occupants of the Dash Reeves site may have utilized these materials for their own purposes. However, the site quite possibly was a major distribution center for certain types of raw materials or finished tools, including blades. Such materials may have been exported to other settlements through established exchange networks, or people may have traveled to Dash Reeves to acquire them at the source. It should be pointed out that red cherts were found at the Holding site far to the north in the American Bottom and have been found at the Twenhafel site in southern Illinois, far beyond known sources for such material. This suggests the existence of exchange involving red chert, at least within the American Bottom and perhaps further afield.

Radiocarbon dates are not very useful for determining the duration of the Dash Reeves occupation. The dates span the entire range of the Hill Lake phase, covering a 150-year period. It is possible that Dash Reeves was occupied during this entire period, especially given the quantity of debris and artifacts recovered. There is, however, little or no evidence of feature superpositioning or multiple pit-filling episodes, at least in the area excavated. Feature density is not particularly high, and outside of the main creek midden artifact density is also not very high. The settlement, therefore, could have been occupied for a period considerably shorter than indicated by the span of radiocarbon dates. We are left with the apparently unresolvable dilemma: did a few people leave behind this incredibly large assemblage of debitage, pottery, and tools from 150 years of accumulated activity, or did many produce it over a shorter period of time?

TECHNOLOGICAL TRADITION AND DIVERSITY

The technological innovations of Middle Woodland peoples throughout the Midwest were truly spectacular and involved a wide variety of material mediums. Experimentation in metallurgy and the use of exotic minerals, the development of blade technology in multiple formats, sophisticated pottery manufacture and design execution, the creation of new woodworking and gardening tools, elaborate pipe manufacture, and the construction of chambered burial tombs are among the most visible technological achievements of Middle Woodland peoples. Remarkably, many of these developments spread over thousands of miles of the Eastern Woodlands and into the Plains. Even more remarkable is the virtual disappearance of these technological patterns by the end of the Middle Woodland period. This disappearing act was probably initiated during the Middle Woodland period, just about the time the Dash Reeves settlement came into being. Yet, in the Dash Reeves assemblage one can still see the kind of technological diversity typifying the Middle Woodland tradition. This is manifested particularly in the blade industry and in the number of different tool types produced and utilized at the site.

In the prehistoric Midwest the production of lamellar blades from prepared blade cores was unique to Middle Woodland peoples. Presumably, it was an efficient way to manufacture large numbers of small tools from minimal raw resources. Such blades could be produced from a variety of blade core types, and several techniques (e.g., Fulton, Cobden) are known to have existed. As discussed in Chapter 8, the origins of this unique technology are unknown, although it appears associated with obsidian use. Therefore, a possible western connection is proposed.

Dash Reeves contains the largest assemblage of blades and blade cores ever recovered from a Middle Woodland site in the American Bottom. A wide variety of tools were made from lamellar blades, suggesting that this was a generalized industry. In this sense, blade tools were no more specialized than their flake tool counterparts. Even though this technology was no doubt acquired from outside the region, it was quickly adapted to midwestern mediums and tool themes. This is why its origins have been so difficult to trace.

The disappearance of this industry is enigmatic. There is no obvious technological reason for abandoning blade production. Blades made ideal cutting and scraping tools, were lightweight and easily transportable, and had more than tripled previous tool inventories. The disappearance of blade manufacture is clearly tied to the disappearance of other aspects of Middle Woodland technology, such as the production of platform pipes, disk scrapers, microlithic tools, clay figurines and ear spools, copper and mica artifacts, elaborately decorated pottery vessels, and numerous tool types and projectile point forms. Quite possibly, blade technology was associated with a specific social group or

sociocultural framework whose ideas were no longer supported or with whom people no longer wished to be associated. It is worth noting that in addition to the disappearance of many artifact types, elaborate burial programs involving tombed formats were no longer enacted at the end of Middle Woodland times. Settlements by the end of that period, as represented by the Truck #7 site, were small and lacking the kinds of technologies enumerated above. The breakdown of technological traditions and associated symbolic or sociopolitical networks, along with the collapse of technological diversity, is remarkable and one of the great remaining problems to resolve in American Bottom prehistory.

SUBSISTENCE

A major discontinuity in subsistence patterns, at least as indicated by archaeobotanical remains, marked the onset of the Holding phase at 50 B.C. Present evidence indicates that at that time an important shift occurred toward intensive horticulture, contributing to a tenfold increase in plant utilization. Excavations at the Holding site, for example, yielded a wide array of plant remains, including new cultigens such as maize (Riley et al. 1994). The occurrence of hoes, bell-shaped pestles, and grinding stones and an increase in serving vessels no doubt were related to the expansion in horticultural activity. It appears that the Middle Woodland was a period of subsistence as well as technological innovation. This may or may not apply to exploitation of animal resources. Thus far, poor preservation has not allowed us to say much about the relative contribution of animal species to Middle Woodland diets. We do know that the deep earth ovens (communal steamers?) of the Late Woodland period had not yet made their appearance in the American Bottom and that shallow hearths and small open fire pits apparently were utilized exclusively as cookers. Largely as a result of cooking practices most faunal remains recovered from Middle Woodland sites in the American Bottom occur as fragments of unidentifiable calcined bone and are most often recovered from open midden contexts.

The archaeobotanical assemblage recovered from Dash Reeves is generally typical of post-50 B.C. sites in this area, particularly in terms of the presence of starchy seeds and the low nut-to-seed ratios. Interestingly, however, despite the extensive nature of the occupation and the presence of Hopewell-type artifacts (e.g., the ear spool and the figurine), the Dash Reeves assemblage indicates a plant procurement pattern more similar to earlier Middle Woodland assemblages than to its immediate Holding phase predecessors. This similarity is especially apparent in the types of nuts procured and the large number of nondomesticated seeds. In terms of nut procurement, the Dash Reeves occupants followed a typical Hill Lake phase pattern, emphasizing hickory nuts rather than hazelnuts. In fact, peak use of hazelnuts during the middle portion of the Middle Woodland stage and the subsequent decline in their use at the end of this stage follows a regional trend, noted in the American Bottom as well as in the lower Illinois River valley (D. Asch and N. Asch 1985; Maher 1996:158; Parker 1989). The scarcity of domesticated seeds, however, is somewhat unusual for Hill Lake plant assemblages.

Two of the main problems that we face today in the American Bottom when we compare archaeobotanical assemblages from different Middle Woodland sites or phases are sampling and differential site size and function. For example, it is difficult to compare the Dash Reeves and Holding assemblages (Parker 1989), since so little of the Dash Reeves site was actually investigated. Comparison with Meridian Hills is also difficult, as only a few features could be excavated and analyzed for subsistence remains at that site, and sampling was undertaken under the worst salvage conditions (Williams 1993; Williams et al. 1987). The assemblage from Nochta is based on only one pit (Higgins 1990:156). Truck #7, a site that was coeval with Dash Reeves, is known from a small assemblage, derived from a single household probably only occupied for one season (Fortier 1985a). At Dash Reeves only the outer edge of the occupation fell within the right-of-way and was therefore investigated. Are the features in that area typical of what might have been recovered from the (presumably) more densely occupied central portion of the site?

Middle Woodland subsistence studies are still in their infancy in the American Bottom, primarily because so few sites have been excavated. Settlement/subsistence models are crude at best. The Dash Reeves site does not seem to represent the same kind of long-term horticultural hamlet that Holding or Meridian

Hills represented. The scarcity of grinding stones and the low quantities of domesticated seeds at Dash Reeves are patterns that are reversed at the aforementioned sites. Perhaps, however, this contrast in apparent site function would not be as clear-cut had we excavated in the area of the main village at Dash Reeves.

MANIPULATION OF THE PHYSICAL WORLD

Middle Woodland cultures of the American Bottom are generally known to have procured and utilized a wide variety of raw materials from local, nonlocal American Bottom, and extraregional sources. Although this phenomenon appears to have been greatly magnified during the middle (Holding phase) portion of the sequence, there is growing evidence that it characterized the Middle Woodland period in general. For example, the use, albeit in small quantities, of southern Illinois cherts such as Dongola/Cobden, occurred in early, middle, and late Middle Woodland times. Exotic materials, such as mica, obsidian, and fluorite, have thus far only been recovered from Holding phase assemblages. However, copper has been found in both Cement Hollow phase (Bonnie Gums, personal communication 1995, regarding the Petite Michele site) and Holding phase contexts, while galena appears in contexts dating to all phases of the Middle Woodland period. The acquisition of exotic extraregional materials apparently occurred mostly, but not strictly, during the height of Hopewellian Interaction Sphere exchanges, or from 50 B.C. to A.D. 150. However, the use of nonlocal American Bottom resources apparently was common throughout the Middle Woodland period.

The occurrence of exotic minerals or rocks is perhaps not the best gauge for characterizing diversity in Middle Woodland material assemblages in this area. Middle Woodland peoples also utilized a wide variety of local cherts, perhaps more so than during any other period of prehistory in this area. The use of relatively low-quality as well as high-quality cherts for blade manufacture at Dash Reeves is striking. The Middle Woodland preference for colorful cherts is well known, and heat-treating cherts to achieve certain colors was common (Fortier 1992). Clays used for ceramic manufacture were tempered with a wide variety of materials, including grit, sand, grog, and (rarely) limestone. There is some reason to believe that even glacial till was selectively utilized for certain kinds of tools (see Meinkoth's analysis of glacial tools from Holding in Williams 1989:326–327). In terms of the procurement and use of stone materials, this period was clearly a time of great experimentation.

The Dash Reeves assemblage certainly typifies the kind of procurement diversity expected of a Middle Woodland context, although it is also important to note that the lithic assemblage is mostly locally derived, more so than the assemblage recovered from the Holding site. The predominance of local Salem and Ste. Genevieve cherts at Dash Reeves, many types of which could be acquired within a 5-km radius of the site, is striking and atypical of earlier Holding phase procurement patterns. It is not known at this time whether the Dash Reeves situation reflects the birth of a trend toward localized resource procurement in the area, a trend that is more clearly observable in Late Woodland assemblages, or is merely a product of the specialized nature of the site, i.e., a lithic production center. In this regard, the smaller, Hill Lake phase settlement at the Truck #7 site displays a very similar local resource use profile, suggesting that the localization process had indeed been initiated by middle to late Middle Woodland times.

Just as Middle Woodland peoples followed diverse procurement and use practices, their manipulation of natural site environs was also complex. This facet of their life is highlighted by their refuse discard patterns and their choice of settlement niches that often accommodated those patterns. Middle Woodland habitation areas often appear cluttered and the refuse pattern unordered, especially by comparison with Late Woodland standards. Initially, the Dash Reeves site appeared to fit this pattern. However, it became apparent, particularly during analysis, that the discard pattern at Dash Reeves was more ordered than anticipated. Although materials were distributed over most of the living area, it was also clear that most refuse had been systematically dumped into restricted areas, mostly in old creek swales adjacent to living surfaces. In short, the Dash Reeves inhabitants apparently made periodic efforts to clear refuse from the main living areas of the site. It is possible that individual households were cleaned and the resulting debris moved into localized "dead zones" at the site.

This idea is suggested by the contents of Feature 29 and by the concentration of southern Illinois-related artifacts in several creek midden units. Caching of chert debitage in pits within Middle Woodland houses has previously been recognized at the Truck #7 site (Fortier 1985a:205) and indicates that Hill Lake phase people were perhaps not as untidy as previously thought. It also means that in future excavations of sites from this period, we need to be aware of specialized refuse deposits situated away from feature or household concentrations. It is perhaps significant that most of the Middle Woodland sites known today in floodplain environments in the American Bottom are located either on stream banks or near paleochannel swales, both ideal depositories for the kinds of high-density refuse generated by the sites' occupants. It is apparent that the vast majority of the material assemblage recovered from middle to late Middle Woodland occupations from this area is found in such midden contexts and not in feature contexts.

REGIONAL INTERACTION AND SETTLEMENT SYSTEMATICS

Evidence for regional interaction at the Dash Reeves site is minimal and almost exclusively focused on southern Illinois relationships. Unlike Holding, which produced such extraregional materials as copper, obsidian, mica, and fluorite, Dash Reeves contained few exotics. The only nonlocal rock or mineral recovered from the site is galena, a lead ore that is not common but tends to be ubiquitous throughout the prehistoric sequence in this area (Walthall 1981). Other indications of affiliation with the so-called Hopewell Interaction Sphere are sparse but might include the elaborate figurine head fragment, several clay ear spool fragments, and the two Brangenburg vessel rims. These artifacts are difficult to evaluate, but their presence does indicate some outside contact or, at least, interaction with local groups who themselves had direct contacts with the sources of such materials. In the Holding site report the authors proposed that such items were most probably obtained at special exchange centers or regional transaction centers (Fortier et al. 1989:574–577), perhaps during specific times of the year. Unfortunately, to date we have identified no candidates for such centers in the American Bottom. Given the paucity of exotic items in Hill Lake phase assemblages (Fortier et al. 1989:559), it is apparent that few, if any, such centers existed in the area after A.D. 150. It is possible that a number of southern Illinois artifacts in the Dash Reeves assemblage came to the site through direct interaction with southern Illinois peoples, who perhaps in turn had acquired the materials through interactions at sites such as Twenhafel in Jackson County. This, of course, is pure conjecture, and other alternatives, such as the heirlooming of older artifacts, are equally viable explanations for the occurrence of exotics on Hill Lake phase sites. The entire question of exchange during this period will be difficult to resolve until major excavations are undertaken at some of the larger Middle Woodland interaction centers in the region.

The issue of possible blade trade during the Holding phase was raised in the Holding site report (Fortier et al. 1989:577), and others have considered the exchange of Burlington and Ste. Genevieve red cherts for such southern Illinois cherts as Cobden/Dongola, Kaolin, Mill Creek, Mansker, and Blair (Morrow 1987). Were the red Ste. Genevieve blades manufactured at Dash Reeves produced for consumption elsewhere in the region? A small percentage of Ste. Genevieve red cherts occur at the Holding site and at other Middle Woodland sites in the area and most probably did come either directly or indirectly from sites or quarries located in Monroe County. Just how far these cherts traveled outside of the American Bottom is unclear. I inspected a sizable collection of chert from the Twenhafel site in Jackson County in southern Illinois but could identify only a small number of blades and one blade core as Ste. Genevieve red chert. It is clear that this site at least did not participate in major blade trade involving this kind of chert. There were, however, numerous white Burlington blades in the Twenhafel collection that could have originated from American Bottom sources or quite possibly Missouri sources such as the Crescent Hills quarry southwest of St. Louis.

Conversely, it is interesting that the southern Illinois cherts recovered from Dash Reeves most often occur as complete artifacts rather than as raw resources and that they rarely take the form of blades. Given the occurrence of Crab Orchard pottery on the site and tools and a little debitage made of southern cherts, it is clear that any exchange between the American Bottom and

southern Illinois involved direct contact between individuals at the site itself. It is not known whether such interaction occurred primarily as a result of formal exchange transactions, or whether such artifacts were the byproducts of other kinds of social interactions, such as intermarriage, calumet-like associations, or transient hunting party or collecting visits. It is perhaps significant, however, that such interactions occurred at Dash Reeves often enough to produce specific refuse disposal episodes involving southern materials, a fact that indicates a longer period of contact than expected from short-term trading associations. It should also be pointed out that the occurrence of Crab Orchard pottery and southern Illinois cherts is widespread in the American Bottom during the Middle Woodland period, suggesting that strong bonds of more than a transient nature existed between the two areas.

The issues of regional interaction and settlement systematics are closely connected during the Middle Woodland period. Unfortunately, Middle Woodland settlement systematics are poorly known and mostly hypothetical in nature. Each new excavation has essentially provided us with a new settlement type. A relatively complex Middle Woodland settlement model was presented in the Holding site report (Fortier et al. 1989:562–569) involving a hierarchy of site types based primarily on size and proposed economic function. Site types included extractive loci, individual households, horticultural hamlets, residence camps, and local rendezvous or transaction centers. It was thought that transaction centers comprised the hub of the system during the Holding phase and theoretically functioned as mediators of regional exchange. Although specific sites were identified as representing each of these site types, the existence of some, such as transaction centers, is clearly hypothetical. A more recent analysis of the Middle Woodland settlement system has argued that this category of settlement should be removed from the model (Fortier and Ghosh 2000), since such centers have not been documented in the American Bottom. Other sites were assigned a type identity based on partial knowledge of site limits. Others were fit into the hierarchy on the basis of unanalyzed site assemblages. Still others were considered likely but untested representatives of specific types. This model has been rightly criticized for these reasons (Farnsworth 1990:119–120). Since the model was introduced, only a handful of Middle Woodland sites, including Dash Reeves, Bosque

Medio (Fortier and Ghosh 2000), and Petite Michele, have been excavated in the American Bottom, and attempts to resolve the issue of the existence of major centers or mounds associated with this period have, thus far, met with ambiguous results (Maher 1994, 1996).

Petite Michele, presently being analyzed, dates to the Cement Hollow phase and probably best fits the residential camp site type proposed in the 1989 Fortier et al. model. Dash Reeves, on the other hand, does not clearly meet the criteria of any site type proposed in that model; at the time of the Holding report, the Dash Reeves site was regarded as a horticultural hamlet. It is now interpreted as a specialized lithic production center, a site type we did not anticipate. There is no clear evidence of dwellings (although we infer their presence north of the excavated area), and the archaeobotanical assemblage is far less diverse than would be expected from a horticulturally based settlement. Perhaps *specialized residential camp* would better characterize the Dash Reeves settlement. In future models it might be best if we designated all sizable settlements such as Dash Reeves and Holding specialized residential camps and subcategorized them according to their primary functions, for example, as horticultural or lithic manufacturing foci. Since we do not yet have the means of determining whether such settlements were occupied on a year-round basis, it would probably be premature to call these *permanent* residential camps. Moreover, as our knowledge of exchange and interaction during this period becomes more sophisticated, the concept of transaction centers as prime movers of exchange and as centers of a settlement system may have to be modified. It is quite possible that specialized residential camps such as Holding and Dash Reeves will prove to have been more important to the functioning of the overall settlement system in this area than previously anticipated.

SITE SIGNIFICANCE

The Dash Reeves site has yielded one of the largest Middle Woodland material culture assemblages ever excavated in the American Bottom. It has provided us with new information about technology, tool forms, pottery formats, and artifact distributions dating to the poorly known Hill Lake phase. The site dates to A.D. 150–300, following a period of cultural florescence in the prehistoric sequence in the Eastern Woodlands often referred to as the Hopewell climax. During the Hopewell era exchange networks covered vast areas of the Eastern United States, and even small settlements seemed to be touched by material goods, technologies, and ideas of nonlocal origin. It is clear that the Dash Reeves inhabitants were direct descendants of that era and carried on many of its cultural traditions, technologies, and perhaps, symbols. At Dash Reeves this is highlighted particularly by the presence of massive blade production and microtool industries.

Conversely, the Dash Reeves assemblage lacks many of the classic Hopewell traits found in the American Bottom, including exotic minerals, that presumably entered the area earlier through the Hopewell Interaction Sphere network. The Dash Reeves ceramic assemblage lacks many of the finely executed vessels and zoned design motifs observed, for example, in the Holding assemblage. Exotic trade ware (Marksville) is absent at Dash Reeves. The archaeobotanical assemblage is not diverse and few cultigens were identified. This is in striking contrast to the pattern observed at Holding phase sites in the area. The Dash Reeves lithic assemblage indicates a heavy reliance on cherts and other rocks procured within 5 km of the site, a pattern that is generally more common during the Late Woodland period in this area. Similar material assemblage patterns were observed at the Truck #7 site, where the disassociation from the Hopewell world is even more pronounced, given the absence of a blade technology and the extremely poorly executed ceramic assemblage. In short, the Dash Reeves site provides us with significant insights into the so-called collapse of Hopewell in the American Bottom, a collapse that was apparently not abrupt, but gradual in nature. The reader is cautioned that such a process of decline may have been peculiar to the American Bottom rather than regional in scope. It certainly warrants continued study and documentation in the American Bottom itself.

As a final footnote, we are indeed fortunate to have been able to investigate the Dash Reeves site when we did. Three years after completion of field investigations, the remaining portion of the site north of the highway was sold to private land developers. A gas station and a convenience store were constructed over the central portion of the site, and numerous water and sewer lines have been excavated in the area in anticipation of further development. In addition, loessal fill from the nearby bluffs now covers most of the site area so that surface remains are completely obscured. There are only a handful of sites like Dash Reeves now remaining in the American Bottom, and none are known to be as potentially productive in terms of artifact content. Therefore, the data presented in this report and the materials currently curated at the University of Illinois have taken on an added significance that we could not have anticipated at the outset of the project.

SITE SUMMARY

Archaeological investigations were conducted at the Dash Reeves site by the University of Illinois in 1990 as part of a proposed IDOT road project in the Palmer Creek locality, situated about 1–2 km north of Columbia in northern Monroe County, Illinois. The Dash Reeves site encompasses approximately 30,000 m², of which nearly 6,000 m² fell within the proposed construction area. Surface collections had indicated that the site represented one of the largest Middle Woodland occupations in the area and that it dated almost exclusively to the Hill Lake phase (A.D. 150–300). Excavation, aided by the use of heavy machinery, was undertaken to define the depth and extent of midden materials and subsurface features. Eventually, 53 features, including hearths, cooking pits, and refuse pits, were exposed and excavated. In addition, a sheet midden over the entire occupation area and a more specialized creek refuse deposit were defined. The creek midden was excavated in its entirety, while the sheet midden was sampled. Most of the features were located along the inner portions of two paleochannels, one of which may have been active for a short period during the occupation. In all probability, the main portion of the community lay north of the excavation area, outside of the right-of-way limits. The site appears to have been ringed on the north and east by a curving paleochannel swale. This channel was filled with refuse, so that the occupation area was actually surrounded by a ring midden, a portion of which is visible on modern aerial photographs.

Excavations produced the largest assemblage of artifacts ever recovered from a Hill Lake phase site in this area. Diagnostic pottery and lithics and a series of radiocarbon dates have confirmed the Hill Lake affiliation of the occupation. The massive lithic assemblage, including several thousand blades and over 300 blade cores, indicates that the site functioned primarily as a specialized residential camp for the production of chert tools. It is also apparent, given the diversity of recovered tool types, that a wide variety of other tasks were undertaken here, including meat and hide processing, woodworking, nut harvesting, and limited gardening. Investigations at the Dash Reeves site have contributed a great deal of new information concerning what previously had been a poorly known phase at the end of the Middle Woodland continuum. Investigations also have provided some insight into the process of Hopewellian collapse in the American Bottom.

Appendix A. Materials Inventory by Feature

	N	Wt(g)
Feature 1		
Ceramics	4	24.4
Chert Debitage	7	4.0
Feature 2		
Ceramics	1	2.5
Chert Debitage	11	6.2
Feature 3		
Ceramics	7	7.9
Chert Debitage	13	2.9
Sandstone	1	93.2
Feature 4		
Ceramics	4	7.5
Chert Debitage	16	45.0
Utilized Blade	1	1.4
Feature 5		
Chert Debitage	72	10.5
Utilized Flakes	2	0.9
Feature 6		
Ceramics	1	0.6
Chert Debitage	29	34.0
Sandstone	1	1.7
Utilized Flakes	3	7.5
Feature 7		
Ceramics	29	66.5
Daub/Burned Clay	5	3.3
Chert Debitage	56	47.6
Limestone	15	806.8
Feature 8		
Ceramics	55	51.9
Daub/Burned Clay	22	14.9
Chert Debitage	193	77.8
Limestone	3	40.0
Flake Perforator	1	1.8
Utilized Flake	1	3.3
Utilized Blades	2	6.1
Feature 9 (PM4)		
Ceramics	1	5.3
Chert Debitage	3	0.1
Feature 10		
Ceramics	3	6.6
Daub/Burned Clay	14	20.8
Chert Debitage	174	414.7
Limestone	31	215.2
Utilized Flake	1	1.3
Utilized Blade	1	5.0
Blade Graver	1	10.6
Polished Flake	1	0.3

	N	Wt(g)
Feature 11		
Ceramics	22	112.7
Daub/Burned Clay	4	4.7
Chert Debitage	103	152.4
Sandstone	1	7.8
Utilized Flakes	4	2.9
Flake Graver	1	5.0
Flake Perforator	1	1.5
Polished Flakes	3	0.9
Feature 12		
Ceramics	1	36.4
Chert Debitage	19	7.6
Feature 13		
Ceramics	6	52.2
Chert Debitage	1	0.1
Feature 14		
Chert Debitage	4	0.9
Blade Graver	1	5.0
Feature 15		
Ceramics	1	1.4
Chert Debitage	5	4.0
Feature 17		
Chert Debitage	6	5.7
Feature 19		
Chert Debitage	11	159.9
Limestone	25	632.1
Feature 20		
Ceramics	30	137.4
Daub/Burned Clay	1	12.8
Chert Debitage	52	205.4
Limestone	12	269.4
Sandstone	2	92.1
Utilized Flakes	2	4.5
Core Denticulate	1	23.7
Flake Scraper	1	20.0
Feature 21		
Quartzite	1	20.5
Quartzite HS	1	21.0
Biface Frag.	1	0.1
Feature 22		
Chert Debitage	13	2.1
Feature 23		
Ceramics	14	9.0
Chert Debitage	21	3.0

	N	Wt(g)
Feature 24		
Ceramics	1	8.8
Chert Debitage	20	4.5
Feature 25		
Ceramics	35	77.0
Daub/Burned Clay	7	9.4
Chert Debitage	122	134.2
Limestone	4	6.3
Utilized Flake	1	1.4
Flake Perforator	1	1.1
Flake Graver	1	3.4
Bifacial Flake Scraper	1	19.4
Feature 26		
Ceramics	83	397.8
Daub/Burned Clay	6	12.3
Chert Debitage	216	336.6
Limestone	90	1,551.8
Sandstone	3	141.1
Rough Rock/Gravel	3	7.4
Utilized Flakes	6	13.3
Utilized Blade	1	1.1
Core Edge Tool	1	14.4
Core Edge Tool Frags.	3	47.4
Igneous PS	1	160.5
Quartzite GS	1	133.1
Cobble HS	1	133.5
Schist HS/GS Frag.	1	214.7
Schist HS/GS	1	445.2
Feature 27		
Ceramics	4	6.2
Chert Debitage	7	9.2
Feature 28		
Ceramics	36	511.1
Daub/Burned Clay	22	36.5
Chert Debitage	388	586.9
Limestone	28	236.4
Fire Cracked Rock	1	35.3
Utilized Flakes	4	19.1
Utilized Blades	3	10.0
Flake Perforator	1	1.5
Flake Side Scrapers	2	44.4
Ovate Flake Scrapers	2	33.1
Micro-drill	1	0.4
Projectile Point Tip	1	10.0
Core Edge Tool Frag.	1	31.8
Polished Flakes	5	3.5
Igneous GS	1	410.7

	N	Wt(g)
Feature 29		
Ceramics	267	1,898.4
Daub/Burned Clay	20	27.8
Chert Debitage	1,763	2,691.9
Limestone	12	136.1
Sandstone	4	154.9
Rough Rock/Gravel	1	0.8
Quartzite	1	45.0
Utilized Flakes	14	42.9
Utilized Blades	2	6.5
Flake Gravers	2	20.1
Drill	1	7.0
Flake Scrapers	2	14.6
Ovate Flake Scrapers	2	88.4
Blade Perforators	2	3.9
Chert Hoe	1	425.2
Triangular Knives	2	63.2
Chert HS	1	101.4
Projectile Points	3	49.1
Projectile Point Frag.	1	1.4
Bifacial Knives	3	42.1
Flat Gouge	1	25.0
Spurs	2	20.7
Polished Flakes	15	6.9
Worked Igneous Rock	1	45.2
Igneous GS	1	391.8
Sandstone Slot Abrader	1	122.9
Feature 30		
Ceramics	15	70.3
Daub/Burned Clay	201	13,457.8
Chert Debitage	15	33.2
Limestone	4	48.0
Utilized Flakes	2	0.6
Core Edge Tool	1	23.5
Core Graver	1	23.0
Feature 31		
Ceramics	4	12.3
Daub/Burned Clay	1	1.0
Chert Debitage	11	49.6
Utilized Flake	1	1.2
Feature 32		
Ceramics	10	16.0
Daub/Burned Clay	2	3.0
Chert Debitage	107	169.4
Limestone	3	36.4
Utilized Flake	1	0.3
Utilized Blade	1	4.2
Flake Perforators	1	18.3

	N	Wt(g)
Feature 33		
Ceramics	13	23.6
Chert Debitage	15	8.5
Limestone	4	12.4
Rough Rock/Gravel	1	9.2
Feature 34		
Ceramics	65	394.1
Daub/Burned Clay	1	2.8
Chert Debitage	121	98.0
Ochre/Hematite	1	39.5
Utilized Flakes	2	2.9
Polished Flakes	3	3.1
Worked Sandstone	1	113.3
Feature 35 (stain)		
Ceramics	27	81.9
Chert Debitage	5	5.7
Feature 36		
Ceramics	40	109.5
Daub/Burned Clay	7	7.1
Chert Debitage	183	113.1
Limestone	15	265.9
Sandstone	2	3.8
Rough Rock/Gravel	1	0.7
Utilized Flakes	3	6.1
Drill	1	0.7
Projectile Point Tip	1	2.8
Bifacial Frag.	1	11.8
Polished Flake	1	2.4
Feature 37		
Chert Debitage	153	57.5
Feature 38		
Chert Debitage	6	3.8
Utilized Flake	1	2.2
Feature 40		
Chert Debitage	11	109.8
Feature 41		
Chert Debitage	37	3.2
Feature 42		
Ceramics	1	2.6
Chert Debitage	21	3.1
Limestone	6	2.5
Utilized Flakes	1	1.0

	N	Wt(g)
Feature 43		
Ceramics	2	3.2
Chert Debitage	116	93.1
Limestone	55	235.1
Sandstone	2	12.2
Utilized Flakes	2	10.4
Utilized Blade	1	0.5
Blade Perforator	1	2.9
Feature 44		
Chert Debitage	19	14.9
Utilized Blade	1	0.7
Feature 45		
Ceramics	1	129.0
Chert Debitage	24	2.8
Limestone	51	524.5
Feature 46		
Chert Debitage	2	0.7
Spur	1	1.7
Feature 47		
Daub/Burned Clay	1	4.1
Chert Debitage	190	166.3
Limestone	2	1.4
Sandstone	16	286.2
Hematite	1	0.3
Utilized Flakes	2	16.2
Projectile Point Frag.	1	29.2
Core Edge Tool Frag.	1	25.4
Feature 48		
Ceramics	1	7.7
Chert Debitage	11	12.3
Sandstone	1	1.5
Feature 49		
Ceramics	14	39.0
Daub/Burned Clay	1	0.7
Chert Debitage	43	27.5
Limestone	53	89.5
Sandstone	1	29.3
Polished Flake	1	0.2
Feature 50		
Ceramics	33	58.3
Daub/Burned Clay	19	21.1
Chert Debitage	174	218.2
Limestone	16	6.0
Sandstone	3	7.6
Rough Rock/Gravel	4	4.9
Igneous Rock	1	1.3
Utilized Flakes	3	0.8
Flake Perforator	1	3.2

	N	Wt(g)
Feature 51		
Ceramics	2	7.1
Chert Debitage	14	14.5
Feature 52		
Ceramics	1	6.3
Chert Debitage	383	126.3
Schist	1	485.0
Utilized Flakes	3	20.4
Flake Graver	1	9.4
Drill	1	4.7
Feature 53		
Chert Debitage	95	37.8
Feature 54		
Chert Debitage	169	105.2
Utilized Flakes	3	7.4
Feature 55		
Chert Debitage	484	234.2
Sandstone	1	91.7
Utilized Flakes	4	6.8
Triangular Knife	1	29.0
Drill	1	1.2
Blade Perforator	1	0.9
Biface Frags.	2	6.1
Feature 56		
Ceramics	7	12.5
Chert Debitage	13	2.4

Appendix B. Ceramic Inventory

Table 1. Diagnostics from Test Units

	N	Wt (g)
Unit A		
Crab Orchard Fabric Marked (grit)	1	30.0
Havana Cordmarked, *var. Bottoms*	1	38.4
Havana Cordmarked, *var. Unsp.*	1	27.4
Hopewell Cross Hatched, *var. Mississippi*	1	2.1
Hopewell Zoned Stamped, *var. Ferry*	2	172.8
Hopewell Zoned Stamped, *var. Unsp.*	1	54.5
Indeterminate (grog)	1	0.5
Indeterminate (no temper)	1	0.5
Pike Rocker Stamped, *var. Black Lane*	3	19.9
Untyped	1	5.2
Total	13	351.3
Unit B		
Indeterminate (grog)	2	3.6
Pike Brushed, *var. Pike*	1	7.7
Total	3	11.3
Unit E		
Crab Orchard Fabric Marked (grit)	1	3.2
Indeterminate (grog)	3	8.4
Pike Rocker Stamped, *var. Black Lane*	3	22.5
Pike Rocker Stamped, *var. Fairmount*	1	7.5
Untyped	1	3.8
Total	9	45.4
Unit F		
Fournie Plain, *var. Fournie*	1	1.5
Havana Plain, *var. Collinsville*	1	12.2
Hopewell Zoned Incised, *var. Cross*	1	21.2
Pike Rocker Stamped, *var. Black Lane*	1	8.7
Total	4	43.6
Unit G		
Indeterminate (grog)	1	9.4
Pike Brushed, *var. Pike*	1	2.8
Pike Rocker Stamped, *var. Black Lane*	3	7.9
Total	5	20.1
Unit J		
Pike Rocker Stamped, *var. Black Lane*	1	2.6
Total	1	2.6
Unit K		
Pike Rocker Stamped, *var. Black Lane*	1	13.6
Total	1	13.6

Table 2. Rim Fragments from Test Units

	N	Wt (g)
Unit E		
Indeterminate (grog)	5	1.8
Sherdlets	2	0.9
Total	7	2.7
Unit F		
Indeterminate (limestone)	1	0.8
Total	1	0.8
Unit G		
Indeterminate (grit)	2	2.1
Indeterminate (grog)	3	2.3
Total	5	4.4
Unit J		
Indeterminate (grit)	1	0.7
Indeterminate (grog)	1	2.0
Total	2	2.7
Unit K		
Indeterminate (grit)	1	0.7
Indeterminate (grog/limestone)	1	1.1
Total	2	1.8
Unit L		
Indeterminate (limestone)	1	0.6
Total	1	0.6
Unit M		
Indeterminate (grog)	1	1.8
Total	1	1.8

Table 3. Body Sherds from Test Units

	N	Wt (g)
Unit A		
Cordmarked (limestone)	1	13.2
Crab Orchard Fabric Marked (grit)	4	38.9
Fournie Plain, *var. Fournie*	15	23.5
Havana Cordmarked, *var. Bottoms*	9	36.6
Havana Plain, *var. Collinsville*	2	7.2
Hopewell Plain	3	12.4
Hopewell Zoned Stamped, *var. Casey*	1	5.2
Hopewell Zoned Stamped, *var. Ferry*	1	1.6
Hopewell Zoned Stamped, *var. Unsp.*	1	1.0
Indeterminate (grit)	30	47.5
Indeterminate (grog)	49	56.9
Indeterminate (limestone)	19	16.1
Pike Brushed, *var. Pike*	1	1.2
Pike Brushed, *var. Robinson*	1	0.9
Pike Rocker Stamped, *var. Black Lane*	85	287.2
Pike Rocker Stamped, *var. Calhoun*	19	68.0
Pike Rocker Stamped, *var. Fairmount*	3	6.7
Pike Rocker Stamped, *var. Unsp.*	1	2.7
Sherdlets	534	174.7
Total	779	801.5
Unit B		
Cordmarked (limestone)	3	28.7
Fournie Plain, *var. Fournie*	20	36.6
Hopewell Plain	3	3.7
Indeterminate (grit)	6	4.5
Indeterminate (grog)	26	36.1
Indeterminate (limestone)	11	10.7
Pike Brushed, *var. Pike*	12	34.1
Pike Brushed, *var. Robinson*	6	17.1
Pike Rocker Stamped, *var. Black Lane*	4	9.8
Plain (no temper)	1	1.0
Sherdlets	173	62.7
Total	265	245.0
Unit C		
Historic	1	4.5
Hopewell Plain	1	2.2
Indeterminate (grit)	5	3.4
Indeterminate (grog)	3	5.1
Indeterminate (limestone)	2	2.1
Sherdlets	27	9.0
Total	39	26.3

	N	Wt (g)
Unit D		
Fournie Plain, *var. Fournie*	3	3.1
Havana Plain, *var. Collinsville*	1	0.9
Havana Plain, *var. Unsp.*	1	1.0
Indeterminate (grit)	3	4.7
Indeterminate (grog)	11	14.4
Indeterminate (limestone)	2	3.5
Pike Brushed, *var. Robinson*	2	1.2
Pike Rocker Stamped, *var. Black Lane*	1	2.9
Sherdlets	50	16.8
Total	74	48.5
Unit E		
Baehr Zoned Brushed	3	18.6
Crab Orchard Fabric Marked (grit)	2	8.0
Fournie Plain, *var. Fournie*	14	17.9
Havana Cordmarked, *var. Bottoms*	1	12.7
Havana Plain, *var. Collinsville*	1	1.8
Havana Plain, *var. Unsp.*	2	2.4
Indeterminate (grit)	31	58.0
Indeterminate (grog)	39	48.3
Indeterminate (limestone)	9	10.5
Pike Brushed, *var. Pike*	3	4.4
Pike Brushed, *var. Robinson*	37	109.8
Pike Brushed, *var. Unsp.*	9	33.6
Pike Rocker Stamped, *var. Black Lane*	37	85.7
Pike Rocker Stamped, *var. Calhoun*	8	40.1
Pike Rocker Stamped, *var. Fairmount*	10	80.0
Sherdlets	385	132.6
Total	591	664.4
Unit F		
Baehr Zoned Brushed	7	58.2
Fournie Plain, *var. Fournie*	7	27.6
Havana Cordmarked, *var. Bottoms*	1	9.8
Havana Plain, *var. Collinsville*	1	5.8
Hopewell Plain	1	1.0
Indeterminate (grit)	13	15.5
Indeterminate (grog)	21	38.5
Indeterminate (limestone)	10	7.0
Pike Brushed, *var. Pike*	14	41.2
Pike Brushed, *var. Robinson*	4	15.8
Pike Brushed, *var. Unsp.*	6	52.2
Pike Rocker Stamped, *var. Black Lane*	8	45.3
Pike Rocker Stamped, *var. Calhoun*	4	18.7
Sherdlets	240	89.8
Total	337	426.4

Table 3. Body Sherds from Test Units, continued

	N	Wt (g)
Unit G		
Baehr Zoned Brushed	2	11.8
Cordmarked (grog)	1	9.3
Crab Orchard Fabric Marked (grit)	4	27.0
Crab Orchard Fabric Marked (grog)	1	4.2
Fournie Plain, *var. Fournie*	17	37.6
Havana Cordmarked, var. Bottoms	4	51.9
Havana Plain, *var. Collinsville*	9	19.9
Hopewell Plain	5	8.7
Hopewell Zoned Stamped, *var. Casey*	2	7.6
Indeterminate (grit)	29	55.0
Indeterminate (grog)	46	68.7
Indeterminate (limestone)	12	19.5
Pike Brushed, *var. Pike*	6	12.7
Pike Brushed, *var. Robinson*	43	215.2
Pike Brushed, *var. Unsp.*	5	11.9
Pike Rocker Stamped, *var. Black Lane*	81	415.0
Pike Rocker Stamped, *var. Calhoun*	17	40.8
Pike Rocker Stamped, *var. Fairmount*	19	117.5
Pike Rocker Stamped, *var. Unsp.*	2	21.5
Sherdlets	553	212.8
Untyped	1	3.1
Total	859	1,371.7
Unit H		
Havana Cordmarked, *var. Bottoms*	1	0.6
Historic	1	0.8
Indeterminate (grit)	3	3.6
Sherdlets	5	1.4
Total	10	6.4
Unit J		
Cordmarked (grog)	1	1.5
Fournie Plain, *var. Fournie*	4	5.0
Havana Cordmarked, *var. Bottoms*	2	7.8
Havana Plain, *var. Collinsville*	1	2.3
Hopewell Plain	1	2.3
Indeterminate (grit)	8	11.4
Indeterminate (grog)	18	29.9
Indeterminate (limestone)	10	13.7
Pike Rocker Stamped, *var. Black Lane*	4	9.0
Pike Rocker Stamped, *var. Calhoun*	1	2.3
Pike Rocker Stamped, *var. Fairmount*	1	1.4
Sherdlets	118	49.6
Total	169	136.2

	N	Wt (g)
Unit K		
Cordmarked (limestone)	1	1.7
Havana Cordmarked, *var. Bottoms*	2	3.2
Havana Plain, *var. Collinsville*	1	2.1
Havana Plain, *var. Unsp.*	1	1.6
Hopewell Plain	2	5.1
Indeterminate (grit)	9	14.5
Indeterminate (grog)	17	20.6
Indeterminate (limestone)	20	21.8
Pike Rocker Stamped, *var. Black Lane*	3	7.5
Pike Rocker Stamped, *var. Fairmount*	1	3.9
Sherdlets	91	36.7
Total	148	118.7
Unit L		
Fournie Plain, *var. Fournie*	1	1.1
Hopewell Plain	3	4.1
Indeterminate (grit)	6	6.7
Indeterminate (grog)	14	18.9
Indeterminate (limestone)	8	6.7
Pike Rocker Stamped, *var. Black Lane*	9	13.8
Pike Rocker Stamped, *var. Fairmount*	3	20.6
Sherdlets	78	32.6
Total	122	104.5
Unit M		
Fournie Plain, *var. Fournie*	6	9.9
Hopewell Plain	3	3.3
Indeterminate (grit)	2	1.0
Indeterminate (grog)	10	8.9
Indeterminate (limestone)	5	4.5
Pike Brushed, *var. Pike*	1	1.6
Sherdlets	58	18.0
Total	85	47.2
Unit N		
Fournie Plain, *var. Fournie*	3	2.5
Havana Plain, *var. Collinsville*	1	2.0
Indeterminate (grit)	3	2.2
Indeterminate (grog)	9	8.2
Indeterminate (limestone)	6	5.6
Pike Brushed, *var. Robinson*	1	7.5
Pike Rocker Stamped, *var. Black Lane*	1	1.5
Pike Rocker Stamped, *var. Calhoun*	1	1.8
Sherdlets	64	18.6
Total	89	49.9

Table 4. Diagnostics from Features

	N	Wt (g)
Feature 8		
Untyped	1	4.7
Total	1	4.7
Feature 9		
Havana Cordmarked, *var. Bottoms*	1	5.3
Total	1	5.3
Feature 12		
Crab Orchard Fabric Marked (grit)	1	36.4
Total	1	36.4
Feature 20		
Hopewell Rocker Rim, *var. West*	1	22.1
Indeterminate (grog)	1	4.8
Total	2	26.9
Feature 25		
Hopewell Zoned Stamped, *var. Unsp.*	1	27.8
Pike Brushed, var. Pike	1	2.5
Total	2	30.3
Feature 26		
Indeterminate (grog)	1	3.6
Pike Brushed, *var. Pike*	1	64.8
Untyped	1	4.3
Total	3	72.7
Feature 28		
Crab Orchard Fabric Marked (grit)	1	37.4
Hopewell Rocker Rim, *var. West*	1	1.3
Hopewell Zoned Stamped, *var. Unsp.*	1	14.5
Indeterminate (grit)	1	8.7
Pike Rocker Stamped, *var. Black Lane*	1	14.1
Total	5	76.0

	N	Wt (g)
Feature 29		
Havana Cordmarked, *var. Bottoms*	1	20.3
Hopewell Cross Hatched, *var. Mississippi*	1	19.3
Indeterminate (grog)	1	3.8
Pike Rocker Stamped, *var. Black Lane*	1	13.0
Pike Rocker Stamped, *var. Calhoun*	1	104.0
Untyped	2	113.5
Total	7	273.9
Feature 30		
Havana Cordmarked, *var. Bottoms*	1	7.9
Total	1	7.9
Feature 34		
Crab Orchard Fabric Marked (grit)	1	140.4
Havana Cordmarked, *var. Bottoms*	1	7.8
Total	2	148.2
Feature 36		
Indeterminate (grit)	1	6.3
Total	1	6.3
Feature 47		
Pike Rocker Stamped, *var. Calhoun*	1	7.3
Total	1	7.3
Feature 50		
Hopewell Cross Hatched, *var. Mississippi*	1	6.0
Total	1	6.0

Table 5. Rim Fragments from Features

	N	Wt (g)
Feature 7		
Indeterminate (limestone)	1	1.4
Total	1	1.4
Feature 15		
Indeterminate (grog)	1	1.4
Total	1	1.4

Table 6. Body Sherds from Features

	N	Wt (g)
Feature 1		
Indeterminate (grog)	1	8.9
Pike Rocker Stamped, *var. Black Lane*	2	13.1
Pike Rocker Stamped, *var. Fairmount*	1	2.4
Total	4	24.4
Feature 2		
Indeterminate (limestone)	1	2.5
Total	1	2.5
Feature 3		
Indeterminate (grog)	1	0.3
Pike Brushed, *var. Pike*	1	3.1
Pike Brushed, *var. Unsp.*	1	1.6
Pike Rocker Stamped, *var. Black Lane*	1	2.1
Sherdlets	3	0.8
Total	7	7.9
Feature 4		
Fournie Plain, *var. Fournie*	2	3.9
Pike Brushed, *var. Robinson*	1	2.5
Pike Rocker Stamped, *var. Black Lane*	1	1.1
Total	4	7.5
Feature 6		
Indeterminate (grog)	1	0.6
Total	1	0.6

	N	Wt (g)
Feature 7		
Fournie Plain, *var. Fournie*	1	27.8
Fournie Plain, *var. Unsp.*	2	7.4
Indeterminate (grog)	3	2.4
Pike Brushed, *var. Pike*	2	6.8
Pike Brushed, *var. Robinson*	2	3.1
Pike Brushed, *var. Unsp.*	1	8.1
Pike Rocker Stamped, *var. Calhoun*	1	5.9
Sherdlets	16	3.6
Total	28	65.1
Feature 8		
Indeterminate (limestone)	5	4.5
Pike Brushed, *var. Pike*	26	22.4
Pike Brushed, *var. Unsp.*	2	10.9
Pike Rocker Stamped, *var. Fairmount*	1	3.5
Red Slip (limestone)	1	1.1
Sherdlets	19	4.8
Total	54	47.2
Feature 10		
Indeterminate (limestone)	1	0.5
Pike Rocker Stamped, *var. Black Lane*	2	6.1
Total	3	6.6
Feature 11		
Crab Orchard Fabric Marked (grit)	3	35.1
Havana Cordwrapped Stick	1	2.9
Hopewell Plain	1	5.6
Indeterminate (grit)	2	2.1
Indeterminate (grog)	1	1.1
Pike Rocker Stamped, *var. Black Lane*	1	12.9
Pike Rocker Stamped, *var. Unsp.*	2	46.4
Sherdlets	11	6.6
Total	22	112.7

Table 6. Body Sherds from Features, continued

	N	Wt (g)
Feature 13		
Pike Rocker Stamped, *var. Black Lane*	6	52.2
Total	6	52.2
Feature 20		
Fournie Plain, *var. Fournie*	1	2.1
Havana Cordmarked, *var. Bottoms*	1	2.1
Hopewell Plain	1	1.4
Indeterminate (grit)	3	2.7
Indeterminate (grog)	1	3.2
Indeterminate (limestone)	2	2.5
Pike Brushed, *var. Pike*	3	31.5
Pike Brushed, *var. Robinson*	1	3.0
Pike Brushed, *var. Unsp.*	1	44.1
Pike Rocker Stamped, *var. Black Lane*	2	9.3
Pike Rocker Stamped, *var. Calhoun*	2	5.1
Sherdlets	10	3.5
Total	28	110.5
Feature 23		
Fournie Plain, *var. Fournie*	1	2.1
Indeterminate (limestone)	13	6.9
Total	14	9.0
Feature 24		
Pike Rocker Stamped, *var. Black Lane*	1	8.8
Total	1	8.8
Feature 25		
Pike Brushed, *var. Pike*	24	44.0
Sherdlets	9	2.7
Total	33	46.7
Feature 26		
Cordmarked (limestone)	3	85.2
Fournie Plain, *var. Fournie*	6	19.9
Havana Plain, *var. Collinsville*	6	14.8
Hopewell Plain	3	9.9
Indeterminate (grit)	9	18.0
Indeterminate (grog)	4	12.2
Indeterminate (limestone)	1	2.1
Pike Brushed, *var. Pike*	10	55.3
Pike Brushed, *var. Robinson*	13	43.7
Pike Rocker Stamped, *var. Black Lane*	1	51.2
Sherdlets	24	12.8
Total	80	325.1

	N	Wt (g)
Feature 27		
Cordmarked (limestone)	1	2.2
Hopewell Zoned Incised, *var. Cross*	1	2.2
Indeterminate (grog)	2	1.8
Total	4	6.2
Feature 28		
Havana Cordmarked, *var. Bottoms*	4	39.4
Indeterminate (grog)	1	0.8
Pike Rocker Stamped, *var. Black Lane*	12	202.1
Pike Rocker Stamped, *var. Calhoun*	2	55.7
Pike Rocker Stamped, *var. Fairmount*	7	77.8
Pike Rocker Stamped, *var. Unsp.*	4	58.9
Sherdlets	1	0.4
Total	31	435.1
Feature 29		
Crab Orchard Fabric Marked (grit)	6	221.9
Havana Cordmarked, *var. Bottoms*	50	572.4
Havana Plain, *var. Collinsville*	3	6.9
Hopewell Zoned Stamped, *var. Casey*	12	55.1
Hopewell Zoned Stamped, *var. Unsp.*	2	2.1
Indeterminate (grit)	7	15.5
Indeterminate (grog)	1	7.2
Indeterminate (limestone)	1	1.2
Pike Rocker Stamped, *var. Black Lane*	47	190.4
Pike Rocker Stamped, *var. Calhoun*	30	423.6
Pike Rocker Stamped, *var. Fairmount*	5	76.4
Sherdlets	96	51.8
Total	260	1,624.5
Feature 30		
Crab Orchard Fabric Marked (grog)	1	17.1
Indeterminate (grog)	7	5.7
Indeterminate (grog/limestone)	1	4.8
Indeterminate (limestone)	2	8.1
Pike Brushed, *var. Robinson*	1	20.9
Pike Rocker Stamped, *var. Black Lane*	1	3.3
Plain (no temper)	1	2.5
Total	14	62.4
Feature 31		
Indeterminate (grit)	2	6.1
Pike Brushed, *var. Robinson*	2	6.2
Total	4	12.3

Table 6. Body Sherds from Features, continued

	N	Wt (g)
Feature 32		
Indeterminate (grog)	3	3.2
Pike Brushed, *var. Robinson*	2	3.6
Pike Rocker Stamped, *var. Calhoun*	1	7.7
Sherdlets	4	1.5
Total	10	16.0
Feature 33		
Fournie Plain, *var. Fournie*	1	2.7
Indeterminate (grog)	1	3.2
Indeterminate (limestone)	1	1.9
Pike Rocker Stamped, *var. Black Lane*	2	11.3
Sherdlets	8	4.5
Total	13	23.6
Feature 34		
Fournie Plain, *var. Fournie*	1	3.5
Havana Cordmarked, *var. Bottoms*	7	34.3
Havana Plain, *var. Collinsville*	3	34.6
Indeterminate (grit)	3	6.0
Indeterminate (grog)	6	12.8
Indeterminate (limestone)	1	2.1
Pike Brushed, *var. Pike*	1	29.1
Pike Brushed, *var. Robinson*	1	4.8
Pike Brushed, *var. Unsp.*	2	24.5
Pike Rocker Stamped, *var. Black Lane*	16	85.0
Sherdlets	22	9.2
Total	63	245.9
Feature 35		
Indeterminate (grit)	2	3.4
Indeterminate (grog)	4	4.8
Pike Rocker Stamped, *var. Black Lane*	2	3.8
Pike Rocker Stamped, *var. Fairmount*	9	66.3
Sherdlets	10	3.6
Total	27	81.9
Feature 36		
Crab Orchard Fabric Marked (grit)	1	5.4
Fournie Plain, *var. Fournie*	3	4.2
Havana Plain, *var. Collinsville*	1	16.5
Indeterminate (grit)	1	5.2
Indeterminate (grog)	3	2.8
Pike Brushed, *var. Pike*	1	0.9
Pike Brushed, *var. Robinson*	4	36.9
Pike Rocker Stamped, *var. Black Lane*	3	20.9
Pike Rocker Stamped, *var. Fairmount*	1	2.3
Sherdlets	21	8.1
Total	39	103.2

	N	Wt (g)
Feature 42		
Pike Brushed, *var. Robinson*	1	2.6
Total	1	2.6
Feature 43		
Fournie Plain, *var. Fournie*	1	2.0
Indeterminate (limestone)	1	1.2
Total	2	3.2
Feature 45		
Pike Brushed, *var. Robinson*	1	129.0
Total	1	129.0
Feature 47		
Havana Plain, *var. Collinsville*	1	6.3
Indeterminate (grog)	2	3.1
Pike Brushed, *var. Pike*	1	3.4
Pike Rocker Stamped, *var. Black Lane*	13	111.6
Sherdlets	2	0.7
Total	19	125.1
Feature 48		
Pike Rocker Stamped, *var. Black Lane*	1	7.7
Total	1	7.7
Feature 49		
Cordmarked (grog)	1	1.7
Havana Plain, *var. Collinsville*	1	8.4
Hopewell Zoned Stamped, *var. Casey*	1	1.9
Indeterminate (grit)	3	10.0
Indeterminate (grog)	2	1.7
Pike Rocker Stamped, *var. Black Lane*	2	12.2
Pike Rocker Stamped, *var. Calhoun*	1	1.5
Sherdlets	3	1.6
Total	14	39.0
Feature 50		
Indeterminate (grog)	2	12.2
Indeterminate (limestone)	1	7.0
Pike Brushed, *var. Pike*	1	13.5
Pike Rocker Stamped, *var. Black Lane*	3	13.5
Pike Rocker Stamped, *var. Calhoun*	1	1.1
Sherdlets	24	5.0
Total	32	52.3

Table 6. Body Sherds from Features, continued

	N	Wt (g)
Feature 51		
Indeterminate (limestone)	1	0.5
Pike Rocker Stamped, *var. Black Lane*	1	6.6
Total	2	7.1
Feature 52		
Pike Rocker Stamped, *var. Black Lane*	1	6.3
Total	1	6.3
Feature 56		
Indeterminate (grit)	1	2.1
Indeterminate (grog)	1	2.7
Indeterminate (limestone)	4	2.2
Pike Brushed, *var. Unsp.*	1	5.5
Total	7	12.5

Table 7. Diagnostics from Excavation Block Units★

	N	Wt (g)			N	Wt (g)
Unit 1				**Unit 5**		
Crab Orchard Fabric Marked (grit)	1	56.2		Fournie Plain, *var. Fournie*	1	1.9
Pike Rocker Stamped, *var. Black Lane*	1	4.0		Hopewell Cross Hatched, *var. Unsp.*	1	8.3
Total	2	60.2		Indeterminate (grog)	1	5.9
				Pike Rocker Stamped, *var. Black Lane*	1	67.7
Unit 2				Pike Rocker Stamped, *var. Calhoun*	3	45.1
Havana Cordmarked, *var. Unsp.*	1	9.7		Total	7	128.9
Hopewell Cross Hatched, *var. Mississippi*	3	25.1				
Hopewell Rocker Rim, *var. West*	2	16.1		**Unit 6**		
Indeterminate (grit)	1	5.4		Fournie Plain, *var. Fournie*	1	7.0
Indeterminate (grog)	3	34.1		Hopewell Cross Hatched, *var. Mississippi*	2	4.9
Indeterminate (limestone)	1	6.2		Hopewell Plain	1	1.7
Montezuma Punctate, *var. Montezuma*	1	4.1		Hopewell Zoned Stamped, *var. Casey*	1	113.4
Pike Brushed, *var. Pike*	1	3.3		Hopewell Zoned Stamped, *var. Ferry*	1	60.0
Pike Brushed, *var. Robinson*	1	2.1		Pike Rocker Stamped, *var. Black Lane*	4	151.6
Pike Rocker Stamped, *var. Black Lane*	2	30.1		Total	10	338.6
Pike Rocker Stamped, *var. Fairmount*	1	2.7				
Pike Rocker Stamped, *var. Unsp.*	1	38.6		**Unit 7**		
Untyped	1	6.4		Hopewell Zoned Incised, *var. Fulton*	1	11.2
Total	19	183.9		Indeterminate (grit)	1	39.7
				Indeterminate (grog)	1	25.0
Unit 4				Pike Brushed, *var. Robinson*	1	4.9
Indeterminate (grog)	2	29.6		Total	4	80.8
Pike Brushed, *var. Robinson*	2	32.5				
Total	4	62.1				

Table 7. Diagnostics from Excavation Block Units, continued

	N	Wt (g)
Unit 8		
Crab Orchard Fabric Marked (grit)	1	27.4
Hopewell Cross Hatched, *var. Mississippi*	1	5.3
Hopewell Zoned Incised, *var. Cross*	1	10.3
Indeterminate (grog)	1	1.4
Pike Brushed, *var. Robinson*	3	36.4
Pike Rocker Stamped, *var. Black Lane*	1	75.9
Untyped	1	2.3
Total	9	159.0
Unit 9		
Crab Orchard Fabric Marked (grit)	4	97.9
Fournie Plain, *var. Fournie*	1	55.0
Hopewell Cross Hatched, *var. Illinois*	1	15.5
Hopewell Cross Hatched, *var. Mississippi*	1	25.5
Hopewell Rocker Rim, *var. West*	2	25.8
Hopewell Zoned Stamped, *var. Unsp.*	1	16.1
Indeterminate (grit)	1	3.5
Indeterminate (grit/grog)	1	9.9
Indeterminate (grog)	3	28.8
Indeterminate (limestone)	2	9.6
Pike Brushed, *var. Pike*	2	18.7
Pike Brushed, *var. Robinson*	3	100.9
Pike Brushed, *var. Unsp.*	1	70.4
Pike Rocker Stamped, *var. Black Lane*	6	260.7
Pike Rocker Stamped, *var. Unsp.*	1	6.0
Total	30	744.3
Unit 10		
Havana Plain, *var. Collinsville*	1	10.0
Indeterminate (limestone)	1	2.1
Pike Rocker Stamped, *var. Black Lane*	2	23.4
Pike Rocker Stamped, *var. Calhoun*	1	16.8
Total	5	52.3
Unit 11		
Havana Cordmarked, *var. Bottoms*	1	13.0
Hopewell Cross Hatched, *var. Mississippi*	1	6.0
Hopewell Zoned Stamped, *var. Ferry*	1	64.7
Pike Brushed, *var. Robinson*	1	31.5
Total	4	15.2
Unit 12		
Hopewell Cross Hatched, *var. Snyder*	1	5.9
Hopewell Zoned Stamped, *var. Casey*	1	9.8
Indeterminate (limestone)	2	5.8
Pike Brushed, *var. Pike*	1	4.9
Pike Brushed, *var. Robinson*	1	9.7
Total	6	36.1

	N	Wt (g)
Unit 13		
Indeterminate (grit)	1	4.5
Indeterminate (grog)	1	5.2
Indeterminate (limestone)	1	9.0
Pike Brushed, *var. Robinson*	1	9.3
Pike Rocker Stamped, *var. Fairmount*	1	19.0
Untyped	1	3.1
Total	6	50.1
Unit 14		
Baehr Zoned Punctated	1	11.5
Hopewell Zoned Stamped, *var. Unsp.*	1	10.4
Indeterminate (grit)	1	10.1
Pike Rocker Stamped, *var. Calhoun*	1	4.0
Total	4	36.0
Unit 15		
Indeterminate (grit)	1	28.2
Pike Rocker Stamped, *var. Black Lane*	2	56.6
Pike Rocker Stamped, *var. Calhoun*	1	22.6
Total	4	107.4
Unit 16		
Havana Plain, *var. Collinsville*	1	3.9
Indeterminate (grit)	1	19.6
Pike Rocker Stamped, *var. Black Lane*	3	27.9
Untyped	1	42.4
Total	6	93.8
Unit 18		
Baehr Zoned Brushed	1	21.2
Crab Orchard Fabric Marked (grit)	1	26.2
Hopewell Cross Hatched, *var. Mississippi*	1	4.2
Hopewell Rocker Rim, *var. West*	1	5.1
Hopewell Zoned Incised, *var. Cross*	1	14.8
Indeterminate (grog)	1	9.6
Pike Brushed, *var. Robinson*	3	83.3
Pike Brushed, *var. Unsp.*	1	6.2
Pike Rocker Stamped, *var. Black Lane*	2	120.4
Total	12	291.0
Unit 19		
Hopewell Cross Hatched, *var. Mississippi*	1	1.3
Indeterminate (grit)	1	3.8
Pike Rocker Stamped, *var. Calhoun*	1	66.5
Total	3	71.6

Table 7. Diagnostics from Excavation Block Units, continued

	N	Wt (g)
Unit 20		
Baehr Zoned Brushed	1	18.1
Hopewell Zoned Stamped, *var. Ferry*	1	39.0
Indeterminate (grog)	1	6.0
Pike Rocker Stamped, *var. Black Lane*	1	10.3
Pike Rocker Stamped, *var. Calhoun*	1	49.0
Untyped	1	9.7
Total	6	132.1
Unit 21		
Pike Rocker Stamped, *var. Calhoun*	1	5.1
Total	1	5.1
Unit 22		
Untyped	1	4.2
Total	1	4.2
Unit 23		
Pike Rocker Stamped, *var. Unsp.*	1	4.5
Total	1	4.5
Unit 24		
Hopewell Rocker Rim, *var. West*	1	16.4
Hopewell Zoned Stamped, *var. Casey*	1	15.8
Pike Rocker Stamped, *var. Black Lane*	2	42.1
Total	4	74.3
Unit 25		
Indeterminate (grog)	1	10.4
Total	1	10.4
Unit 26		
Pike Brushed, *var. Pike*	2	22.3
Total	2	22.3
Unit 27		
Hopewell Zoned Stamped, *var. Ferry*	1	26.4
Total	1	26.4
Unit 30		
Pike Rocker Stamped, *var. Fairmount*	1	46.5
Total	1	46.5

	N	Wt (g)
Unit 31		
Pike Brushed, *var. Pike*	1	6.1
Total	1	6.1
Unit 37		
Pike Rocker Stamped, *var. Fairmount*	1	14.5
Total	1	14.5
Unit 38		
Indeterminate (grit)	1	2.7
Indeterminate (grit/limestone)	1	2.5
Pike Rocker Stamped, *var. Black Lane*	1	3.6
Total	3	8.8
Unit 39		
Crab Orchard Fabric Marked (grit)	1	18.1
Pike Rocker Stamped, *var. Black Lane*	1	30.7
Total	2	48.8
Unit 40		
Pike Brushed, *var. Pike*	1	42.5
Total	1	42.5
Unit 41		
Hopewell Cross Hatched, *var. Illinois*	1	17.7
Total	1	17.7
Unit 42		
Havana Plain, *var. Collinsville*	1	19.1
Pike Brushed, *var. Unsp.*	1	17.6
Pike Rocker Stamped, *var. Black Lane*	1	2.2
Total	3	38.9
Unit 44		
Pike Brushed, *var. Pike*	2	27.0
Total	2	27.0
Unit 45		
Brangenburg Plain	1	2.7
Indeterminate (grog/limestone)	1	1.8
Pike Brushed, *var. Pike*	1	18.8
Pike Rocker Stamped, *var. Calhoun*	1	4.3
Total	4	27.6

Table 7. Diagnostics from Excavation Block Units, continued

	N	Wt (g)
Unit 46		
Crab Orchard Fabric Marked (grit)	1	21.2
Crab Orchard Fabric Marked (grog)	1	10.9
Indeterminate (grog)	1	3.5
Pike Rocker Stamped, *var. Unsp.*	1	21.0
Total	4	56.6
Unit 47		
Montezuma Punctate, *var. Granite*	1	4.5
Pike Rocker Stamped, *var. Black Lane*	1	42.7
Total	2	47.2
Unit 48		
Hopewell Cross Hatched, *var. Illinois*	1	8.1
Total	1	8.1

⋆ Includes all unscreened block excavation units

Table 8. Rim Fragments from Excavation Block Units⋆

	N	Wt (g)			N	Wt (g)
Unit 1				**Unit 11**		
Indeterminate (limestone)	1	1.0		Indeterminate (grog)	2	3.7
Total	1	1.0		Total	2	3.7
Unit 6				**Unit 13**		
Indeterminate (grog)	1	0.9		Indeterminate (grog)	1	1.2
Indeterminate (limestone)	1	1.5		Total	1	1.2
Total	2	2.4				
Unit 8				**Unit 14**		
Indeterminate (grog)	2	5.0		Indeterminate (grit)	1	3.1
Total	2	5.0		Indeterminate (grog)	3	4.8
				Total	4	7.9
Unit 9				**Unit 15**		
Indeterminate (grog)	2	2.2		Indeterminate (grit)	1	4.0
Indeterminate (limestone)	2	3.2		Indeterminate (grog)	1	1.5
Total	4	5.4		Total	2	5.5
Unit 10				**Unit 16**		
Indeterminate (grit)	1	0.9		Indeterminate (grog)	3	5.5
Indeterminate (limestone)	1	0.9		Total	3	5.5
Total	2	1.8				

Table 8. Rim Fragments from Excavation Block Units, continued

	N	Wt (g)
Unit 17		
Indeterminate (grog)	1	0.6
Total	1	0.6
Unit 18		
Indeterminate (grog)	3	3.8
Total	3	3.8
Unit 20		
Indeterminate (limestone)	1	0.5
Total	1	0.5
Unit 23		
Indeterminate (grog)	1	0.5
Total	1	0.5
Unit 26		
Indeterminate (grit)	1	1.1
Total	1	1.1

	N	Wt (g)
Unit 38		
Indeterminate (grit)	1	3.4
Indeterminate (limestone)	1	1.9
Total	2	5.3
Unit 42		
Indeterminate (grog)	1	2.5
Total	1	2.5
Unit 46		
Indeterminate (grit)	1	1.2
Indeterminate (limestone)	2	2.4
Total	3	3.6

★ All unscreened excavation blocks

Table 9. Body Sherds from Excavation Block Units⋆

	N	Wt (g)
Unit 1		
Fournie Plain, *var. Fournie*	2	7.5
Havana Cordmarked, *var. Bottoms*	1	3.0
Indeterminate (grit)	5	8.5
Indeterminate (grog)	6	12.9
Indeterminate (limestone)	6	7.1
Pike Brushed, var. Pike	1	4.6
Pike Brushed, *var. Robinson*	3	7.9
Pike Rocker Stamped, *var. Black Lane*	3	9.3
Sherdlets	21	7.5
Total	48	68.3
Unit 2		
Cordmarked (grog)	1	5.6
Crab Orchard Fabric Marked (grit)	3	17.7
Fournie Plain, *var. Fournie*	6	36.3
Havana Cordmarked, *var. Bottoms*	5	91.6
Havana Plain, *var. Collinsville*	1	16.1
Hopewell Plain	10	41.5
Indeterminate (grit)	10	53.9
Indeterminate (grog)	12	35.7
Indeterminate (limestone)	19	42.0
Pike Brushed, *var. Pike*	9	73.2
Pike Brushed, *var. Robinson*	4	2.3
Pike Brushed, *var. Unsp.*	3	108.8
Pike Rocker Stamped, *var. Black Lane*	19	164.5
Pike Rocker Stamped, *var. Calhoun*	8	81.9
Pike Rocker Stamped, *var. Fairmount*	1	9.0
Sherdlets	62	41.0
Total	173	841.1
Unit 3		
Hopewell Plain	2	4.6
Indeterminate (grit)	4	6.3
Indeterminate (grog)	2	3.3
Indeterminate (grog/limestone)	1	1.6
Pike Brushed, *var. Pike*	1	2.2
Pike Brushed, *var. Robinson*	2	8.6
Pike Rocker Stamped, *var. Black Lane*	1	5.8
Sherdlets	4	1.1
Total	17	34.0
Unit 4		
Fournie Plain, *var. Fournie*	2	9.9
Havana Plain, *var. Collinsville*	1	34.6
Hopewell Plain	2	2.3
Indeterminate (grit)	6	11.2
Indeterminate (grog)	11	18.1
Indeterminate (limestone)	10	14.6
Pike Brushed, *var. Pike*	8	49.3
Pike Brushed, *var. Robinson*	3	20.4
Pike Rocker Stamped, *var. Black Lane*	10	61.3
Pike Rocker Stamped, *var. Fairmount*	1	8.0
Sherdlets	89	32.5
Total	143	262.2

	N	Wt (g)
Unit 5		
Crab Orchard Fabric Marked (grit)	1	8.9
Fournie Plain, *var. Fournie*	13	49.1
Havana Cordmarked, *var. Bottoms*	4	43.8
Havana Plain, *var. Collinsville*	7	31.5
Hopewell Plain	2	0.8
Hopewell Zoned Stamped, *var. Ferry*	1	15.8
Indeterminate (grit)	7	17.4
Indeterminate (grog)	21	41.2
Indeterminate (limestone)	17	27.6
Pike Brushed, *var. Pike*	10	90.8
Pike Brushed, *var. Robinson*	8	25.5
Pike Rocker Stamped, *var. Black Lane*	55	339.6
Pike Rocker Stamped, *var. Calhoun*	18	128.1
Pike Rocker Stamped, *var. Fairmount*	1	13.8
Sherdlets	68	28.9
Total	233	863.8
Unit 6		
Cordmarked (grog)	1	1.9
Crab Orchard Fabric Marked (grit)	9	79.0
Fournie Plain, *var. Fournie*	6	23.2
Havana Cordmarked, *var. Bottoms*	6	33.0
Havana Plain, *var. Collinsville*	11	76.7
Hopewell Plain	7	20.1
Hopewell Zoned Incised, *var. Unsp.*	1	4.1
Hopewell Zoned Stamped, *var. Casey*	2	6.9
Hopewell Zoned Stamped, *var. Ferry*	3	18.2
Hopewell Zoned Stamped, *var. Unsp.*	3	5.6
Indeterminate (grit)	12	19.4
Indeterminate (grog)	27	0.2
Indeterminate (limestone)	22	48.2
Pike Brushed, *var. Pike*	5	32.7
Pike Brushed, *var. Robinson*	2	9.7
Pike Brushed, *var. Unsp.*	2	15.3
Pike Rocker Stamped, *var. Black Lane*	56	356.0
Pike Rocker Stamped, *var. Calhoun*	28	240.8
Pike Rocker Stamped, *var. Fairmount*	4	17.2
Pike Rocker Stamped, *var. Unsp.*	1	1.2
Sherdlets	95	46.6
Total	303	1,095.0
Unit 7		
Crab Orchard Fabric Marked (grit)	6	34.6
Havana Cordmarked, *var. Bottoms*	2	29.6
Hopewell Plain	1	1.4
Hopewell Zoned Stamped, *var. Ferry*	2	3.1
Indeterminate (grit)	6	8.7
Indeterminate (grog)	9	21.4
Indeterminate (limestone)	8	14.9
Pike Brushed, *var. Robinson*	3	17.5
Pike Rocker Stamped, *var. Black Lane*	15	61.3
Pike Rocker Stamped, *var. Calhoun*	5	34.5
Pike Rocker Stamped, *var. Fairmount*	2	12.4
Sherdlets	38	17.3
Total	97	256.7

Table 9. Body Sherds from Excavation Block Units, continued

	N	Wt (g)
Unit 8		
Baehr Zoned Brushed	1	9.6
Crab Orchard Fabric Marked (grit)	2	20.4
Fournie Plain, *var. Fournie*	1	1.9
Havana Cordmarked, *var. Bottoms*	1	19.6
Havana Plain, *var. Collinsville*	1	6.0
Hopewell Plain	1	1.2
Indeterminate (grit)	4	7.3
Indeterminate (grog)	17	40.5
Indeterminate (limestone)	3	4.6
Pike Brushed, *var. Pike*	6	28.9
Pike Brushed, *var. Robinson*	7	19.2
Pike Brushed, *var. Unsp.*	6	168.4
Pike Rocker Stamped, *var. Black Lane*	5	30.5
Pike Rocker Stamped, *var. Calhoun*	5	63.4
Pike Rocker Stamped, *var. Fairmount*	7	81.6
Sherdlets	114	70.6
Total	181	573.7
Unit 9		
Baehr Zoned Brushed	2	14.0
Cordmarked (grog)	2	45.2
Crab Orchard Fabric Marked (grit)	15	173.9
Crab Orchard Fabric Marked (grog)	2	8.3
Fournie Plain, *var. Fournie*	23	196.5
Havana Cordmarked, *var. Bottoms*	8	181.0
Havana Plain, *var. Collinsville*	9	65.8
Hopewell Plain	5	9.8
Hopewell Zoned Incised, *var. Cross*	2	7.6
Hopewell Zoned Incised, *var. Fulton*	1	1.5
Hopewell Zoned Stamped, *var. Casey*	1	4.4
Hopewell Zoned Stamped, *var. Ferry*	1	11.1
Hopewell Zoned Stamped, *var. Unsp.*	1	1.7
Indeterminate (grit)	38	121.3
Indeterminate (grog)	55	127.6
Indeterminate (limestone)	21	30.8
Montezuma Punctate, *var. Granite*	1	5.6
Pike Brushed, *var. Pike*	4	36.7
Pike Brushed, *var. Robinson*	85	538.0
Pike Brushed, *var. Unsp.*	14	85.6
Pike Rocker Stamped, *var. Black Lane*	71	540.6
Pike Rocker Stamped, *var. Calhoun*	22	104.3
Pike Rocker Stamped, *var. Fairmount*	8	427.1
Pike Rocker Stamped, *var. Unsp.*	1	6.4
Sherdlets	200	211.7
Total	592	2,956.5
Unit 10		
Crab Orchard Fabric Marked (grit)	2	6.5
Havana Cordmarked, *var. Bottoms*	2	15.2
Havana Plain, *var. Collinsville*	1	18.8
Hopewell Plain	1	1.5
Hopewell Zoned Stamped, *var. Bluff*	1	19.8

	N	Wt (g)
Hopewell Zoned Stamped, *var. Ferry*	2	23.8
Indeterminate (grit)	11	19.6
Indeterminate (grog)	16	36.6
Indeterminate (limestone)	8	9.7
Pike Brushed, *var. Robinson*	1	4.2
Pike Rocker Stamped, *var. Black Lane*	36	102.3
Pike Rocker Stamped, *var. Calhoun*	17	114.7
Pike Rocker Stamped, *var. Fairmount*	4	19.8
Sherdlets	110	59.7
Untyped	1	9.6
Total	213	461.8
Unit 11		
Cordmarked (grog)	2	3.6
Crab Orchard Fabric Marked (grit)	36	216.9
Crab Orchard Fabric Marked (grog)	1	4.4
Fournie Plain, *var. Fournie*	1	2.3
Havana Cordmarked, *var. Bottoms*	6	49.5
Havana Plain, *var. Collinsville*	1	2.6
Hopewell Zoned Stamped, *var. Unsp.*	1	2.2
Indeterminate (grit)	7	14.5
Indeterminate (grog)	11	24.8
Indeterminate (limestone)	16	25.0
Pike Brushed, *var. Robinson*	1	7.0
Pike Rocker Stamped, *var. Black Lane*	26	114.4
Pike Rocker Stamped, *var. Calhoun*	21	243.9
Sherdlets	130	60.4
Total	260	771.5
Unit 12		
Crab Orchard Fabric Marked (grit)	2	5.1
Fournie Plain, *var. Fournie*	3	19.8
Havana Cordmarked, *var. Bottoms*	1	3.6
Havana Plain, *var. Collinsville*	2	5.9
Hopewell Zoned Stamped, *var. Ferry*	1	0.7
Indeterminate (grit)	9	26.6
Indeterminate (grog)	8	13.9
Indeterminate (limestone)	3	2.8
Pike Brushed, *var. Pike*	3	30.4
Pike Brushed, *var. Robinson*	1	12.4
Pike Brushed, *var. Unsp.*	1	18.1
Pike Rocker Stamped, *var. Black Lane*	12	88.5
Pike Rocker Stamped, *var. Calhoun*	2	7.6
Sherdlets	52	24.6
Total	100	260.0
Unit 13		
Crab Orchard Fabric Marked (grit)	4	82.3
Crab Orchard Fabric Marked (grog)	1	8.8
Fournie Plain, *var. Fournie*	6	19.4
Havana Plain, *var. Collinsville*	3	27.3
Hopewell Plain	1	2.3
Hopewell Zoned Incised, *var. Hertzog*	1	8.4
Hopewell Zoned Stamped, *var. Ferry*	2	3.1
Indeterminate (grit)	8	27.5
Indeterminate (grit/grog)	1	9.8

Table 9. Body Sherds from Excavation Block Units, continued

	N	Wt (g)
Indeterminate (grog)	14	45.9
Indeterminate (limestone)	7	13.6
Pike Brushed, *var. Pike*	2	5.5
Pike Brushed, *var. Robinson*	14	80.8
Pike Brushed, *var. Unsp.*	1	2.5
Pike Rocker Stamped, *var. Black Lane*	30	191.5
Pike Rocker Stamped, *var. Calhoun*	2	8.4
Pike Rocker Stamped, *var. Fairmount*	12	259.8
Sherdlets	116	72.4
Total	225	869.3

Unit 14

	N	Wt (g)
Baehr Zoned Brushed	1	1.5
Fournie Plain, *var. Fournie*	2	2.9
Hopewell Plain	1	1.2
Indeterminate (grit)	6	18.6
Indeterminate (grog)	11	21.4
Indeterminate (limestone)	1	1.8
Pike Brushed, *var. Pike*	1	1.7
Pike Brushed, *var. Robinson*	12	65.7
Pike Brushed, *var. Unsp.*	1	4.7
Pike Rocker Stamped, *var. Black Lane*	6	37.4
Pike Rocker Stamped, *var. Fairmount*	5	32.2
Sherdlets	28	15.6
Total	75	204.7

Unit 15

	N	Wt (g)
Cordmarked (grog)	1	0.8
Crab Orchard Fabric Marked (grit)	5	32.7
Fournie Plain, *var. Fournie*	1	1.4
Havana Cordmarked, *var. Bottoms*	5	39.0
Indeterminate (grit)	2	4.9
Indeterminate (grog)	13	22.7
Indeterminate (limestone)	3	4.6
Pike Brushed, *var. Pike*	1	1.1
Pike Brushed, *var. Robinson*	5	13.5
Pike Rocker Stamped, *var. Black Lane*	14	39.8
Pike Rocker Stamped, *var. Calhoun*	3	21.1
Pike Rocker Stamped, *var. Fairmount*	1	8.9
Sherdlets	88	34.0
Total	142	224.5

Unit 16

	N	Wt (g)
Cordmarked (grog)	11	50.3
Crab Orchard Fabric Marked (grit)	7	63.3
Havana Cordmarked, *var. Bottoms*	8	68.5
Hopewell Zoned Stamped, *var. Ferry*	1	2.8
Hopewell Zoned Stamped, *var. Unsp.*	1	5.0
Indeterminate (grit)	13	40.0
Indeterminate (grog)	28	107.4
Indeterminate (limestone)	7	22.9
Pike Brushed, *var. Pike*	7	69.5
Pike Brushed, *var. Robinson*	31	107.4
Pike Brushed, *var. Unsp.*	1	9.3
Pike Rocker Stamped, *var. Black Lane*	55	403.6
Pike Rocker Stamped, *var. Calhoun*	10	51.0

	N	Wt (g)
Pike Rocker Stamped, *var. Fairmount*	1	4.6
Pike Rocker Stamped, *var. Unsp.*	1	5.1
Sherdlets	114	90.9
Total	296	1,101.6

Unit 17

	N	Wt (g)
Havana Plain, *var. Collinsville*	3	17.2
Indeterminate (grit)	2	1.4
Indeterminate (grog)	2	2.1
Pike Rocker Stamped, *var. Black Lane*	2	4.4
Pike Rocker Stamped, *var. Calhoun*	1	4.9
Sherdlets	34	7.2
Total	44	37.2

Unit 18

	N	Wt (g)
Baehr Zoned Brushed	1	1.7
Crab Orchard Fabric Marked (grit)	7	37.4
Fournie Plain, *var. Fournie*	14	29.2
Havana Cordmarked, *var. Bottoms*	1	32.9
Hopewell Plain	3	14.6
Hopewell Zoned Incised, *var. Hertzog*	1	11.5
Hopewell Zoned Stamped, *var. Casey*	1	4.0
Indeterminate (grit)	19	42.5
Indeterminate (grog)	34	104.6
Indeterminate (limestone)	8	7.9
Pike Brushed, *var. Pike*	14	82.6
Pike Brushed, *var. Robinson*	40	247.0
Pike Brushed, *var. Unsp.*	3	17.8
Pike Rocker Stamped, *var. Black Lane*	35	203.4
Pike Rocker Stamped, *var. Calhoun*	9	78.9
Pike Rocker Stamped, *var. Fairmount*	8	57.2
Sherdlets	175	94.3
Total	373	1,067.5

Unit 19

	N	Wt (g)
Crab Orchard Fabric Marked (grit)	6	53.2
Havana Cordmarked, *var. Bottoms*	4	47.9
Havana Plain, *var. Collinsville*	2	19.5
Hopewell Plain	3	5.5
Hopewell Zoned Stamped, *var. Casey*	2	8.0
Hopewell Zoned Stamped, *var. Unsp.*	1	2.1
Indeterminate (grit)	6	29.7
Indeterminate (grog)	2	3.7
Indeterminate (limestone)	5	10.0
Pike Brushed, *var. Robinson*	2	22.9
Pike Rocker Stamped, *var. Black Lane*	30	100.5
Pike Rocker Stamped, *var. Calhoun*	11	83.9
Sherdlets	57	26.8
Total	131	413.7

Unit 20

	N	Wt (g)
Crab Orchard Fabric Marked (grit)	6	42.4
Fournie Plain, *var. Fournie*	1	3.9
Havana Cordmarked, *var. Bottoms*	1	4.4
Havana Plain, *var. Collinsville*	7	44.3

Table 9. Body Sherds from Excavation Block Units, continued

	N	Wt (g)
Hopewell Plain	1	1.0
Hopewell Zoned Stamped, *var. Ferry*	1	4.8
Indeterminate (grit)	13	41.2
Indeterminate (grog)	14	34.0
Indeterminate (limestone)	12	31.7
Pike Brushed, *var. Pike*	5	27.5
Pike Rocker Stamped, *var. Black Lane*	30	162.5
Pike Rocker Stamped, *var. Calhoun*	19	151.1
Pike Rocker Stamped, *var. Fairmount*	2	14.2
Sherdlets	51	18.1
Total	163	581.1
Unit 21		
Crab Orchard Fabric Marked (grit)	1	7.2
Fournie Plain, *var. Fournie*	4	11.2
Havana Plain, *var. Collinsville*	1	11.7
Indeterminate (grog)	6	28.2
Indeterminate (limestone)	2	9.6
Pike Brushed, *var. Robinson*	5	17.3
Pike Rocker Stamped, *var. Black Lane*	3	16.7
Pike Rocker Stamped, *var. Fairmount*	2	54.1
Sherdlets	17	8.4
Total	41	164.4
Unit 22		
Crab Orchard Fabric Marked (grit)	1	4.8
Fournie Plain, *var. Fournie*	1	3.5
Havana Plain, *var. Collinsville*	1	29.7
Hopewell Zoned Incised, *var. Fulton*	1	3.7
Indeterminate (grit)	1	1.8
Indeterminate (grog)	4	13.8
Indeterminate (limestone)	5	29.7
Pike Brushed, *var. Robinson*	2	8.8
Pike Rocker Stamped, *var. Black Lane*	4	23.8
Sherdlets	22	11.0
Total	42	130.6
Unit 23		
Fournie Plain, *var. Fournie*	3	65.5
Hopewell Cross Hatched, *var. Mississippi*	1	0.7
Indeterminate (grit)	1	7.5
Indeterminate (grog)	19	29.1
Indeterminate (limestone)	4	12.4
Pike Brushed, *var. Robinson*	3	8.1
Pike Rocker Stamped, *var. Black Lane*	7	95.0
Pike Rocker Stamped, *var. Fairmount*	1	5.3
Sherdlets	24	10.0
Total	63	233.6
Unit 24		
Crab Orchard Fabric Marked (grit)	4	54.5
Fournie Plain, *var. Fournie*	1	12.7
Havana Plain, *var. Collinsville*	3	9.2
Hopewell Plain	2	8.5
Indeterminate (grit)	7	25.7

	N	Wt (g)
Indeterminate (grog)	16	22.2
Indeterminate (limestone)	13	20.1
Pike Rocker Stamped, *var. Black Lane*	15	63.5
Pike Rocker Stamped, *var. Calhoun*	8	54.7
Pike Rocker Stamped, *var. Fairmount*	3	7.8
Sherdlets	36	16.6
Total	108	295.5
Unit 25		
Crab Orchard Fabric Marked (grit)	1	8.4
Indeterminate (grit)	1	4.2
Indeterminate (grog)	2	14.5
Pike Brushed, *var. Pike*	1	3.2
Sherdlets	9	3.4
Total	14	33.7
Unit 26		
Crab Orchard Fabric Marked (grit)	1	7.7
Fournie Plain, *var. Fournie*	1	3.6
Havana Cordmarked, *var. Bottoms*	1	2.9
Hopewell Plain	2	4.8
Hopewell Zoned Stamped, *var. Casey*	1	1.4
Indeterminate (grit)	12	33.3
Indeterminate (grog)	1	7.3
Pike Brushed, *var. Robinson*	2	3.3
Pike Brushed, *var. Unsp.*	2	13.9
Pike Rocker Stamped, *var. Black Lane*	4	43.7
Sherdlets	33	21.5
Total	60	143.4
Unit 27		
Cordmarked (grog)	1	13.4
Crab Orchard Fabric Marked (grog)	1	7.6
Fournie Plain, *var. Fournie*	3	9.1
Havana Plain, *var. Collinsville*	3	193.4
Indeterminate (grit)	3	8.9
Indeterminate (grog)	11	21.8
Indeterminate (limestone)	7	9.4
Pike Brushed, *var. Pike*	4	18.4
Pike Brushed, *var. Robinson*	2	25.8
Pike Brushed, *var. Unsp.*	1	38.6
Pike Rocker Stamped, *var. Black Lane*	4	54.3
Pike Rocker Stamped, *var. Fairmount*	1	4.4
Sherdlets	54	26.8
Total	95	431.9
Unit 28		
Hopewell Zoned Stamped, *var. Unsp.*	1	2.6
Indeterminate (grit)	3	5.0
Indeterminate (grog)	4	8.1
Indeterminate (limestone)	1	3.3
Pike Rocker Stamped, *var. Black Lane*	1	2.0
Pike Rocker Stamped, *var. Fairmount*	1	31.7
Sherdlets	9	1.4
Total	20	54.1

Table 9. Body Sherds from Excavation Block Units, continued

	N	Wt (g)
Unit 29		
Indeterminate (grog)	2	1.8
Total	2	1.8
Unit 30		
Fournie Plain, *var. Fournie*	3	10.9
Havana Plain, *var. Collinsville*	1	5.8
Hopewell Plain	3	23.1
Indeterminate (grog)	6	25.2
Indeterminate (limestone)	9	9.5
Pike Brushed, *var. Unsp.*	3	8.0
Pike Rocker Stamped, *var. Black Lane*	4	23.7
Pike Rocker Stamped, *var. Calhoun*	2	7.2
Sherdlets	72	28.5
Total	103	141.9
Unit 31		
Fournie Plain, *var. Fournie*	1	5.6
Indeterminate (grit)	2	3.1
Indeterminate (grog)	2	2.3
Indeterminate (limestone)	2	2.2
Pike Brushed, *var. Robinson*	3	6.0
Sherdlets	12	2.8
Total	22	22.0
Unit 32		
Cordmarked (grog)	1	0.8
Fournie Plain, *var. Fournie*	1	2.1
Indeterminate (grit)	1	1.1
Indeterminate (grog)	4	12.7
Indeterminate (limestone)	1	0.7
Pike Brushed, *var. Robinson*	1	1.7
Sherdlets	20	7.6
Total	29	26.7
Unit 33		
Indeterminate (grit)	1	1.3
Sherdlets	12	2.1
Total	13	3.4
Unit 34		
Indeterminate (grit)	3	4.0
Indeterminate (grog)	5	8.9
Indeterminate (limestone)	2	1.7
Sherdlets	9	5.4
Total	19	20.0
Unit 35		
Crab Orchard Fabric Marked (grit)	1	5.0
Indeterminate (grit)	1	1.7
Indeterminate (grog)	2	6.3
Indeterminate (limestone)	1	3.4
Sherdlets	4	1.2
Total	9	17.6

	N	Wt (g)
Unit 36		
Indeterminate (grit)	1	2.9
Sherdlets	4	1.3
Total	5	4.2
Unit 37		
Cordmarked (grog)	1	13.9
Fournie Plain, *var. Fournie*	2	3.7
Indeterminate (grog)	2	19.7
Indeterminate (limestone)	2	6.0
Pike Brushed, *var. Pike*	1	3.0
Pike Brushed, *var. Robinson*	1	2.0
Sherdlets	1	0.5
Total	10	48.8
Unit 38		
Cordmarked (grog)	3	9.9
Crab Orchard Fabric Marked (grit)	3	24.0
Crab Orchard Fabric Marked (grog)	3	22.6
Crab Orchard Fabric Marked (limestone)	1	32.5
Fournie Plain, *var. Fournie*	3	18.1
Havana Cordmarked, *var. Bottoms*	1	15.6
Havana Plain, *var. Collinsville*	1	3.8
Hopewell Plain	6	22.5
Indeterminate (grit)	7	19.9
Indeterminate (grog)	9	27.7
Indeterminate (limestone)	3	4.6
Pike Brushed, *var. Pike*	3	15.3
Pike Brushed, *var. Unsp.*	1	5.8
Pike Rocker Stamped, *var. Black Lane*	1	17.8
Pike Rocker Stamped, *var. Calhoun*	3	276.0
Sherdlets	56	27.8
Total	104	295.5
Unit 39		
Crab Orchard Fabric Marked (grit)	1	4.9
Fournie Plain, *var. Fournie*	1	13.3
Havana Cordmarked, *var. Bottoms*	1	5.4
Indeterminate (grit)	2	0.4
Indeterminate (grog)	3	14.0
Indeterminate (limestone)	6	17.5
Pike Brushed, *var. Pike*	1	4.4
Pike Brushed, *var. Robinson*	2	1.8
Pike Rocker Stamped, *var. Black Lane*	3	26.8
Pike Rocker Stamped, *var. Calhoun*	1	8.5
Sherdlets	12	4.8
Total	33	105.9
Unit 40		
Crab Orchard Fabric Marked (grog)	3	54.5
Havana Plain, *var. Collinsville*	1	30.8
Hopewell Plain	2	17.5
Indeterminate (grit)	1	2.7
Indeterminate (grog)	19	53.4

Table 9. Body Sherds from Excavation Block Units, continued

	N	Wt (g)
Indeterminate (limestone)	4	8.1
Pike Brushed, *var. Pike*	2	12.3
Pike Brushed, *var. Robinson*	10	28.9
Pike Brushed, *var. Unsp.*	2	20.9
Pike Rocker Stamped, *var. Calhoun*	1	2.6
Sherdlets	110	51.7
Total	155	283.4

Unit 41

	N	Wt (g)
Cordmarked (grog)	1	1.1
Crab Orchard Fabric Marked (grit)	5	45.0
Crab Orchard Fabric Marked (grog)	1	6.5
Fournie Plain, *var. Fournie*	1	0.8
Havana Cordmarked, *var. Bottoms*	2	20.6
Havana Plain, *var. Collinsville*	2	14.9
Hopewell Plain	3	9.2
Hopewell Zoned Incised, *var. Fulton*	2	8.7
Hopewell Zoned Stamped, *var. Casey*	1	5.7
Indeterminate (grit)	7	22.6
Indeterminate (grog)	11	41.2
Indeterminate (limestone)	6	13.8
Pike Brushed, *var. Pike*	2	15.7
Pike Brushed, *var. Robinson*	3	12.4
Pike Rocker Stamped, *var. Black Lane*	22	102.5
Pike Rocker Stamped, *var. Calhoun*	12	44.5
Pike Rocker Stamped, *var. Fairmount*	2	11.2
Sherdlets	97	36.9
Untyped	1	14.2
Total	181	427.5

Unit 42

	N	Wt (g)
Cordmarked (grog)	3	17.4
Cordmarked (limestone)	1	6.3
Crab Orchard Fabric Marked (grit)	7	34.6
Fournie Plain, *var. Fournie*	2	20.7
Havana Cordmarked, *var. Bottoms*	2	9.2
Havana Plain, *var. Unsp.*	1	19.5
Hopewell Plain	5	38.6
Hopewell Zoned Stamped, *var. Ferry*	1	5.2
Indeterminate (grit)	7	24.6
Indeterminate (grog)	8	29.8
Indeterminate (limestone)	7	20.0
Pike Brushed, *var. Pike*	8	34.7
Pike Brushed, *var. Robinson*	2	5.4
Pike Rocker Stamped, *var. Black Lane*	17	148.1
Pike Rocker Stamped, *var. Calhoun*	7	48.4
Sherdlets	81	49.6
Total	159	512.1

Unit 43

	N	Wt (g)
Crab Orchard Fabric Marked (grit)	1	3.3
Havana Cordmarked, *var. Bottoms*	1	5.0
Hopewell Plain	2	3.6
Indeterminate (grit)	1	6.0
Indeterminate (grog)	5	8.9
Pike Brushed, *var. Pike*	2	5.9

	N	Wt (g)
Pike Brushed, *var. Robinson*	2	3.1
Pike Rocker Stamped, *var. Black Lane*	4	9.0
Pike Rocker Stamped, *var. Calhoun*	3	61.1
Pike Rocker Stamped, *var. Fairmount*	2	5.2
Sherdlets	23	9.9
Total	46	121.0

Unit 44

	N	Wt (g)
Fournie Plain, *var. Fournie*	4	16.8
Havana Plain, *var. Collinsville*	4	9.6
Indeterminate (grit)	4	8.6
Indeterminate (grog)	5	14.3
Pike Rocker Stamped, *var. Black Lane*	4	32.9
Pike Rocker Stamped, *var. Calhoun*	1	8.1
Sherdlets	30	12.5
Total	52	102.8

Unit 45

	N	Wt (g)
Fournie Plain, *var. Fournie*	2	4.9
Indeterminate (grit)	4	8.7
Indeterminate (grog)	7	8.8
Indeterminate (limestone)	6	14.8
Pike Brushed, *var. Pike*	4	12.2
Pike Brushed, *var. Robinson*	3	4.1
Pike Rocker Stamped, *var. Black Lane*	9	53.0
Pike Rocker Stamped, *var. Calhoun*	2	3.6
Pike Rocker Stamped, *var. Fairmount*	1	2.8
Sherdlets	31	16.2
Total	69	129.1

Unit 46

	N	Wt (g)
Cordmarked (grog)	1	7.0
Crab Orchard Fabric Marked (grit)	2	27.8
Fournie Plain, *var. Fournie*	2	2.7
Havana Plain, *var. Collinsville*	3	12.0
Indeterminate (grit)	1	3.8
Indeterminate (grog)	5	19.8
Pike Brushed, *var. Pike*	2	20.1
Pike Brushed, *var. Robinson*	4	12.4
Pike Brushed, *var. Unsp.*	1	7.0
Pike Rocker Stamped, *var. Black Lane*	9	81.5
Pike Rocker Stamped, *var. Calhoun*	2	10.6
Pike Rocker Stamped, *var. Fairmount*	2	6.5
Sherdlets	28	15.2
Total	62	226.4

Unit 47

	N	Wt (g)
Havana Cordmarked, *var. Bottoms*	1	6.4
Indeterminate (grit)	4	6.1
Indeterminate (limestone)	3	16.4
Pike Brushed, *var. Robinson*	2	2.2
Pike Rocker Stamped, *var. Black Lane*	12	121.3
Pike Rocker Stamped, *var. Calhoun*	1	3.5
Pike Rocker Stamped, *var. Unsp.*	1	50.7
Sherdlets	26	9.2
Total	50	215.8

Table 9. Body Sherds from Excavation Block Units, continued

	N	Wt (g)
Unit 48		
Crab Orchard Fabric Marked (grog)	1	21.5
Fournie Plain, *var. Fournie*	2	5.8
Havana Cordmarked, *var. Bottoms*	1	3.5
Havana Cordmarked, *var. Unsp.*	1	14.1
Hopewell Plain	1	5.5
Indeterminate (grit)	4	10.6
Indeterminate (grog)	5	10.7
Indeterminate (limestone)	3	9.0
Pike Brushed, *var. Unsp.*	1	21.5
Pike Rocker Stamped, *var. Black Lane*	11	67.4
Pike Rocker Stamped, *var. Fairmount*	4	20.7
Sherdlets	35	15.9
Total	69	206.2

★ Includes all unscreened block excavations

Table 10. Ceramics from Geomorphological Trenches

	N	Wt (g)
Trench #1		
Diagnostics:		
Pike Brushed, *var. Pike*	1	798.3
Body sherds:		
Cordmarked (limestone)	1	1.3
Fournie Plain, *var. Fournie*	2	30.3
Pike Rocker Stamped, *var. Black Lane*	2	18.1
Pike Rocker Stamped, *var. Calhoun*	1	11.6
Sherdlets	2	2.2
Total	9	861.8
Trench #2		
Diagnostics:		
Fournie Plain, *var. Fournie*	1	130.6
Body sherds:		
Crab Orchard Fabric Marked (grog)	2	48.6
Havana Plain, *var. Collinsville*	2	23.8
Hopewell Plain	1	15.2
Hopewell Zoned Incised, *var. Fulton*	1	6.8
Indeterminate (grit)	4	57.2
Indeterminate (grog)	1	11.9
Pike Brushed, *var. Robinson*	2	26.8
Pike Rocker Stamped, *var. Black Lane*	5	79.9
Pike Rocker Stamped, *var. Calhoun*	1	4.5
Pike Rocker Stamped, *var. Fairmount*	4	49.1
Sherdlets	5	3.7
Total	29	458.1

Table 11. Surface, Subplowzone Piece Plot, and Machine Excavation Diagnostics from the 1990 Season

	N	Wt (g)
Surface (Bag: 700s)		
Fournie Plain, *var. Fournie*	1	6.2
Havana Plain, *var. Unsp.*	1	10.0
Hopewell Cross Hatched, *var. Mississippi*	1	1.4
Indeterminate (grit)	2	7.5
Indeterminate (grog)	3	19.6
Pike Rocker Stamped, var. *Black Lane*	2	8.3
Pike Rocker Stamped, var. *Calhoun*	1	3.8
Pike Rocker Stamped, var. *Fairmount*	1	18.2
Untyped	1	8.5
Total	13	83.5
Subplowzone Piece Plot (Bag: 800s)		
Cordmarked (grog)	1	22.7
Fournie Plain, *var. Fournie*	1	9.8
Hopewell Zoned Stamped, *var. Unsp.*	1	19.1
Indeterminate (limestone)	1	4.8
Pike Brushed, *var. Pike*	1	14.9
Pike Brushed, *var. Robinson*	2	22.4
Pike Brushed, *var. Unsp.*	1	30.8
Pike Rocker Stamped, *var. Black Lane*	5	98.1
Pike Rocker Stamped, *var. Calhoun*	2	44.7
Pike Rocker Stamped, *var. Fairmount*	1	27.1
Pike Rocker Stamped, *var. Unsp.*	2	26.1
Total	18	320.5
Machine Excavation (Bag: 900s)		
Baehr Zoned Brushed	1	12.5
Cordmarked (limestone)	1	8.0
Crab Orchard Fabric Marked (grit)	1	8.1
Fournie Plain, *var. Fournie*	3	17.1
Havana Cordmarked, *var. Unsp.*	1	3.2
Havana Plain, *var. Unsp.*	1	13.4
Hopewell Cross Hatched, *var. Mississippi*	2	8.4
Hopewell Plain	3	11.5
Hopewell Zoned Red, *var. Unsp.*	1	10.8
Indeterminate (grit)	1	4.1
Indeterminate (grog)	8	40.9
Indeterminate (limestone)	1	19.2
Pike Rocker Stamped, *var. Black Lane*	3	23.0
Pike Rocker Stamped, *var. Calhoun*	2	13.3
Pike Rocker Stamped, *var. Fairmount*	1	47.5
Untyped	3	57.3
Total	33	298.3

Table 12. Surface, Subplowzone Piece Plot, and Machine Excavation Rim Fragments from the 1990 Season

	N	Wt (g)
Surface (Bag: 700s)		
Indeterminate (grog)	3	10.2
Indeterminate (limestone)	1	4.9
Total	4	15.1
Subplowzone Piece Plot (Bag: 800s)		
Indeterminate (grog)	3	66.3
Total	3	66.3
Machine Excavation (Bag: 900s)		
Indeterminate (grit)	1	3.3
Indeterminate (grog)	11	23.2
Indeterminate (grog/limestone)	1	1.7
Indeterminate (limestone)	1	1.3
Sherdlet	1	1.3
Total	15	30.8

Table 13. Surface, Subplowzone Piece Plot, and Machine Excavation Body Sherds from the 1990 Season

	N	Wt (g)
Surface (Bag: 700s)		
Cordmarked (grog)	1	1.7
Cordmarked (limestone)	2	9.4
Crab Orchard Fabric Marked (grit)	8	46.1
Crab Orchard Fabric Marked (limestone)	1	10.1
Fournie Plain, *var. Fournie*	20	136.8
Havana Cordmarked, *var. Bottoms*	9	37.3
Havana Plain, *var. Collinsville*	7	25.7
Hopewell Plain	6	41.1
Hopewell Zoned Stamped, *var. Casey*	1	3.8
Hopewell Zoned Stamped, *var. Ferry*	1	3.2
Hopewell Zoned Stamped, *var. Unsp.*	3	11.6
Indeterminate (grit)	43	157.4
Indeterminate (grog)	49	116.4
Indeterminate (grog/limestone)	1	1.7
Indeterminate (limestone)	35	55.8
Pike Brushed, *var. Pike*	9	41.4
Pike Brushed, *var. Robinson*	16	100.6
Pike Brushed, *var. Unsp.*	1	5.1
Pike Rocker Stamped, *var. Black Lane*	58	263.9
Pike Rocker Stamped, *var. Calhoun*	15	62.8
Pike Rocker Stamped, *var. Fairmount*	7	27.9
Pike Rocker Stamped, *var. Unsp.*	1	4.0
Sherdlets	116	58.0
Total	410	1,221.8
Subplowzone Piece Plot (Bag: 800s)		
Baehr Zoned Brushed	1	1.4
Cordmarked (grog)	1	2.8
Crab Orchard Fabric Marked (grit)	2	16.2
Fournie Plain, *var. Fournie*	4	36.8
Havana Cordmarked, *var. Bottoms*	2	25.7
Hopewell Plain	2	13.8
Hopewell Zoned Stamped, *var. Casey*	1	1.6
Indeterminate (grit)	5	12.1
Indeterminate (grog)	5	12.8
Indeterminate (limestone)	5	12.7
Pike Brushed, *var. Robinson*	1	7.0
Pike Brushed, *var. Unsp.*	2	13.6
Pike Rocker Stamped, *var. Black Lane*	15	89.0
Pike Rocker Stamped, *var. Calhoun*	3	22.0
Pike Rocker Stamped, *var. Fairmount*	3	19.3
Sherdlets	11	6.2
Total	63	293.0

	N	Wt (g)
Machine Excavation (Bag: 900s)		
Cordmarked (grog)	9	87.7
Cordmarked (limestone)	10	92.8
Cordmarked (no temper)	1	4.5
Crab Orchard Fabric Marked (grit)	27	158.2
Crab Orchard Fabric Marked (limestone)	2	12.5
Fournie Plain, *var. Fournie*	63	201.0
Havana Cordmarked, *var. Bottoms*	15	133.6
Havana Cordmarked, *var. Unsp.*	2	15.2
Havana Plain, *var. Collinsville*	24	133.5
Havana Plain, *var. Unsp.*	3	20.1
Historic	4	42.6
Hopewell Plain	47	184.7
Hopewell Zoned Incised, *var. Cross*	2	7.0
Hopewell Zoned Stamped, *var. Unsp.*	1	3.8
Indeterminate (grit)	73	263.8
Indeterminate (grog)	117	356.2
Indeterminate (grog/limestone)	3	18.1
Indeterminate (limestone)	85	228.7
Montezuma Punctate, *var. Granite*	1	3.2
Pike Brushed, *var. Pike*	48	244.3
Pike Brushed, *var. Robinson*	58	277.9
Pike Brushed, *var. Unsp.*	8	59.4
Pike Rocker Stamped, *var. Black Lane*	112	585.4
Pike Rocker Stamped, *var. Calhoun*	32	183.2
Pike Rocker Stamped, *var. Fairmount*	19	207.5
Sherdlets	410	265.0
Total	1,176	3,789.9

Appendix C. Description of Chert Types

Material Type	Color	Texture	Impurities	Luster	Workability	Effects of Heat Treatment	Comments
1 (Burlington)	Homogenous white (10YR 8/1)	Fine grain, occasionally patches of grainier texture	15X magnification: small fossil fragments common but density is low	Generally glossy	Medium to good	Slightly pink to reddish pink; after knapping exhibits faintly rippled flake scars	Source: Keokuk-Burlington Formation
2 (Burlington)	Predominantly white (10YR 8/1.5) with irregular medium to large mottles of gray (10YR 6/1 and N 6/0)	Medium grain	Not present	White area is dull, gray areas exhibit slight luster	Poor	Color becomes pinkish or reddish	Source: Keokuk-Burlington Formation
3 (Burlington/ Salem)	Predominantly light gray (10YR 7/2) with frequent small mottles of white (10YR 8/1)	Coarse grain	Frequent small fossils	Dull	Poor to fair	Color becomes pinkish or reddish	Source: Keokuk-Burlington or Salem Formation
4 (Burlington/ Salem)	Variable, but predominantly gray (10YR 6/1 to 10YR 5/1, also 10YR 7/1)	Slightly to very grainy	Small fossils and impurities frequent	Slightly glossy	Poor to fair	Color becomes pinkish or reddish	Source: Keokuk-Burlington or Salem Formation
5 (Burlington/ Salem)	Matrix between white and light gray (10YR 7.5/2) with horizontal bands (5–15 mm) of gray and gray-brown (10YR 7/1 to 10YR 6/1 to 10YR 6/2)	Fine grain	15X magnification small fossils occur rarely	Moderately glossy	Good	Bands remain distinct, becoming various shades of red	Source: Keokuk-Burlington or Salem Formation
6 (Burlington)	Yellowish brown (10YR 5/4), intermixing of yellows and browns within each piece	Fine grain	Not present	Glossy	Medium to good	Color becomes same reddish tint observed on Type 1	Source: Possibly Keokuk-Burlington Formation
7 (Root Beer/ Ste. Genevieve Red)	Reddish brown to dark reddish brown (2.5YR 5/4 to 2.5YR 3/4), also pale brown to dark brown (10YR 6/3 to 10YR 3/3). No particular pattern of colors	Fine grain	Fossils are seldom observed, other impurities are occasionally present	Moderately to highly glossy	Medium to good	Unknown	Characteristic cortex is thin, tan or light brown, only slightly rough in texture. Source is assumed to be Ste. Genevieve Formation.

303

Material Type	Color	Texture	Impurities	Luster	Workability	Effects of Heat Treatment	Comments
8 (Root Beer)	Significant variety but predominantly pale or yellowish brown or even olive. Narrow concentric bands of brownish yellow to red (10YR 6/6 to 2.5YR 3/6)	Fine to medium grain	Fossils are seldom observed	Moderately glossy	Medium to good	Unknown	Characteristic cortex is thin, tan or light brown, only slightly rough in texture. Source is assumed to be Ste. Genevieve Formation.
9 (Mill Creek)	Gray, light gray (10YR 7/2 to 10YR 5/1)	Coarse grain, "peppered" appearance	Recognizable fossils are rare but "peppered" appearance probably due to presence of extremely small fossil fragments (cf. May 1980)	Dull unless "polished" from use	Tabular nature. Makes it excellent for hoes and large excavation tools	Unknown	Source: Salem Formation outcropping in Union and Alexander counties in southern Illinois (cf. May 1980)
10 (Fern Glen)	Mixture of greenish (5YR 5/1) and reddish (2.5YR 6/2 to 2.5YR 4/2) shades in no apparent pattern	Medium grain	Small crystalline inclusions and small fossils are occasional to frequent in occurrence	Some are dull, others exhibit a slight to medium luster	Quality is medium, impurities make hinge fractures frequent	Unclear at this time	Sources: Fern Glen Formation in Jefferson and Ste. Genevieve counties in Missouri and possibly Monroe County in Illinois.
11 (Old Blue)	Various shades of blue (N 7/0 to N 5/0). Some samples are homogeneous in color, others have thread-like veins of white running through them	Fine grain, smooth	Not present	Highly glossy	Good, although only small nodules or small tabular pieces have been found	Not found in heat-treated form	Cortex is thin, white or light tan in color and only slightly rough. Source: Assumed to be Ste. Genevieve
12 (Dongola)	Light-colored samples range from light gray (10YR 7/1) to dark gray (10YR 4/1). Very dark grayish brown (10YR 3/2) and lighter shades of grayish brown are not uncommon	Very fine grain and smooth	Fossils are rare	Moderately to highly glossy	Nodular form common, exceptionally good	Not found in heat-treated form	Source: St. Louis Formation in Union and Hardin counties of southern Illinois (cf. May 1980)

Material Type	Color	Texture	Impurities	Luster	Workability	Effects of Heat Treatment	Comments
13 (Cobden Ball)	Very similar in color to Dongola, often exhibits alternating gray to black concentric bands (N 5/0 to N 2.5/0)	Fine grain	Not present	Moderately to highly glossy	Very good	Not found in heat-treated form	Source: St. Louis Formation in Union and Hardin counties of southern Illinois (cf. May 1980)
14 (Gray Oolitic)	Gray to dark gray (N 4/0) with some areas of grayish brown (10YR 5/2)	Medium grain	15X magnification: impurities scattered throughout	Moderately glossy	Poor, hinge fractures are common	Turns dusky red (10YR 3/4), also lighter shades of red	Assumed to be from St. Louis or Ste. Genevieve Formation
15 (Kaolin)	Yellow or brownish with areas of pale brown (10YR 7/6 or 10YR 6/6), yellow sometimes appears as tiny veins	Grainy in structure	Fossils are frequent	Frosty and translucent	Good	Not found in heat-treated form	Source: Bluffs near Clear Creek, Illinois
16 (Mansker)	Ranges from tan to dark brown or gray	Medium to coarse grain	Microscopic oolitic fossil fragments are common	Dull to moderately glossy	Fair to good	Uncertain	Source: One is the creek beds near Rockwood, Illinois. This chert is similar to Kincaid chert.
17	Unidentifiable						
18	Predominantly light gray (10YR 7/1) with 10–12 mm band of darker gray (N 4/1), overall peppered and banded	Fine grain	15X magnification: numerous small gray and white fossils	Moderately glossy	Fair to good	Color becomes pinkish with the band remaining distinct	Source: Possibly St. Louis Formation
19	Ranges from light gray (N 7/1) to gray (N5/1) speckled surface	Medium fine grain	Mixed small gray and white crystalline mottles	Slightly glossy	Fair to good	Unknown	Source: Possibly St. Louis Formation

Material Type	Color	Texture	Impurities	Luster	Workability	Effects of Heat Treatment	Comments
20	White (10YR 8/1) to light gray (10YR 7/1), some samples shade into darker gray (5Y 5/1)	Readily visible medium to coarse oolitic grains. Further from the cortex the texture becomes less markedly oolitic		Slightly gray	Poor to fair	Unknown	Cortex is white with coarsely angular and smaller round oolitic grains. Source: Possibly Salem or Keokuk–Burlington Formation
21	Light gray (10YR 7/1) to gray (10YR 6/1)	Medium fine grain	Small fossil fragments evenly distributed; visible at 15X	Dull to slightly glossy	Poor to fair	Color becomes pinkish	Source: Possibly Salem Formation
22	Light olive gray with lighter mottles of gray	Medium–coarse grain	Numerous small fossils	Slightly glossy	Fair to good	Unknown	Source: Possibly Salem Formation
23 (Burlington)	Dull white (10YR 8/1) to 10YR 8/3)	Medium–fine to medium–coarse grain	Network of very fine fossil fragments	Usually dull, occasionally will exhibit a slight gloss	Fair to good	Color becomes slightly pinkish, does not become glossy	Source: Possibly Burlington Formation
24 (Salem Coarse)	Highly variable, ranges from light gray (10YR 7/2) through very pale brown (10YR 7/3) to brown (10YR 6/3)	Medium–coarse grain	Interlocking net-work of coarse fossil fragments	Dull (some specimens exhibit strong brown (7.5YR 4/6) patina	Fair to good	Color becomes slightly pinkish, does not become glossy	This chert may be a coarser variety of the following type. Source: Possibly Salem Formation
25 (Salem Creamy)	Similar to those of Type 24, ranges from light gray (10YR 7/2) to a pale brown (10YR 6/3)	Fine micro-crystalline to medium grain	All but the most finely crystalline contain abundant fossil fragments	Ranges from glossy to slightly glossy	Fair to good	Unknown	Source: Possibly Salem or Ste. Genevieve Formation. Thick limestone-like cortex varies from white (10YR 8/1) to very pale brown (10YR 8/4). (See also Type 34)
26 (Silicified Sediment)	Various shades of brown and tan	Medium–fine to medium–coarse grain	Fossils usually not present	Slightly glossy	Fair	Unknown	Silicified sediment

Material Type	Color	Texture	Impurities	Luster	Workability	Effects of Heat Treatment	Comments
27 (Cortical)	Limestone-like white (10YR 8/2)	Extremely coarse and granular	Relatively non-fossiliferous	Dull	Very poor quality although the material retains the characteristic conchoidal fracture	Becomes pinkish or reddish in color	This material appears very limestone-like. Source: Probably Keokuk-Burlington Formation.
28 (Ste. Genevieve Orange-Speckled)	Distinctive irregularly patterned and mottled appearance due to the blending of light reddish brown (2.5YR 6/4) with various reddish shades (2.5YR 5/6, 6/6)	Fine microcrystalline	Numerous small crystal inclusions	Highly glossy	Fair; nodules are very small	Color darkens, only rarely encountered	Cortex is very thin (1-2 mm) and smooth, bright white in color. Source: Possibly Ste. Genevieve Formation
29 (Ste. Genevieve Purple)	Multi-hued, each piece exhibits a wide range of natural gray (N 7/ to N 3/)	Usually fine-grained	Cloudy white quartz inclusions are not uncommon	Dull	Fair to good	Color becomes a reddish violet	Cortex is very thin (1-2 mm) smooth and white. Source: Possibly Ste. Genevieve Formation
31 (Light yellowish brown)	Light yellowish brown (10YR 6/4) to a very pale brown (10YR 7/3). Some samples exhibit a stain or patina of strong brown (7.5YR 5/6)	Fine microcrystalline to medium fine	Few random fossils	Highly glossy to slightly less glossy	Fair to good	Color becomes reddish	Source: Possibly Ste. Genevieve Formation
32 (Knappable limestone)	Dull gray	Very coarse grain	May or may not be present	Dull	Fractures conchoidally but poor quality	Unknown	
34 (Salem Banded)	Alternating gray (10YR 6/1) to light gray (10YR 7/2) to light brownish gray (10YR 6/2) horizontal bands of approximately 1-8 mm	Very fine to medium	Interlocking network of fossil fragments visible at 15X	Ranges from slightly glossy to glossy	Fair to good	Unknown	Related to Types 24 and 5. Source: Possibly Salem Formation
35	Light gray (5YR 7/1), somewhat mottled appearance with diffuse whitish areas	Fine to medium grain	Small needle-like fossils visible at 15X	Glossy	Good	Unknown	Source: Possibly Salem Formation

Material Type	Color	Texture	Impurities	Luster	Workability	Effects of Heat Treatment	Comments
36 (Blair)	(N 6/) gray	Fine grain	Needle-like fossils form bands	Highly glossy	Good	Unknown	Appears similar to Blair chert from southern Illinois.
38	(N 4/) dark gray	Medium–coarse grain	Small fragments scattered throughout visible at 15X	Dull	Good	Unknown	Source: Possibly St. Louis Formation
39 (St. Louis)	(10YR 7/1) light gray	Coarse grain, almost limestone-like grain	None	Dull	Very poor	Unknown	Source: Possibly St. Louis Formation
40	Gray (N 6/1) to light gray (N 7/–2.5YR 7/2)	Medium–coarse grain	Coarse white fragments scattered liberally, observable with naked eye	Dull	Poor to fair	Becomes purplish and slightly glossy	Cortex is 3–12 mm wide, coarser grained but rather worn, white (2.5Y 8/2) in color. Source: Possibly St. Louis Formation
41	Homogeneous gray (10YR 6/1)	Medium–coarse grain	None	Dull	Fair	Unknown	Cortex is chalky-white in color, coarse grained, and very thin (1–3 mm). Source: Possibly Salem Formation
42	Probably light gray (all our samples have been thermally altered)	Very coarse grain	Large broken fossil fragments (some crinoids) protruding on the surface	Slightly glossy	Poor	Color becomes a weak red (2.5YR 5/2)	
45	Background color (10YR 8/1) white with small irregular mottles of dark brown (7.5YR 4/2 or 4/4)	Medium–coarse	15X magnification: small, white interlocking fossil fragments	Dull to slightly glossy	Poor to fair	Becomes somewhat darker and glossier	Source: Possibly Salem Formation
46	Background: dark gray (N 4/) with 1–3 mm horizontal bands of white (N 8/)	Medium–coarse grain	Not present	Dull	Poor	Unknown	Source: Unknown

Material Type	Color	Texture	Impurities	Luster	Workability	Effects of Heat Treatment	Comments
47	Reddish brown (5YR 5/4)	Very fine microcrystalline	Very, very fine network of fossil fragments visible at 15X	Very glossy	Good	Unknown	Source: Unknown
49	Background: light gray (2.5Y 7/2) with thin (0.5 mm–2 mm) horizontal bands of olive gray (5Y 5/2)	Medium grain	Not present	Dull	Fair to good	Becomes pinkish gray and slightly glossy	Cortex is 0.5 to 1 mm thick, of medium–coarse grain, and is white (10YR 8/1). Source: Possibly Salem Formation
54	Light gray (N 7/)	Coarse grain	Bryozoa, brachiopods, and other whole fossils on the surface	Dull	Very poor	Becomes light reddish brown (2.5YR 6/4) but not glossy	Source: Probably Keokuk-Burlington Formation
57	Ranges from white (5YR 8/1) to pinkish white (5YR 8/2), speckled and sometimes banded appearance	Medium–fine grain fossils scattered throughout	15X magnification: finely fragmented	Slightly glossy	Good	Becomes pale red (10Y 6/4) and very glossy	Source: Possibly Salem or Keokuk-Burlington Formation
58	Pinkish gray (5YR 6/2)	Medium–coarse grain	15X magnification: coarseness of texture obscures identification but it is highly probable that fossils are present	Slightly glossy	Fair	Color becomes light reddish brown (5YR 6/3) and more glossy	Source: Probably Salem Formation
59	Gray (10YR 5/1)	Medium–coarse grain	Visible at 15X: scattered fossil fragments	Slightly glossy	Good	Unknown	Source: Probably Salem Formation
60	White (10YR 8/1) and light gray (10YR 7/1), salt-and-pepper appearance	Coarse grain	Ubiquitous irregular-shaped fossil fragments visible at 15X	Dull	Fair to good	Unknown	Source: Probably Salem or Keokuk-Burlington Formation

Material Type	Color	Texture	Impurities	Luster	Workability	Effects of Heat Treatment	Comments
62	Bright white	Coarse grain	Not present	Chalky	Poor	Unknown	Appears to be identical to cortex on pieces of Types 25 and 34. Source: Probably Salem Formation
63	Black (N 2/) speckled appearance	Fine to medium grain	Small white oolitic fossil fragments, 1.5 mm in size and visible to the naked eye	Glossy	Fine to good	Unknown	Source: Unknown
64	Gray (10YR 6/1)	Very fine micro-crystalline	Unidentified inclusions apparent at 15X	Highly glossy	Good	Unknown	Source: Unknown
65	Gray (10YR 6/1) to pinkish gray (5YR 6/2) appearance somewhat mottled	Medium-coarse granular	Numerous fossil fragments scattered throughout	Slightly glossy	Fair to good	Color does not change, becomes somewhat glossier	Source: Probably Salem Formation
68 (Bluff Buff)	Light gray (2.5Y 7/2) to light brownish gray (2.5Y 6)	Very fine to medium-fine grain	Not present	Glossy	Fair to good	Becomes slightly darker and glossier	Source: Unknown
69 (Burlington-Crescent Hills)	Variable reddish gray (10R 6/1)	Fine grain	None	Generally glossy	Good	Accentuates natural reds	Source: Keokuk-Burlington Formation in Crescent Hills, Missouri locality
70 (Burlington)	Reddish brown (5YR 5/4), pink (7.5 YR 7/4), brown (7.5YR /4)	Medium to fine grain glossy	None	Slightly	Good	Accentuates redness	Source: Keokuk-Burlington Formation
71 (Rhyolite)	Dark red (10YR 3/4) with many small to medium white inclusions and streaks of quartzite	Very coarse grain	Many small to medium white inclusions and streaks of quartzite	Dull	Medium	Unknown	Source: Not a chert; presumably obtained from glacial till
72 (Quartzite)	Light gray (7.5YR 7/0) with patches of white	Medium-coarse grain	Not applicable	Dull	Fair	Unknown	Source: Not a chert; presumably obtained from glacial till

Material Type	Color	Texture	Impurities	Luster	Workability	Effects of Heat Treatment	Comments
73 (Burlington)	Pinkish white (5YR 8/2) and light reddish brown (2.5YR 6/4) banded with light gray (5YR 6/1)	Fine grain	None	Slightly glossy	Good	Turns pink	Source: Keokuk-Burlington Formation in Crescent Hills, Missouri, locality
81 (Grimes Hill)	White (10YR 8/10) with bands of gray (2.5YR 5/0–6/8) with many black and white specks	Fine to medium grain	Small fossils and white crystalline inclusions frequent	Generally glossy	Good	Turns pink, red, purple	Source: West-central Illinois in the Keokuk-Burlington Formation
82 (Grover Gravel)	Brown (7.5YR 4/6) cortex with white (10YR 8/1) and/or light gray (10YR 6/1) and/or dark yellowish brown (10YR 4/6)	Medium to fine grain	Quartz inclusions	Slightly glossy	Poor	Unknown	Source: West of St. Louis, Missouri, creek beds; beneath glacial loess deposits in western and northern Illinois
83 (Chert Gravel)	Variable	Fine to coarse grain	Variable	Dull	Fair to poor	Unknown	Source: Local glacial till deposits
84 (Chouteau)	Light gray (N 7/0) to dark gray (N3/0), splotchy	Medium-fine to medium grain	Unknown	Dull	Unknown	Gains pink rusty hue and gains luster	Source: Chouteau Formation in the vicinity of the lower Illinois River valley. (cf. Meyer 1970; Rick 1978)
86 (Pine Hills)	Predominately white (10YR 8/1) with discrete circular patches of yellowish brown (10YR 5/4)	Fine grain	Not present in white matrix, small fossils	Generally glossy	Good	Possibly pink or same only more lustrous	Source: Unknown, possibly southern Illinois
88 (Dover)	Gray (N 5/0) with streaks of dark grayish brown (2.5Y 4/2)	Fine grain	None	Glossy	Good	Becomes dull, occasionally light pink	Source: Formation unknown; source area in western Tennessee and Kentucky (Nance 1984); similar to Elco chert of southern Illinois

Material Type	Color	Texture	Impurities	Luster	Workability	Effects of Heat Treatment	Comments
89 (Attica)	Light greenish gray banded (5YR 5/1) and (10YR 7/1)	Grainy	Nonfossiliferous	Slightly glossy	Good	Unknown	Source: Mississippian system chert in Floyds Knob limestone formations near Attica, Indiana
90 (Moline)	Black to bluish gray (5Y 2.5/1) and (N 5/0 to N 7/0), sometimes banded or with small blue fossils	Grainy	Small fossils	Slightly glossy	Good	Unknown	Source: Pennsylvanian system Seville limestone formation in northwestern Illinois
91 (Creek Gravel)	White to brown with waterworn skin and remnants	Grainy to fine grain	Many fossils	Dull to glossy	Poor	Possibly pink	Source: Creek beds; parental sources variable

Appendix D. Chert Blade Attribute Code

Qualitative Attributes

Completeness
- 0   Fragment
- 1   Whole (Distal & Proximal Ends)

Blade Type
- 0   Segment
- 1   Classic (Flat, Prox. & Distal Ends)
- 2   Crested (*Lame à Crete*)
- 3   *Outrepassé*

Chert Type
- 00   (by Chert Type #)

Heat Alteration
- 0   Absent
- 1   Present

Nature of Heat Alteration
- 0   Color Change Only
- 1   Luster/Sheen Only
- 2   Pot Lid Fractures Only
- 3   Color/Luster
- 4   Color/Pot Lid
- 5   Luster/Pot Lid

Platform
Cross Section
- 0   Indet.
- 1   Triangular
- 2   Trapezoidal or Polyzoidal
- 3   Irregular
- 4   Elliptical

Platform
- 0   Absent
- 1   Present-intact
- 2   Present-broken or partially missing

Platform Type
- 0   Proximal-Regular
- 1   Bipolar

Platform Modification
- 0   Unmodified
- 1   Trimming
- 2   Grinding
- 3   Battering

Distal Shape
- 0   Pointed
- 1   Flat
- 2   Broken
- 3   Remodified

Blade Modification
- 0   Unmodified
- 1   Formal Retouch Scars
- 2   Isolated, Random Use Scars

Dorsal Position of Modificatin Scars
(Proximal End Up)
- 0   Left, Proximal
- 1   Left, Medial
- 2   Left, Distal
- 3   Right, Proximal
- 4   Right, Medial
- 5   Right, Distal
- 6   Proximal End
- 7   Distal End
- 8   Right, Distal, Medial
- 9   Left, Distal, Medial
- 10   Right, Proximal, Medial
- 11   Left, Proximal, Medial

Ventral Position of Modification Scars
(Proximal End Up)
- 0   Left, Proximal
- 1   Left, Medial
- 2   Left, Distal
- 3   Right, Proximal
- 4   Right, Medial
- 5   Right, Distal
- 6   Proximal End
- 7   Distal End
- 8   Right, Distal, Medial
- 9   Left, Distal, Medial
- 10   Right, Proximal, Medial
- 11   Left, Proximal, Medial

Evidence of Bifacial Modification
   0 Absent
   1 Present

Blade Notching
   0 Absent
   1 Present

Presence of Blade Cortex
   0 Absent
   1 Present

Presence of Platform Cortex
   0 Absent
   1 Present

Termination Break

		Distal End
0	Feather	Thin, Pinched
1	Step (Crenulated)	Crenulated
2	Hinge	Bulbar-Hinge-Like
3	Plunging	Thick, Curved
4	Axial	Axial Fracture
5	Snapped	Straight

Appendix E. Diagnostic Hafted Biface Attributes

Hafted Biface Type	Provenience	Chert Type	Heat Altered	Complete/ Fragment	Stem Shape	Base Width (cm)	Stem Width (cm)	Stem Length (cm)	Stem Thickness (cm)	Shoulder Width (cm)	Blade Thickness (cm)	Blade Length (cm)	Maximum Length (cm)	Wt(g)
Manker Corner Notched	surface	69	yes	complete	expand	2.41	1.77	1.27	0.45	3.04	0.68	4.02	5.29	9.5
	surface	3	yes	complete	expand	2.61	1.94	1.23	0.40	na	0.97	4.36	5.44	14.5
	surface	1	no	complete	expand	2.55	1.78	1.34	0.32	3.49	0.64	4.04	5.39	12.8
	surface	3	yes	complete	expand	2.59	1.80	1.62	0.65	3.11	0.99	4.33	5.95	19.9
	BPZ	17	yes	complete	expand	2.67	1.89	1.53	0.53	3.43	0.62	3.80	5.33	12.4
	BPZ	16	no	complete	expand	2.19	1.88	1.37	0.54	3.35	0.85	4.26	5.53	13.4
	EXC 8	7	no	complete	expand	2.64	1.89	1.41	0.53	2.79	0.64	2.62	4.03	7.8
	EXC 6	7	no	complete	expand	3.02	1.87	1.64	0.56	2.87	0.59	3.34	4.98	11.0
	Fea 29	7	no	complete	expand	3.07	1.97	1.63	0.59	3.84	0.71	4.37	6.00	17.8
	surface	3	no	fragment	expand	na	1.71	1.29	0.50	na	0.75	4.11	5.40	11.3
	surface	17	yes	fragment	expand	na	1.80	1.34	0.56	na	0.62	na	na	3.6
	BPZ	10	no	fragment	expand	2.97	1.90	1.57	0.51	3.72	0.62	na	na	12.9
	BPZ	7	no	fragment	expand	na	2.04	1.64	0.59	3.73	0.72	na	na	12.2
	BPZ	1	no	fragment	expand	na	2.53	na	0.49	3.61	na	3.59	na	15.9
	BPZ	60	yes	fragment	expand	2.19	1.90	0.97	0.61	3.59	0.89	na	na	13.7
	EXC 9	12	yes	fragment	indet	na	1.75	na	0.46	3.94	0.73	4.55	na	16.7
	EXC 9	7	no	fragment	expand	2.41	1.50	1.49	0.57	2.96	0.75	na	na	8.1
	EXC 20	29	yes	fragment	expand	2.58	1.79	1.78	0.76	3.61	na	na	na	9.8
	EXC 39	10	no	fragment	expand	2.70	1.82	1.42	0.51	3.14	0.58	na	na	11.0
	Fea 28	17	no	fragment	expand	2.72	1.71	1.73	0.68	3.54	0.72	na	na	16.2
	Fea 29	7	no	fragment	expand	3.29	2.02	1.68	0.64	2.78	1.04	na	na	19.8
	Fea 29	17	yes	fragment	expand	na	1.77	1.61	0.63	3.39	na	na	na	11.5
Manker Stemmed	surface	46	no	complete	straight	1.63	1.51	1.10	0.54	2.52	0.37	2.51	3.61	7.2
	surface	24	yes	complete	straight	2.19	1.69	1.27	0.48	3.13	1.01	3.90	5.17	12.5
	EXC 4	7	no	complete	expand	2.26	1.60	1.49	0.49	3.69	0.83	3.74	5.23	14.9
	surface	3	yes	fragment	expand	2.78	2.10	1.30	0.60	na	0.39	na	na	11.4
	BPZ	12	no	fragment	expand	na	1.91	1.45	0.54	3.28	0.64	na	na	5.8
	BPZ	19	no	fragment	expand	2.52	1.55	1.84	0.57	3.15	na	na	na	8.1
Gibson	BPZ	57	no	fragment	expand	na	1.88	1.69	0.48	3.21	0.78	5.70	7.39	18.0
	EXC 3	7	no	fragment	expand	3.48	2.12	1.51	0.45	3.42	0.60	na	na	11.5
	EXC 13	24	no	fragment	expand	2.49	1.69	1.47	0.49	3.43	0.55	na	na	10.3
	EXC 38	10	yes	fragment	expand	2.67	1.61	1.48	0.48	3.29	0.64	na	na	14.2
Ansell	surface	7	no	fragment	expand	na	2.03	1.48	0.59	3.19	0.87	3.80	5.28	13.5
	BPZ	3	yes	complete	expand	2.39	1.72	1.40	0.60	3.01	0.82	3.52	4.92	11.5
	BPZ	12	no	fragment	expand	2.28	1.57	1.16	0.57	2.70	0.72	na	na	16.3
	BPZ	7	yes	fragment	expand	2.50	1.84	1.62	0.59	na	na	na	na	6.1

Hafted Biface Type	Provenience	Chert Type	Heat Altered	Complete/ Fragment	Stem Shape	Base Width (cm)	Stem Width (cm)	Stem Length (cm)	Stem Thickness (cm)	Shoulder Width (cm)	Blade Thickness (cm)	Blade Length (cm)	Maximum Length (cm)	Wt (g)
	EXC 5	3	yes	complete	expand	1.81	1.59	1.04	0.42	2.00	1.00	3.24	4.28	8.7
	EXC 16	25	yes	fragment	expand	2.21	1.38	1.93	0.62	na	na	na	na	4.3
Burkett	surface	7	no	complete	straight	1.01	1.87	2.08	0.61	3.23	0.86	4.68	6.76	17.2
	surface	3	no	complete	contract	1.28	2.17	1.53	0.56	4.06	0.74	3.64	5.36	14.2
	surface	11	no	complete	straight	0.91	1.92	1.64	0.72	2.78	0.92	2.91	5.55	14.2
	surface	1	no	fragment	contract	1.48	1.99	1.50	0.59	2.80	na	na	na	7.8
	surface	3	yes	fragment	unknown	na	na	na	na	na	0.75	na	na	15.4
Steuben	surface	3	yes	fragment	expand	2.62	1.79	1.89	0.58	na	na	na	na	5.2
	surface	3	yes	fragment	expand	1.54	1.43	1.56	0.61	na	1.05	na	na	8.2
	BPZ	15	no	fragment	expand	na	na	1.17	0.78	na	1.13	4.87	6.04	19.1
	EXC 24	3	yes	complete	expand	1.91	1.67	1.65	0.79	2.81	1.12	3.22	4.89	12.6
Snyders	BPZ	11	no	fragment	expand	2.51	2.11	1.23	0.48	3.84	0.65	na	na	7.2
Dickson/Waubesa	surface	57	yes	complete	contract	1.03	2.25	1.95	0.60	2.69	1.00	3.50	5.45	11.6
	surface	69	yes	complete	contract	1.01	2.01	1.46	0.74	3.05	0.86	4.22	5.68	19.7
	BPZ	17	no	complete	contract	1.41	2.46	2.34	0.67	3.42	0.97	6.61	8.95	27.5
	BPZ	39	yes	fragment	contract	na	2.38	1.97	0.71	3.10	1.91	na	na	13.5
	EXC 9	24	no	complete	contract	1.20	2.23	2.26	0.59	3.49	0.78	4.59	6.85	13.0
Adena/Mason	surface	7	no	fragment	ind	na	na	na	0.61	3.20	0.71	na	na	11.6
	surface	17	yes	fragment	straight	1.64	1.73	1.33	0.59	3.27	0.71	na	na	8.9
	BPZ	25	no	complete	expand	1.90	1.64	1.57	0.56	3.43	0.83	4.49	6.13	16.1
	BPZ	3	yes	complete	expand	1.76	1.53	1.32	0.45	3.00	0.68	5.60	6.92	15.7
	BPZ	13	yes	fragment	expand	na	na	1.64	0.61	na	0.96	5.09	6.73	22.6
	BPZ	10	yes	fragment	straight	na	1.98	1.77	0.64	na	0.72	na	na	15.2
Clear Lake Side Notched	surface	1	no	complete	expand	2.68	1.81	1.29	0.55	2.81	0.79	4.74	6.03	13.9
	surface	1	yes	complete	expand	2.56	1.91	1.42	0.49	3.22	0.82	3.80	5.08	11.0
	surface	11	no	fragment	ind	na	na	na	na	na	0.77	4.83	na	12.2
	surface	1	yes	fragment	expand	2.47	1.99	1.14	0.47	na	na	na	na	9.3
	surface	29	no	fragment	expand	2.68	2.07	1.02	0.30	2.91	0.75	na	na	10.8
	surface	7	no	fragment	expand	2.64	1.97	1.50	0.57	3.11	0.64	na	na	5.5
	BPZ	3	no	complete	expand	2.40	1.81	1.26	0.39	3.39	0.87	4.64	5.90	14.2
	BPZ	1	yes	fragment	ind	2.54	1.84	1.31	0.39	na	0.45	2.40	3.71	4.8
	BPZ	8	no	fragment	expand	2.67	1.62	1.43	0.53	na	0.69	3.02	4.45	8.6
	BPZ	11	no	fragment	expand	2.12	1.63	1.45	0.49	2.87	0.65	na	na	10.6

Hafted Biface Type	Provenience	Chert Type	Heat Altered	Complete/Fragment	Stem Shape	Base Width (cm)	Stem Width (cm)	Stem Length (cm)	Stem Thickness (cm)	Shoulder Width (cm)	Blade Thickness (cm)	Blade Length (cm)	Maximum Length (cm)	Wt(g)
	BPZ	12	no	fragment	expand	na	1.54	1.17	0.36	na	na	na	na	1.7
	BPZ	17	no	fragment	expand	2.39	1.73	1.77	0.62	na	0.98	na	na	7.6
	EXC 6	19	no	complete	expand	2.67	1.72	1.69	0.44	3.17	0.75	4.11	5.80	12.7
	EXC 42	1	yes	complete	expand	2.50	1.64	1.37	0.49	2.79	0.71	3.24	4.61	8.3
	EXC 4	1	yes	fragment	expand	3.02	2.04	1.50	0.42	3.31	0.56	na	na	6.9
	EXC 5	3	yes	fragment	expand	2.55	1.82	1.67	0.59	2.85	0.61	na	na	9.0
	EXC 9	7	yes	fragment	expand	na	1.90	1.49	0.55	3.07	0.81	na	na	8.4
	EXC 18	36	no	fragment	expand	2.43	1.75	1.18	0.44	2.31	0.55	na	na	5.4
Manker Side Notched	surface	3	yes	complete	expand	1.89	1.49	1.23	0.48	2.44	0.84	3.80	5.07	10.0
	surface	10	no	fragment	expand	2.76	1.64	1.73	0.52	3.08	0.68	na	na	8.1
	surface	7	no	fragment	expand	na	1.83	1.77	0.55	na	0.62	na	na	9.4
	surface	34	yes	fragment	expand	na	1.58	1.74	0.47	2.85	0.74	3.62	5.36	11.7
	surface	3	yes	fragment	expand	2.49	1.88	1.71	0.61	na	0.94	na	na	13.6
	surface	7	yes	fragment	expand	2.34	1.59	1.44	0.68	2.78	na	na	na	7.7
	surface	2	yes	fragment	expand	na	na	na	0.39	na	0.73	na	na	3.7
	surface	1	yes	fragment	expand	3.09	2.17	1.48	0.52	na	na	na	na	4.9
	surface	10	no	fragment	expand	na	1.69	1.26	0.70	2.70	0.89	na	na	9.2
	BPZ	7	no	fragment	expand	2.73	1.76	1.49	0.52	3.14	1.09	4.40	5.82	17.6
	BPZ	10	no	complete	expand	2.52	1.63	1.17	0.45	2.64	0.55	1.14	3.31	5.1
	BPZ	36	no	complete	expand	2.31	1.65	1.56	0.68	2.78	0.73	4.08	5.64	14.1
	BPZ	29	no	complete	expand	2.71	1.87	1.75	0.59	2.40	0.75	3.97	5.72	12.8
	BPZ	7	no	complete	expand	2.94	1.77	-1.63	0.75	3.22	0.94	3.77	5.40	14.3
	BPZ	16	no	fragment	expand	2.32	1.69	1.65	0.67	na	0.72	na	na	6.0
	BPZ	24	no	fragment	expand	2.29	1.39	1.74	0.74	2.52	0.75	na	na	7.2
	BPZ	7	no	fragment	expand	2.71	na	1.61	0.55	na	0.56	3.24	4.85	9.4
	BPZ	3	no	fragment	expand	3.18	2.13	1.39	0.49	3.28	0.68	na	na	9.2
	BPZ	7	no	fragment	expand	2.69	1.48	1.49	0.46	3.03	0.67	na	na	6.6
	BPZ	3	yes	fragment	expand	2.96	1.92	1.54	0.63	2.99	0.59	na	na	7.7
	BPZ	7	no	fragment	expand	3.25	1.93	1.55	0.72	3.62	0.77	na	na	18.9
	BPZ	7	no	fragment	expand	2.53	1.90	1.41	0.58	3.03	0.75	na	na	8.5
	EXC 3	17	yes	fragment	expand	2.86	1.77	1.69	0.59	2.75	0.74	na	na	9.1
	EXC 10	3	yes	complete	expand	2.28	1.64	1.62	0.54	3.18	1.02	3.60	5.22	13.2
	EXC 13	7	no	complete	expand	3.10	2.04	1.43	0.60	3.42	0.74	3.50	4.93	13.7
	EXC 16	1	yes	complete	expand	2.49	2.16	1.33	0.37	3.00	0.53	2.71	4.04	6.2
	EXC 22	34	no	complete	expand	2.91	1.60	1.93	0.53	2.76	0.83	1.94	3.87	9.5
	EXC 24	3	yes	complete	expand	3.12	1.83	1.76	0.62	3.32	0.69	3.56	5.32	11.4
	EXC 24	7	no	complete	expand	2.20	1.86	1.49	0.66	3.37	0.79	4.29	5.78	16.1
	EXC 40	69	yes	complete	expand	3.26	2.28	1.94	0.57	3.66	0.91	3.80	5.74	15.4
	EXC 44	34	yes	complete	expand	3.01	1.86	1.69	0.56	2.82	0.85	5.11	6.80	15.6
	EXC 46	7	no	complete	expand	2.57	1.85	1.48	0.54	2.86	0.64	3.72	5.20	9.8
	EXC 36	57	yes	fragment	expand	2.69	1.73	1.54	0.45	na	0.76	na	na	6.2

Appendix F. Inventory of Plant Remains

FEATURES

Feature	1		2		3		4		5		6				7	
Provenience	SW1/2, ZA1		SW1/2, ZA1		SW1/2, ZA1		W1/2, ZA		E1/2, ZA		S1/2,ZA		S1/2,ZA		N1/2, ZA	
Type	open basin cook pit		open basin cook pit		open basin cook pit		open basin cook pit		open basin cook pit		open basin cook pit				open basin cook pit	
Volume	7L		6L		6L		7L		5L		6L		6L		8L	
	count	weight	count	weight	count	weight	count	weight	count	weight	count	weight	count	weight	count	weight
Nutshell Total	0	0.00	0	0.00	0	0.00	0	0.00	0	0.00	2	0.02	0	0.00	1	0.01
Carya sp. (hickory)	-	-	-	-	-	-	-	-	-	-	-	-	-	-	1	0.01
Corylus americana (hazelnut)	-	-	-	-	-	-	-	-	-	-	-	-	-	-	-	-
Juglandaceae (walnut family)	-	-	-	-	-	-	-	-	-	-	2	0.02	-	-	-	-
Juglans nigra (walnut)	-	-	-	-	-	-	-	-	-	-	-	-	-	-	-	-
Quercus sp. (acorn)	-	-	-	-	-	-	-	-	-	-	-	-	-	-	-	-
Unidentifiable	-	-	-	-	-	-	-	-	-	-	-	-	-	-	-	-
Wood Total	1	0.01	2	0.01	-	-	6	0.13	-	-	42	0.26	1	0.04	8	0.02
Carya sp. (hickory)	-	-	-	-	-	-	1	-	-	-	-	-	-	-	-	-
Fraxinus sp. (ash)	-	-	-	-	-	-	-	-	-	-	-	-	-	-	-	-
Juglans sp. (walnut)	-	-	-	-	-	-	-	-	-	-	-	-	-	-	-	-
Morus sp. (mulberry)	-	-	-	-	-	-	-	-	-	-	-	-	-	-	..	-
Plantanus sp. (sycamore)	-	-	-	-	-	-	2	-	-	-	-	-	-	-	-	-
Populus sp.	-	-	-	-	-	-	-	-	-	-	-	-	-	-	-	-
Prunus sp. (cherry)	-	-	-	-	-	-	-	-	-	-	-	-	-	-	-	-
Quercus sp. (oak)	-	-	-	-	-	-	-	-	-	-	2	-	1	-	-	-
Quercus sp. (red)	-	-	-	-	-	-	-	-	-	-	-	-	-	-	-	-
Quercus sp. (white oak)	-	-	-	-	-	-	-	-	-	-	-	-	-	-	-	-
Betulaceae (birch)	-	-	-	-	-	-	-	-	-	-	-	-	-	-	-	-
cf. Betulaceae sp. (birch)	-	-	-	-	-	-	-	-	-	-	-	-	-	-	-	-
Salicaceae (willow)	-	-	-	-	-	-	-	-	-	-	-	-	-	-	-	-
ct. *Ulmus rubus*	-	-	-	-	-	-	-	-	-	-	-	-	-	-	-	-
Ulmaceae (elm)	-	-	-	-	-	-	-	-	-	-	-	-	-	-	-	-
Total identified	0	0.00	0	0.00	0	0.00	3	0.00	0	0.00	2	0.00	1	0.00	0	0.00
Semi-ring porous	1	0.01	-	-	-	-	-	-	-	-	-	-	-	-	-	-
Diffuse porous	-	-	1	-	-	-	1	-	-	-	-	-	-	-	-	-
Ring porous	-	-	-	-	-	-	2	-	-	-	14	-	-	-	2	-
Unidentifiable	-	-	1	-	-	-	-	-	-	-	4	-	-	-	6	-
Identifications attempted	1	0.01	2	0.00	0	0.00	6	0.00	0	0.00	20	0.00	1	0.00	8	0.00
Bark	-	-	-	-	-	-	-	-	-	-	-	-	-	-	-	-
Total Seed	0	0.00	0	0.00	0	0.00	0	0.00	0	0.00	2	0.00	0	0.00	2	0.00
C. berlandieri (goosefoot)	-	-	-	-	-	-	-	-	-	-	1	-	-	-	-	-
P. caroliniana (maygrass)	-	-	-	-	-	-	-	-	-	-	-	-	-	-	-	-
P. erectum (erect knotweed)	-	-	-	-	-	-	-	-	-	-	-	-	-	-	-	-
H. pusillum (little barley)	-	-	-	-	-	-	-	-	-	-	-	-	-	-	-	-
Subtotal starchy cultigen	0	0.00	0	0.00	0	0.00	0	0.00	0	0.00	1	0.00	0	0.00	0	0.00
Amaranthus sp.	-	-	-	-	-	-	-	-	-	-	-	-	-	-	-	-
Chenopodium sp.	-	-	-	-	-	-	-	-	-	-	-	-	-	-	-	-
Compositae	-	-	-	-	-	-	-	-	-	-	-	-	-	-	-	-
Fabaceae sp. (bean)	-	-	-	-	-	-	-	-	-	-	-	-	-	-	-	-
Galium sp. (bedstraw)	-	-	-	-	-	-	-	-	-	-	-	-	-	-	-	-
Gramineae 6F	-	-	-	-	-	-	-	-	-	-	-	-	-	-	-	-
Gramineae sp. (grass)	-	-	-	-	-	-	-	-	-	-	-	-	-	-	-	-
Hordeum sp. (barley)	-	-	-	-	-	-	-	-	-	-	-	-	-	-	-	-
cf. *Hordeum* sp.	-	-	-	-	-	-	-	-	-	-	-	-	-	-	-	-
Panicum sp. (panic grass)	-	-	-	-	-	-	-	-	-	-	-	-	-	-	-	-
Polygonaceae sp. (knotweed)	-	-	-	-	-	-	-	-	-	-	-	-	-	-	-	-
Portulaca oleracea	-	-	-	-	-	-	-	-	-	-	-	-	-	-	-	-
Unknown	-	-	-	-	-	-	-	-	-	-	-	-	-	-	-	-
Subtotal other seed	0	0.00	0	0.00	0	0.00	0	0.00	0	0.00	0	0.00	0	0.00	0	0.00
Unidentifiable	-	-	-	-	-	-	-	-	-	-	-	-	-	-	-	-
Unidentifiable seed coat	-	-	-	-	-	-	-	-	-	-	-	-	-	-	-	-
Total Other	0	0.00	0	0.00	0	0.00	0	0.00	0	0.00	0	0.00	0	0.00	0	0.00
Fruit (?)	-	-	-	-	-	-	-	-	-	-	-	-	-	-	-	-
Monocot stem	-	-	-	-	-	-	-	-	-	-	-	-	-	-	-	-
Amorphous	-	-	-	-	-	-	-	-	-	-	-	-	-	-	-	-
Total-all	1	0.01	2	0.01	0	0.00	6	0.13	0	0.00	46	0.28	1	0.04	11	0.03

FEATURES

Feature	8					Post Mold 4		10		11		12		13	
Provenience	SE1/2, ZA		SE1/2, ZA		SE1/2, ZA		SW1/2, ZA		SW1/2, ZA		W1/2, ZA		NW1/2, ZA,B		E1/2, ZA	
Type	cooking/refuse pit						postmold		cooking/refuse pit		activity stain		sunken cook pit		fire stain	
Volume	7L		6L		8L		4L		7L		8L		6L		5L	
	count	weight	count	weight	count	weight	count	weight	count	weight	count	weight	count	weight	count	weight
Nutshell Total	6	0.04	72	0.63	141	1.23	0	0.00	64	0.64	0	0.00	0	0.00	0	0.00
Carya sp. (hickory)	6	0.04	2	0.01	74	0.88	-	-	54	0.42	-	-	-	-	-	-
Corylus americana (hazelnut)	-	-	-	-	-	-	-	-	-	-	-	-	-	-	-	-
Juglandaceae (walnut family)	-	-	-	-	40	0.24	-	-	1	0.01	-	-	-	-	-	-
Juglans nigra (walnut)	-	-	-	-	-	-	-	-	4	0.15	-	-	-	-	-	-
Quercus sp. (acorn)	-	-	2	0.01	27	0.11	-	-	-	-	-	-	-	-	-	-
Unidentifiable	-	-	-	-	-	-	-	-	5	0.06	-	-	-	-	-	-
Wood Total	2	0.01	11	0.05	49	0.27	-	-	52	0.29	2	0.08	86	1.39	3	0.02
Carya sp. (hickory)	-	-	-	-	2	-	-	-	3	-	-	-	6	-	-	-
Fraxinus sp. (ash)	-	-	-	-	-	-	-	-	1	-	-	-	-	-	-	-
Juglans sp. (walnut)	-	-	-	-	-	-	-	-	-	-	-	-	2	-	-	-
Morus sp. (mulberry)	-	-	2	-	1	-	-	-	-	-	2	-	-	-	-	-
Plantanus sp. (sycamore)	-	-	-	-	-	-	-	-	-	-	-	-	-	-	-	-
Populus sp.	-	-	-	-	-	-	-	-	-	-	-	-	-	-	-	-
Prunus sp. (cherry)	-	-	-	-	-	-	-	-	-	-	-	-	-	-	-	-
Quercus sp. (oak)	-	-	-	-	-	-	-	-	-	-	-	-	-	-	-	-
Quercus sp. (red)	-	-	-	-	-	-	-	-	-	-	-	-	-	-	-	-
Quercus sp. (white oak)	-	-	-	-	-	-	-	-	-	-	-	-	-	-	-	-
Betulaceae (birch)	-	-	-	-	-	-	-	-	-	-	-	-	-	-	-	-
cf. Betulaceae sp. (birch)	-	-	-	-	-	-	-	-	-	-	-	-	-	-	-	-
Salicaceae (willow)	-	-	-	-	-	-	-	-	-	-	-	-	-	-	-	-
ct. *Ulmus rubus*	-	-	-	-	-	-	-	-	-	-	-	-	-	-	-	-
Ulmaceae (elm)	-	-	-	-	-	-	-	-	-	-	-	-	-	-	-	-
Total identified	0	0.00	2	0.00	3	0.00	0	0.00	4	0.00	2	0.00	8	0.00	0	0.00
Semi-ring porous	-	-	-	-	-	-	-	-	-	-	-	-	-	-	-	-
Diffuse porous	1	-	-	-	-	-	-	-	-	-	-	-	-	-	-	-
Ring porous	-	-	3	-	7	-	-	-	11	-	-	-	12	-	1	-
Unidentifiable	1	-	6	-	10	-	-	-	4	-	-	-	-	-	2	-
Identifications attempted	2	0.00	11	0.00	20	0.00	0	0.00	19	0.00	2	0.00	20	0.00	3	0.00
Bark	-	-	-	-	15	0.04	-	-	5	0.02	-	-	-	-	1	0.01
Total Seed	27	0.00	20	0.00	32	0.00	0	0.00	9	0.00	1	0.00	3	0.00	7	0.00
C. berlandieri (goosefoot)	-	-	-	-	-	-	-	-	-	-	-	-	-	-	-	-
P. caroliniana (maygrass)	-	-	-	-	-	-	-	-	-	-	-	-	-	-	-	-
P. erectum (erect knotweed)	11	-	5	-	12	-	-	-	-	-	-	-	-	-	-	-
H. pusillum (little barley)	-	-	-	-	-	-	-	-	-	-	-	-	-	-	-	-
Subtotal starchy cultigen	11	0.00	5	0.00	12	0.00	0	0.00	4	0.00	0	0.00	0	0.00	0	0.00
Amaranthus sp.	2	-	-	-	-	-	-	-	-	-	-	-	1	-	-	-
Chenopodium sp.	-	-	-	-	-	-	-	-	-	-	-	-	-	-	1	-
Compositae	-	-	-	-	1	-	-	-	-	-	-	-	-	-	-	-
Fabaceae sp. (bean)	-	-	-	-	1	-	-	-	-	-	-	-	-	-	-	-
Galium sp. (bedstraw)	-	-	-	-	1	-	-	-	-	-	-	-	-	-	-	-
Gramineae 6F	1	-	-	-	-	-	-	-	-	-	-	-	-	-	-	-
Gramineae sp. (grass)	-	-	-	-	-	-	-	-	-	-	-	-	-	-	-	-
Hordeum sp. (barley)	-	-	-	-	-	-	-	-	-	-	-	-	-	-	-	-
cf. *Hordeum* sp.	-	-	-	-	-	-	-	-	-	-	-	-	-	-	-	-
Panicum sp. (panic grass)	-	-	-	-	2	-	-	-	1	-	-	-	-	-	-	-
Polygonaceae sp. (knotweed)	3	-	-	-	1	-	-	-	-	-	1	-	-	-	-	-
Portulaca oleracea	-	-	-	-	-	-	-	-	-	-	-	-	-	-	-	-
Unknown	3	-	-	-	-	-	-	-	-	-	-	-	-	-	-	-
Subtotal other seed	9	0.00	0	0.00	6	0.00	0	0.00	1	0.00	1	0.00	1	0.00	1	0.00
Unidentifiable	7	-	2	-	14	-	-	-	4	-	-	-	2	-	6	-
Unidentifiable seed coat	-	-	13	-	-	-	-	-	-	-	-	-	-	-	-	-
Total Other	2	0.01	14	0.05	7	0.04	0	0.00	20	0.14	0	0.00	1	0.01	0	0.00
Fruit (?)	-	-	-	-	-	-	-	-	-	-	-	-	-	-	-	-
Monocot stem	-	-	-	-	-	-	-	-	-	-	-	-	-	-	-	-
Amorphous	2	0.01	14	0.05	7	0.04	-	-	20	0.14	-	-	1	0.01	-	-
Total-all	37	0.06	117	0.73	244	1.58	0	0.00	150	1.09	3	0.08	90	1.40	11	0.03

FEATURES

Feature	14		15				16		Postmold 5		18					
Provenience	W1/2		N1/2, ZA		N1/2, ZA		S1/2, ZA		N1/2, ZA		S1/2		S1/2		S1/2	
Type	fire stain		sunken cook pit				fire stain		postmold		extended hearth					
Volume	7L		7L		7L		5L		4L		7L		6L		7L	
	count	weight	count	weight	count	weight	count	weight	count	weight	count	weight	count	weight	count	weight
Nutshell Total	0	0.00	0	0.00	0	0.00	0	0.00	0	0.00	0	0.00	0	0.00	0	0.00
Carya sp. (hickory)	-	-	-	-	-	-	-	-	-	-	-	-	-	-	-	-
Corylus americana (hazelnut)	-	-	-	-	-	-	-	-	-	-	-	-	-	-	-	-
Juglandaceae (walnut family)	-	-	-	-	-	-	-	-	-	-	-	-	-	-	-	-
Juglans nigra (walnut)	-	-	-	-	-	-	-	-	-	-	-	-	-	-	-	-
Quercus sp. (acorn)	-	-	-	-	-	-	-	-	-	-	-	-	-	-	-	-
Unidentifiable	-	-	-	-	-	-	-	-	-	-	-	-	-	-	-	-
Wood Total	-	-	5	0.04	4	0.11	82	0.85	6	0.06	11	0.10	6	0.03	15	0.25
Carya sp. (hickory)	-	-	-	-	-	-	5	-	-	-	2	-	1	-	7	-
Fraxinus sp. (ash)	-	-	-	-	-	-	-	-	-	-	-	-	-	-	-	-
Juglans sp. (walnut)	-	-	-	-	-	-	7	-	-	-	-	-	-	-	2	-
Morus sp. (mulberry)	-	-	-	-	-	-	-	-	-	-	-	-	-	-	-	-
Plantanus sp. (sycamore)	-	-	-	-	-	-	-	-	-	-	-	-	-	-	-	-
Populus sp.	-	-	-	-	-	-	-	-	-	-	-	-	-	-	-	-
Prunus sp. (cherry)	-	-	-	-	-	-	-	-	-	-	-	-	-	-	-	-
Quercus sp. (oak)	-	-	-	-	-	-	-	-	2	-	-	-	-	-	-	-
Quercus sp. (red)	-	-	-	-	-	-	-	-	-	-	-	-	-	-	-	-
Quercus sp. (white oak)	-	-	-	-	-	-	-	-	-	-	-	-	-	-	-	-
Betulaceae (birch)	-	-	-	-	-	-	-	-	-	-	-	-	-	-	-	-
cf. Betulaceae sp. (birch)	-	-	-	-	-	-	-	-	-	-	-	-	-	-	-	-
Salicaceae (willow)	-	-	-	-	-	-	-	-	-	-	-	-	-	-	-	-
ct. Ulmus rubus	-	-	-	-	-	-	-	-	-	-	-	-	-	-	-	-
Ulmaceae (elm)	-	-	-	-	-	-	-	-	-	-	-	-	-	-	-	-
Total identified	0	0.00	0	0.00	0	0.00	12	0.00	2	0.00	2	0.00	1	0.00	9	0.00
Semi-ring porous	-	-	-	-	-	-	-	-	-	-	-	-	-	-	-	-
Diffuse porous	-	-	-	-	-	-	-	-	-	-	-	-	-	-	-	-
Ring porous	-	-	4	-	4	-	8	-	4	-	9	-	5	-	6	-
Unidentifiable	-	-	1	-	-	-	-	-	-	-	-	-	-	-	-	-
Identifications attempted	0	0.00	5	0.00	4	0.00	20	0.00	6	0.00	11	0.00	6	0.00	15	0.00
Bark	-	-	-	-	-	-	-	-	-	-	-	-	-	-	-	-
Total Seed	0	0.00	1	0.00	2	0.00	6	0.00	4	0.00	0	0.00	0	0.00	0	0.00
C. berlandieri (goosefoot)	-	-	-	-	2	-	-	-	-	-	-	-	-	-	-	-
P. caroliniana (maygrass)	-	-	-	-	-	-	-	-	-	-	-	-	-	-	-	-
P. erectum (erect knotweed)	-	-	-	-	-	-	-	-	-	-	-	-	-	-	-	-
H. pusillum (little barley)	-	-	-	-	-	-	-	-	-	-	-	-	-	-	-	-
Subtotal starchy cultigen	0	0.00	0	0.00	2	0.00	0	0.00	0	0.00	0	0.00	0	0.00	0	0.00
Amaranthus sp.	-	-	-	-	-	-	-	-	-	-	-	-	-	-	-	-
Chenopodium sp.	-	-	-	-	-	-	-	-	1	-	-	-	-	-	-	-
Compositae	-	-	-	-	-	-	-	-	-	-	-	-	-	-	-	-
Fabaceae sp. (bean)	-	-	-	-	-	-	-	-	-	-	-	-	-	-	-	-
Galium sp. (bedstraw)	-	-	-	-	-	-	-	-	-	-	-	-	-	-	-	-
Gramineae 6F	-	-	-	-	-	-	-	-	-	-	-	-	-	-	-	-
Gramineae sp. (grass)	-	-	-	-	-	-	-	-	-	-	-	-	-	-	-	-
Hordeum sp. (barley)	-	-	-	-	-	-	-	-	-	-	-	-	-	-	-	-
cf. Hordeum sp.	-	-	-	-	-	-	-	-	-	-	-	-	-	-	-	-
Panicum sp. (panic grass)	-	-	-	-	-	-	-	-	-	-	-	-	-	-	-	-
Polygonaceae sp. (knotweed)	-	-	-	-	-	-	-	-	-	-	-	-	-	-	-	-
Portulaca oleracea	-	-	-	-	-	-	-	-	-	-	-	-	-	-	-	-
Unknown	-	-	-	-	-	-	-	-	-	-	-	-	-	-	-	-
Subtotal other seed	0	0.00	0	0.00	0	0.00	0	0.00	1	0.00	0	0.00	0	0.00	0	0.00
Unidentifiable	-	-	1	-	-	-	6	-	3	-	-	-	-	-	-	-
Unidentifiable seed coat	-	-	-	-	-	-	-	-	-	-	-	-	-	-	-	-
Total Other	0	0.00	4	0.03	0	0.00	1	0.01	0	0.00	0	0.00	0	0.00	0	0.00
Fruit (?)	-	-	-	-	-	-	-	-	-	-	-	-	-	-	-	-
Monocot stem	-	-	-	-	-	-	-	-	-	-	-	-	-	-	-	-
Amorphous	-	-	4	0.03	-	-	1	0.01	-	-	-	-	-	-	-	-
Total-all	0	0.00	10	0.07	6	0.11	89	0.86	10	0.06	11	0.10	6	0.03	15	0.25

FEATURES

Feature	19		20		21		22		23		24		25		26	
Provenience	N1/2, ZA		NE1/2, ZA		S1/2, ZA		NW1/2, ZA		N1/2, ZA		NE1/2, ZA		NE1/2, ZA		W1/2, ZA	
Type	open basin cook pit		cooking/refuse pit		open basin cook pit		open basin cook pit		open basin cook pit		open basin cook pit		cooking/refuse pit		cooking/refuse pit	
Volume	8L		5L		6L		5L		5L		5L		6L		8L	
	count	weight	count	weight	count	weight	count	weight	count	weight	count	weight	count	weight	count	weight
Nutshell Total	0	0.00	0	0.00	0	0.00	0	0.00	5	0.03	0	0.00	9	0.07	0	0.00
Carya sp. (hickory)	-	-	-	-	-	-	-	-	3	0.02	-	-	7	0.06	-	-
Corylus americana (hazelnut)	-	-	-	-	-	-	-	-	-	-	-	-	-	-	-	-
Juglandaceae (walnut family)	-	-	-	-	-	-	-	-	-	-	-	-	2	0.01	-	-
Juglans nigra (walnut)	-	-	-	-	-	-	-	-	-	-	-	-	-	-	-	-
Quercus sp. (acorn)	-	-	-	-	-	-	-	-	2	0.01	-	-	-	-	-	-
Unidentifiable	-	-	-	-	-	-	-	-	-	-	-	-	-	-	-	-
Wood Total	-	-	1	0.11	8	0.51	-	-	18	0.15	22	0.36	24	0.21	2	0.01
Carya sp. (hickory)	-	-	-	-	-	-	-	-	-	-	-	-	-	-	-	-
Fraxinus sp. (ash)	-	-	-	-	-	-	-	-	-	-	-	-	-	-	-	-
Juglans sp. (walnut)	-	-	-	-	-	-	-	-	-	-	-	-	-	-	-	-
Morus sp. (mulberry)	-	-	-	-	-	-	-	-	-	-	-	-	-	-	-	-
Plantanus sp. (sycamore)	-	-	-	-	-	-	-	-	-	-	-	-	1	-	-	-
Populus sp.	-	-	-	-	-	-	-	-	-	-	-	-	-	-	-	-
Prunus sp. (cherry)	-	-	-	-	-	-	-	-	-	-	-	-	-	-	-	-
Quercus sp. (oak)	-	-	-	-	-	-	-	-	2	-	1	-	-	-	-	-
Quercus sp. (red)	-	-	-	-	-	-	-	-	-	-	-	-	-	-	-	-
Quercus sp. (white oak)	-	-	-	-	-	-	-	-	-	-	-	-	-	-	-	-
Betulaceae (birch)	-	-	-	-	-	-	-	-	-	-	-	-	-	-	-	-
cf. Betulaceae sp. (birch)	-	-	-	-	-	-	-	-	-	-	-	-	-	-	-	-
Salicaceae (willow)	-	-	-	-	-	-	-	-	-	-	-	-	1	-	-	-
ct. *Ulmus rubus*	-	-	-	-	3	-	-	-	-	-	-	-	-	-	-	-
Ulmaceae (elm)	-	-	-	-	3	-	-	-	3	-	9	-	-	-	-	-
Total identified	0	0.00	0	0.00	6	0.00	0	0.00	5	0.00	10	0.00	2	0.00	0	0.00
Semi-ring porous	-	-	-	-	-	-	-	-	-	-	-	-	-	-	-	-
Diffuse porous	-	-	-	-	-	-	-	-	-	-	-	-	4	-	-	-
Ring porous	-	-	-	-	1	-	-	-	10	-	9	-	8	-	-	-
Unidentifiable	-	-	1	-	1	-	-	-	4	-	1	-	6	-	2	-
Identifications attempted	0	0.00	1	0.00	8	0.00	0	0.00	19	0.00	20	0.00	20	0.00	2	0.00
Bark	-	-	-	-	-	-	-	-	-	-	-	-	-	-	-	-
Total Seed	6	0.00	0	0.00	0	0.00	0	0.00	0	0.00	0	0.00	6	0.00	0	0.00
C. berlandieri (goosefoot)	-	-	-	-	-	-	-	-	-	-	-	-	5	-	-	-
P. caroliniana (maygrass)	-	-	-	-	-	-	-	-	-	-	-	-	-	-	-	-
P. erectum (erect knotweed)	-	-	-	-	-	-	-	-	-	-	-	-	-	-	-	-
H. pusillum (little barley)	-	-	-	-	-	-	-	-	-	-	-	-	-	-	-	-
Subtotal starchy cultigen	0	0.00	0	0.00	0	0.00	0	0.00	0	0.00	0	0.00	5	0.00	0	0.00
Amaranthus sp.	-	-	-	-	-	-	-	-	-	-	-	-	-	-	-	-
Chenopodium sp.	-	-	-	-	-	-	-	-	-	-	-	-	-	-	-	-
Compositae	-	-	-	-	-	-	-	-	-	-	-	-	-	-	-	-
Fabaceae sp. (bean)	-	-	-	-	-	-	-	-	-	-	-	-	-	-	-	-
Galium sp. (bedstraw)	-	-	-	-	-	-	-	-	-	-	-	-	-	-	-	-
Gramineae 6F	-	-	-	-	-	-	-	-	-	-	-	-	-	-	-	-
Gramineae sp. (grass)	-	-	-	-	-	-	-	-	-	-	-	-	-	-	-	-
Hordeum sp. (barley)	-	-	-	-	-	-	-	-	-	-	-	-	-	-	-	-
cf. *Hordeum* sp.	-	-	-	-	-	-	-	-	-	-	-	-	-	-	-	-
Panicum sp. (panic grass)	-	-	-	-	-	-	-	-	-	-	-	-	-	-	-	-
Polygonaceae sp. (knotweed)	-	-	-	-	-	-	-	-	-	-	-	-	-	-	-	-
Portulaca oleracea	-	-	-	-	-	-	-	-	-	-	-	-	-	-	-	-
Unknown	2	-	-	-	-	-	-	-	-	-	-	-	-	-	-	-
Subtotal other seed	2	0.00	0	0.00	0	0.00	0	0.00	0	0.00	0	0.00	0	0.00	0	0.00
Unidentifiable	4	-	-	-	-	-	-	-	-	-	-	-	1	-	-	-
Unidentifiable seed coat	-	-	-	-	-	-	-	-	-	-	-	-	-	-	-	-
Total Other	0	0.00	0	0.00	0	0.00	0	0.00	0	0.00	0	0.00	0	0.00	0	0.00
Fruit (?)	-	-	-	-	-	-	-	-	-	-	-	-	-	-	-	-
Monocot stem	-	-	-	-	-	-	-	-	-	-	-	-	-	-	-	-
Amorphous	-	-	-	-	-	-	-	-	-	-	-	-	-	-	-	-
Total-all	6	0.00	1	0.11	8	0.51	0	0.00	23	0.18	22	0.36	39	0.28	2	0.01

FEATURES

Feature		27				28			29	
Provenience	W1/2, ZA	S1/2, ZA	S1/2, ZA1	S1/2, ZA2	W1/2, ZA1		W1/2, ZA2	W1/2, ZA		W1/2, ZA
Type		open basin cook pit			cooking/refuse pit			cache pit		
Volume	8L	6L	8L	8L	6L		5L	6L		6L
	count weight	count weight	count weight	count weight	count weight		count weight	count weight		count weight
Nutshell Total	4 0.025	0 0.00	0 0.00	0 0.00	0 0.00		0 0.00	0 0.00		0 0.00
Carya sp. (hickory)	1 0.005	- -	- -	- -	- -		- -	- -		- -
Corylus americana (hazelnut)	3 0.020	- -	- -	- -	- -		- -	- -		- -
Juglandaceae (walnut family)	- -	- -	- -	- -	- -		- -	- -		- -
Juglans nigra (walnut)	- -	- -	- -	- -	- -		- -	- -		- -
Quercus sp. (acorn)	- -	- -	- -	- -	- -		- -	- -		- -
Unidentifiable	- -	- -	- -	- -	- -		- -	- -		- -
Wood Total	20 0.180	- -	8 0.05	8 0.04	2 0.01		5 0.07	14 0.20		7 0.04
Carya sp. (hickory)	2 -	- -	- -	- -	- -		- -	2 -		1 -
Fraxinus sp. (ash)	- -	- -	- -	- -	- -		- -	- -		- -
Juglans sp. (walnut)	- -	- -	- -	- -	- -		- -	- -		- -
Morus sp. (mulberry)	- -	- -	- -	- -	- -		- -	- -		- -
Plantanus sp. (sycamore)	- -	- -	- -	- -	- -		- -	- -		- -
Populus sp.	- -	- -	- -	- -	- -		- -	- -		- -
Prunus sp. (cherry)	- -	- -	- -	- -	- -		- -	- -		- -
Quercus sp. (oak)	5 -	- -	- -	- -	- -		3 -	1 -		- -
Quercus sp. (red)	- -	- -	- -	- -	- -		- -	- -		- -
Quercus sp. (white oak)	- -	- -	- -	- -	- -		- -	- -		- -
Betulaceae (birch)	- -	- -	- -	- -	- -		- -	- -		- -
cf. Betulaceae sp. (birch)	- -	- -	- -	- -	- -		- -	- -		- -
Salicaceae (willow)	- -	- -	- -	- -	- -		- -	- -		- -
cf. *Ulmus rubus*	- -	- -	- -	- -	- -		- -	- -		- -
Ulmaceae (elm)	- -	- -	- -	- -	- -		- -	- -		- -
Total identified	7 0.000	0 0.00	0 0.00	0 0.00	0 0.00		3 0.00	3 0.00		1 0.00
Semi-ring porous	- -	- -	- -	- -	- -		- -	- -		- -
Diffuse porous	- -	- -	- -	- -	- -		- -	- -		- -
Ring porous	1 -	- -	8 -	5 -	1 -		1 -	4 -		3 -
Unidentifiable	12 -	- -	- -	3 -	1 -		1 -	7 -		3 -
Identifications attempted	20 0.000	0 0.00	8 0.00	8 0.00	2 0.00		5 0.00	14 0.00		7 0.00
Bark	1 0.005	- -	- -	- -	- -		- -	- -		- -
Total Seed	0 0.000	0 0.00	0 0.00	2 0.00	2 0.00		0 0.00	4 0.00		0 0.00
C. berlandieri (goosefoot)	- -	- -	- -	- -	- -		- -	- -		- -
P. caroliniana (maygrass)	- -	- -	- -	- -	- -		- -	- -		- -
P. erectum (erect knotweed)	- -	- -	- -	- -	- -		- -	- -		- -
H. pusillum (little barley)	- -	- -	- -	- -	- -		- -	- -		- -
Subtotal starchy cultigen	0 0.000	0 0.00	0 0.00	0 0.00	0 0.00		0 0.00	0 0.00		0 0.00
Amaranthus sp.	- -	- -	- -	- -	- -		- -	- -		- -
Chenopodium sp.	- -	- -	- -	- -	- -		- -	- -		- -
Compositae	- -	- -	- -	- -	- -		- -	- -		- -
Fabaceae sp. (bean)	- -	- -	- -	- -	- -		- -	- -		- -
Galium sp. (bedstraw)	- -	- -	- -	- -	- -		- -	- -		- -
Gramineae 6F	- -	- -	- -	- -	- -		- -	- -		- -
Gramineae sp. (grass)	- -	- -	- -	- -	- -		- -	- -		- -
Hordeum sp. (barley)	- -	- -	- -	- -	- -		- -	- -		- -
cf. *Hordeum* sp.	- -	- -	- -	- -	- -		- -	- -		- -
Panicum sp. (panic grass)	- -	- -	- -	- -	- -		- -	- -		- -
Polygonaceae sp. (knotweed)	- -	- -	- -	- -	1 -		- -	- -		- -
Portulaca oleracea	- -	- -	- -	- -	- -		- -	4 -		- -
Unknown	- -	- -	- -	1 -	1 -		- -	- -		- -
Subtotal other seed	0 0.000	0 0.00	0 0.00	1 0.00	2 0.00		0 0.00	4 0.00		0 0.00
Unidentifiable	- -	- -	- -	1 -	- -		- -	- -		- -
Unidentifiable seed coat	- -	- -	- -	- -	- -		- -	- -		- -
Total Other	0 0.000	0 0.00	0 0.00	1 0.01	1 0.01		0 0.00	0 0.00		0 0.00
Fruit (?)	- -	- -	- -	- -	- -		- -	- -		- -
Monocot stem	- -	- -	- -	- -	- -		- -	- -		- -
Amorphous	- -	- -	- -	1 0.01	1 0.01		- -	- -		- -
Total-all	25 0.210	0 0.00	8 0.05	11 0.05	5 0.02		5 0.07	18 0.20		7 0.04

FEATURES

Feature			30		31		32		33		34		36		37	
Provenience	W1/2, ZA		W1/2, ZA1		W1/2, ZA		E1/2, ZA		NW1/2		E1/2, ZA		W1/2, ZA		W1/2, ZA	
Type			special purpose pit		open basin cook pit		cooking/refuse pit		open basin cook pit		cooking/refuse pit		cooking/refuse pit		open basin cook pit	
Volume	7L		7L		7L		10L		5L		10L		6L		7L	
	count	weight	count	weight	count	weight	count	weight	count	weight	count	weight	count	weight	count	weight
Nutshell Total	0	0.00	0	0.00	12	0.22	12	0.20	0	0.00	0	0.00	0	0.00	1	0.005
Carya sp. (hickory)	-	-	-	-	12	0.22	12	0.20	-	-	-	-	-	-	1	0.005
Corylus americana (hazelnut)	-	-	-	-	-	-	-	-	-	-	-	-	-	-	-	-
Juglandaceae (walnut family)	-	-	-	-	-	-	-	-	-	-	-	-	-	-	-	-
Juglans nigra (walnut)	-	-	-	-	-	-	-	-	-	-	-	-	-	-	-	-
Quercus sp. (acorn)	-	-	-	-	-	-	-	-	-	-	-	-	-	-	-	-
Unidentifiable	-	-	-	-	-	-	-	-	-	-	-	-	-	-	-	-
Wood Total	7	0.05	1	0.09	9	0.06	4	0.03	1	0.01	4	0.02	3	0.02	29	0.260
Carya sp. (hickory)	-	-	-	-	4	-	-	-	-	-	-	-	1	-	-	-
Fraxinus sp. (ash)	-	-	-	-	-	-	-	-	-	-	-	-	-	-	-	-
Juglans sp. (walnut)	-	-	-	-	-	-	-	-	-	-	-	-	-	-	-	-
Morus sp. (mulberry)	-	-	-	-	1	-	-	-	-	-	-	-	-	-	-	-
Plantanus sp. (sycamore)	-	-	-	-	-	-	-	-	-	-	-	-	-	-	-	-
Populus sp.	-	-	-	-	-	-	-	-	-	-	-	-	-	-	-	-
Prunus sp. (cherry)	-	-	-	-	-	-	-	-	-	-	-	-	-	-	-	-
Quercus sp. (oak)	-	-	-	-	-	-	-	-	-	-	-	-	-	-	2	-
Quercus sp. (red)	-	-	-	-	-	-	-	-	-	-	-	-	-	-	-	-
Quercus sp. (white oak)	1	-	-	-	-	-	-	-	-	-	-	-	-	-	-	-
Betulaceae (birch)	-	-	-	-	-	-	-	-	-	-	-	-	-	-	-	-
cf. Betulaceae sp. (birch)	-	-	-	-	1	-	-	-	-	-	-	-	-	-	-	-
Salicaceae (willow)	-	-	-	-	-	-	-	-	-	-	-	-	-	-	-	-
ct. *Ulmus rubus*	-	-	-	-	-	-	-	-	-	-	-	-	-	-	-	-
Ulmaceae (elm)	-	-	-	-	-	-	-	-	-	-	-	-	-	-	-	-
Total identified	1	0.00	0	0.00	6	0.00	0	0.00	0	0.00	0	0.00	1	0.00	2	0.000
Semi-ring porous	-	-	-	-	-	-	-	-	-	-	-	-	-	-	-	-
Diffuse porous	1	-	-	-	-	-	-	-	-	-	-	-	-	-	-	-
Ring porous	-	-	-	-	1	-	1	-	-	-	1	-	2	-	3	-
Unidentifiable	5	-	1	-	2	-	3	-	1	-	3	-	-	-	15	-
Identifications attempted	7	0.00	1	0.00	9	0.00	4	0.00	1	0.00	4	0.00	3	0.00	20	0.000
Bark	-	-	1	0.01	2	0.01	-	-	-	-	-	-	1	0.01	113	1.330
Total Seed	0	0.00	0	0.00	3	0.00	15	0.00	1	0.00	4	0.00	38	0.00	13	0.000
C. berlandieri (goosefoot)	-	-	-	-	-	-	5	-	-	-	-	-	2	-	-	-
P. caroliniana (maygrass)	-	-	-	-	-	-	2	-	-	-	3	-	22	-	4	-
P. erectum (erect knotweed)	-	-	-	-	-	-	-	-	-	-	-	-	-	-	-	-
H. pusillum (little barley)	-	-	-	-	-	-	1	-	-	-	-	-	-	-	1	-
Subtotal starchy cultigen	0	0.00	0	0.00	0	0.00	8	0.00	0	0.00	3	0.00	24	0.00	5	0.000
Amaranthus sp.	-	-	-	-	-	-	-	-	-	-	-	-	-	-	-	-
Chenopodium sp.	-	-	-	-	-	-	-	-	-	-	-	-	-	-	-	-
Compositae	-	-	-	-	-	-	-	-	-	-	-	-	-	-	-	-
Fabaceae sp. (bean)	-	-	-	-	-	-	-	-	-	-	-	-	-	-	-	-
Galium sp. (bedstraw)	-	-	-	-	-	-	-	-	-	-	-	-	-	-	-	-
Gramineae 6F	-	-	-	-	-	-	-	-	-	-	-	-	-	-	-	-
Gramineae sp. (grass)	-	-	-	-	-	-	2	-	-	-	-	-	-	-	-	-
Hordeum sp. (barley)	-	-	-	-	-	-	-	-	-	-	-	-	-	-	-	-
cf. *Hordeum* sp.	-	-	-	-	-	-	-	-	-	-	-	-	-	-	-	-
Panicum sp. (panic grass)	-	-	-	-	1	-	-	-	-	-	-	-	-	-	-	-
Polygonaceae sp. (knotweed)	-	-	-	-	-	-	-	-	-	-	-	-	-	-	-	-
Portulaca oleracea	-	-	-	-	-	-	-	-	-	-	-	-	-	-	-	-
Unknown	-	-	-	-	-	-	-	-	-	-	-	-	-	-	-	-
Subtotal other seed	0	0.00	0	0.00	1	0.00	2	0.00	0	0.00	0	0.00	0	0.00	0	0.000
Unidentifiable	-	-	-	-	2	-	5	-	1	-	1	-	14	-	8	-
Unidentifiable seed coat	-	-	-	-	-	-	-	-	-	-	-	-	-	-	-	-
Total Other	0	0.00	0	0.00	4	0.02	0	0.00	0	0.00	0	0.00	0	0.00	3	0.020
Fruit (?)	-	-	-	-	-	-	-	-	-	-	-	-	-	-	-	-
Monocot stem	-	-	-	-	-	-	-	-	-	-	-	-	-	-	-	-
Amorphous	-	-	-	-	4	0.02	-	-	-	-	-	-	-	-	3	0.020
Total-all	7	0.05	2	0.10	30	0.31	31	0.23	2	0.01	8	0.02	42	0.03	159	1.615

FEATURES

Feature	38		39		40		41		42		43		44		45	
Provenience	N1/2, ZA1-2		W1/2, ZA		S1/2, ZA		S1/2, ZA		N1/2, ZA		E1/2, ZA		E1/2, ZA		N1/2, ZA	
Type	open basin cook pit		fire stain		fire stain		open basin cook pit		open basin cook pit		cooking/refuse pit		open basin cook pit		open basin cook pit	
Volume	7L		10L		9L		8L		9L		10L		10L		7L	
	count	weight	count	weight	count	weight	count	weight	count	weight	count	weight	count	weight	count	weight
Nutshell Total	0	0.00	2	0.01	4	0.15	0	0.00	0	0.00	9	0.090	0	0.00	0	0.00
Carya sp. (hickory)	-	-	2	0.01	3	0.14	-	-	-	-	5	0.030	-	-	-	-
Corylus americana (hazelnut)	-	-	-	-	-	-	-	-	-	-	1	0.010	-	-	-	-
Juglandaceae (walnut family)	-	-	-	-	-	-	-	-	-	-	1	0.005	-	-	-	-
Juglans nigra (walnut)	-	-	-	-	1	0.01	-	-	-	-	1	0.040	-	-	-	-
Quercus sp. (acorn)	-	-	-	-	-	-	-	-	-	-	1	0.005	-	-	-	-
Unidentifiable	-	-	-	-	-	-	-	-	-	-	-	-	-	-	-	-
Wood Total	76	0.28	4	0.04	3	0.01	-	-	3	0.02	12	0.230	13	0.13	-	-
Carya sp. (hickory)	-	-	-	-	-	-	-	-	-	-	-	-	-	-	-	-
Fraxinus sp. (ash)	-	-	-	-	-	-	-	-	-	-	-	-	-	-	-	-
Juglans sp. (walnut)	-	-	-	-	-	-	-	-	-	-	-	-	-	-	-	-
Morus sp. (mulberry)	-	-	-	-	-	-	-	-	-	-	-	-	-	-	-?	-
Plantanus sp. (sycamore)	-	-	-	-	-	-	-	-	-	-	-	-	-	-	-	-
Populus sp.	-	-	-	-	-	-	-	-	-	-	-	-	-	-	-	-
Prunus sp. (cherry)	-	-	-	-	-	-	-	-	-	-	-	-	-	-	-	-
Quercus sp. (oak)	3	-	-	-	-	-	-	-	-	-	2	-	2	-	-	-
Quercus sp. (red)	-	-	-	-	-	-	-	-	-	-	1	-	-	-	-	-
Quercus sp. (white oak)	-	-	-	-	-	-	-	-	-	-	-	-	-	-	-	-
Betulaceae (birch)	-	-	-	-	-	-	-	-	-	-	-	-	-	-	-	-
cf. Betulaceae sp. (birch)	-	-	-	-	-	-	-	-	-	-	-	-	-	-	-	-
Salicaceae (willow)	-	-	-	-	-	-	-	-	-	-	-	-	-	-	-	-
ct. *Ulmus rubus*	-	-	-	-	-	-	-	-	-	-	-	-	-	-	-	-
Ulmaceae (elm)	-	-	-	-	-	-	-	-	-	-	-	-	-	-	-	-
Total identified	3	0.00	0	0.00	0	0.00	0	0.00	0	0.00	3	0.000	2	0.00	0	0.00
Semi-ring porous	-	-	-	-	-	-	-	-	-	-	-	-	-	-	-	-
Diffuse porous	-	-	-	-	-	-	-	-	-	-	-	-	-	-	-	-
Ring porous	12	-	3	-	1	-	-	-	2	-	6	-	1	-	-	-
Unidentifiable	5	-	1	-	2	-	-	-	1	-	3	-	10	-	-	-
Identifications attempted	20	0.00	4	0.00	3	0.00	0	0.00	3	0.00	12	0.000	13	0.00	0	0.00
Bark	-		-		-		-		-		-		-		-	
Total Seed	4	0.00	0	0.00	1	0.00	2	0.00	3	0.00	2	0.000	1	0.00	0	0.00
C. berlandieri (goosefoot)	-	-	-	-	-	-	-	-	-	-	-	-	-	-	-	-
P. caroliniana (maygrass)	1	-	-	-	-	-	-	-	1	-	1	-	-	-	-	-
P. erectum (erect knotweed)	-	-	-	-	-	-	-	-	-	-	-	-	-	-	-	-
H. pusillum (little barley)	-	-	-	-	-	-	-	-	-	-	-	-	-	-	-	-
Subtotal starchy cultigen	1	0.00	0	0.00	0	0.00	0	0.00	1	0.00	1	0.000	0	0.00	0	0.00
Amaranthus sp.	-	-	-	-	-	-	-	-	-	-	-	-	-	-	-	-
Chenopodium sp.	-	-	-	-	-	-	-	-	-	-	-	-	-	-	-	-
Compositae	-	-	-	-	-	-	-	-	-	-	-	-	-	-	-	-
Fabaceae sp. (bean)	-	-	-	-	-	-	-	-	-	-	-	-	-	-	-	-
Galium sp. (bedstraw)	-	-	-	-	-	-	-	-	-	-	-	-	-	-	-	-
Gramineae 6F	-	-	-	-	-	-	-	-	-	-	-	-	-	-	-	-
Gramineae sp. (grass)	-	-	-	-	-	-	-	-	-	-	-	-	-	-	-	-
Hordeum sp. (barley)	-	-	-	-	-	-	-	-	-	-	-	-	-	-	-	-
cf. *Hordeum* sp.	-	-	-	-	-	-	-	-	-	-	-	-	-	-	-	-
Panicum sp. (panic grass)	-	-	-	-	-	-	-	-	-	-	-	-	-	-	-	-
Polygonaceae sp. (knotweed)	-	-	-	-	-	-	-	-	-	-	-	-	-	-	-	-
Portulaca oleracea	-	-	-	-	-	-	-	-	-	-	-	-	-	-	-	-
Unknown	-	-	-	-	-	-	-	-	-	-	-	-	-	-	-	-
Subtotal other seed	0	0.00	0	0.00	0	0.00	0	0.00	0	0.00	0	0.000	0	0.00	0	0.00
Unidentifiable	3	-	-	-	1	-	2	-	2	-	1	-	1	-	-	-
Unidentifiable seed coat	-	-	-	-	-	-	-	-	-	-	-	-	-	-	-	-
Total Other	10	0.05	0	0.00	3	0.01	1	0.01	0	0.00	0	0.000	5	0.02	0	0.00
Fruit (?)	-	-	-	-	-	-	-	-	-	-	-	-	-	-	-	-
Monocot stem	-	-	-	-	-	-	-	-	-	-	-	-	-	-	-	-
Amorphous	10	0.05	-	-	3	0.01	1	0.01	-	-	-	-	5	0.02	-	-
Total-all	90	0.33	6	0.05	11	0.17	3	0.01	6	0.02	23	0.320	19	0.15	0	0.00

FEATURES

Feature	46		47		48		49		50		51		52		53	
Provenience	NE1/2, ZA		N, ZA		N1/2, ZA		SE1/2, ZA		NE1/2, ZA		N1/2, ZA		E1/2, ZA		N1/2, ZA	
Type	extended hearth		cooking/refuse pit		extended hearth		cooking/refuse pit		cooking/refuse pit		extended hearth		special purpose pit		special purpose pit	
Volume	9L		10L		10L		10L		10L		10L		7L		7L	
	count	weight	count	weight	count	weight	count	weight	count	weight	count	weight	count	weight	count	weight
Nutshell Total	0	0.000	0	0.00	0	0.00	13	0.12	16	0.18	0	0.00	0	0.00	0	0.00
Carya sp. (hickory)	-	-	-	-	-	-	4	0.08	10	0.14	-	-	-	-	-	-
Corylus americana (hazelnut)	-	-	-	-	-	-	-	-	-	-	-	-	-	-	-	-
Juglandaceae (walnut family)	-	-	-	-	-	-	-	0.04	5	0.03	-	-	-	-	-	-
Juglans nigra (walnut)	-	-	-	-	-	-	-	-	-	-	-	-	-	-	-	-
Quercus sp. (acorn)	-	-	-	-	-	-	-	-	-	-	-	-	-	-	-	-
Unidentifiable	-	-	-	-	-	-	-	-	1	0.01	-	-	-	-	-	-
Wood Total	54	0.340	-	-	10	0.08	12	0.30	77	0.70	10	0.19	-	-	5	0.05
Carya sp. (hickory)	3	-	-	-	7	-	3	-	-	-	-	-	-	-	-	-
Fraxinus sp. (ash)	-	-	-	-	-	-	1	-	-	-	-	-	-	-	-	-
Juglans sp. (walnut)	-	-	-	-	-	-	-	-	-	-	4	-	-	-	-	-
Morus sp. (mulberry)	-	-	-	-	-	-	-	-	-	-	-	-	-	-	-	-
Platanus sp. (sycamore)	-	-	-	-	-	-	-	-	-	-	-	-	-	-	-	-
Populus sp.	-	-	-	-	-	-	-	-	-	-	-	-	-	-	-	-
Prunus sp. (cherry)	-	-	-	-	-	-	-	-	-	-	-	-	-	-	-	-
Quercus sp. (oak)	-	-	-	-	-	-	-	-	6	-	-	-	-	-	-	-
Quercus sp. (red)	-	-	-	-	-	-	-	-	-	-	-	-	-	-	-	-
Quercus sp. (white oak)	-	-	-	-	-	-	-	-	-	-	-	-	-	-	-	-
Betulaceae (birch)	-	-	-	-	-	-	-	-	-	-	-	-	-	-	-	-
cf. Betulaceae sp. (birch)	-	-	-	-	-	-	-	-	-	-	-	-	-	-	-	-
Salicaceae (willow)	-	-	-	-	-	-	-	-	-	-	-	-	-	-	-	-
cf. *Ulmus rubus*	-	-	-	-	-	-	-	-	-	-	-	-	-	-	-	-
Ulmaceae (elm)	-	-	-	-	-	-	-	-	-	-	-	-	-	-	-	-
Total identified	3	0.000	0	0.00	7	0.00	4	0.00	6	0.00	4	0.00	0	0.00	0	0.00
Semi-ring porous	-	-	-	-	-	-	-	-	-	-	-	-	-	-	-	-
Diffuse porous	-		-		-		-		-		-		-		-	
Ring porous	15	-	-	-	1	-	1	-	6	-	5	-	-	-	-	-
Unidentifiable	2	-	-	-	2	-	7	-	8	-	1	-	1	-	5	-
Identifications attempted	20	0.000	0	0.00	10	0.00	12	0.00	20	0.00	10	0.00	1	0.00	5	0.00
Bark	-	-	-	-	-	-	-	-	6	0.01	-	-	-	-	-	-
Total Seed	0	0.000	0	0.00	0	0.00	2047	0.00	45	0.00	0	0.00	0	0.00	0	0.00
C. berlandieri (goosefoot)	-	-	-	-	-	-	-	-	-	-	-	-	-	-	-	-
P. caroliniana (maygrass)	-	-	-	-	-	-	-	-	5	-	-	-	-	-	-	-
P. erectum (erect knotweed)	-	-	-	-	-	-	27	-	1	-	-	-	-	-	-	-
H. pusillum (little barley)	-	-	-	-	-	-	-	-	-	-	-	-	-	-	-	-
Subtotal starchy cultigen	0	0.000	0	0.00	0	0.00	27	0.00	6	0.00	0	0.00	0	0.00	0	0.00
Amaranthus sp.	-	-	-	-	-	-	25	-	-	-	-	-	-	-	-	-
Chenopodium sp.	-	-	-	-	-	-	2	-	12	-	-	-	-	-	-	-
Compositae	-	-	-	-	-	-	-	-	-	-	-	-	-	-	-	-
Fabaceae sp. (bean)	-	-	-	-	-	-	-	-	-	-	-	-	-	-	-	-
Galium sp. (bedstraw)	-	-	-	-	-	-	-	-	-	-	-	-	-	-	-	-
Gramineae 6F	-	-	-	-	-	-	-	-	-	-	-	-	-	-	-	-
Gramineae sp. (grass)	-	-	-	-	-	-	25	-	-	-	-	-	-	-	-	-
Hordeum sp. (barley)	-	-	-	-	-	-	-	-	-	-	-	-	-	-	-	-
cf. *Hordeum* sp.	-	-	-	-	-	-	-	-	-	-	-	-	-	-	-	-
Panicum sp. (panic grass)	-	-	-	-	-	-	-	-	1	-	-	-	-	-	-	-
Polygonaceae sp. (knotweed)	-	-	-	-	-	-	11	-	-	-	-	-	-	-	-	-
Portulaca oleracea	-	-	-	-	-	-	1948	-	-	-	-	-	-	-	-	-
Unknown	-	-	-	-	-	-	-	-	-	-	-	-	-	-	-	-
Subtotal other seed	0	0.000	0	0.00	0	0.00	2011	0.00	13	0.00	0	0.00	0	0.00	0	0.00
Unidentifiable	-	-	-	-	-	-	9	-	26	-	-	-	-	-	-	-
Unidentifiable seed coat	-	-	-	-	-	-	-	-	-	-	-	-	-	-	-	-
Total Other	2	0.005	0	0.00	0	0.00	2	0.02	3	0.01	0	0.00	0	0.00	2	0.01
Fruit (?)	-	-	-	-	-	-	-	-	-	-	-	-	-	-	-	-
Monocot stem	-	-	-	-	-	-	-	-	1	-	-	-	-	-	-	-
Amorphous	2	0.005	-	-	-	-	2	0.02	2	0.01	-	-	-	-	2	0.01
Total-all	56	0.345	0	0.00	10	0.08	2074	0.44	147	0.90	10	0.19	0	0.00	7	0.06

FEATURES

Feature	54		55		56			
Provenience	E1/2, ZA		N1/2, ZA		ZA			
Type	special purpose pit		special purpose pit		open basin cook pit		**FEATURE**	**TOTALS**
Volume	7L		8L		6L		476 L	
	count	weight	count	weight	count	weight	Total Ct	Total Wt
Nutshell Total	0	0.00	0	0.00	0	0.00	373	3.670
Carya sp. (hickory)	-	-	-	-	-	-	197	2.270
Corylus americana (hazelnut)	-	-	-	-	-	-	4	0.030
Juglandaceae (walnut family)	-	-	-	-	-	-	60	0.355
Juglans nigra (walnut)	-	-	-	-	-	-	6	0.200
Quercus sp. (acorn)	-	-	-	-	-	-	32	0.135
Unidentifiable	-	-	-	-	-	-	6	0.070
Wood Total	-	-	2	0.04	1	0.01	873	8.920
Carya sp. (hickory)	-	-	-	-	-	-	50	0.000
Fraxinus sp. (ash)	-	-	-	-	-	-	6	0.000
Juglans sp. (walnut)	-	-	-	-	-	-	11	0.000
Morus sp. (mulberry)	-	-	-	-	-	-	6	0.000
Platanus sp. (sycamore)	-	-	-	-	-	-	3	0.000
Populus sp.	-	-	-	-	-	-	0	0.000
Prunus sp. (cherry)	-	-	-	-	-	-	0	0.000
Quercus sp. (oak)	-	-	-	-	-	-	32	0.000
Quercus sp. (red)	-	-	-	-	-	-	1	0.000
Quercus sp. (white oak)	-	-	-	-	-	-	1	0.000
Betulaceae (birch)	-	-	-	-	-	-	0	0.000
cf. Betulaceae sp. (birch)	-	-	-	-	-	-	1	0.000
Salicaceae (willow)	-	-	-	-	-	-	1	0.000
cf. *Ulmus rubus*	-	-	-	-	-	-	3	0.000
Ulmaceae (elm)	-	-	-	-	-	-	15	0.000
Total identified	0	0.00	0	0.00	0	0.00	130	0.000
Semi-ring porous	-						1	0.010
Diffuse porous	-						8	0.000
Ring porous	-		2				206	0.000
Unidentifiable	-	-			1		156	0.000
Identifications attempted	0	0.00	2	0.00	1	0.00	501	0.010
Bark	-	-	-	-	-	-	145	1.440
Total Seed	0	0.00	0	0.00	0	0.00	2,315	0.000
C. berlandieri (goosefoot)	-	-	-	-	-	-	19	0.000
P. caroliniana (maygrass)	-	-	-	-	-	-	39	0.000
P. erectum (erect knotweed)	-	-	-	-	-	-	56	0.000
H. pusillum (little barley)	-	-	-	-	-	-	2	0.000
Subtotal starchy cultigen	0	0.00	0	0.00	0	0.00	116	0.000
Amaranthus sp.	-	-	-	-	-	-	28	0.000
Chenopodium sp.	-	-	-	-	-	-	16	0.000
Compositae	-	-	-	-	-	-	1	0.000
Fabaceae sp. (bean)	-	-	-	-	-	-	1	0.000
Galium sp. (bedstraw)	-	-	-	-	-	-	1	0.000
Gramineae 6F	-	-	-	-	-	-	1	0.000
Gramineae sp. (grass)	-	-	-	-	-	-	27	0.000
Hordeum sp. (barley)	-	-	-	-	-	-	0	0.000
cf. *Hordeum* sp.	-	-	-	-	-	-	0	0.000
Panicum sp. (panic grass)	-	-	-	-	-	-	5	0.000
Polygonaceae sp. (knotweed)	-	-	-	-	-	-	17	0.000
Portulaca oleracea	-	-	-	-	-	-	1,952	0.000
Unknown	-	-	-	-	-	-	7	0.000
Subtotal other seed	0	0.00	0	0.00	0	0.00	2,056	0.000
Unidentifiable	-	-	-	-	-	-	130	0.000
Unidentifiable seed coat	-	-	-	-	-	-	13	0.000
Total Other	0	0.00	0	0.00	0	0.00	86	0.485
Fruit (?)	-	-	-	-	-	-	0	0.000
Monocot stem	-	-	-	-	-	-	1	0.000
Amorphous	-	-	-	-	-	-	85	0.485
Total-all	0	0.00	2	0.04	1	0.01	3,792	14.515

CREEK MIDDEN UNITS

Feature Provenience Type	Exc. U. 5		Exc. U. 6		Exc. U. 10				Exc. U. 20				Exc. U. 24			
Volume	10L		8L		9L		10L		9L		8L		10L		10L	
	count	weight	count	weight	count	weight	count	weight	count	weight	count	weight	count	weight	count	weight
Nutshell Total	5	0.030	1	0.01	1	0.01	3	0.05	1	0.01	24	0.30	0	0.00	2	0.02
Carya sp. (hickory)	5	0.030	1	0.01	1	0.01	3	0.05	1	0.01	17	0.14	-	-	2	0.02
Corylus americana (hazelnut)	-	-	-	-	-	-	-	-	-	-	1	0.01	-	-	-	-
Juglandaceae (walnut family)	-	-	-	-	-	-	-	-	-	-	1	0.01	-	-	-	-
Juglans nigra (walnut)	-	-	-	-	-	-	-	-	-	-	5	0.14	-	-	-	-
Quercus sp. (acorn)	-	-	-	-	-	-	-	-	-	-	-	-	-	-	-	-
Unidentifiable	-	-	-	-	-	-	-	-	-	-	-	-	-	-	-	-
Wood Total	1	0.010	5	0.02	-	-	7	0.08	9	0.06	18	0.12	2	0.02	7	0.07
Carya sp. (hickory)	-	-	-	-	-	-	-	-	1	-	3	-	-	-	2	-
Fraxinus sp. (ash)	-	-	-	-	-	-	-	-	-	-	4	-	-	-	-	-
Juglans sp. (walnut)	-	-	-	-	-	-	-	-	-	-	-	-	-	-	-	-
Morus sp. (mulberry)	-	-	1	-	-	-	-	-	-	-	-	-	-	-	-	-
Plantanus sp. (sycamore)	-	-	-	-	-	-	-	-	-	-	-	-	-	-	-	-
Populus sp.	-	-	-	-	-	-	-	-	-	-	-	-	1	-	-	-
Prunus sp. (cherry)	-	-	-	-	-	-	-	-	-	-	-	-	-	-	-	-
Quercus sp. (oak)	-	-	-	-	-	-	2	-	-	-	-	-	-	-	-	-
Quercus sp. (red)	-	-	-	-	-	-	-	-	-	-	-	-	-	-	-	-
Quercus sp. (white oak)	-	-	-	-	-	-	-	-	-	-	-	-	-	-	-	-
Betulaceae (birch)	-	-	-	-	-	-	-	-	-	-	-	-	-	-	-	-
cf. Betulaceae sp. (birch)	-	-	-	-	-	-	-	-	-	-	-	-	-	-	-	-
Salicaceae (willow)	-	-	-	-	-	-	-	-	-	-	-	-	-	-	-	-
cf. *Ulmus rubus*	-	-	-	-	-	-	-	-	-	-	-	-	-	-	-	-
Ulmaceae (elm)	-	-	-	-	-	-	1	-	-	-	-	-	-	-	-	-
Total identified	0	0.000	1	0.00	0	0.00	3	0.00	1	0.00	7	0.00	1	0.00	2	0.00
Semi-ring porous	-	-	-	-	-	-	-	-	-	-	-	-	-	-	-	-
Diffuse porous	-	-	-	-	-	-	-	-	-	-	-	-	1	-	1	-
Ring porous	1	-	3	-	-	-	-	-	3	-	6	-	-	-	2	-
Unidentifiable	-	-	1	-	-	-	4	-	5	-	5	-	-	-	2	-
Identifications attempted	1	0.000	5	0.00	0	0.00	7	0.00	9	0.00	18	0.00	2	0.00	7	0.00
Bark	-	-	-	-	-	-	-	-	-	-	-	-	-	-	-	-
Total Seed	1	0.000	1	0.00	10	0.00	0	0.00	2	0.00	3	0.00	0	0.00	0	0.00
C. berlandieri (goosefoot)	-	-	-	-	-	-	-	-	-	-	-	-	-	-	-	-
P. caroliniana (maygrass)	1	-	1	-	3	-	-	-	1	-	2	-	-	-	-	-
P. erectum (erect knotweed)	-	-	-	-	-	-	-	-	-	-	-	-	-	-	-	-
H. pusillum (little barley)	-	-	-	-	-	-	-	-	-	-	-	-	-	-	-	-
Subtotal starchy cultigen	1	0.000	1	0.00	3	0.00	0	0.00	1	0.00	2	0.00	0	0.00	0	0.00
Amaranthus sp.	-	-	-	-	-	-	-	-	-	-	-	-	-	-	-	-
Chenopodium sp.	-	-	-	-	-	-	-	-	-	-	-	-	-	-	-	-
Compositae	-	-	-	-	-	-	-	-	-	-	-	-	-	-	-	-
Fabaceae sp. (bean)	-	-	-	-	-	-	-	-	-	-	-	-	-	-	-	-
Galium sp. (bedstraw)	-	-	-	-	-	-	-	-	-	-	-	-	-	-	-	-
Gramineae 6F	-	-	-	-	-	-	-	-	-	-	-	-	-	-	-	-
Gramineae sp. (grass)	-	-	-	-	-	-	-	-	-	-	-	-	-	-	-	-
Hordeum sp. (barley)	-	-	-	-	-	-	-	-	-	-	-	-	-	-	-	-
cf. *Hordeum* sp.	-	-	-	-	-	-	-	-	-	-	-	-	-	-	-	-
Panicum sp. (panic grass)	-	-	-	-	-	-	-	-	-	-	-	-	-	-	-	-
Polygonaceae sp. (knotweed)	-	-	-	-	-	-	-	-	-	-	-	-	-	-	-	-
Portulaca oleracea	-	-	-	-	-	-	-	-	-	-	-	-	-	-	-	-
Unknown	-	-	-	-	-	-	-	-	-	-	-	-	-	-	-	-
Subtotal other seed	0	0.000	0	0.00	0	0.00	0	0.00	0	0.00	0	0.00	0	0.00	0	0.00
Unidentifiable	-	-	-	-	7	-	-	-	1	-	1	-	-	-	-	-
Unidentifiable seed coat	-	-	-	-	-	-	-	-	-	-	-	-	-	-	-	-
Total Other	1	0.005	0	0.00	0	0.00	0	0.00	0	0.00	1	0.05	0	0.00	0	0.00
Fruit (?)	-	-	-	-	-	-	-	-	-	-	1	0.05	-	-	-	-
Monocot stem	-	-	-	-	-	-	-	-	-	-	-	-	-	-	-	-
Amorphous	1	0.005	-	-	-	-	-	-	-	-	-	-	-	-	-	-
Total-all	8	0.045	7	0.03	11	0.01	10	0.13	12	0.07	46	0.47	2	0.02	9	0.09

CREEK MIDDEN UNITS

Feature	Exc. U. 43		Exc. U. 44		Exc. U. 45		Exc. U. 7	Exc. U. 11
Provenience Type								
Volume	5L	10L	9L	8L	7L	10L	10L	10L
	count / weight	count / weight	count / weight	count / weight	count / weight	count / weight	count / weight	count / weight
Nutshell Total	0 0.00	3 0.02	3 0.02	1 0.01	5 0.04	0 0.00	0 0.00	0 0.00
Carya sp. (hickory)	- -	3 0.02	3 0.02	1 0.01	5 0.04	- -	- -	- -
Corylus americana (hazelnut)	- -	- -	- -	- -	- -	- -	- -	- -
Juglandaceae (walnut family)	- -	- -	- -	- -	- -	- -	- -	- -
Juglans nigra (walnut)	- -	- -	- -	- -	- -	- -	- -	- -
Quercus sp. (acorn)	- -	- -	- -	- -	- -	- -	- -	- -
Unidentifiable	- -	- -	- -	- -	- -	- -	- -	- -
Wood Total	- -	- -	- -	2 0.01	5 0.02	- -	- -	8 0.11
Carya sp. (hickory)	- -	- -	- -	- -	- -	- -	- -	- -
Fraxinus sp. (ash)	- -	- -	- -	- -	- -	- -	- -	- -
Juglans sp. (walnut)	- -	- -	- -	- -	- -	- -	- -	- -
Morus sp. (mulberry)	- -	- -	- -	- -	- -	- -	- -	- -
Platanus sp. (sycamore)	- -	- -	- -	- -	- -	- -	- -	- -
Populus sp.	- -	- -	- -	- -	- -	- -	- -	- -
Prunus sp. (cherry)	- -	- -	- -	- -	- -	- -	- -	- -
Quercus sp. (oak)	- -	- -	- -	- -	1	- -	- -	- -
Quercus sp. (red)	- -	- -	- -	- -	- -	- -	- -	- -
Quercus sp. (white oak)	- -	- -	- -	- -	- -	- -	- -	- -
Betulaceae (birch)	- -	- -	- -	- -	- -	- -	- -	- -
cf. Betulaceae sp. (birch)	- -	- -	- -	- -	- -	- -	- -	- -
Salicaceae (willow)	- -	- -	- -	- -	- -	- -	- -	- -
cf. *Ulmus rubus*	- -	- -	- -	- -	- -	- -	- -	- -
Ulmaceae (elm)	- -	- -	- -	- -	- -	- -	- -	- -
Total identified	0 0.00	0 0.00	0 0.00	0 0.00	1 0.00	0 0.00	0 0.00	0 0.00
Semi-ring porous	- -	- -	- -	- -	- -	- -	- -	- -
Diffuse porous	- -	- -	- -	- -	- -	- -	- -	- -
Ring porous	- -	- -	- -	1 -	1 -	- -	- -	3 -
Unidentifiable	- -	- -	- -	1 -	3 -	- -	- -	5 -
Identifications attempted	0 0.00	0 0.00	0 0.00	2 0.00	5 0.00	0 0.00	0 0.00	8 0.00
Bark	- -	- -	- -	- -	- -	- -	- -	- -
Total Seed	0 0.00	1 0.00	0 0.00	3 0.00	0 0.00	0 0.00	1 0.00	0 0.00
C. berlandieri (goosefoot)	- -	- -	- -	1 -	- -	- -	- -	- -
P. caroliniana (maygrass)	- -	1 -	- -	- -	- -	- -	- -	- -
P. erectum (erect knotweed)	- -	- -	- -	- -	- -	- -	- -	- -
H. pusillum (little barley)	- -	- -	- -	- -	- -	- -	- -	- -
Subtotal starchy cultigen	0 0.00	1 0.00	0 0.00	1 0.00	0 0.00	0 0.00	0 0.00	0 0.00
Amaranthus sp.	- -	- -	- -	- -	- -	- -	- -	- -
Chenopodium sp.	- -	- -	- -	- -	- -	- -	- -	- -
Compositae	- -	- -	- -	- -	- -	- -	- -	- -
Fabaceae sp. (bean)	- -	- -	- -	- -	- -	- -	- -	- -
Galium sp. (bedstraw)	- -	- -	- -	- -	- -	- -	- -	- -
Gramineae 6F	- -	- -	- -	- -	- -	- -	- -	- -
Gramineae sp. (grass)	- -	- -	- -	- -	- -	- -	- -	- -
Hordeum sp. (barley)	- -	- -	- -	- -	- -	- -	- -	- -
cf. *Hordeum* sp.	- -	- -	- -	- -	- -	- -	- -	- -
Panicum sp. (panic grass)	- -	- -	- -	- -	- -	- -	1 -	- -
Polygonaceae sp. (knotweed)	- -	- -	- -	- -	- -	- -	- -	- -
Portulaca oleracea	- -	- -	- -	- -	- -	- -	- -	- -
Unknown	- -	- -	- -	- -	- -	- -	- -	- -
Subtotal other seed	0 0.00	0 0.00	0 0.00	0 0.00	0 0.00	0 0.00	1 0.00	0 0.00
Unidentifiable	- -	- -	- -	2 -	- -	- -	- -	- -
Unidentifiable seed coat	- -	- -	- -	- -	- -	- -	- -	- -
Total Other	0 0.00	0 0.00	0 0.00	0 0.00	0 0.00	0 0.00	0 0.00	0 0.00
Fruit (?)	- -	- -	- -	- -	- -	- -	- -	- -
Monocot stem	- -	- -	- -	- -	- -	- -	- -	- -
Amorphous	- -	- -	- -	- -	- -	- -	- -	- -
Total-all	0 0.00	4 0.02	3 0.02	6 0.02	10 0.06	0 0.00	1 0.00	8 0.11

CREEK MIDDEN UNITS

Feature	Exc. U. 15				Exc. U. 16				Exc. U. 19				Exc. U. 8		Exc. U. 9	
Provenience									ZA		L-4		ZA		L-A	
Type																
Volume	10L		10L		10L		10L		8L		10L		10L		9L	
	count	weight	count	weight	count	weight	count	weight	count	weight	count	weight	count	weight	count	weight
Nutshell Total	0	0.00	1	0.01	0	0.00	2	0.01	0	0.00	0	0.00	0	0.00	14	0.13
Carya sp. (hickory)	-	-	1	0.01	-	-	2	0.01	-	-	-	-	-	-	11	0.11
Corylus americana (hazelnut)	-	-	-	-	-	-	-	-	-	-	-	-	-	-	-	-
Juglandaceae (walnut family)	-	-	-	-	-	-	-	-	-	-	-	-	-	-	-	-
Juglans nigra (walnut)	-	-	-	-	-	-	-	-	-	-	-	-	-	-	-	-
Quercus sp. (acorn)	-	-	-	-	-	-	-	-	-	-	-	-	-	-	3	0.02
Unidentifiable	-	-	-	-	-	-	-	-	-	-	-	-	-	-	-	-
Wood Total	-	-	6	0.03	-	-	1	0.01	1	0.02	-	-	-	-	21	0.12
Carya sp. (hickory)	-	-	-	-	-	-	-	-	-	-	-	-	-	-	-	-
Fraxinus sp. (ash)	-	-	-	-	-	-	-	-	-	-	-	-	-	-	-	-
Juglans sp. (walnut)	-	-	-	-	-	-	-	-	-	-	-	-	-	-	-	-
Morus sp. (mulberry)	-	-	-	-	-	-	-	-	-	-	-	-	-	-	-	-
Platanus sp. (sycamore)	-	-	-	-	-	-	-	-	-	-	-	-	-	-	-	-
Populus sp.	-	-	-	-	-	-	-	-	-	-	-	-	-	-	-	-
Prunus sp. (cherry)	-	-	-	-	-	-	-	-	-	-	-	-	-	-	-	-
Quercus sp. (oak)	-	-	-	-	-	-	-	-	-	-	-	-	-	-	-	-
Quercus sp. (red)	-	-	-	-	-	-	-	-	-	-	-	-	-	-	-	-
Quercus sp. (white oak)	-	-	-	-	-	-	-	-	-	-	-	-	-	-	-	-
Betulaceae (birch)	-	-	-	-	-	-	-	-	-	-	-	-	-	-	-	-
cf. Betulaceae sp. (birch)	-	-	2	-	-	-	-	-	-	-	-	-	-	-	-	-
Salicaceae (willow)	-	-	-	-	-	-	-	-	-	-	-	-	-	-	-	-
cf. *Ulmus rubus*	-	-	-	-	-	-	-	-	-	-	-	-	-	-	-	-
Ulmaceae (elm)	-	-	-	-	-	-	-	-	-	-	-	-	-	-	-	-
Total identified	0	0.00	2	0.00	0	0.00	0	0.00	0	0.00	0	0.00	0	0.00	0	0.00
Semi-ring porous	-	-	-	-	-	-	-	-	-	-	-	-	-	-	-	-
Diffuse porous	-	-	2	-	-	-	-	-	-	-	-	-	-	-	-	-
Ring porous	-	-	-	-	-	-	-	-	-	-	-	-	-	-	12	-
Unidentifiable	-	-	2	-	-	-	1	-	1	-	-	-	-	-	8	-
Identifications attempted	0	0.00	6	0.00	0	0.00	1	0.00	1	0.00	0	0.00	0	0.00	20	0.00
Bark	-	-	-	-	-	-	-	-	-	-	-	-	-	-	1	0.01
Total Seed	0	0.00	0	0.00	0	0.00	3	0.00	2	0.00	0	0.00	1	0.00	261	0.00
C. berlandieri (goosefoot)	-	-	-	-	-	-	-	-	-	-	-	-	-	-	9	-
P. caroliniana (maygrass)	-	-	-	-	-	-	-	-	-	-	-	-	-	-	168	-
P. erectum (erect knotweed)	-	-	-	-	-	-	-	-	-	-	-	-	-	-	-	-
H. pusillum (little barley)	-	-	-	-	-	-	-	-	-	-	-	-	-	-	-	-
Subtotal starchy cultigen	0	0.00	0	0.00	0	0.00	0	0.00	0	0.00	0	0.00	0	0.00	177	0.00
Amaranthus sp.	-	-	-	-	-	-	-	-	-	-	-	-	-	-	-	-
Chenopodium sp.	-	-	-	-	-	-	-	-	-	-	-	-	-	-	-	-
Compositae	-	-	-	-	-	-	-	-	-	-	-	-	-	-	-	-
Fabaceae sp. (bean)	-	-	-	-	-	-	-	-	-	-	-	-	-	-	-	-
Galium sp. (bedstraw)	-	-	-	-	-	-	-	-	-	-	-	-	-	-	2	-
Gramineae 6F	-	-	-	-	-	-	-	-	-	-	-	-	-	-	-	-
Gramineae sp. (grass)	-	-	-	-	-	-	-	-	-	-	-	-	-	-	-	-
Hordeum sp. (barley)	-	-	-	-	-	-	-	-	-	-	-	-	-	-	-	-
cf. *Hordeum* sp.	-	-	-	-	-	-	-	-	-	-	-	-	1	-	-	-
Panicum sp. (panic grass)	-	-	-	-	-	-	-	-	-	-	-	-	-	-	-	-
Polygonaceae sp. (knotweed)	-	-	-	-	-	-	1	-	1	-	-	-	-	-	-	-
Portulaca oleracea	-	-	-	-	-	-	-	-	-	-	-	-	-	-	-	-
Unknown	-	-	-	-	-	-	-	-	-	-	-	-	-	-	-	-
Subtotal other seed	0	0.00	0	0.00	0	0.00	1	0.00	1	0.00	0	0.00	1	0.00	2	0.00
Unidentifiable	-	-	-	-	-	-	2	-	1	-	-	-	-	-	82	-
Unidentifiable seed coat	-	-	-	-	-	-	-	-	-	-	-	-	-	-	-	-
Total Other	0	0.00	0	0.00	0	0.00	0	0.00	0	0.00	0	0.00	0	0.00	0	0.00
Fruit (?)	-	-	-	-	-	-	-	-	-	-	-	-	-	-	-	-
Monocot stem	-	-	-	-	-	-	-	-	-	-	-	-	-	-	-	-
Amorphous	-	-	-	-	-	-	-	-	-	-	-	-	-	-	-	-
Total-all	0	0.00	7	0.04	0	0.00	6	0.02	3	0.02	0	0.00	1	0.00	297	0.26

CREEK MIDDEN UNITS

Feature	Exc. U. 13				Exc. U. 14 ZA		Exc. U. 18							
Provenience / Type	ECU-N				ECU-N		ECU-N							
Volume	7L		7L		10L		7L		10L		10L			
	count	weight	count	weight	count	weight	count	weight	count	weight	count	weight	Total Ct	Total Wt
Nutshell Total	1	0.03	1	0.005	0	0.00	2	0.02	8	0.10	0	0.00	78	0.825
Carya sp. (hickory)	1	0.03	-	-	-	-	1	0.01	8	0.10	-	-	66	0.630
Corylus americana (hazelnut)	-	-	-	-	-	-	-	-	-	-	-	-	1	0.010
Juglandaceae (walnut family)	-	-	-	-	-	-	-	-	-	-	-	-	1	0.010
Juglans nigra (walnut)	-	-	-	-	-	-	-	-	-	-	-	-	5	
Quercus sp. (acorn)	-	-	1	0.005	-	-	-	-	-	-	-	-	4	0.025
Unidentifiable	-	-	-	-	-	-	1	0.01	-	-	-	-	1	0.010
Wood Total	5	0.06	-	-	-	-	-	-	48	0.39	2	0.01	148	1.155
Carya sp. (hickory)	-	-	-	-	-	-	-	-	1	-	-	-	7	0.000
Fraxinus sp. (ash)	-	-	-	-	-	-	-	-	-	-	-	-	4	0.000
Juglans sp. (walnut)	-	-	-	-	-	-	-	-	-	-	-	-	0	0.000
Morus sp. (mulberry)	-	-	-	-	-	-	-	-	-	-	-	-	1	0.000
Plantanus sp. (sycamore)	-	-	-	-	-	-	-	-	-	-	-	-	0	0.000
Populus sp.	-	-	-	-	-	-	-	-	-	-	-	-	1	0.000
Prunus sp. (cherry)	-	-	-	-	-	-	-	-	-	-	-	-	0	0.000
Quercus sp. (oak)	-	-	-	-	-	-	-	-	-	-	-	-	3	0.000
Quercus sp. (red)	-	-	-	-	-	-	-	-	2	-	-	-	2	0.000
Quercus sp. (white oak)	-	-	-	-	-	-	-	-	-	-	-	-	0	0.000
Betulaceae (birch)	-	-	-	-	-	-	-	-	-	-	-	-	0	0.000
cf. Betulaceae sp. (birch)	-	-	-	-	-	-	-	-	-	-	-	-	2	0.000
Salicaceae (willow)	-	-	-	-	-	-	-	-	-	-	-	-	0	0.000
cf. Ulmus rubus	-	-	-	-	-	-	-	-	-	-	-	-	0	0.000
Ulmaceae (elm)	-	-	-	-	-	-	-	-	1	-	-	-	2	0.000
Total identified	0	0.00	0	0.000	0	0.00	0	0.00	4	0.00	0	0.00	22	0.000
Semi-ring porous	-	-	-	-	-	-	-	-	-	-	-	-	0	0.000
Diffuse porous	3	-	-	-	-	-	-	-	1	-	-	-	8	0.000
Ring porous	-	-	-	-	-	-	-	-	9	-	1	-	42	0.000
Unidentifiable	2	-	-	-	-	-	-	-	6	-	1	-	47	0.000
Identifications attempted	5	0.00	0	0.000	0	0.00	0	0.00	20	0.00	2	0.00	119	0.000
Bark													1	0.010
Total Seed	1	0.00	0	0.000	0	0.00	2	0.00	0	0.00	1	0.00	293	0.000
C. berlandieri (goosefoot)	-	-	-	-	-	-	-	-	-	-	-	-	10	0.000
P. caroliniana (maygrass)	-	-	-	-	-	-	-	-	-	-	1	-	178	0.000
P. erectum (erect knotweed)	-	-	-	-	-	-	-	-	-	-	-	-	0	0.000
H. pusillum (little barley)	-	-	-	-	-	-	-	-	-	-	-	-	0	0.000
Subtotal starchy cultigen	0	0.00	0	0.000	0	0.00	0	0.00	0	0.00	1	0.00	188	0.000
Amaranthus sp.	-	-	-	-	-	-	-	-	-	-	-	-	0	0.000
Chenopodium sp.	-	-	-	-	-	-	-	-	-	-	-	-	0	0.000
Compositae	-	-	-	-	-	-	-	-	-	-	-	-	0	0.000
Fabaceae sp. (bean)	-	-	-	-	-	-	-	-	-	-	-	-	0	0.000
Galium sp. (bedstraw)	-	-	-	-	-	-	-	-	-	-	-	-	2	0.000
Gramineae 6F	-	-	-	-	-	-	-	-	-	-	-	-	0	0.000
Gramineae sp. (grass)	-	-	-	-	-	-	-	-	-	-	-	-	0	0.000
Hordeum sp. (barley)	-	-	-	-	-	-	-	-	-	-	-	-	0	0.000
cf. Hordeum sp.	-	-	-	-	-	-	-	-	-	-	-	-	1	0.000
Panicum sp. (panic grass)	-	-	-	-	-	-	-	-	-	-	-	-	1	0.000
Polygonaceae sp. (knotweed)	-	-	-	-	-	-	-	-	-	-	-	-	2	0.000
Portulaca oleracea	-	-	-	-	-	-	-	-	-	-	-	-	0	0.000
Unknown	-	-	-	-	-	-	-	-	-	-	-	-	0	0.000
Total other seed	0	0.00	0	0.000	0	0.00	0	0.00	0	0.00	0	0.00	6	0.000
Unidentifiable	1	-	-	-	-	-	-	-	-	-	-	-	99	0.000
Unidentifiable seed coat	-	-	-	-	-	-	-	-	-	-	-	-	0	0.000
Total Other	0	0.00	0	0.000	0	0.00	0	0.00	5	0.03	0	0.00	7	0.085
Fruit (?)	-	-	-	-	-	-	-	-	-	-	-	-	1	0.050
Monocot stem	-	-	-	-	-	-	-	-	-	-	-	-	0	0.000
Amorphous	-	-	-	-	-	-	-	-	5	0.03	-	-	6	0.035
Total-all	7	0.09	1	0.005	0	0.00	4	0.02	61	0.52	3	0.01	527	2.075

SHEET MIDDEN UNITS

Feature Provenience Type Volume	Exc. U. 1 7L		Exc. U. 41 7L		Exc. U. 17 7L		Exc. U. 30 8L		Exc. U. 36 10L		Exc. U. 4 7L		Exc. U. 37 6L		SHEET MIDDEN TOTALS 52 L	
	count	weight	count	weight	count	weight	count	weight	count	weight	count	weight	count	weight	Total Ct	Total Wt
Nutshell Total	0	0.00	0	0.00	0	0.00	0	0.00	0	0.00	0	0.00	0	0.00	0	0.000
Carya sp. (hickory)	-	-	-	-	-	-	-	-	-	-	-	-	-	-	0	0.000
Corylus americana (hazelnut)	-	-	-	-	-	-	-	-	-	-	-	-	-	-	0	0.000
Juglandaceae (walnut family)	-	-	-	-	-	-	-	-	-	-	-	-	-	-	0	0.000
Juglans nigra (walnut)	-	-	-	-	-	-	-	-	-	-	-	-	-	-	0	0.000
Quercus sp. (acorn)	-	-	-	-	-	-	-	-	-	-	-	-	-	-	0	0.000
Unidentifiable	-	-	-	-	-	-	-	-	-	-	-	-	-	-	0	0.000
Wood Total	4	0.02	-	-	2	0.01	-	-	-	-	1	0.01	-	-	7	0.040
Carya sp. (hickory)	-	-	-	-	-	-	-	-	-	-	-	-	-	-	0	0.000
Fraxinus sp. (ash)	-	-	-	-	-	-	-	-	-	-	-	-	-	-	0	0.000
Juglans sp. (walnut)	-	-	-	-	-	-	-	-	-	-	-	-	-	-	0	0.000
Morus sp. (mulberry)	-	-	-	-	-	-	-	-	-	-	-	-	-	-	0	0.000
Plantanus sp. (sycamore)	-	-	-	-	-	-	-	-	-	-	-	-	-	-	0	0.000
Populus sp.	4	-	-	-	-	-	-	-	-	-	-	-	-	-	4	0.000
Prunus sp. (cherry)	-	-	-	-	-	-	-	-	-	-	-	-	-	-	0	0.000
Quercus sp. (oak)	-	-	-	-	-	-	-	-	-	-	-	-	-	-	0	0.000
Quercus sp. (red)	-	-	-	-	-	-	-	-	-	-	-	-	-	-	0	0.000
Quercus sp. (white oak)	-	-	-	-	-	-	-	-	-	-	-	-	-	-	0	0.000
Betulaceae (birch)	-	-	-	-	-	-	-	-	-	-	-	-	-	-	0	0.000
cf. Betulaceae sp. (birch)	-	-	-	-	-	-	-	-	-	-	-	-	-	-	0	0.000
Salicaceae (willow)	-	-	-	-	-	-	-	-	-	-	-	-	-	-	0	0.000
cf. *Ulmus rubus*	-	-	-	-	-	-	-	-	-	-	-	-	-	-	0	0.000
Ulmaceae (elm)	-	-	-	-	-	-	-	-	-	-	-	-	-	-	0	0.000
Total identified	4	0.00	0	0.00	0	0.00	0	0.00	0	0.00	0	0.00	0	0.00	4	0.000
Semi-ring porous	-	-	-	-	-	-	-	-	-	-	-	-	-	-	0	0.000
Diffuse porous	-	-	-	-	2	-	-	-	-	-	1	-	-	-	3	0.000
Ring porous	-	-	-	-	-	-	-	-	-	-	-	-	-	-	0	0.000
Unidentifiable	-	-	-	-	-	-	-	-	-	-	-	-	-	-	0	0.000
Identifications attempted	4	0.00	0	0.00	2	0.00	0	0.00	0	0.00	1	0.00	0	0.00	7	0.000
Bark	-	-	-	-	-	-	-	-	-	-	-	-	-	-	0	0.000
Total Seed	0	0.00	0	0.00	1	0.00	0	0.00	0	0.00	0	0.00	0	0.00	1	0.000
C. berlandieri (goosefoot)	-	-	-	-	-	-	-	-	-	-	-	-	-	-	0	0.000
P. caroliniana (maygrass)	-	-	-	-	-	-	-	-	-	-	-	-	-	-	0	0.000
P. erectum (erect knotweed)	-	-	-	-	-	-	-	-	-	-	-	-	-	-	0	0.000
H. pusillum (little barley)	-	-	-	-	-	-	-	-	-	-	-	-	-	-	0	0.000
Subtotal starchy cultigen	0	0.00	0	0.00	0	0.00	0	0.00	0	0.00	0	0.00	0	0.00	0	0.000
Amaranthus sp.	-	-	-	-	-	-	-	-	-	-	-	-	-	-	0	0.000
Chenopodium sp.	-	-	-	-	-	-	-	-	-	-	-	-	-	-	0	0.000
Compositae	-	-	-	-	-	-	-	-	-	-	-	-	-	-	0	0.000
Fabaceae sp. (bean)	-	-	-	-	-	-	-	-	-	-	-	-	-	-	0	0.000
Galium sp. (bedstraw)	-	-	-	-	-	-	-	-	-	-	-	-	-	-	0	0.000
Gramineae 6F	-	-	-	-	-	-	-	-	-	-	-	-	-	-	0	0.000
Gramineae sp. (grass)	-	-	-	-	-	-	-	-	-	-	-	-	-	-	0	0.000
Hordeum sp. (barley)	-	-	-	-	-	-	-	-	-	-	-	-	-	-	0	0.000
cf. *Hordeum* sp.	-	-	-	-	-	-	-	-	-	-	-	-	-	-	0	0.000
Panicum sp. (panic grass)	-	-	-	-	-	-	-	-	-	-	-	-	-	-	0	0.000
Polygonaceae sp. (knotweed)	-	-	-	-	1	-	-	-	-	-	-	-	-	-	1	0.000
Portulaca oleracea	-	-	-	-	-	-	-	-	-	-	-	-	-	-	0	0.000
Unknown	-	-	-	-	-	-	-	-	-	-	-	-	-	-	0	0.000
Subtotal other seed	0	0.00	0	0.00	1	0.00	0	0.00	0	0.00	0	0.00	0	0.00	1	0.000
Unidentifiable	-	-	-	-	-	-	-	-	-	-	-	-	-	-	0	0.000
Unidentifiable seed coat	-	-	-	-	-	-	-	-	-	-	-	-	-	-	0	0.000
Total Other	0	0.00	0	0.00	1	0.01	0	0.00	0	0.00	1	0.01	0	0.00	2	0.020
Fruit (?)	-	-	-	-	-	-	-	-	-	-	-	-	-	-	0	0.000
Monocot stem	-	-	-	-	1	0.01	-	-	-	-	-	-	-	-	1	0.010
Amorphous	-	-	-	-	-	-	-	-	-	-	1	0.01	-	-	1	0.010
Total-all	4	0.02	0	0.00	4	0.02	0	0.00	0	0.00	2	0.02	0	0.00	10	0.060

TEST UNITS

Feature	T.U. A						T.U. E					
Provenience												
Type												
Volume	10L		8L		7L		5L		7L		6L	
	count	weight	count	weight	count	weight	count	weight	count	weight	count	weight
Nutshell Total	1	0.01	0	0.00	0	0.00	24	0.27	0	0.00	27	0.19
Carya sp. (hickory)	1	0.01	-	-	-	-	14	0.11	-	-	18	0.14
Corylus americana (hazelnut)	-	-	-	-	-	-	-	-	-	-	-	-
Juglandaceae (walnut family)	-	-	-	-	-	-	5	0.03	-	-	8	0.04
Juglans nigra (walnut)	-	-	-	-	-	-	5	0.13	-	-	-	-
Quercus sp. (acorn)	-	-	-	-	-	-	-	-	-	-	1	0.01
Unidentifiable	-	-	-	-	-	-	-	-	-	-	-	-
Wood Total	2	0.02	-	-	1	0.01	27	0.23	2	0.01	8	0.04
Carya sp. (hickory)	-	-	-	-	-	-	-	-	-	-	2	
Fraxinus sp. (ash)	-	-	-	-	-	-	-	-	-	-	-	-
Juglans sp. (walnut)	-	-	-	-	-	-	-	-	-	-	-	-
Morus sp. (mulberry)	-	-	-	-	-	-	-	-	-	-	-	-
Plantanus sp. (sycamore)	-	-	-	-	-	-	-	-	-	-	-	-
Populus sp.	-	-	-	-	-	-	-	-	-	-	-	-
Prunus sp. (cherry)	-	-	-	-	-	-	-	-	-	-	-	-
Quercus sp. (oak)	-	-	-	-	-	-	3	-	-	-	-	-
Quercus sp. (red)	-	-	-	-	-	-	2	-	-	-	-	-
Quercus sp. (white oak)	-	-	-	-	-	-	-	-	-	-	-	-
Betulaceae (birch)	-	-	-	-	-	-	-	-	-	-	-	-
cf. Betulaceae sp. (birch)	-	-	-	-	-	-	-	-	-	-	-	-
Salicaceae (willow)	-	-	-	-	-	-	-	-	-	-	-	-
cf. *Ulmus rubus*	-	-	-	-	-	-	-	-	-	-	-	-
Ulmaceae (elm)	-	-	-	-	-	-	-	-	-	-	-	-
Total identified	0	0.00	0	0.00	0	0.00	5	0.00	0	0.00	2	0.00
Semi-ring porous	-	-	-	-	-	-	-	-	-	-	-	-
Diffuse porous	-	-	-	-	-	-	-	-	-	-	-	-
Ring porous	1	-	-	-	-	-	10	-	-	-	2	-
Unidentifiable	1	-	-	-	1	-	5	-	2	-	4	-
Identifications attempted	2	0.00	0	0.00	1	0.00	20	0.00	2	0.00	8	0.00
Bark	-	-	-	-	-	-	-	-	-	-	-	-
Total Seed	2	0.00	1	0.00	0	0.00	3	0.00	1	0.00	1	0.00
C. berlandieri (goosefoot)	-	-	-	-	-	-	-	-	-	-	-	-
P. caroliniana (maygrass)	-	-	-	-	-	-	2	-	-	-	1	-
P. erectum (erect knotweed)	-	-	-	-	-	-	1	-	1	-	-	-
H. pusillum (little barley)	-	-	1	-	-	-	-	-	-	-	-	-
Subtotal starchy cultigen	0	0.00	0	0.00	0	0.00	2	0.00	1	0.00	1	0.00
Amaranthus sp.	-	-	-	-	-	-	-	-	-	-	-	-
Chenopodium sp.	1	-	-	-	-	-	-	-	-	-	-	-
Compositae	-	-	-	-	-	-	-	-	-	-	-	-
Fabaceae sp. (bean)	-	-	-	-	-	-	-	-	-	-	-	-
Galium sp. (bedstraw)	-	-	-	-	-	-	-	-	-	-	-	-
Gramineae 6F	-	-	-	-	-	-	-	-	-	-	-	-
Gramineae sp. (grass)	-	-	- .	-	-	-	-	-	-	-	-	-
Hordeum sp. (barley)	-	-	-	-	-	-	-	-	-	-	-	-
cf. *Hordeum* sp.	-	-	-	-	-	-	-	-	-	-	-	-
Panicum sp. (panic grass)	-	-	-	-	-	-	-	-	-	-	-	-
Polygonaceae sp. (knotweed)	-	-	-	-	-	-	-	-	-	-	-	-
Portulaca oleracea	-	-	-	-	-	-	-	-	-	-	-	-
Unknown	-	-	-	-	-	-	-	-	-	-	-	-
Subtotal other seed	1	0.00	1	0.00	0	0.00	1	0.00	0	0.00	0	0.00
Unidentifiable	1	-	-	-	-	-	-	-	-	-	-	-
Unidentifiable seed coat	-	-	-	-	-	-	-	-	-	-	-	-
Total Other	0	0.00	1	0.01	0	0.00	0	0.00	0	0.00	0	0.00
Fruit (?)	-	-	-	-	-	-	-	-	-	-	-	-
Monocot stem	-	-	-	-	-	-	-	-	-	-	-	-
Amorphous	-	-	1	0.01	-	-	-	-	-	-	-	-
Total-all	5	0.03	2	0.01	1	0.01	54	0.50	3	0.01	36	0.23

TEST UNITS

Feature	T.U. G							
Provenience								
Type							**TEST UNIT TOTALS**	
Volume	7L		7L		6L		25 L	
	count	weight	count	weight	count	weight	Total ct	Total Wt.
Nutshell Total	0	0.00	3	0.02	1	0.01	56	0.500
Carya sp. (hickory)	-	-	3	0.02	-	-	36	0.280
Corylus americana (hazelnut)	-	-	-	-	-	-	0	0.000
Juglandaceae (walnut family)	-	-	-	-	1	0.01	14	0.080
Juglans nigra (walnut)	-	-	-	-	-	-	5	0.130
Quercus sp. (acorn)	-	-	-	-	-	-	1	0.010
Unidentifiable	-	-	-	-	-	-	0	0.000
Wood Total	12	0.24	38	0.49	-	-	90	1.040
Carya sp. (hickory)	-	-	1	.-	-	-	3	0.000
Fraxinus sp. (ash)	2	-	2	-	-	-	4	0.000
Juglans sp. (walnut)	-	-	-	-	-	-	0	0.000
Morus sp. (mulberry)	1	-	-	-	-	-	1	0.000
Plantanus sp. (sycamore)	-	-	-	-	-	-	0	0.000
Populus sp.	-	-	-	-	-	-	0	0.000
Prunus sp. (cherry)	-	-	-	-	-	-	0	0.000
Quercus sp. (oak)	-	-	2	-	-	-	5	0.000
Quercus sp. (red)	-	-	-	-	-	-	2	0.000
Quercus sp. (white oak)	1	-	1	-	-	-	2	0.000
Betulaceae (birch)	-	-	-	-	-	-	0	0.000
cf. Betulaceae sp. (birch)	-	-	-	-	-	-	0	0.000
Salicaceae (willow)	-	-	-	-	-	-	0	0.000
cf. *Ulmus rubus*	-	-	-	-	-	-	0	0.000
Ulmaceae (elm)	-	-	-	-	-	-	0	0.000
Total identified	4	0.00	6	0.00	0	0.00	17	0.000
Semi-ring porous	-	-	-	-	-	-	0	0.000
Diffuse porous	-	-	-	-	-	-	0	0.000
Ring porous	2	-	7	-	-	-	22	0.000
Unidentifiable	6	-	7	-	-	-	26	0.000
Identifications attempted	12	0.00	20	0.00	0	0.00	65	0.000
Bark	-	-	-	-	2	0.02	2	0.020
Total Seed	1	0.00	10	0.00	1	0.00	20	0.000
C. berlandieri (goosefoot)	-	-	3	-	-	-	3	0.000
P. caroliniana (maygrass)	-	-	1	-	-	-	4	0.000
P. erectum (erect knotweed)	-	-	-	-	-	-	2	0.000
H. pusillum (little barley)	-	-	5	-	-	-	6	0.000
Subtotal starchy cultigen	0	0.00	9	0.00	0	0.00	13	0.000
Amaranthus sp.	-	-	-	-	-	-	0	0.000
Chenopodium sp.	-	-	-	-	-	-	1	0.000
Compositae	-	-	-	-	-	-	0	0.000
Fabaceae sp. (bean)	-	-	-	-	-	-	0	0.000
Galium sp. (bedstraw)	-	-	-	-	-	-	0	0.000
Gramineae 6F	-	-	-	-	-	-	0	0.000
Gramineae sp. (grass)	-	-	-	-	-	-	0	0.000
Hordeum sp. (barley)	1	-	-	-	-	-	1	0.000
cf. *Hordeum* sp.	-	-	-	-	-	-	0	0.000
Panicum sp. (panic grass)	-	-	-	-	-	-	0	0.000
Polygonaceae sp. (knotweed)	-	-	-	-	-	-	0	0.000
Portulaca oleracea	-	-	-	-	-	-	0	0.000
Unknown	-	-	-	-	-	-	0	0.000
Subtotal other seed	1	0.00	0	0.00	0	0.00	4	0.000
Unidentifiable	-	-	1	-	1	-	3	0.000
Unidentifiable seed coat	-	-	-	-	-	-	0	0.000
Total Other	0	0.00	1	0.02	0	0.00	2	0.030
Fruit (?)	-	-	-	-	-	-	0	0.000
Monocot stem	-	-	-	-	-	-	0	0.000
Amorphous	-	-	1	0.02	-	-	2	0.030
Total-all	13	0.24	52	0.53	4	0.03	170	1.590

GEOTRENCH

Feature	GT 1						GEOTRENCH TOTALS	
Provenience								
Type								
Volume		6L					**GEOTRENCH TOTALS**	
	count	weight	count	weight	count	weight	Total Ct	Total Wt
Nutshell Total	1	0.01	0	0.00	0	0.00	1	0.010
Carya sp. (hickory)	1	0.01	-	-	-	-	1	0.010
Corylus americana (hazelnut)	-	-	-	-	-	-	0	0.000
Juglandaceae (walnut family)	-	-	-	-	-	-	0	0.000
Juglans nigra (walnut)	-	-	-	-	-	-	0	0.000
Quercus sp. (acorn)	-	-	-	-	-	-	0	0.000
Unidentifiable	-	-	-	-	-	-	0	0.000
Wood Total	32	0.33	-	-	-	-	32	0.330
Carya sp. (hickory)	-	-	-	-	-	-	0	0.000
Fraxinus sp. (ash)	-	-	-	-	-	-	0	0.000
Juglans sp. (walnut)	-	-	-	-	-	-	0	0.000
Morus sp. (mulberry)	-	-	-	-	-	-	0	0.000
Plantanus sp. (sycamore)	1	-	-	-	-	-	1	0.000
Populus sp.	-	-	-	-	-	-	0	0.000
Prunus sp. (cherry)	-	-	-	-	-	-	0	0.000
Quercus sp. (oak)	4	-	-	-	-	-	4	0.000
Quercus sp. (red)	-	-	-	-	-	-	0	0.000
Quercus sp. (white oak)	-	-	-	-	-	-	0	0.000
Betulaceae (birch)	-	-	-	-	-	-	0	0.000
cf. Betulaceae sp. (birch)	-	-	-	-	-	-	0	0.000
Salicaceae (willow)	-	-	-	-	-	-	0	0.000
cf. *Ulmus rubus*	-	-	-	-	-	-	0	0.000
Ulmaceae (elm)							0	0.000
Total identified	5	0.00	0	0.00	0	0.00	5	0.000
Semi-ring porous	-	-	-	-	-	-	0	0.000
Diffuse porous	-	-	-	-	-	-	0	0.000
Ring porous	10	-	-	-	-	-	10	0.000
Unidentifiable	5	-	-	-	-	-	5	0.000
Identifications attempted	20	0.00	0	0.00	0	0.00	20	0.000
Bark	-	-	-	-	-	-	0	0.000
Total Seed	0	0.00	0	0.00	0	0.00	0	0.000
C. berlandieri (goosefoot)	-	-	-	-	-	-	0	0.000
P. caroliniana (maygrass)	-	-	-	-	-	-	0	0.000
P. erectum (erect knotweed)	-	-	-	-	-	-	0	0.000
H. pusillum (little barley)	-	-	-	-	-	-	0	0.000
Subtotal starchy cultigen	0	0.00	0	0.00	0	0.00	0	0.000
Amaranthus sp.	-	-	-	-	-	-	0	0.000
Chenopodium sp.	-	-	-	-	-	-	0	0.000
Compositae	-	-	-	-	-	-	0	0.000
Fabaceae sp. (bean)	-	-	-	-	-	-	0	0.000
Galium sp. (bedstraw)	-	-	-	-	-	-	0	0.000
Gramineae 6F	-	-	-	-	-	-	0	0.000
Gramineae sp. (grass)	-	-	-	-	-	-	0	0.000
Hordeum sp. (barley)	-	-	-	-	-	-	0	0.000
cf. *Hordeum* sp.	-	-	-	-	-	-	0	0.000
Panicum sp. (panic grass)	-	-	-	-	-	-	0	0.000
Polygonaceae sp. (knotweed)	-	-	-	-	-	-	0	0.000
Portulaca oleracea	-	-	-	-	-	-	0	0.000
Unknown	-	-	-	-	-	-	0	0.000
Subtotal other seed	0	0.00	0	0.00	0	0.00	0	0.000
Unidentifiable	-	-	-	-	-	-	0	0.000
Unidentifiable seed coat	-	-	-	-	-	-	0	0.000
Total Other	0	0.00	0	0.00	0	0.00	0	0.000
Fruit (?)	-	-	-	-	-	-	0	0.000
Monocot stem	-	-	-	-	-	-	0	0.000
Amorphous	-	-	-	-	-	-	0	0.000
Total-all	33	0.34	0	0.00	0	0.00	33	0.340

REFERENCES

Ackerman, Robert E.
1980 Microblades and Prehistory: Technological and Cultural Considerations for the North Pacific Coast. In *Early Native Americans, Prehistoric Demography, Economy, and Technology*, edited by David L. Browman, pp. 189–197. Mouton, The Hague.

Adrosko, Rita J.
1971 *Natural Dyes and Home Dyeing.* Dover Publications, New York.

Ahler, Stanley A., and Julieann Van Nest
1985 Temporal Change in Knife River Flint Reduction Strategies. In *Lithic Resource Procurement: Proceedings from the Second Conference on Prehistoric Chert Exploitation*, edited by Susan C. Vehik, pp. 183–198. Occasional Paper No. 4. Center for Archaeological Investigations, Southern Illinois University at Carbondale.

American Ornithologists' Union
1983 *Check-List of North American Birds.* 6th ed. American Ornithologists' Union, Lawrence, Kansas.

Anderson, Douglas D.
1970 Microblade Traditions in Northwestern Alaska. *Arctic Anthropology* 7(2):2–16.

Asch, David L., and Nancy B. Asch
1985 Archeobotany. In *Smiling Dan: Structure and Function at a Middle Woodland Settlement in the Illinois Valley*, edited by Barbara D. Stafford and Mark B. Sant, pp. 327–401. Kampsville Archeological Research Series Vol. 2. Center for American Archeology, Kampsville, Illinois.

Asch, Nancy B., and David L. Asch
1985 Archaeobotany. In *The Hill Creek Homestead and the Late Mississippian Settlement in the Lower Illinois Valley*, edited by Michael D.

Conner, pp. 115–165. Kampsville Archeological Center Research Series Vol. 1. Center for American Archeology, Kampsville, Illinois.

1986 Woodland Period Archeobotany of the Napoleon Hollow Site. In *Woodland Period Occupations of the Napoleon Hollow Site in the Lower Illinois Valley*, edited by Michael D. Wiant and Charles R. McGimsey, pp. 427–526. Kampsville Archeological Research Series Vol. 6. Center for American Archeology, Kampsville, Illinois.

Baerreis, David A.
1953 The Airport Village Site, Dane County. *The Wisconsin Archeologist* 34:149–164.

Bareis, Charles J., and James W. Porter (editors)
1984 *American Bottom Archaeology, A Summary of the FAI-270 Project Contribution to the Culture History of the Mississippi River Valley.* University of Illinois Press, Urbana.

Bailey, Reeve M., Carl E. Bond, James R. Brooker, Ernest A. Lachner, Robert N. Lea, and W. B. Scott
1991 *Common and Scientific Names of Fishes from the United States and Canada.* 5th ed. Special Publication 20. American Fisheries Society, Bethesda, Maryland.

Bell, Robert E.
1958 *Guide to the Identification of Certain American Indian Projectile Points.* Special Bulletin 1. Oklahoma Anthropological Society, Oklahoma City.

Binford, Lewis R., Sally R. Binford, Robert C. Whallon, and Margaret A. Hardin
1970 *Archaeology at Hatchery West.* Memoir 24. Society for American Archaeology, Washington, D.C.

Braun, David P.
1979   Illinois Hopewell Burial Practices and Social Organization: A Re-examination of the Klunk-Gibson Mound Group. In *Hopewell Archaeology, The Chillicothe Conference*, edited by David S. Brose and N'omi Greber, pp. 66–79. Kent State University Press, Kent, Ohio.
1985   Absolute Seriation: A Time-Series Approach. In *For Concordance in Archaeological Analysis: Bridging Data Structure, Quantitative Technique, and Theory*, edited by Christopher Carr, pp. 509–539. Westport Press, New York.

Browman, David, and David Munsell
1969   Columbia Plateau Prehistory: Cultural Development and Impinging Influences. *American Antiquity* 34:249–264.

Butler, Brian M.
1979   Hopewellain Contacts in Southern Middle Tennessee. In *Hopewell Archaeology, The Chillicothe Conference*, edited by David S. Brose and N'omi Greber, pp. 150–156. Kent State University Press, Kent, Ohio.

Butler, Brian M., and Richard W. Jefferies
1986   Crab Orchard and Early Woodland Cultures in the Middle South. In *Early Woodland Archeology*, edited by Kenneth B. Farnsworth and Thomas E. Emerson, pp. 523–534. Kampsville Seminars in Archeology No. 2. Center for American Archeology, Kampsville, Illinois.

Cambron, James W.
1958   Projectile Point Types, Part III. *Journal of Alabama Archaeology* 4(2):10–12.

Cantwell, Anne-Marie
1980   *Dickson Camp and Pond: Two Early Havana Tradition Sites in the Central Illinois Valley.* Reports of Investigations No. 36. Illinois State Museum, Springfield.
1981   Middle Woodland Dog Ceremonialism in Illinois. *The Wisconsin Archeologist* 61:480–497.

Collins, Henry B.
1956   The T1 Site at Native Point, Southampton Island, N.W.T. *Anthropological Papers of the University of Alaska* 4(2):63–69.

Cook, Thomas G.
1976   *Koster: An Artifact Analysis of Two Archaic Phases in West Central Illinois.* Koster Research Reports 3. Northwestern University Archeological Program, Kampsville, Illinois.

Core, Harold A., Wilfred A. Cote, and Arnold C. Day
1979   *Wood Structure and Identification.* 2nd ed. Wood Science Series 6. Syracuse University Press, Syracuse, New York.

Cowan, C. Wesley
1978   The Prehistoric Use and Distribution of Maygrass in Eastern North America: Cultural and Phytogeographical Implications. In *The Nature and Status of Ethnobotany*, edited by Richard I. Ford, pp. 263–288. Anthropological Papers No. 67. Museum of Anthropology, University of Michigan, Ann Arbor.

Crabtree, Don E.
1968   Mesoamerican Polyhedral Cores and Prismatic Blades. *American Antiquity* 33:446–478.

Cross, Paula G.
1983   Faunal Remains from the Mund Phase. In *The Mund Site (11-S-435)*, by Andrew C. Fortier, Fred A. Finney, and Richard B. Lacampagne, pp. 318–341. American Bottom Archaeology FAI-270 Site Reports Vol. 5. University of Illinois Press, Urbana.

Dumond, D. E.
1962   Blades and Cores in Oregon. *American Antiquity* 27:419–424.

Elston, Robert G.
1986   Prehistory of the Western Area. In *Great Basin*, edited by Warren L. D'Azevedo, pp. 135–148. Handbook of North American Indians, Vol. 11, W. C. Sturtevant, general editor. Smithsonian Institution, Washington, D.C.

Emerson, Thomas E.
1984   The Dyroff (11-S-463) and Levin Sites (11-S-462). In *The Go-Kart North Site (11-Mo-552N)*, by Andrew C. Fortier, and *The Dyroff (11-S-463) and Levin (11-S-462) Sites*, by

Thomas E. Emerson, pp. 201–362. American Bottom Archaeology FAI-270 Site Reports Vol. 9. University of Illinois Press, Urbana.

Emerson, Thomas E., George R. Milner, and Douglas K. Jackson
1983 *The Florence Street Site (11-S-485)*. American Bottom Archaeology FAI-270 Site Reports Vol. 2. University of Illinois Press, Urbana.

Farnsworth, Kenneth B.
1990 The Evidence for Specialized Middle Woodland Camps in Western Illinois. *Illinois Archaeology* 2:109–132.

Farnsworth, Kenneth B., and David L. Asch
1986 Early Woodland Chronology, Artifact Styles, and Settlement Distribution in the Lower Illinois Valley Region. In *Early Woodland Archeology*, edited by Kenneth B. Farnsworth and Thomas E. Emerson, pp. 326–457. Kampsville Seminars in Archeology Vol. 2. Center for American Archeology, Kampsville, Illinois.

Farnsworth, Kenneth B., and Ann L. Koski
1985 *Massey and Archie, A Study of Two Hopewellian Homesteads in the Western Illinois Uplands*. Kampsville Archeological Research Series Vol. 3. Center for American Archeology, Kampsville, Illinois.

Faulkner, Charles H., and Major C. R. McCollough (editors)
1974 *Excavations and Testing, Normandy Reservoir Salvage Project: 1972 Season*. Normandy Archaeological Project Vol. 2. Reports of Investigations No. 12. Department of Anthropology, University of Tennessee, Knoxville.

Fecht, William G.
1961 The Snyders Mound Group and Village Site. *Central States Archaeological Journal* 8:84–93.

Finney, Fred A.
1983 Middle Woodland Cement Hollow Phase. In *The Mund Site (11-S-435)*, by Andrew C. Fortier, Fred A. Finney, and Richard B.

Lacampagne, pp. 40–94. American Bottom Archaeology FAI-270 Site Reports Vol. 5. University of Illinois Press, Urbana.

Ford, James A., Philip Phillips, and William G. Haag
1955 *The Jaketown Site in West-Central Mississippi*. Anthropological Papers Vol. 45, Pt. I. American Museum of Natural History, New York.

Fortier, Andrew C.
1984 The Go-Kart North Site (11-Mo-552N). In *The Go-Kart North Site (11-Mo-552N)*, by Andrew C. Fortier, and *The Dyroff (11-S-463) and Levin (11-S-462) Sites*, by Thomas E. Emerson, pp. 1–197. American Bottom Archaeology FAI-270 Site Reports Vol. 9. University of Illinois Press, Urbana.

1985a *Selected Sites in the Hill Lake Locality*. American Bottom Archaeology FAI-270 Site Reports Vol. 13. University of Illinois Press, Urbana.

1985b The Robert Schneider Site (11-Ms-1177). In *The Carbon Dioxide Site (11-M0-594)*, by Fred A. Finney, and *The Robert Schneider Site (11-Ms-1177)*, by Andrew C. Fortier, pp. 169–313. American Bottom Archaeology FAI-270 Site Reports Vol. 11. University of Illinois Press, Urbana.

1988 Archaeological Testing at the Dash Reeves (11-Mo-80) and Marge (11-Mo-99) Sites in the Columbia Interchange on FAP 14. Report submitted to the Illinois Department of Transportation, Springfield. Illinois Transportation Archaeological Research Program, University of Illinois, Urbana-Champaign.

1992 A People of Colors: The World of American Bottom Hopewell, Their Middens, Blades, and Other Profanities. Paper presented at the 37th annual Midwest Archaeological Conference, Grand Rapids, Michigan.

1996 *The Marge Site (11-Mo-99): Late Archaic and Emergent Mississippian Occupations in the Palmer Creek Locality*. American Bottom Archaeology FAI-270 Site Reports Vol. 27. University of Illinois Press, Urbana.

2000 The Emergence and Demise of the Middle Woodland Small-Tool Tradition in the American Bottom. *Midcontinental Journal of Archaeology* 25:191–213.

2001 A Tradition of Discontinuity: American Bottom Early and Middle Woodland Culture History Reexamined. In *The Archaeology of Traditions: The Southeast Before and After Columbus*, edited by Timothy Pauketat. In press. University Press of Florida, Gainesville.

Fortier, Andrew C., Fred A. Finney, and Richard B. Lacampagne
1983 *The Mund Site (11-S-435)*. American Bottom Archaeology FAI-270 Site Reports Vol. 5. University of Illinois Press, Urbana.

Fortier, Andrew C., and Swastika Ghosh
2000 The Bosque Medio Site: A Hopewellian Campsite in the American Bottom Uplands. *Illinois Archaeology* 12:1–57.

Fortier, Andrew C., Thomas O. Maher, Joyce A. Williams, Michael C. Meinkoth, Kathryn E. Parker, and Lucretia S. Kelly
1989 *The Holding Site (11-Ms-118): A Hopewell Community in the American Bottom*. American Bottom Archaeology FAI-270 Site Reports Vol. 19. University of Illinois Press, Urbana.

Fowke, Gerard
1928 Archaeological Investigations II. *Forty-fourth Annual Report of the Bureau of American Ethnology*, pp. 530–532. Smithsonian Institution, Washington, D.C.

Fowler, Melvin L.
1952 The Clear Lake Site: Hopewellian Occupation. In *Hopewellian Communities in Illinois*, edited by Thorne Deuel, pp. 131–174. Scientific Papers Vol. 5. Illinois State Museum, Springfield.

Fritz, Gayle
1984 Identification of Cultigen Amaranth and Chenopod from Rockshelter Sites in Northwest Arkansas. *American Antiquity* 49:558–572.

Greber, N'omi, Richard S. Davis, and Ann S. DuFresne
1981 The Micro Component of the Ohio Hopewell Lithic Technology: Bladelets. *Annals of the New York Academy of Sciences* 376:489–528.

Gregg, Michael L.
1974 Flintknapping as a Mortuary Activity: Evidence from Mound 72 at Cahokia. Paper presented at the 39th Annual Meeting of the Society for American Archaeology, Washington, D.C.

Griffin, James B.
1952 Some Early and Middle Woodland Pottery Types in Illinois. In *Hopewellian Communities in Illinois*, edited by Thorne Deuel, pp. 93–129. Scientific Papers, Vol. 5. Illinois State Museum, Springfield.

Griffin, James B., Richard E. Flanders, and Paul F. Titterington
1970 *The Burial Complexes of the Knight and Norton Mounds in Illinois and Michigan*. Memoirs No. 2. Museum of Anthropology, University of Michigan, Ann Arbor.

Haag, William G., and Clarence H. Webb
1953 Microblades at Poverty Point Sites. *American Antiquity* 18:245–248.

Hajic, Edward
1988 Appendix A. Preliminary Geomorphological Investigations at the FAP 14 (Ill 3) Interchange with Palmer Road and CH-6, Central Mississippi Valley. In Archaeological Testing at the Dash Reeves (11-Mo-80) and Marge (11-Mo-99) Sites in the Columbia Interchange on FAP 14, by Andrew C. Fortier, pp. 23–32. Report submitted to the Illinois Department of Transportation, Springfield. Illinois Transportation Archaeological Research Program, University of Illinois, Urbana-Champaign.

Hall, Robert L.
1981 Radiocarbon Chronology for the Labras Lake Site. In *Labras Lake, Investigations into the Prehistoric Occupations of a Mississippi Floodplain Locality in St. Clair County, Illinois*, edited by James L. Phillips and Robert L. Hall, pp. 383–414. Department of Anthropology, University of Illinois at Chicago Circle.

Higgins, Michael J.

1990   *The Nochta Site: The Early, Middle, and Late Archaic Occupations.* American Bottom Archaeology FAI-270 Site Reports Vol. 21. University of Illinois Press, Urbana.

Hoffmeister, Donald F.

1989   *Mammals of Illinois.* University of Illinois Press, Urbana.

Hofman, Jack L.

1987   Hopewell Blades from Twenhafel: Distinguishing Local and Foreign Core Technology. In *Organization of Core Technology*, edited by Jay K. Johnson and Carol A. Morrow, pp. 87–117. Westview Press, Boulder, Colorado.

Hughes, Richard E., and James A. Bennyhoff

1986   Early Trade. In *Great Basin*, edited by Warren L. D'Azevedo, pp. 238–255. Handbook of North American Indians, Vol. 11, W. C. Sturtevant, general editor. Smithsonian Institution, Washington, D.C.

Hughes, Richard E., and Andrew C. Fortier

1997   Identification of the Geologic Sources for Obsidian Artifacts from Three Middle Woodland Sites in the American Bottom, Illinois. *Illinois Archaeology* 9:79–92.

Hurlburt, Isobel

1977   *Faunal Remains from Fort White Earth NW Co. (1810–1813).* Human History Occasional Paper 1. Provincial Museum of Alberta, Edmonton.

Irving, William N.

1957   An Archaeological Survey of the Susitna Valley. *Anthropological Papers of the University of Alaska* 6(1):37–52.

Ives, David J.

1975   *The Crescent Hills Prehistoric Quarrying Area.* Museum Brief 22. University of Missouri, Columbia.

Jackson, Douglas K.

1990   The Willoughby Site (11-Ms-610). In *Selected Early Mississippian Household Sites in the Ameri-can Bottom*, by Douglas K. Jackson and Ned H. Hanenberger, pp. 17–90. American Bottom Archaeology FAI-270 Site Reports Vol. 22. University of Illinois Press, Urbana.

Johannessen, Sissel

1983   Plant Remains from the Cement Hollow Phase. In *The Mund Site*, by Andrew C. Fortier, Fred A. Finney, and Richard B. Lacampagne, pp. 94–104. American Bottom Archaeology FAI-270 Site Reports Vol. 5. University of Illinois Press, Urbana.

1984   Paleoethnobotany. In *American Bottom Archaeology, A Summary of the FAI-270 Project Contribution to the Culture History of the Mississippi River Valley*, edited by Charles J. Bareis and James W. Porter, pp. 197–214. University of Illinois Press, Urbana.

1985   Plant Remains. In *Selected Sites in the Hill Lake Locality*, by Andrew C. Fortier, pp. 281–308. American Bottom Archaeology FAI-270 Site Reports Vol. 13. University of Illinois Press, Urbana.

1988   Plant Remains and Culture Change: Are Paleoethnobotanical Data Better Than We Think? In *Current Paleoethnobotany*, edited by Chirstine A. Hastorf and Virginia S. Popper, pp. 145–166. University of Chicago Press, Chicago.

Johnson, Alfred E.

1979   Kansas City Hopewell. In *Hopewell Archaeology, The Chillicothe Conference*, edited by David S. Brose and N'omi Greber, pp. 86–93. Kent State University Press, Kent, Ohio.

Johnson, Jay K.

1983   Poverty Point Period Blade Technology in the Yazoo Basin, Mississippi. *Lithic Technology* 12(3):49–56.

Kay, Marvin

1980   *The Central Missouri Hopewell Subsistence-Settlement System.* Research Series No. 15. Missouri Archaeological Society, Columbia.

Kellar, James H.

1979   The Mann Site and "Hopewell" in the Lower Wabash-Ohio Valley. In *Hopewell Archaeology,*

The Chillicothe Conference, edited by David S. Brose and N'omi Greber, pp. 100–107. Kent State University Press, Kent, Ohio.

Kelly, John E.

1984   Late Bluff Chert Utilization on the Merrell Tract, Cahokia. In *Prehistoric Chert Exploitation: Studies from the Midcontinent*, edited by Brian M. Butler and Ernest E. May, pp. 23–44. Occasional Paper No. 2. Center for Archaeological Investigations, Southern Illinois University at Carbondale.

1990   The Emergence of Mississippian Culture in the American Bottom. In *The Mississippian Emergence*, edited by Bruce D. Smith, pp. 113–152. Smithsonian Institution Press, Washington, D.C.

Kelly, John E., Andrew C. Fortier, Steven J. Ozuk, and Joyce A. Williams

1987   *The Range Site (11-S-47): Archaic through Late Woodland Occupations.* American Bottom Archaeology FAI-270 Site Reports Vol. 16. University of Illinois Press, Urbana.

Kelly, Lucretia S.

1989   Faunal Assemblage. In *The Holding Site (11-Ms-118): A Hopewell Community in the American Bottom*, by Andrew C. Fortier, Thomas O. Maher, Joyce A. Williams, Michael C. Meinkoth, Kathryn E. Parker, and Lucretia S. Kelly, pp. 465–482. American Bottom Archaeology FAI-270 Site Reports Vol. 19. University of Illinois Press, Urbana.

King, Frances B., and Donna C. Roper

1976   Floral Remains from Two Middle to Early Late Woodland Sites in Central Illinois and Their Implications. *The Wisconsin Archeologist* 57:142–151.

Kneberg, Madeline

1956   Some Important Projectile Point Types Found in the Tennessee Area. *Tennessee Archaeologist* 12(1):17–28.

Lacampagne, Richard B., and Charles Bentz

1988   The Rosewood Phase Occupation at the Steinberg Site. In *Late Woodland Sites in the American Bottom Uplands*, by Charles Bentz, Dale L. McElrath, Fred A. Finney, and Richard B. Lacampagne, pp. 75–106. American Bottom Archaeology FAI-270 Site Reports Vol. 18. University of Illinois Press, Urbana.

Leechman, Douglas

1951   Bone Grease. *American Antiquity* 16:355–356.

Leigh, Steven R.

1988   Comparative Analysis of the Elizabeth Middle Woodland Artifact Assemblage. In *The Archaic and Woodland Cemeteries at the Elizabeth Site in the Lower Illinois Valley*, edited by Douglas K. Charles, Steven R. Leigh, and Jane E. Buikstra, pp. 191–217. Kampsville Archeological Center Research Series Vol. 7. Center for American Archeology, Kampsville, Illinois.

Lopinot, Neal H.

1990   *Archaeology of the Little Hills Expressway Site (23SC572), St. Charles County, Missouri.* Archaeology Program Research Report No. 6. Contract Archaeology Program, Southern Illinois University at Edwardsville.

1991   Archaeobotanical Remains. In *The Archaeology of the Cahokia Mounds ICT-II: Biological Remains*, by Neal H. Lopinot, Lucretia S. Kelly, George R. Milner, and Richard Paine. Illinois Cultural Resources Study No. 13, Part I. Illinois Historic Preservation Agency, Springfield.

MacNeish, Richard S., Antoinette Nelken-Turner, and Irmgard W. Johnson

1967   Blades and Poyhedral Cores. In *The Prehistory of the Tehuacan Valley, Vol. 2, Nonceramic Artifacts, Pt. 1, Chipped Stone Tools*, pp. 17–29. University of Texas Press, Austin.

Maher, Thomas O.

1989   The Middle Woodland Ceramic Assemblage. In *The Holding Site (11-Ms-118): A Hopewell Community in the American Bottom*, by Andrew C. Fortier, Thomas O. Maher, Joyce A. Williams, Michael C. Meinkoth, Kathryn E. Parker, and Lucretia S. Kelly, pp. 125–318. American Bottom Archaeology FAI-270 Site

Reports Vol. 19. University of Illinois Press, Urbana.

1991   Time and Community Patterns at Holding, A Middle Woodland Site in the American Bottom. *Southeastern Archaeology* 10(2):114–133.

1994   Middle Woodland Mounds of the American Bottom, Test Excavations in Five Potential Middle Woodland Mounds. Manuscript on file, Illinois Transportation Archaeological Research Program, Univesity of Illinois, Urbana-Champaign.

1996   *Time, Space, and Social Dynamics during the Hopewell Occupation of the American Bottom.* Ph.D. dissertation, Department of Anthropology, University of North Carolina, Chapel Hill.

Markman, Charles W.
1988   *Putney Landing, Archaeological Investigations at a Havana-Hopewell Settlement on the Mississippi River in West-Central Illinois.* Reports of Investigations No. 15. Department of Anthropology, Northern Illinois University, DeKalb.

Martin, Alexander C., and William D. Barkley
1961   *Seed Identification Manual.* University of California Press, Berkeley.

Maxwell Moreau S.
1951   *The Woodland Cultures in Southern Illinois: Archaeological Excavations in the Carbondale Area.* Bulletin 7, Logan Museum Publications in Anthropology. Beloit College, Beloit, Wisconsin.

McElrath, Dale L.
1986   *The McLean Site (11-S-640).* American Bottom FAI-270 Site Reports Vol. 14. University of Illinois Press, Urbana.

McElrath, Dale L., and Andrew C. Fortier
1983   *The Missouri Pacific #2 Site (11-S-46).* American Bottom FAI-270 Site Reports Vol. 3. University of Illinois Press, Urbana.

2000   The Early Late Woodland Occupation of the American Bottom. In *Late Woodland Societies, Tradition and Transformation Across the Midcontinent*, edited by Thomas E. Emerson, Dale L. McElrath, and Andrew C. Fortier, pp.

91–121. University of Nebraska Press, Lincoln.

McGhee, Robert
1970   A Quantitative Comparison of Dorset Culture Microblade Samples. *Arctic Anthropology* 7(2):89–96.

McGimsey, Charles R.
1988   *The Haw Creek Site (11-Kx-3), Knox County, Illinois, A Middle Woodland Occupation in the Upper Spoon River Valley.* Technical Report 88-257-7. Quaternary Studies Center, Archaeological Research Program, Illinois State Museum, Springfield.

McGimsey, Charles R., and Michael D. Wiant
1986   Middle Woodland Features. In *Woodland Period Occupations of the Napoleon Hollow Site in the Lower Illinois Valley*, edited by Michael D. Wiant and Charles R. McGimsey, pp. 114–170. Kampsville Archeological Center Research Series Vol. 6. Center for American Archeology, Kampsville, Illinois.

McGregor, John C.
1958   *The Pool and Irving Villages, A Study of Hopewell Occupation in the Illinois River Valley.* University of Illinois Press, Urbana.

McNerney, Michael J.
1987   Crab Orchard Technology at the Consol Site, Jackson County, Illinois. In *The Organization of Core Technology*, edited by Jay K. Johnson and Carol A. Morrow, pp. 63–85. Westview Press, Boulder, Colorado.

Mitchell, Donald H.
1968   Microblades: A Long-Standing Gulf of Georgia Tradition. *American Antiquity* 33:11–15.

Mohlenbrock, Robert
1986   *Guide to the Vascular Flora of Illinois.* Southern Illinois University Press, Carbondale.

Montet-White, Anta
1963   Analytic Description of the Chipped-Stone Industry from the Snyders Site, Calhoun County, Illinois. In *Miscellaneous Studies in Typology and Classification*, by Anta Montet-

White, Lewis R. Binford, and Mark L. Papworth, pp. 1–70. Anthropological Papers No. 19. Museum of Anthropology, University of Michigan, Ann Arbor.

1968   *The Lithic Industries of the Illinois Valley in the Early and Middle Woodland Period.* Anthropological Papers No. 35. Museum of Anthropology, University of Michigan, Ann Arbor.

Morgan, David T.

1985   Ceramic Analysis. In *Smiling Dan: Structure and Function at a Middle Woodland Settlement in the Illinois Valley*, edited by Barbara D. Stafford and Mark B. Sant, pp. 183–257. Kampsville Archeological Research Series Vol. 2. Center for American Archeology, Kampsville, Illinois.

1986   Ceramics. In *Woodland Period Occupations of the Napoleon Hollow Site in the Lower Illinois Valley*, edited by Michael D. Wiant and Charles R. McGimsey, pp. 364–426. Kampsville Archeological Research Series Vol. 6. Center for American Archeology, Kampsville, Illinois.

Morrow, Carol A.

1987   Blades and Cobden Chert: A Technological Argument for Their Role as Makers of Regional Identification during the Hopewell Period in Illinois. In *The Organization of Core Technology*, edited by Jay K. Johnson and Carol A. Morrow, pp. 119–149. Westview Press, Boulder, Colorado.

Morse, Dan F.

1963   *The Steuben Village and Mounds: A Multicomponent Late Hopewell Site in Illinois.* Anthropological Papers No. 21. Museum of Anthropology, University of Michigan, Ann Arbor.

Nash, Ronald J.

1969   *The Arctic Small Tool Tradition in Manitoba.* Occasional Paper No. 2. Department of Anthropology, University of Manitoba, Winnipeg.

Newcomer, M. H.

1971   Some Quantitative Experiments in Hand-Axe Manufacture. *World Archaeology* 3:85–94.

Parker, Kathryn E.

1986   Appendix 1. Plant Remains from the Irish Hollow and North Hanover Sites. In *Archaeological Investigations of Four Sites along the Great River Road in Jo Daviess County, Illinois: Late Woodland Occupation in the Apple River Drainage*, by Norm Meinholz, pp. 48–51. Resource Investigation Program Research Reports No. 23. Department of Anthropology, University of Illinois, Urbana.

1989   Archaeobotanical Assemblage In *The Holding Site (11-Ms-118): A Hopewell Community in the American Bottom*, by Andrew C. Fortier, Thomas O. Maher, Joyce A. Williams, Michael C. Meinkoth, Kathryn E. Parker, and Lucretia S. Kelly, pp. 429–464. American Bottom Archaeology FAI-270 Site Reports Vol. 19. University of Illinois Press, Urbana.

1991   Sponemann Phase Archaeobotany. In *The Sponemann Site: The Formative Emergent Mississippian Sponemann Phase Occupations*, by Andrew C. Fortier, Thomas O. Maher, and Joyce A. Williams, pp. 377–419. American Bottom Archaeology FAI-270 Site Reports Vol. 23. University of Illinois Press, Urbana.

Parker, Kathryn E., and Mary Simon

1994   Prehistoric Plant Use in the American Bottom Region of Illinois. Paper presented at the Joint 51st Southeastern Archaeological Conference and 39th Midwest Archaeological Conference, Lexington, Kentucky.

Parry, William J.

1994   Prismatic Blade Technologies in North America. In *The Organization of North American Prehistoric Chipped Stone Tool Technologies*, edited by Philip J. Carr, pp. 87–98. Archaeological Series 7, International Monographs in Prehistory. Ann Arbor, Michigan.

Patterson, Leland W.

1973   Some Texas Blade Technology. *Bulletin of the Texas Archeological Society* 44:89–111.

Phillippe, Joseph S.

1993   The Robert Watts Site: Archaeological Excavations of a Late Eighteenth/Early Nineteenth Century Euroamerican Farmstead. In

Highways to the Past, Essays on Illinois Archaeology in Honor of Charles J. Bareis, edited by Thomas E. Emerson, Andrew C. Fortier, and Dale L. McElrath. *Illinois Archaeology* 5:527–536.

Pi-Sunyer, Oriol
1965 The Flint Industry. In *The McGraw Site, A Study in Hopewellian Dyanmics*, by Olaf H. Prufer, pp. 60–89. Scientific Publications Vol. 3, No. 1. Cleveland Museum of Natural History, Cleveland, Ohio.

Porter, James W.
1971 An Archaeological Survey of the Mississippi Valley in St. Clair, Monroe, and Randolph Counties. In *Preliminary Report of 1971 Historic Sites Survey Archaeological Reconnaissance of Selected Areas in the State of Illinois, Part I, Summary Section A*, pp. 28–32. Illinois Archaeological Survey, Urbana.
1972 An Archaeological Survey of the Mississippi Valley in St. Clair, Monroe, and Randolph Counties. In *Preliminary Report of 1972 Historic Sites Survey Archaeological Reconnaissance of Selected Areas in the State of Illinois, Part I, Summary Section A*, pp. 25–31. Illinois Archaeological Survey, Urbana.
1974 *Cahokia Archaeology as Viewed from the Mitchell Site: A Satellite Community at AD 1150–1200*. Ph.D. dissertation, University of Wisconsin–Madison. University Microfilms, Ann Arbor, Michigan.

Prufer, Olaf H.
1965 *The McGraw Site, A Study in Hopewellian Dyanmics*. Scientific Publications Vol. 3, No. 1. Cleveland Museum of Natural History, Cleveland, Ohio.

Reeves, Dache M.
1936 Aerial Photography and Archaeology. *American Antiquity* 2:102–107.

Reid, Kenneth C.
1976 Prehistoric Trade in the Lower Missouri River Valley: An Analysis of Middle Woodland Bladelets. In *Hopewellian Archaeology in the Lower Missouri Valley*, edited by Alfred E. Johnson, pp. 63–99. Publications in Anthropology No. 8. University of Kansas, Lawrence.

Riley, Thomas J., Gregory R. Waltz, Charles J. Bareis, Andrew C. Fortier, and Kathryn E. Parker
1994 Accelerator Mass Spectrometry (AMS) Dates Confirm Early *Zea mays* in the Mississippi River Valley. *American Antiquity* 59:490–498.

Ritchie, William A.
1929 *Hammerstones, Anvils, and Certain Pitted Stones*. Researches and Transactions Vol. 7, No. 2. New York State Archaeological Association, Rochester.

Sanger, David
1968a Prepared Core and Blade Traditions in the Pacific Northwest. *Arctic Anthropology* 5(1):92–120.
1968b The High River Microblade Industry, Alberta. *Plains Anthropologist* 13:190–208.
1969 Cultural Traditions in the Interior of British Columbia. *Syesis* 2(2):189–200.
1970 Mid-Latitude Core and Blade Traditions. *Arctic Anthropology* 7(2):106–114.

Schiffer, Michael B.
1976 *Behavioral Archeology*. Academic Press, New York.
1985 Is There a "Pompeii Premise" in Archaeology? *Journal of Anthropological Research* 41(1):18–41.

Scully, Edward G.
1951 Some Central Mississippi Valley Projectile Point Types. Manuscript on file, Museum of Anthropology, University of Michigan, Ann Arbor.

Seeman, Mark F.
1979a Feasting with the Dead: Ohio Hopewell Charnel House Ritual as a Context for Redistribution. In *Hopewell Archaeology, The Chillicothe Conference*, edited by David S. Brose and N'omi Greber, pp. 39–46. Kent State University Press, Kent, Ohio.

1979b The Hopewell Interaction Sphere: The Evidence for Interregional Trade and Structural Complexity. *Prehistory Research Series* 5(2):237–438. Indiana Historical Society, Indianapolis.

Simon, Mary
1996 Emergent Mississippian Plant Remains. In *The Marge Site (11-Mo-99): Late Archaic and Emergent Mississippian Occupations in the Palmer Creek Locality*, by Andrew C. Fortier, pp. 263–306. American Bottom Archaeology FAI-270 Site Reports Vol. 27. University of Illinois Press, Urbana.

Smith, Bruce D.
1985 *Chenopodium berlandieri* ssp. *jonesianum*: Evidence for a Hopewellian Domesticate from Ash Cave, Ohio. *Southeastern Archaeology* 4:107–132.

Smith, Philip W.
1961 *The Amphibians and Reptiles of Illinois*. Bulletin 28. Illinois Natural History Survey, Champaign.

Spaulding, Albert C.
1958 The Significance of Differences Between Radiocarbon Dates. *American Antiquity* 23:309–311.

Spence, Michael W., William D. Finlayson, and Robert H. Pihl
1979 Hopewellian Influences on Middle Woodland Cultures in Southern Ontario. In *Hopewell Archaeology, The Chillicothe Conference*, edited by David S. Brose and N'omi Greber, pp. 115–121. Kent State University Press, Kent, Ohio.

Stafford, Barbara D.
1985 Middle Woodland Midden Analysis. In *Smiling Dan: Structure and Function at a Middle Woodland Settlement in the Illinois Valley*, edited by Barbara D. Stafford and Mark B. Sant, pp. 95–112. Kampsville Archeological Research Series Vol. 2. Center for American Archeology, Kampsville, Illinois.

Stafford, Barbara D., amd Mark B. Sant (editors)
1985 *Smiling Dan: Structure and Function at a Middle Woodland Settlement in the Illinois Valley*. Kampsville Archeological Research Series Vol. 2. Center for American Archeology, Kampsville, Illinois.

Struever, Stuart
1964 The Hopewell Interaction Sphere in Riverine-Western Great Lakes Culture History. In *Hopewellian Studies*, edited by Joseph R. Caldwell and Robert L. Hall, pp. 85–106. Scientific Papers Vol. 12. Illinois State Museum, Springfield.

Stuiver, Minze, and Gordon W. Pearson
1986 High-Precision Calibration of the Radiocarbon Time Scale, AD 1950–500 BC. *Radiocarbon* 28(2B):805–838.

Stuiver, Minze, and Paula J. Reimer
1986 A Computer Program for Radiocarbon Age Calibration. *Radiocarbon* 28:1022–1030.
1993 Extended 14C Database and Revised CALIB Radiocarbon Calibration Program. *Radiocarbon* 35:215–230.

Syles, Bonnie W., and James R. Purdue
1986 Woodland Faunal Exploitation. In *Woodland Period Occupations of the Napoleon Hollow Site in the Lower Illinois Valley*, edited by Michael D. Wiant and Charles R. McGimsey, pp. 513–526. Kampsville Archeological Research Series Vol. 6. Center for American Archeology, Kampsville, Illinois.

Styles, Bonnie W., James R. Purdue, and Mona L. Colburn
1985 Faunal Exploitation at the Smiling Dan Site. In *Smiling Dan: Structure and Function at a Middle Woodland Settlement in the Illinois Valley*, edited by Barbara D. Stafford and Mark B. Sant, pp. 402–446. Kampsville Archeological Research Series Vol. 2. Center for American Archeology, Kampsville, Illinois.

Taylor, William E.
1968 *The Arnapik and Tyara Sites: An Archaeological Study of Dorset Culture Origins*. Memoirs No.

22. Society for American Archaeology, Salt Lake City, Utah.

Telford, Clarence J.
1926 Third Report on a Forest Survey of Illinois. *Bulletin* 16:1–102. Illinois Natural History Survey, Urbana.

Theler, James L.
1987 *Woodland Tradition Economic Strategies.* Report No. 17. Office of the State Archaeologist, University of Iowa, Iowa City.

Thomas, Cyrus
1891 *Catalogue of Prehistoric Works East of the Rocky Mountains.* Bulletin No. 12. Bureau of American Ethnology, Smithsonian Institution, Washington, D.C.

Titterington, Paul F.
1938 *The Cahokia Mound Group and Its Village Site Materials.* Reprint of privately published volume. Copies available through Cahokia Mounds Museum Society, Collinsville, Illinois.

Tomelleri, Joseph R., and Mark E. Eberle
1990 *Fishes of the Central United States.* University Press of Kansas, Lawrence.

Wagner, Gail
1976 IDOT Flotation Procedure Manual. Manuscript on file, Illinois Department of Transportation, District 8, Fairview Heights, Illinois.

Walthall, John A.
1981 *Galena and Aboriginal Trade in Eastern North America.* Scientific Papers No. 17. Illinois State Museum, Springfield.

Webb, Clarence H.
1982 *The Poverty Point Culture.* Geoscience and Man, Vol. 17. 2nd ed., revised. School of Geoscience, Louisiana State University, Baton Rouge.

Webb, Clarence H., and John L. Gibson
1981 Studies of the Microflint Industry at Poverty Point Site. *Geoscience and Man* 22:85–101.

Whelpley, Henry M.
1915 A Rare Illinois Flint Artifact. *Journal of the Illinois State Historical Society* 8:137–138.

White, Theodore E.
1953 A Method for Calculating Dietary Percentage of Various Food Animals Utilized by Aboriginal Peoples. *American Antiquity* 18:396–398.

White, William P., Sissel Johannessen, Paula G. Cross, and Lucretia S. Kelly
1984 Environmental Setting. In *American Bottom Archaeology, A Summary of the FAI-270 Project Contribution to the Culture History of the Mississippi River Valley*, edited by Charles J. Bareis and James W. Porter, pp. 15–33. University of Illinois Press, Urbana.

Wiant, Michael D., and Charles R. McGimsey (editors)
1986 *Woodland Period Occupations of the Napoleon Hollow Site in the Lower Illinois Valley.* Kampsville Archeological Research Series Vol. 6. Center for American Archeology, Kampsville, Illinois.

Williams, Joyce A.
1989 Lithic Assemblage. In *The Holding Site (11-Ms-118): A Hopewell Community in the American Bottom*, by Andrew C. Fortier, Thomas O. Maher, Joyce A. Williams, Michael C. Meinkoth, Kathryn E. Parker, and Lucretia S. Kelly, pp. 319–428. American Bottom Archaeology FAI-270 Site Reports Vol. 19. University of Illinois Press, Urbana.
1993 Meridian Hills: An Upland Holding Phase Middle Woodland Habitation Site. In *Highways to the Past, Essays on Illinois Archaeology in Honor of Charles J. Bareis*, edited by Thomas E. Emerson, Andrew C. Fortier, and Dale E. McElrath. *Illinois Archaeology* 5:193–200.

Williams, Joyce A., Thomas O. Maher, and Kathryn E. Parker

1987   The Meridian Hills Site (11-S-1258): An Upland Middle Woodland Extractive Site. Paper presented at the 32nd Midwest Archaeological Conference, Milwaukee, Wisconsin.

Williams, Kenneth R., and William I. Woods

1977   An Archaeological Reconnaissance of FAP-310 (Bypass 50 to Pinckneyville). Report submitted to the Illinois Department of Transportation, Springfield. Department of Anthropology, Southern Illinois University at Edwardsville.

Winters, Howard D.

1963   An Archaeological Survey of the Wabash Valley in Illinois. Reports of Investigations No. 10. Illinois State Museum, Springfield.

1969   The Riverton Culture, A Second Millenium Occupation in the Central Wabash Valley. Reports of Investigations No. 13, Illinois State Museum, Springfield, and Monograph No. 1, Illinois Archaeological Survey, Urbana.

Wittry, Warren L.

1981   An Archaeological Survey of the Proposed Fish Lake Interchange (FAI-270) and the Adjacent Proposed Industrial Park Area. Report submitted to the Illinois Department of Transportation, Springfield. Department of Anthropology, University of Illinois at Urbana-Champaign.

Wolforth, Thomas, Mary Simon, and Richard Alvey

1993   The Widman Site (11-Ms-866): A Small Middle Woodland Settlement in the Wood River Valley, Illinois. Illinois Archaeology 2:45–69.

Yarnell, Richard A.

1969   Contents of Human Paleofeces. In The Prehistory of Salts Cave, Kentucky, by Patty Jo Watson, pp. 41–54. Reports of Investigations No. 16. Illinois State Museum, Springfield.

Yarnell, Richard A., and Jean M. Black

1985   Temporal Trends Indicated by a Survey of Archaic and Woodland Plant Food Remains from Southeastern North America. Southeastern Archaeology 4:93–106.

Yerkes, Richard W.

1994   A Consideration of the Function of Ohio Hopewell Bladelets. Lithic Technology 19(2):110–127.